THIRD EDITION

EXPLORER'S GUIDE

Starting Your College Journey with a Sense of Purpose

BILL MILLARD

Kendall Hunt
publishing company

Book Team

Chairman and Chief Executive Officer   Mark C. Falb
President and Chief Operating Officer   Chad M. Chandlee
Vice President, Higher Education   David L. Tart
Director of Publishing Partnerships   Paul B. Carty
Editorial Manager   Georgia Botsford
Senior Developmental Editor   Lynnette M. Rogers
Vice President, Operations   Timothy J. Beitzel
Assistant Vice President, Production Services   Christine E. O'Brien
Senior Production Editor   Laura Bies
Permissions Editor   Renae Horstman
Cover Designer   Suzanne Millius

Unless otherwise indicated, all Scripture quotations in this publication are taken from the HOLY BIBLE, TODAY'S NEW INTERNATIONAL VERSION. Copyright © 2001, 2005 by International Bible Society. Used under permission of International Bible Society. All rights reserved worldwide.

"TNIV" and "Today's New International Version" are trademarks registered in the United States Patent and Trademark Office by International Bible Society. Use of either trademark requires the permission of International Bible Society.

The story in this book is a work of fiction. Names, characters, businesses, organizations, places, events, and incidents either are the product of the author's imagination or are used fictitiously. Any resemblance to actual persons, living or dead, events, or locales is entirely coincidental.

Cover image used under license from Shutterstock, Inc.

www.kendallhunt.com
Send all inquiries to:
4050 Westmark Drive
Dubuque, IA 52004-1840

Dedication

To Anita, who has patiently traveled the Life Calling exploration road with me for many years;

to Jim, my philosophical and conceptual colleague and good friend;

to Evrett, true supporter, friend and fellow explorer for Life Calling;

to Bud, Todd, By, Judy, Kay, Dan, Burt, Connie, and Rick, who served on the Board of Directors of the Life Calling Initiative, a grant funded by the Lilly Endowment, Inc. These individuals held me accountable during the development of this project and added valuable insight to my investigations;

to Latrese, Cindy, Ellen, Kay, Dan, Amy, Nancy, Megan, Heather, Nicole, Jill, Stephanie, Karen, and Petros, faithful life coaches who have served alongside me during much of my theoretical musings.

to Kristy and Susanna who served as creative and thorough editors for my manuscript

Brief Contents

Contents

SECTION III   Personal Leadership

Features of the Book

There is a universal need found among people for meaning, significance and hope in their lives that can lead to a sense of purpose. The high school and college experience can and should be one that takes students along the path to those discoveries. But that will happen only if they follow the right map!

Exploration and discovery in the Life Calling journey have just become a lot easier. Life explorer Bill Millard, a leading theorist in calling and purpose, has developed *Explorer's Guide* to help students discover the components for a sense of calling and develop the tools for unleashing the power of purpose in their lives and in their college experience.

Explorer's Guide combines theory and spiritual insight with storytelling and exercises to create a unique approach to this important area of study. It provides a contemporary framework for studying an age-old dilemma for every student entering college.

> "It's kind of weird. It only took us a few minutes to figure out where we wanted to go on this summer adventure, and yet it seems so difficult to figure out where we are going in life after graduation," Adam, a soon-to-graduate reflected to his five companions. College is important to me, sure, but it is only one part of my life. It just seems like there ought to be a bigger purpose to my life than just going to college, getting a degree, then getting a job and ending up bored like half our parents."
> — *Explorer's Guide*

About the Author

Bill Millard is the founding theorist and Executive Director of the Center for Life Calling and Leadership at Indiana Wesleyan University. This Center enables students to find a higher purpose in their life that draws and guides them in all aspects of their life, equips them to make life decisions based on this purpose, and empowers them to develop this purpose into world changing leadership. He brings together nearly three decades of research, experience and application as a life explorer and leading theorist in calling and purpose that has helped people discover the components that go into a sense of calling and develop the tools for unleashing the power of purpose in their lives. Bill is also the creator of the *Intrinsic Motivation Assessment Guide & Evaluation (IMAGE)*, an assessment tool that has guided thousands of people on their unique journeys through life. It provides a service compass to pilot individuals toward fulfilling goals in response to people, locations, opportunities and problems in the world, and to help people map out roles to adopt as they interact with others and gain a greater understanding of themselves.

Bill is also a Professor of Leadership Studies at IWU, chairing the undergraduate program. He was also one of the chief developers of IWU's doctoral program in leadership. Bill also has served as an advisor to businesses and nonprofit organizations in the area of leadership assessment, organizational mobilization, strategic planning, and change implementation. He has extensive professional experience in the corporate and nonprofit sectors as well as in church and education sectors.

Bill earned his doctorate in Organizational Leadership from Pepperdine University. He completed his Bachelor of Arts in History, Greek, and Pre-Law and also earned graduate degrees in Secondary Education, Religion, and in Geology.

Bill was born in Honolulu, Hawaii, but lived the majority of his life in California. His wife Anita is a registered nurse working in hospice, and they now live in Indiana. They have two adult sons. Bill is an avid adventurer who has explored all fifty states and five different continents, climbing mountains, rafting whitewater rivers, hiking through dense jungles, enduring scorching deserts, and investigating geological, archeological and other natural wonders of the world.

Introduction

What if you knew you could live a life that was filled with meaning, significance, and hope? Would you be interested in finding out about it? I have had the opportunity throughout my life to dialogue with thousands of people in all fifty of the United States and in nearly thirty countries on five different continents of the world. I have discovered three important insights through these conversations. First of all, I have come to the conclusion that the desire for meaning, significance, and hope is nearly universal across all cultures—no matter how rich or how poor the circumstances are. Second of all, I have discovered that in spite of their desires, many people live their lives without any compelling feelings of meaning, significance, or hope. As these people age and enter the last stages of their lives, feelings of despair often overwhelm them. Third of all, as I have been engaged in conversation with these people, I have heard continuous themes emerge from their words that signify that there actually *was a purpose* in their lives that could have given them meaning, significance, and hope.

Ironically, very few people recognize this purpose, even though it is right there in their hands; as a result they live their lives without realizing their true calling. The reason people are not able to recognize a purpose in their lives is that society has encouraged them to chase after jobs by pursuing the typical career development model. But the problem is that this model tends to put too much emphasis on careers instead of focusing on a higher purpose in their lives—a Life Calling.

This career-development process plays out in what I call the *Tale of Two Kingdoms*. In the philosophy and teachings of Jesus, he identified those two kingdoms. The first one he called the *kingdom of this world*. He characterized it as a kingdom where people strive to save their lives, but in the end they lose their lives. It's a kingdom where the goal is to gain the whole world, but people in this kingdom of the world achieve this kind of success at the cost of forfeiting their souls. The second kingdom Jesus called the *kingdom of heaven*. In this kingdom Jesus said people are willing to lose their lives for his sake, but in the end they find life. It's a kingdom where people deny themselves and, instead, take up their cross and follow Jesus. This kingdom of heaven is not a "pie-in-the-sky" approach. Jesus pointed out very emphatically that this kingdom is at hand (which means it is here right now), and that it is in you (in other words, you don't have to look all over to find it).

Unfortunately, typical career development pursues the *kingdom of this world* approach. In this model you are urged to chase after the so-called "best" jobs with the belief that your sense of meaning, significance, and hope will be found in these jobs. The process of promised success goes like this: (1) you are encouraged to follow your interests and select a major in college based on these interests; (2) you are then directed to find a career that goes along with your major, but one that will also give you success and security; (3) you are finally left to make some sense of meaning in your life from what you experience in your job—a struggle that is usually futile. The problem with this approach based on self-interests is that the initial interests have often been aroused, for the most part, by the amount of pay, job availability, and job growth. Although these concerns have some value, if you look at them closely, they very easily lead to a self-centered approach. An entire self-help industry has emerged out of this, with claims to help you pursue this approach successfully and quickly. A recent cover on a magazine associated with a very popular self-help television show claimed to have an "easy-does-it guide in finding and fulfilling your life purpose." But these self-centered, quick-fix approaches are not from the *kingdom of heaven* and never bring long-lasting meaning, significance, and hope.

The self-centered approach that comes out of the *kingdom of this world* is totally backwards. You need to move, instead, to the *kingdom of heaven* to find the better approach. In this kingdom you begin by looking for deeper meaning in your life. You ask, "What is the higher purpose of my life?" While this purpose will be somewhat unique for each person, the fundamental core will be the same: the focus will not be on striving to better yourself, but, in contrast, it focuses on what God is doing and what you can do to join him in his efforts. Once this purpose has been discovered or recognized, then you can decide on a career that will help fulfill this purpose. Finally, a decision on a college major that will help you prepare for that career can be effectively determined. Then, when you graduate and go on to life beyond college, you realize that your Life Calling is to experience all of life, not just a job. And that is where you will begin to find long-lasting meaning, significance, and hope.

So there they are—two kingdoms with two opposite patterns for life. You need to choose wisely which kingdom you will follow. The kingdom we will explore all through this study will be the *kingdom of heaven*. Our theme throughout *Explorer's Guide* will be:

Start your college journey with a sense of purpose.

List of Figures

Getting Started

As you read this book, you are likely in one of two places in life: 1) You are finishing high school and looking ahead, trying to make a decision about whether or not to go to college; or 2) you've arrived on your college campus. You probably have emotions that are a mixture of excitement and apprehension, anticipation and fear, ambition and confusion. You have been told all your life that college is your ticket to the future. The problem is that you're not really sure what that future actually is!

Uncertainty about career futures characterizes an estimated 20 to 50 percent of students entering college (Lewallen, 1995), leading them to postpone selection of a major until they have stronger convictions and instead opting for the "undecided" classification. The actual number in this category may be as high as two-thirds of all first-year students. The reason that number does not show up in statistics stems from the fact that a sizeable percentage of these students go ahead and declare a major because they think or have been advised that this is the preferred way to start, even though they have little reassurance that the chosen major is really the one for them. These same individuals often end up changing their majors several times during their college experience.

In the introduction to this book, we discussed the problem with preparing for life based on a self-centered approach. Unfortunately, colleges often adopt this same approach when advising students. They encourage students to choose a major based on their interests and then go into a career that corresponds to the major. Without meaning and purpose, this approach doesn't work. Studies have shown that one year after graduating from college, 25 percent of college students work in careers unrelated to their college majors. Four years after graduating, 40 percent of people end up working in careers unrelated to their college majors (McCormick and Horn, 1996; McCormick et. al., 1999). If you were buying a new car, you certainly would like to have some hope that the car would have a better chance of working after four years than these numbers. You will be paying more money for your college education than you would for a new car; shouldn't you be able to expect even a higher rate of success than you would for a car?

In this book we will explore a different approach to college and to life. This approach directly challenges the self-centered, what's-in-it-for-me approach to life. It calls us to look for something outside ourselves, something bigger—a Life Calling. This Life Calling is larger than a college major, job, or position. It is more profound than a title or salary. The concept of a Life Calling is simply this: confidence in an overriding purpose for your life...and then living your life consistently with that purpose.

In the past few years, people have GPS navigational systems on their cell phones or in their cars. Most likely you have used such a device. You enter a desired destination, and then as you travel along, a voice informs you of distances you must go and turns you must take. The accuracy is amazing. If you have used one of these devices, you have probably also experienced a secret desire to have a similar device give you specific instructions that would guide you on your personal mission in life. Wouldn't it be great to have a voice saying, "Turn right in point two miles?"

Remember what we discussed in the introduction about Jewish history? Moses saw the burning bush. Gideon put out a fleece—two actually. Elijah heard a still, small voice. A donkey instructed Balaam. A whale redirected Jonah. The prophets, like Isaiah, Jeremiah, and Ezekiel, saw explicit visions. We agreed that those all seem alluring when so many of us get up and face each day with little or no sense of deep purpose or direction. However, when we go out and look at the bush, there is no fire. Our fleeces don't work, our donkeys don't talk, and our visions are dim. There is no Life GPS navigational system that we can plug in.

So is there anything we can do? Is there any hope of direction, mission, or reason for our lives? The answer is yes! It can be found in our Life Calling. Is it discernable? Yes. Is it logical? Yes. Is it mystical? Yes. Is it simple? Yes. Is it complex? Yes.

Those answers may at first seem contradictory and confusing, but they really are not. What they indicate is that the concept of a Life Calling has a great breadth and at the same time a great depth. Here is the question with its answer, however, that can give you the greatest hope. Can a Life Calling be discovered? Yes!

And this is the best place to start as you move from high school to whatever lies ahead for you—whether it be college, training for a trade, or entering immediately into the work world. This time of transition should be more than anything else a discovery of your Life Calling. This will provide you a context that you can use to make sense out of your choices. And if you are college-bound, it provides a valuable context for everything else you study or do in your college experience.

The goal of this book is to help prepare you to make that discovery of a Life Calling. To guide you through the discovery process, we will use an approach similar to a traveler's guide that is often used when visiting other countries. In those guides you have tabbed sections for lodging, meals, attractions, things to do, and many more. In this book, each chapter will be divided into different sections as well, with tabs identifying each section:

1. The Model section will provide a graphic representation of the Life Calling Model indicating where we are in our exploration.

2. The Concepts section will provide an exploration of the theory behind Life Calling.

3. The Insights section will expand the understanding of Life Calling by looking at what the Bible says about the concepts being explored.

4. The Discovery section will give you suggestions of how to explore a specific element of the Life Calling Model using one or more of the seven important discovery guides.

5. The Story section will explore the concept of Life Calling through the telling of a story that follows six students who have just graduated from high school and are looking ahead at issues related to college.

6. The Exercises section will provide practical exercises to help you explore the Life Calling concepts introduced in each chapter and develop habits that will help you implement the concepts into your life.

7. The References section will provide a list of references cited and other resources on the topic of each chapter.

Life Calling Model

Throughout this book, you will have the opportunity to explore your Life Calling using a specific model (Figure 1-1). And just as important, you will have the opportunity to develop tools that will continue to help you discover your Life Calling throughout your lifetime.

FIGURE 1-1
Life Calling Model

The model is comprised of three main components—*Foundational Values, Unique Design*, and *Personal Leadership*. Each of these components has three distinct elements, resulting in nine total elements in the overall model.

Each of the components and elements could be studied independently of the other components and elements. But a sense of an overriding purpose for your life is only found when the components and elements are explored in a manner that in the end brings them all together as indicated by the central light zone in the model. The impact of each main component on the other two components is indicated by the terms and arrows in the smaller shield-shaped areas where two components overlap.

MODEL

▶ Seven Sources to Explore for a Life Calling

Over the last three decades, Indiana Jones has become one of the better-known fictional explorers. The daring archeologist traveled all over the world from one adventure to another, often risking his life, in search of rare items of great importance such as the Ark of the Covenant, the Holy Grail, or as in his latest episode, the Crystal Skull. Discovering your Life Calling requires a similar adventurous search. Dr. Jones often followed a set of clues or a map to guide him to the treasure. You also will need sources of information to guide your discovery of a Life Calling. Here are seven of the most effective ones.

Theory

Many people have already traveled the path before you in search of a Life Calling. As a result, they have been able to leave behind theories that explain how to be effective in the search. Seek out these theories and study them. This will greatly accelerate your own discovery process. These explanations fall into three broad theories:

Scientific Theories.   These theories study human characteristics and dynamics and how this can help you understand what kind of person you are. Psychology, sociology, anthropology, and biology are rich sources of information about what it means to be human.

Philosophical Theories.   These theories study ultimate meaning in the human experience and how this can help you understand the deeper meaning of your life. These theories are often tied directly into religious and theological studies.

Strategic Theories.   These theories study how to create an effective plan of action for your life and how this can provide you a road map to follow as you pursue your Life Calling. Leadership and management studies often look at this in relationship to groups of people and organizations. Self-help and career development studies look at this with an individual focus.

Examples

One of the most common sources that can help you discover your Life Calling can be found in observing the examples of other people. Here are three good groups to watch:

Family.   Most people are around their family members more than any other group. If you follow this pattern, you will have the chance to closely observe them in relationship to Life Calling dynamics. Don't make the mistake, however, of automatically assuming that your Life Calling will be the same as other members of your family.

Modelers.   As you think of areas of work, family, or service that seem to be drawing your attention, look at people around you who model success in these areas.

Mentors.   One of the real blessings that can come into your life is a trusted counselor or teacher who is willing to walk alongside you as you explore your Life Calling. You can learn much from such a person.

Assessments

Social scientists have created numerous assessments that can help you discover the unique characteristics you possess as an individual. These should be used as one set of tools in the discovery process, not the only set of tools. When using assessments, keep in mind the following guidelines:

Strengths-focus.   Look for assessments that emphasize the measurement of your strengths rather than highlighting your weaknesses.

Comprehensive.   Seek information from multiple assessments that measure all aspects of your strengths rather than those that focus on one area only.

Validate.   When you receive results from assessments, do not accept them at face value. Ask yourself if they make sense to you. If they don't, question them. Also ask other people who know you well if the assessment results seem valid.

Counsel

You can learn much about yourself and your sense of calling by working with counselors who are committed to helping you. You can find such counselors in three groupings:

Professional Life Coaches.   These are individuals that are trained to help you in the exploration process as you search for a Life Calling.

Paraprofessionals.   These are individuals such as pastors, youth ministers, and teachers. Though they may not be trained specifically in the area of life coaching, they have training in working with people in life development.

Nonprofessionals.   Family members and friends often have good advice that can help you understand your life better. Their counsel should not be ignored.

History

Discovering what lies ahead of us can many times be found as much in understanding what has already happened behind us as it is in guessing what will happen ahead of us.

Life Mapping.   This process can provide a very effective approach to collecting the events of our lives and trying to make sense of what we collect. We will look at how to do this later on in this book.

Classic Works.   The writings of others throughout history can provide valuable lessons to be learned. These authors often provide insights that we would overlook on our own.

Analyzing Trends.   This can be an interesting way to approach history when *applying* it to our lives. What patterns can be seen in the past and are happening right now? And what do these indicate about the future? Though these trends do not lock the future in place, they do help us be prepared for what might happen.

Experience

One of the most useful sources of information concerning our Life Calling can be gathered from experience. As we evaluate these experiences, we can learn a lot about ourselves and what really connects with us and draws us to a calling.

Circumstantial Experiences. These are experiences that are not necessarily planned, but as they happen allow us to evaluate them to gain information about our Life Calling.

Experimental Experiences. These are activities that we engage in specifically for the purpose of trying to gain information about our Life Calling. We use these experiences like a laboratory.

Job-related Experiences. These experiences provide us direct information from the world of work. Here we can learn a lot about the career aspects of our Life Calling.

Reflection

As we explore our Life Calling, it is very important that we take time to reflect on what we are learning. However, reflection is one of the hardest things for people in our fast-paced culture to do because it requires us to stop and be quiet for a period of time. Here are three valuable habits you should develop to be more effective at reflection.

Listening. The habit of listening is almost more an art than a habit. Most of us don't really know how to do it. Even when we think we are listening, we aren't. Instead, we are judging what the other person is saying and jumping to conclusions about what is being said long before the person has finished the idea; or even worse, we are planning what we are going to say as soon as the other person is finished, though the person is still talking. Patiently listening to another person in a nonjudgmental manner is a difficult skill—one we need to work hard to develop.

Meditating. As we search for our Life Calling through the other sources listed earlier in this section, we need to find time when we can deliberately and thoughtfully study what we have learned and contemplate deeply on its meaning. Meditating requires quiet time, and like listening, this is a difficult habit to develop because of the hectic pace at which most of us live our lives.

Journaling. Finally, a very effective way to make reflection a lasting experience and force in our lives is to journal what we are reflecting on in a written form. This is usually done as a daily routine that chronicles occurrences, experiences, observations, or insights encountered during each day. This activity has the added benefit of providing us a source to which we can return when trying to remember reflections we have had earlier in our lives.

Figure 1-2 shows an easy way to remember these seven sources of information that will help you discover your Life Calling. If you combine the first letter of each of the seven, they combine to spell the word "TEACHER." These sources truly can work together to be a teacher imparting knowledge, skills, wisdom, and understanding that can lead to confidence in an overriding purpose for your life.

FIGURE 1-2
TEACHER Acronym

 **Insight**

Scripture provides insight related to each of the seven guiding sources that will help you discover an overriding purpose for your life.

GUIDING SOURCE 1 *Using Theory to Discover Life Calling*

Teach me knowledge and good judgment, for I trust your commands. Before I was afflicted I went astray, but now I obey your word. PSALM 119:66-67

Here is a good question to explore as we search for direction in our life— Is it better to begin with mystical and transcendental experiences or with solid theoretical information that will allow us to evaluate mystical and transcendental experiences and test their validity? As appealing as the first choice might be, the second choice appears to be the better answer. We will ultimately be led astray in our search for a Life Calling if we ignore the information God has already given us concerning our lives.

How many of us say "I'm just waiting to hear from God," when in reality we already have! Maybe the problem is not so much that we haven't heard from God but that we weren't listening in the right place. Our discovery of a Life Calling will be greatly enhanced by careful study of good theory, especially theory that God has provided us in the Bible.

The theme of Psalm 119 focuses on the concept that God has already communicated with us through scripture. At the time this Psalm was written, the scriptures were restricted to the Torah—what would be the first five books in our Bible today. Two concepts can be seen in the passage quoted for today. First, by starting with a study of God's commands, we can learn knowledge and good judgment. It is not the other way around. Second, when we don't heed God's word, we tend to end up going astray.

So as we approach our search for Life Calling and God's direction, the first Discovery Tool we should employ is the study of theory, and the study of theory should begin with what God has already revealed to us in the Bible. This can then become the standard by which we evaluate other information, including information that might come in mystical and transcendental experiences.

> **PERSONAL REFLECTION** God calls us each day. A Life Calling is the collection of all these daily callings. Have I taken time today to listen to what God has already told me about my life today in his word so that I can evaluate the rest of the day by that message?

GUIDING SOURCE 2 *Using Examples to Discover Life Calling*

Join together in following my example, brothers and sisters, and just as you have us as a model, keep your eyes on those who live as we do. PHILIPPIANS 3:17

I have had the opportunity to explore Life Calling with literally tens of thousands of individuals. If I had to identify one area that has had a greater impact on more people than any other, it would have to be the examples they have been portrayed in their lives by other people. This might be a parent, another relative, a favorite teacher, a pastor, someone working in the community or another country, a sports figure, a government leader, and the list could go on. One of the major reasons this occurs is that most people learn by observation. Even if they are book learners, they often learn a lot by reading the story about someone else's life.

And so it is not surprising that in helping the Christians of Philippi to journey down the right path, Paul encouraged them to follow his example. That was a serious exhortation by Paul because it put the pressure on him to set a good example for the Philippians.

Observing the example of others has, throughout history, been a good source of guidance in discovering a Life Calling. Joshua looked to Moses as his example. Elijah served as an example and mentor for Elisha. Socrates mentored Plato, who, in turn, mentored Aristotle. The philosophical thoughts from that line have had tremendous impact on the thinking of the Western world. They had an impact on the Apostle Paul as well. Jesus instructed his disciples to reproduce his example in their lives after he washed their feet at the Last Supper.

Not all of those we observe always set a good example, so we have to choose wisely when we pick someone's example as a pattern to follow in our lives. The book of Proverbs provides this admonition: "Walk with the wise and become wise, for a companion of fools suffers harm" (Proverbs 13:20). Take time right now to list in your mind people who are having a significant impact on you, especially if that impact is related to what you want to do with your life. You will find several important factors with those who are having a strong positive impact. First of all, they are following a strong positive pattern themselves. No matter how old they are, they always seem to have someone who they look up to. Second, they live consistently, which is why they can provide a good example. Finally, they have a good understanding of themselves. If you haven't found a person like this to observe in your own life, start looking for one.

> **PERSONAL REFLECTION** Everybody has other people who are influencing them. The key to making this a valuable dynamic is taking time to evaluate what kind of influence it is and the kind of impact it is having. Who is God using right now in your life to help guide you in your search for a Life Calling?

GUIDING SOURCE 3 *Using Assessments to Discover Life Calling*

Each of you should test your own actions. Then you can take pride in yourself, without comparing yourself to somebody else, for each of you should carry your own load. GALATIANS 6:4-5

When you are getting ready in the morning and you look in the mirror, how much do you know about the person you see? You might be surprised to know that many people don't know that much about themselves. The problem for those who might fall into this category is that they end up defining themselves by how they think they compare with others. The Apostle Paul warned the Christians of Galatia about relying on such comparisons. He instead advised them to assess themselves. Implied in that advice is the need to accept who we are; that's what Paul meant when he said we should carry our own load. That does not mean we should not grow and improve. But we need to accept our uniqueness as an important part of our Life Calling.

One way to test your own actions is to complete formal assessments that have been designed specifically to help you conduct such a test of actions and individual uniqueness. When correctly taken and understood, these can provide valuable information about how God has created you and made you unique. You need to be careful, however, that you do not allow assessments to imprison you. How can you detect if this is happening? The Bible tells us that when Jesus sets us free, we are free indeed (John 8:36). Anything that starts to take away that freedom and causes you to begin conforming to some blueprint that primarily compares you to someone else and ignores God's design in your life, is likely not something God is using to speak into your life.

What have you learned about yourself through formal assessments lately? How does this information compare with what you find in the Bible and what you believe you have already heard God saying to you?

> **PERSONAL REFLECTION** ⟩ Everybody has unique characteristics that are strengths and assets. What characteristic have you learned about your uniqueness that you believe God wired into you as part of your Life Calling? Have you ever thanked God for these?

GUIDING SOURCE 4 ⟩ *Using Counsel to Discover Life Calling*

Plans fail for lack of counsel, but with many advisers they succeed. PROVERBS 15:22

It is very rare, if not impossible, that a person can pursue the search for a Life Calling alone and then live it out successfully in the same solitary approach. It is easy, then, to understand why it makes good sense to listen to the counsel and advice of others as we search for our Life Calling. The admonition from the Proverbs puts it in clear focus.

A great example of this occurred in the life of Moses. Moses was leading the people of Israel out of Egypt across the desert on their way to the Promised Land in Canaan. So far so good. The problem was that Moses did all the work of leading by himself. He evidently had a hard time delegating the responsibility of judging disputes that arose among the Israelites, and the heavy load was weighing him down. Then Jethro entered the scene. He was Moses' father-in-law. He gave Moses some good counsel: if you keep doing all the judging yourself, it is going to wear you out; train up others who can help you carry the load. Moses listened to the counsel and developed an effective structure to help him.

There are blind spots in your life right now that you will discover only with the help of someone else. There are gifts that you have, yet you are unaware of them. Without the counsel of another person, the chances are good that you will never discover these assets. There are choices you have to make, and you are unsure of what you should do. The counsel of another wise person can help give you a clearer perspective.

Some people are afraid to seek counsel because they have the mistaken belief that this is a sign of weakness. The opposite is actually true. People who seek counsel are strong because they know that a Life Calling was never meant to be lived in isolation from others.

> **PERSONAL REFLECTION** ⟩ Who is offering counsel into your life right now?
> How is God using this counsel to help you understand your Life Calling?

GUIDING SOURCE 5 ⟩ *Using History to Discover Life Calling*

Therefore, since we are surrounded by such a great cloud of witnesses, let us throw off everything that hinders and the sin that so easily entangles. And let us run with perseverance the race marked out for us, fixing our eyes on Jesus, the pioneer and perfecter of faith. For the joy set before him he endured the cross, scorning its shame, and sat down at the right hand of the throne of God. Consider him who endured such opposition from sinners, so that you will not grow weary and lose heart. HEBREWS 12:1-3

Hebrews 11, sometimes referred to as the "Hall of Faith," records the lives of several prominent figures in biblical history. In the first three verses of the chapter that follows, the readers are encouraged to use such examples from history to inspire the way they live their lives.

The old saying, "there is no need to reinvent the wheel," comes to mind. As we search for our Life Calling and ways to live it out as we find it, why not look at the people who have lived before us and discover the secrets from their lives that made them successful in pursuing their Life Calling?

What was it that enabled Abel, Enoch, Noah, Abraham, Isaac, Jacob, Joseph, Moses, Rahab, Gideon, Barak, Samson, Jephthah, David, Samuel and the prophets to all live lives of spiritual strength and God-given purpose? In discovering that answer, we might find important secrets for our own lives. But it is not just the history of Bible characters. We can learn much from other historical figures like Augustine, Martin Luther, Abraham Lincoln, Mother Teresa, Martin Luther King, Jr., and many others. We can also learn from the history of our own parents and grandparents.

Our own history also provides a very important source that can help reveal our path to us. Have you ever noticed that you really can't tell if you are going the wrong way by looking at what is coming ahead? It is more likely detected by looking at where you have already traveled.

> **PERSONAL REFLECTION** ⟩ What person in history has been an inspiration to
> you as you look at what you want to do in life? What events in your own life have
> given you direction in what your Life Calling might be?

GUIDING SOURCE 6 ⟩ *Using Experience to Discover Life Calling*

Test everything. Hold on to the good. 1 THESSALONIANS 5:21

Some of the most useful advice that comes from the Bible can be found in statements that are short and to the point. The Apostle Paul was a great source of such statements. His statement above is one of his best.

While this counsel was primarily aimed at ideas and philosophy, it can be expanded to many aspects of our lives. As we search for a Life Calling through many different activities, one good approach is to try out different things in our lives. In other words, test them. Then if they work, hold on to the good. If not, set them aside and look for something else.

INSIGHT

Have you ever tried to ride a bicycle uphill without pedaling? It doesn't work. You just keep falling over. It is only while you are moving forward that you can actually steer your bike. The same thing holds true in life. Steering your life—finding your Life Calling—will best be revealed as you are moving forward in life. In other words, try different things. Some of them will work out really well, and you will discover that these are paths you will want to continue to follow. Others won't turn out so well. But those aren't wasted experiences either, because you learned that those paths were ones you would be better off not traveling.

The Apostle Paul found direction in such experiences. In the city of Athens he tried a sophisticated and clever approach with philosophers based on an altar to an Unknown God that they had as one of many altars to various gods. He used that for a starting point to talk about Jesus. But in the end this approach resulted in only a few people deciding to follow Jesus. Paul went from Athens to the city of Corinth. He learned something from that Athens experience. In Corinth he followed a different path. He chose not to rely on eloquence or superior wisdom; instead, his message and preaching "were not with wise and persuasive words, but with a demonstration of the Spirit's power, so that your faith might not rest on human wisdom, but on God's power" (1 Corinthians 2:1-5). While no significant Christian church resulted from Paul's work in Athens, a very strong church arose from his work in Corinth. He had learned by experience.

Are you moving forward in your life and trying different ways of doing things as you move? Suppose a person would never go to see a movie unless the person had seen that movie at least one time before. Stop and think about that for a moment. If you followed that pattern, you would never see a movie. That is very similar to what will happen in your life if you only pursue things when you know they will work. In other words, you're afraid to experiment with them by trying them out. You will probably end up not doing anything if that's your approach to life, and you will never discover a Life Calling.

> **PERSONAL REFLECTION**   What are you learning from your life experiences? What is working? What isn't working? Remember, answers to both of those questions are equally important.

GUIDING SOURCE 7   *Using Reflection to Discover Life Calling*

I will remember the deeds of the LORD; yes, I will remember your miracles of long ago. I will meditate on all your works and consider all your mighty deeds. Your ways, O God, are holy. What god is so great as our God? You are the God who performs miracles; you display your power among the peoples. Psalm 77:11-14

Reflection is one of the hardest things for people in our fast-paced culture to do because it requires us to stop and be quiet for a period of time. Think about the way you eat dessert. Let's be honest—none of us eats desserts in order to advance our nutrition or health; we eat dessert for enjoyment. But there's the oddity. Once a spoonful or forkful of the dessert is in your mouth, what do you do with spoon or fork? If you're like most of us, you do not set it down while you take time to savor the taste of the dessert. No, instead you sink the spoon or fork into the next portion that you will be moving toward your mouth. Crazy, isn't it? We eat dessert for enjoyment and yet we don't even take time to actually enjoy it.

That pretty much describes our overall approach to life. We don't take time to consider it or enjoy it. Yet it is very important for us to take time to do this if we are going to make sense of what we are learning about a Life Calling. Think about those words from the Psalms.

Reflection accomplishes several things. First, it helps us remember what we have learned. Second, it helps us put what we have learned into perspective. Finally, reflection can inspire us with a sense of God's power to help us live out what we have learned.

Mary, likely a teenage girl living in the small village of Nazareth, was visited by the angel Gabriel. He tells her that she will give birth to a son, and that she should name the son Jesus. This greatly surprised Mary because she was a virgin, and she had no idea how this could come about. Gabriel told her that this would be made possible by a miracle of the Holy Spirit.

When the baby was born in Bethlehem, shepherds came and told her that a host of angles had appeared to them in the fields while they were watching their sheep. The angels had announced to them that the Savior had been born in Bethlehem.

It is Mary's response that can be an inspiration to us as to how we should respond to meaningful events in our lives. The story is recorded in the second chapter of Luke, and in the nineteenth verse it describes Mary's response: "But Mary treasured up all these things and pondered them in her heart." We need to treasure the things that happen in our lives and ponder them. Ponder means to reflect or consider with thoroughness and care. When we do this we will start to see our Life Calling unfold just as Mary began to understand her Life Calling.

> **PERSONAL REFLECTION** ⟩ Do you take time to think about what is happening in your life right now and then try to make meaning of it? Or are you already reaching for the next "spoonful" of life by put your thoughts into tomorrow? What has happened in your life today? What does this reveal to you about your Life Calling?

INSIGHT

Story

The following story involves six seniors from Seahaven High School. To help you get to know them, we gathered the following information from their Facebook pages.

Adam Collins

Education and Work

Employers

District Attorney's Office
Student Intern

High School

Seahaven High School

Activities and Interests

Activities   Sports, Traveling
Interests   Politics, Philosophy

Basic Information

About Adam

I love football and have been the varsity quarterback for the past two years. But I also enjoyed going to national finals with the debate team this year.

I'm going to college, but I am not sure what I am going to major in. I'll start off exploring my options.

Information from the Facebook Group "Seahaven High School Senior Class"

Senior Class Award   Most likely to be President of the US.

What the Senior   Adam's a natural leader of people who seems more
class survey said   self-aware than anyone else in the class
about Adam

Diana Neimon

Education and Work

Employers

Janelle's Fashion Boutique
Sales associate

High School

Seahaven High School

Activities and Interests

Activities   Horseback Riding, Traveling
Interests   Fashion, Socializing

Basic Information

About Diana

I like hanging out with friends or shopping at the mall.

With grades like mine, I'll be lucky to make it into community college, so that's where I'm headed."

Information from the Facebook Group "Seahaven High School Senior Class"

Senior Class Award	Most likely to make it to Hollywood
What the Senior class survey said about Diana	Diana should be on the runway but is also a great listener. Any guy who gets her is one lucky dude.

Justin Park

Education and Work

Employers

 Seahaven Technology Center
Technician Apprentice

High School

Seahaven High School

Activities and Interests

Activities — Tennis, Golf
Interests — Science and Technology, Chaos Theory

Basic Information

About Justin

I'm not sure how to describe myself. I guess I'm sorta Korean bc my grandparents were both born there. They moved to Socal after the Korean War and are cool.

I'm not really sure what my major will be in college. There's a lot more to life than college majors.

Information from the Facebook Group "Seahaven High School Senior Class"

Senior Class Award	Most likely to put Google out of business.
What the Senior class survey said about Justin	Justin knows how to get along with everybody

Lorena Rodriguez

Education and Work

Employers

 Seahaven Seafood Restaurant
Waitress

High School

Seahaven High School

Activities and Interests

Activities — Learning new things, Reading
Interests — Medicine, World Almanac

Basic Information

About Lorena

Came into the world south of the border in Mexico. Olé! The whole fam became US citizens 10 years ago. Still haven't forgotten Mexico, though.

I plan to study medicine and be a pediatrician.

Information from the Facebook Group "Seahaven High School Senior Class"

Senior Class Award	The smartest person in the class (at least that's what she tells us)
What the Senior class survey said about Lorena	If you're not sure what Lorena's opinion is, just ask her!

Ryan Williams

Education and Work

Employers

 Surf's Up
Retail Associate

High School

Seahaven High School

Activities and Interests

Activities   Surfing
Interests   Surfing

Basic Information

About Ryan

One ride on a bad wave is better than the best day in school.

I sure don't plan on wasting my time in college. My dad got his degree but ended up changing jobs 8 times and still hates his job! I'm planning to spend my life looking for the perfect wave. Hang ten, dudes.

Information from the Facebook Group "Seahaven High School Senior Class"

Senior Class Award	Coolest dude in the class.
What the Senior class survey said about Ryan	If you're not sure you saw Ryan in class, you probably didn't!

Abriella Delaney

Education and Work

Employers

 Seahaven Center for the Arts
Young Artists Mentor

High School

Seahaven High School

Activities and Interests

Activities   Reading, Theater, Painting
Interests   Art, Religion

Basic Information

About Abriella

I'm an African-American and proud of it. I'm also proud of my grandfather bc he marched with Dr. Martin Luther King, Jr. in Selma, Alabama.

I have a lot of interests and I haven't narrowed them down, so I am starting college with no major declared. I wish I could take them all.

Information from the Facebook Group "Seahaven High School Senior Class"

Senior Class Award	Most likely to succeed at anything or everything.
What the Senior class survey said about Abriella	She's the valedictorian. What can we say—she's just plain smart!

A cool, foggy veil hung over McClellan State Beach, but this did not dampen the spirits of the six high school seniors as they slowly walked down the sands periodically slapped by waves. Graduation was less than a month away. Who wouldn't be in a good frame of mind? The K–12 time is exciting for some; for others it is a sentence inflicted on them by parents, the government, or some other authority. No matter what the experience, however, everyone looks forward to graduating and bringing it to a close.

These six were no different. They wanted to celebrate in a big way. Sure, there would be some fun parties on graduation night, but it had to be something bigger than that. This would be their chance to have one last fling together. They had grown up together in the town of Seahaven, a midsize town along the Gold Coast of California. They first met each other in kindergarten and had been classmates and best friends from that point on. Now, with graduation from high school around the corner, they realized that they would all be going in different directions and would probably never be together like this again. So when their parents asked them what they wanted for graduation, they had asked for a trip around the United States. They would leave the day after graduation in a 42-foot motor home owned by Diana Neimon's parents—who would also be accompanying them as hosts for the trip.

Adam Collins kicked at a piece of driftwood washed in by the last wave. "So where are we going?" he asked the others.

"I want to see the Grand Canyon," Lorena Rodriguez replied. "I've wanted to go there ever since Mr. Johnson's earth science class in seventh grade."

"It's just a big ditch, Lorena!" Justin Park laughed.

"I don't care; I like big ditches," Lorena shot back. "Where do *you* want to go?"

"Washington, D.C.," Justin replied firmly. "If we're going to see the country, we have to visit the Capitol. My grandparents were young when their families came to America from Korea after the war. They've always wanted to see the Capitol, and they'd kill me if I didn't do it when I had the chance."

"Makes sense to me," Abriella Delaney said. "And as long as we're on the east coast, I want to go to New York."

STORY

"Yeah," the others all echoed in unison. "My mom was born in Harlem," Abriella continued.

"Really?" asked Adam. "What about your dad?"

"He was born in Birmingham, Alabama," Abriella replied. "But he moved to New York when he was a teenager. He says it wasn't easy growing up in the South as an African American in that time period…not that it is easy now."

"As long as we're going to New York, why can't we go to Boston too?" Ryan Williams added. "Besides, isn't that where the Pilgrims landed and stole this whole country?"

"That was Plymouth…you know, Plymouth Rock," Lorena corrected. She often sounded like a teacher when dealing with the others. "But it *is* close to Boston, so I guess that counts."

"That would be *piedra del plimoth* to you," Ryan replied. He and Lorena were constantly picking away at each other's words, and Ryan loved to tease her about her roots. Lorena had been born in Guadalajara, Mexico. Her parents had moved to Seahaven when she was three.

"That's better than *piedras en la cabeza* for you," Lorena shot back. They all laughed. All six of them had taken four years of Spanish in high school and were well aware that this meant "rocks in the head."

"If we're visiting all these major cities, then we should go to Chicago on our return leg," Diana said, jumping into the conversation. "And why not stop at Niagara Falls on the way from Boston to Chicago?"

"I know," Ryan added. "Let's go to St. Louis from Chicago and see the big Arch. We can ride a paddle wheel boat on the Mississippi there too. I've always wanted to see the Mississippi River."

"Any river with water is better than what we have here!" Diana laughed, making fun of the dry washes along the coast of the southern part of California— all having names and few having water.

The excitement was building. The planning gave all the indications that it would be a great trip.

"Let's go to Pike's Peak from St. Louis," Adam suggested. "I've always wanted to see the view from the top. I think that's where that lady wrote the words to 'America the Beautiful.'"

"Yeah, you're right," Lorena answered. "And then why don't we finish by going north to Yellowstone National Park? We should see Old Faithful. We can see the Grand Teton Mountains too."

And in just a short while, the six had planned a splendid trip—and spent quite a lot of their parents' money as well!

A low sand bank had been formed by the waves' action along the beach. Adam sat down on it, and the others followed suit. "You know, it's kind of weird. It only took us a few minutes to figure out where we wanted to go on a trip clear around the nation," he reflected, "and yet it seems so difficult to figure out where we're going after graduation."

"Speak for yourself," Lorena said sharply. "You might not know where you're going, but I do." Lorena was one of the better students at Seahaven High School and had been accepted into UCLA as a biology major in the premedical studies program. Sometimes her high level of achievement came across with a certain air of elitism, but the others had learned to see beyond that. They knew that underneath all of this she was often a very insecure person.

"I don't even know if I'm going to go to college," Ryan said, staring at the sand as he spoke. "It seems like a big waste of time and money. My dad doesn't even do anything close to what he studied in college. You're better off just getting a job."

"That's crazy, Ryan." Justin's voice was filled with scorn. "What kind of job are you going to get with just a high school diploma?"

"Yeah? Well, what kind of job did my dad get with a college diploma? Obviously not too good of one because he changed it. In fact, he's changed jobs eight different times and none of them have paid him that much money!" Ryan snapped defensively. "So what are you going to do to change that in *your* life, Justin?"

"Hey, man, I think college is about more than getting a job," Justin said, rising to the challenge. "I don't even know what I'm going to major in. I'm just going to explore my first year."

"I read somewhere that most students change their major three or four times anyway," Abriella said. "I'm starting out like you, Justin. I'll choose my major after I've had a chance to look around."

"That still blows my mind." Diana had a puzzled tone to her voice. "If *I* was the valedictorian of my class, I'd think I'd know what I was going to do!"

"Why?" Abriella asked.

"Because you're smarter than all the rest of us." There was frustration as well as envy in Diana's words. "I'll be lucky just to make it through my first two years at Seahaven Community College. Hopefully, I'll be ready for the rest of college."

"What about you, Adam? What do you think you'll do?" Lorena asked. "You've always taken the lead with us, and you're a good student."

"I'm still working it through in my mind, Lorena." Adam looked up from the sand to meet her eyes. "College is important to me, sure, but it's only one part of my life. It just seems like there has to be a bigger purpose to my life than just going to college, getting a degree, then getting a job and ending up bored like half our parents."

"That's exactly what I'm saying, man!" Ryan's voice rose in excitement as he figured he had an ally.

"Yeah, but I'm not ready to throw in the towel like you, Ryan," Adam replied. "I'm still planning on college. I'm just looking at it as a smaller piece in a bigger puzzle…and I'm still trying to figure out that bigger puzzle."

"Me too," the others said one-by-one—all, that is, but Lorena.

"Go ahead and look for your big puzzle if you want." The disdain in her voice could not be masked. "My big puzzle is to be a doctor, pure and simple. And I'm on my way!"

The others rolled their eyes as they looked at each other. They loved Lorena as their friend, but it took a certain amount of patience.

"Speaking of being on your way," Adam laughed, "we'd probably better head back before it gets too dark." He stood up, brushed the sand off, and headed down the beach toward the parking area. The others followed.

STORY

▶ Exercises

Exercises to Get You Started

In whatever path you choose to follow in life, you will need to develop disciplines that will help you succeed in this journey and that also can help lead you to discover your Life Calling. In each of the "Exercises" sections, you will have the opportunity to engage in activities that will help you accomplish this.

If the exploration journey that lies ahead of you in college is to be successful, however, you will need to develop two critical habits—time management and financial management. These will also be important in helping you carry out your Life Calling once you have discovered it.

EXERCISE 1

Time Management

In the college culture, time management may be the greatest predictor and influencer of performance. You will constantly be inundated with a wide number of choices of "good" things to take up your time. Knowing what to pursue and to pursue them will make the difference in succeeding. Most students at college can succeed at quite a few things, so you should be less concerned about failing at the right things and more concerned about succeeding at the wrong things.

All these choices don't disappear when college ends. If anything, they increase. So the ability to manage your time will be very important. If you learn that in college, you will be further ahead.

Time is not a difficult thing to understand. It is simply a linear measurement of life—measured periods when life activities take place or can take place. It is not a commodity that can be stored up. It is more like a temporal current that flows by whether it is used or not. With all the distractions that can come in your college experience, it is easy to let time flow by without effectively using it.

Remember this fact: No matter how smart or successful we are, we all have the exact same amount of time. Everyone has the same number of minutes in an hour and the same number of hours in a day. The key to success in college will be how you use this time.

▶ Time Drains

A good place to begin looking at your time is to recognize the wide variety of activities that combine to use up your time. Most of these are valuable so it can be a difficult thing to know how to manage them. The following chart from the U.S. Department of Labor, Bureau of Labor Statistics summarizes the way time is allocated by the average college student.

EXERCISES

Time use on an average weekday for full-time university and college students

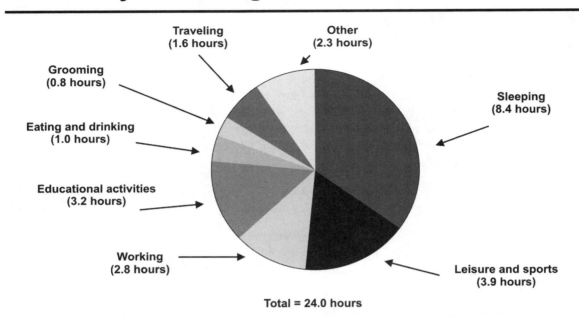

Grooming
(0.8 hours)

Traveling
(1.6 hours)

Other
(2.3 hours)

Sleeping
(8.4 hours)

Eating and drinking
(1.0 hours)

Educational activities
(3.2 hours)

Working
(2.8 hours)

Leisure and sports
(3.9 hours)

Total = 24.0 hours

NOTE: Data include individuals, ages 15 to 49, who were enrolled full time at a university or college. Data include non-holiday weekdays and are an average for 2003-06.

SOURCE: Bureau of Labor Statistics

FIGURE 1-3
American Time Use Survey, 2006

http://www.bls.gov/tus/charts/students.htm

Those averages include students from all types of colleges and universities. How these will occur in your life will depend on your specific situation. As you begin to look at these various drains on your time, it will be useful to add a little more detail beyond that of the Bureau of Labor Statistics survey. The following list provides a more comprehensive approach to evaluating your time.

Educational Activities.   These are scholastic activities that are normally associated with schoolwork and include:
- Class time
- Studying
- Writing papers
- Preparing presentations
- Labs
- Field-trips

Co-curricular Activities.   These are activities that complement the regular curriculum but are engaged in outside of normal class time or class preparation time. They may or may not be required. Some examples of these would be:
- Service-learning
- Internships
- Informational Interviewing
- Job shadowing

Extracurricular Activities.   These are activities you engage in that fall outside the realm of the normal curriculum of a college education. They are generally not scholastic and are not required for classes you are taking.

- Sports – Varsity and Intramural (be sure to account for team and individual practice as well as actual playing)
- Music (be sure to account for group and individual practice as well as actual performing)
- Student government
- Clubs
- Programs, concerts, events

Work.   As the cost of a college education continues to increase, if you are like many students, you will need to maintain a job while you are in college. The Bureau of Labor Statistics reports the following:

> Among recent high school graduates enrolled in college, 92.3 percent were full-time students. Of these full-time students, 40.8 percent were in the labor force, either working or looking for work, in October 2006. In contrast, 81.0 percent of part-time college students participated in the labor force.
>
> *http://www.bls.gov/news.release/hsgec.nr0.htm*
> *last accessed December 9, 2007*

The important thing for you to learn from this is that in managing your time, you should take into account whether or not you will need to work. If you do work, you need to account for that time.

Sleeping.   Adequate sleep is a very important part of your 24-hour day at college. According to the National Sleep Foundation, students in the age group of 18 to 25 require 8 to 9 hours of sleep each night (*Adolescent Sleep Needs and Patterns Research Report and Resource Guide*. National Sleep Foundation. Washington, D.C. 2000).

However, if you are like most college students, you will get only 6 to 7 hours of sleep per night. We will explore later in Chapter 4A how this can present a challenge to college success. Right now what you need to understand is that sleep must be part of your time management program, and you need to allocate time for it.

Eating.   The eating patterns of college students vary widely. Some students will exist on two meals a day, while other will have four. In Chapter 4A we will explore the role of nutrition in relationship to physical strengths. What you need to do in time management is to allocate time for it.

Grooming.   Everyone spends some amount of time each in personal hygiene and getting dressed. The amount of time spent will vary greatly from one person to another. You need to determine what amount of time you need for this activity.

Socializing.   An important part of anyone's college experience is the time they spend making and enjoying relationships with others. The friends made will often last for a lifetime. You will want to make sure you set time aside for this and plan for it in your time management. Socializing includes such activities as:

- Parties
- Dates
- Fraternities/Sororities
- Coffee with others
- Conversation times
- "Hanging out" together

EXERCISES

Electronic Social Networking (ESN).   Though this is really a subset of the "Socializing" realm, it has been listed separately because it has become one of the most significant developments to impact time management. ESN was originally intended to reduce time demands; in many cases, however, it has had the opposite effect. This will be an important activity to monitor in assessing how you spend your time. ESN includes a wide variety of technologies. The most prominent currently are:

- Email
- Text messaging
- Telephones (all categories)
- Voicemail (audio & visual)
- Blogs
- Website hubs (Facebook, MySpace, YouTube, etc.)

Recreation: In everyone's day there is usually some time spent that can best be described as a pastime, diversion, exercise, or other leisure activity that results in relaxation and enjoyment. This is an important part of your college life and will help to make you more successful in other areas. You will want to make sure you make room for this in your daily schedule.

Religion.   The college years usually exhibit the greatest decline in attending religious services. This varies widely, however, from person to person and depending on the type of institution you are attending. A church-run private college may require chapel attendance, and some may require church attendance. In a public college or university, on the other hand, there is no such expectation, and religious activities are totally up to the individual. The important thing in this section is that if this is part of your life, you need to allocate time for it. Activities you should evaluate include:

- Attendance at church, synagogue, or mosque services
- Private devotional/reflection time
- Chapel attendance

Travel.   The final realm listed involves travel to and from school. This will obviously vary greatly depending on whether you are a commuter student or a residential student.

Other.   This category can be used to characterize activities in your life that do not fall into any of the other categories.

▶ Five Steps Toward Managing Your Time

Now that you have identified the major areas that demand your time, you can take five steps that can greatly increase your ability to manage your time and to become much more productive and effective in your college experience.

1. Become Proactive
2. Audit Your time
3. Establish Priorities
4. Set SMART Goals
5. Create a workable Schedule

EXERCISES

FINANCIAL MANAGEMENT

Many students entering college are living on their own for the first time. Once of the biggest challenges in this new independence is the managing of finances. Learning how to do this during your college experience will be a two-fold asset: 1) it will help you make sure you have enough money to stay in school and accomplish the goals you have set for yourself; 2) it will equip you with skills that will help you live more effectively after you complete college. We will look at three of the most important tasks that you will face in managing your finances.

1. Develop a Budget

For a lot of students, budgeting is a pretty simple process. It basically goes like this:

> **MY BUDGET**
>
> I get the money   ⟹   I spend the money

The problem with this approach is that you are never sure where your money is going, and you are never sure you will have the money in the future for things you need or want. On the other hand, if you create a budget that is too elaborate or restrictive, you will likely discard it rather quickly after creating it. The key is to create something simple, yet effective. A monthly budget is usually the best place to start.

Step 1: Collect your information

Over a period of several months, keep careful records of what you are currently spending and what income you are bringing in from various sources. Make sure you include little items as well as the major items; most budgets are destroyed by small items that are ignored rather than by large items that are anticipated.

Your expenses will usually fall into one of the following five categories:

1. *Fixed expenses* (a cost paid on a regular basis that does not change from period to period or that has only slight changes): rent, car payment, insurance, tuition, loan payments, tuition, etc.
2. *Regular unfixed expenses* (a cost paid on a regular basis that can fluctuate up and down from one period to another): food, gasoline, entertainment, charity, etc.
3. *Periodic expenses* (a cost that occurs during the year but cannot necessarily be predicted by month): clothing, books, school supplies, medical check-up, car maintenance, travel home, charity, etc.
4. *Annual expenses*: taxes, etc.
5. *Unanticipated expenses*: medical problem, car repair,

Step 2: Prioritize your expenditures

The information you gather in Step One relates to what you <u>are</u> spending, not what you <u>should be</u> spending. Before you can create a meaningful budget, you need to know which of your expenses are essential and which are not. If your income doesn't cover your expenses, then some of your spending is probably not required—even if you think they are filling a real need.

Use the same categories you established in the Time Management exercise to evaluate the importance of your expenses.

Expense being evaluated	IMPORTANCE			
	Required	Recommended (Beneficial, but not required)	Optional (Enriching but not necessary)	Distracting (Not necessary and no real value)
	1	2	3	4

EXERCISES

Step 3: Set goals for your finances

Budgets are usually more effective when they are created around short-term and long-term goals that provide an incentive. It is better to start with relatively simple goals that will be easier to achieve. Then as you gain more skill in living by a budget, you can begin establishing more difficult goals. An example of a simple goal would be "I want to have enough money left after paying all my expenses so that I can go to a movie or eat out at a restaurant every week." An example of a more difficult goal would be "I want to save enough money so that I can afford to study in another country for a semester."

Step 4: Create your budget

Now you can create a budget with the information you have gathered, taking the following actions.

1. Determine your spendable income level.
   a. Don't overestimate. Include only income you can count on, not income you hope you might get, such as tax refunds or birthday gifts.
   b. A good practice is to set your spendable income no higher than 90 percent of your total income. This way you will have money left to save for bigger items you might want or for unexpected expenses.
   c. Evaluate your goals to see how much more of your income you need to set aside.
2. Now list your expenses in the order you have prioritized them in Step 2.
3. Compare your total expenses with your spendable income
   d. It's pretty simple at this point. If your expenses exceed your income, you are going to have to find ways to cut costs or bring in more income.
      a. Start by eliminating or delaying expenses that have a lower priority.
      b. Use your goals set in Step 3 to give you additional guidance in determining expenses to eliminate or delay.
      c. Don't use a credit card to solve this problem. Credit cards do not provide real income; to the contrary, they add to your expenses with finance charges and interest.

Step 5: Monitor your budget

Track your spending to make sure it stays within the guidelines you have set in your budget. The following tips can help make this easier and more effective:

   e. Use a software program to help you.
      a. A personal-finance program such as *Quicken* will have built-in budget-making tools that can help you create your budget and monitor it.
   f. Concentrate on your main targets.
      a. Avoid getting caught up in the details as you monitor your budget. This is especially easy to do if you use a computer program.
      b. You will be more effective if you focus on the goals you set in Step 2 and the categories you determined to cut back in Step 4.
   g. Beware of cash evaporation.
      a. If you find that you have no idea where the cash you get from an ATM withdrawal has been spent, your budget will be negatively impacted. Find a way to keep better records of your cash expenditures.

EXERCISES

2. Open a Checking Account

You will likely want to open a checking account while you are in college. Usually it will be to your advantage if this account is local to your school's home town. Here are some things to consider as you choose a bank:

- *Fees.* Banks costs can vary greatly from one institution to another. Many offer free checking, but there may be some stipulations. You will want to check these out carefully. Be sure to look at monthly fee, cost of checks, account transfer fees, and overdraft charges.
- *Minimum deposit and balance.* If you are like most students, you will likely be on a tight budget, so you will want a bank with a low minimum deposit and balance required.
- *Branch compatibility.* A local bank that has a branch in your hometown is desirable if all else is equal.
- *Accessibility.* The location of the bank and whether or not it has drive-through banking or an ATM may be important to you.
- Availability. Based on your schedule, you will want to check out the bank's hours of operation—especially whether or not Saturday service is offered.
- *ATM network.* You will want to check out how wide of a network is offered for ATM access and what fees will be charged outside of the network.
- *Online banking.* Online banking is becoming more popular as a way to monitor your account. If this is important to you, you will want to check whether or not it is available.
- *Federal Insurance.* You want to make sure your funds will be insured by a federal agency.

3. Evaluate the Need for a Credit Card

The temptation to have a credit card will be very great. For one thing, banks and credit card companies will inundate you with all sorts of offers. Before you get a credit card, consider carefully the advantages and disadvantages.

- Advantages:
  a. Better than carrying large amounts of cash
  b. Accepted more widely than personal checks
  c. Helps you establish a credit history
- *Disadvantages*
  a. Too easy to use when you really don't have enough money to make a purchase
  b. Number one source of student debt
  c. Interest rates on unpaid balances usually very high
  d. More susceptible to account theft

If you decide that you need a credit card, make sure you know all the features and costs involved. The federal government provides good advice you should follow in evaluating credit card offers. You can find this at the follow website:

> http://www.federalreserve.gov/pubs/shop/

▶ References

The following resources have been cited in this chapter.

American Time Use Survey. (2006). Source: http://www.bls.gov/tus/charts/students.htm.

Lewallen, W.C. (1995). "Students Decided and Undecided about Career Choice: A Comparison of College Achievement and Student Involvement." *NACADA Journal, 15*(1), 22–29.

McCormick, A.C., & Horn, L.J. (1996). *A Descriptive Summary of 1992–93 Bachelor's Degree Recipients 1 Year Later, with an Essay on Time to Degree* (NCES 96-158). U.S. Department of Education, National Center for Education Statistics. Washington, DC: U.S. Government Printing Office.

McCormick, A.C., Nuñez, A.-M., Shah, V., & Choy, S.P. (1999). "Life after College: A Descriptive Summary of 1992–93 Bachelor's Degree Recipients in 1997." *Education Statistics Quarterly, 1*(3), 7–12.

The following resources may be useful as you begin your exploration of Life Calling.

Gardner, J.N., Jewler, A.J., and Barefoot, B.O. (2010). *Your College Experience Concise Edition: Strategies for Success*, 9th ed. New York: Bedford/St. Martins.

Guiness, O. (1998). *The Call: Finding and Fulfilling the Central Purpose of Your Life*. Nashville, TN: Word Publishing.

Patterson, B. (1994) *Serving God: The Grand Essentials of Work and Worship*. Downers Grove, IL: InterVarsity Press.

Foundational Values

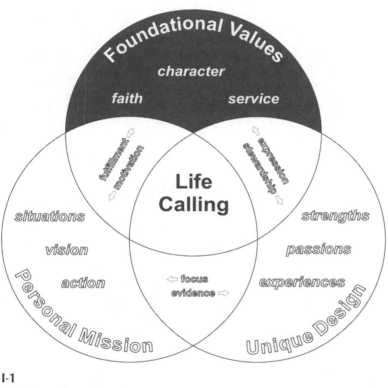

I

FIGURE I-1
Life Calling Model Focusing on Values

Section One deals with the first main component of the Life Calling Model—
Foundational Values.

At the core of each person's life, there exists a set of foundational values
the person holds about reality, themselves, and others. Everybody has these
values. It doesn't matter whether people think of themselves as atheists or
devout fundamentalists. They have developed a personal creed that attempts
to explain the reality of the universe and then from this explanation a valua-
tion of self and others emerges.

A good place to explore for these values during your college experience is
in what may be called general education, liberal learning, core requirements,
or something similar. One big mistake that many college students make is to
dismiss this part of their education as a meaningless waste of time. They have
been misled to believe that the courses specifically training them for a selected
career are the most important. In reality the opposite is the truth.

A good liberal education empowers students with broad knowledge and transferable skills, and a strong sense of values, ethics, civic engagement and social responsibility. Through challenging encounters with important issues, students come to grips with what they really accept as foundational values.

As people search to discover their Life Calling, these foundational values play a major role. In many ways this is really where the search for a Life Calling begins because foundational values form the paradigm that creates the "ground rules" for conducting this search.

In this section we will examine each of these foundational values—reality, self, and others—and discover how these values guide the way in which we discover a Life Calling.

Starting with Faith

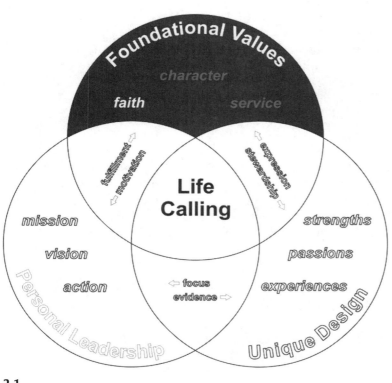

FIGURE 2-1
Life Calling Model Focusing on Faith

The first main component of the Life Calling Model is *Foundational Values*.
The first element of this values component focuses on our **faith**.

CHAPTER OBJECTIVES

1. Understand how your faith forms a mindset that becomes the basis for the rest of your beliefs and actions in life
2. Identify and explain your own faith concerning why you exist
3. Begin explaining the role your faith plays in forming your own concept of a Life Calling

KEY TERMS

Assumption = a statement that is taken for granted or a hypothesis that is assumed to be true and from which a conclusion can be drawn

Belief = mental acceptance of and conviction in the truth, actuality, or validity of something

Chaos = a state of utter confusion or disorder characterized by a total lack of organization

Design = basic plan, scheme, or pattern that guides and controls function or development

Fact = a truth known by actual experience or observation to exist or to have happened

Intentional = something purposely meant to be done or brought about

Mind-set = fundamental, primary mental attitude from which all other aspects of existence are derived, predetermined, and interpreted

Mystical = of, relating to, or stemming from a spiritual reality or import not apparent to the intelligence or external senses

Rational = proceeding or derived from conclusions, judgments, or inferences based on observable facts

Reality = the quality or state of being that is actual or true and exists independent of all other things and from which all other things derive

Spiritual = of or pertaining to the aspect of human existence that is apart and distinguished from the physical nature

▶ Concepts

Have you ever looked in the mirror and asked the question, "Why am I here?" If you are like most other people, you have probably answered "Yes, I have asked that question." Nearly everyone wonders at some time in their life where they came from, why they are here, and what happens to them after this life. The most fundamental of the foundational values we hold is the value we hold about reality that comes from the answers we find in response to those basic questions. Everyone has this value; for most of us it is hard to define and remains some-what mysterious. The dimensions of reality seem infinite. The chronology—past to future—seems infinite. And infinity is something that is hard to measure, let alone comprehend. Furthermore, there is the question of whether or not there is some force behind this reality that causes the reality, yet is separate from the reality. By the very nature of that description, the question is impossible to answer with scientific evidence. So in the end, whether we want to admit it or not, the value we hold about reality comes down to an issue of assumptions—what we presume is true. And these become the *faith* we adopt for our life.

What is a principle?

For some people the idea of a *faith* is hard to face because in their minds faith is associated with religion and in many cases more specifically with a particular religion. That concern arises from a too narrow and distorted understanding of faith. We need to broaden the idea of faith more in the direction of a mind-set that emerges from a combination of facts, assumptions, and beliefs. If we look back at the definitions provided at the beginning of this chapter, we could come up with this definition for *faith:* confident belief in the truth, value, or trustworthiness of a person, idea, or thing that does not rely purely on logical proof or material evidence to arrive at such a conclusion.

When we consider reality as being that state beyond logical proof or material evidence, a philosophical *faith* is pretty much the mindset where we all end up—fundamentalists through atheists. This is because there is no material evidence from the initial Creation, Big Bang, or whatever paradigm one uses for origins. Nor is there material evidence from the future. In the short span of what we call the present, we collect as much evidence as we can. We then use this to construct as sound of a logic as we can. But then we all enter into a world beyond evidence and logic, and from what we encounter there, we make our best guess. This is what the nineteenth-century Danish philosopher Søren Kierkegaard called a leap of faith (verb). And around that process we form our faith (noun).

That leaping process is as much an important part in the development of our faith as is the confidence ultimately developed. Sharon Parks (2000), a nationally recognized scholar in faith and leadership, contends that most discussions of faith place too much emphasis on faith as a noun. She advocates the need to include the verb aspects of faith as well in a discussion such as this one related to Life Calling. "Faith is more adequately recognized as the activity of seeking and discovering meaning in the most comprehensive dimensions of our experience."

As we explore the "comprehensive dimensions" related to the Life Calling Model put forth in this book, the process of clarifying the faith for our own life will constantly need to combine our beliefs (noun) and the seeking-discovering (verb) process we engage in to continually clarify and update these beliefs. Whether conscious intent or subconsciously, this faith will become a mind-set that will ultimately shape every other aspect related to the discovery of our Life Calling. Three concepts within our *faith* in particular stand out because they address questions about reality that set the stage for any exploration related to an overriding purpose in life:

1. **Concept of Design.** What do I believe about the nature and pattern of the universe?

2. **Concept of Intent.** What do I believe about the plan behind the universe?

3. **Concept of Personhood.** What do I believe about the intentionality of my personal place in the universe?

Throughout my life, I have encountered a wide variety of answers to these questions. I have also concluded that the Life Calling Model used as the basis for this book can be used by individuals encountering a variety of answers as well. The only persons who will find no help from the Life Calling Model are those who immediately answer all three of those questions with a certainty of "There is none!" For them the search for a Life Calling or overriding purpose is over—they have none according to their conclusion! The fact that this book continues beyond this point rests on the rejection of the "There is none!" conclusion. Instead, the Life Calling Model is based on the assumption that there is a design to the universe and that each person is a part of that design in some way.

CONCEPTS

Is there a design to the universe?

Evidence supports the conclusion that there is a design to the universe. And this evidence comes from a variety of vantage points. In the science classes you may take, you will find them dependent on a design that can be observed, measured, and predicted. You may take a class in comparative religions. If you do, you will quickly realize that the multitude of religions around the world all derive their explanations around what they see as some definable design of the universe. Even in classes where you study economic, political, and social systems, you will discover that they all base their rationalization on some design. Your classes in philosophy will explore the implications of all this.

Let's go back to the study of science. Theoretical physicists focus on trying to understand this design as a framework for the universe. Einstein saw this framework as designed around relativity. Others saw this framework as designed around what they called quantum physics. And now many scientists are looking at something they call String Theory as a unified framework and theory of the universe that postulates fundamental ingredients of nature are not zero-dimensional point particles, but tiny one-dimensional filaments called strings (Green, 2003).

One fascinating look at design comes from a study of Chaos Theory. A quick dictionary definition might lead us to believe that chaos is a condition or place of great disorder or confusion. Chaos Theory, however, suggests that as we observe apparently random data (the "building blocks" of this disorder or confusion) over time, we will discover an underlying order.

For instance, if we roll a standard die with the numbers 1 through 6 on each face, there is no way to predict which number will come up on each successive roll. However, if we plot these rolls on a graph constructed to transfer the six faces of a three-dimensional die to a two-dimensional hexagon, we will find that these totally random rolls produce a very definite pattern—an underlying order or design.

I programmed a computer to help me do this over what would be equivalent of a year—too long a time for me to roll dice. Figure 2-2 shows the results of that computer program that randomly rolls a die and then plots the resulting number from that roll. The program always plots the point halfway between the last number plotted and the new number rolled. That keeps the

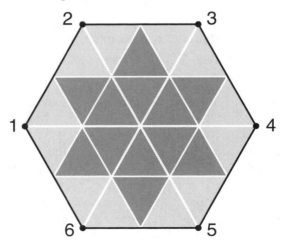

FIGURE 2-2
Roll of the Dice

plots inside the hexagon. The results shown are from a series of 8,640,000 rolls. This is the number of times we would be able to roll a die in a year if we rolled it one time every six seconds. If we were to accept the dictionary definition of chaos, we would expect a random, chaotic plotting pattern, and after just a few rolls, that is what you think you see. But when you are able to amass a large number of rolls, such as year's worth, a definite pattern begins to emerge. There are zones where few to zero plots occur, and there is a zone where a greater density of plots occurs that takes on the shape of a six pointed star (outlined with a solid line for emphasis).

What does this reveal? It reveals that there is some sort of pattern or design underlying the random rolling of dice. It doesn't really reveal to us why there is a design; it just shows us that a design exists.

This same kind of design can be found in many other areas of exploration in theoretical physics. Much of the design comes from the mathematics that underlies all these concepts, and this mathematics may provide the greatest evidence of a design to the universe. To a great extent, mathematics is the very language of design. Does this presence of design prove there is intelligence or God behind the design? It may hint at it, but it does not prove it. It only proves there is a design. An atheist might contend that what we have detected is a self-contained design inherent to the very nature and fabric of the universe free from any outside imposition or influence. An agnostic would agree that there definitely is a design, but would be unsure as to the origins of that design.

To be fair in our discussion, however, we must admit that the majority of the world's population would prefer to attribute this design to God, or at least a god. But even here that approach is widely varied, and that is why we end up with so many religions. The baseline would be what we might call "theistic design"—a definite design with a definite separate designer that has initiated the design and may continue to do so. That designer may be as impersonal as an amorphous power permeating "godness" throughout all aspects of the universe (like the Force described in *Star Wars*) to a very personal, superhuman-like God found in many fundamental religions.

So why go to this extent in answering the question, "Is there a design of the universe?" The reason for this extensive answer is that it shows belief in a design to the universe is widespread, even though the philosophy of the one holding that belief may vary widely. Once we realize this and accept it, this *principle of design* will become the starting point for all subsequent explorations into philosophical questions such as Life Calling.

Earlier we said that we needed to understand that forming the *faith* element of Life Calling contains both a noun and verb component. So what does that mean related to design? Here are two *faith* actions we should take in forming our mind-set:

NOUN-ACTION

Describe as clearly as you can what you believe right now concerning the design of the universe. Be careful to describe what is truly your belief rather than someone else's.

VERB-ACTION

Continually pursue activities of exploration that will expand your understanding of the design of the universe. Here are some possible classes that can help you:

- Science classes can help you learn how to explore the design of the universe using an objective methodology.

- Philosophy classes can help you learn critical thinking that will enable you to develop conclusion based on cause-to-effect logic.
- Religion classes can help you explore these deeper questions from a more mystical approach. They can also help you explore how others have worked through this subject.

What do I believe about the intentionality of the universe?

The discovery of a Life Calling begins with the assumption that there is a design to the universe. The intensity and utility of that discovery increases exponentially, however, corresponding to what we assume related to how intentional that design is. In other words, the greater the likelihood of an intention underlying the design, the greater the likelihood there is for a "purpose" to our lives. Here is the reason this is true. Design without intention answers only the question of *how* the universe will occur. Design with intention answers not only *how* it will occur, but also *why* the universe will occur in that manner. Thus, the greater the intention, the greater the *why*, and this greatly increases the likelihood of *purpose*.

The challenge in answering the question of intent, however, is that it requires significantly more speculation than does the question of design by itself. Design is far easier to detect than intention. You may have gone on a field trip to an art museum sometime in your school experience. During the tour your teacher or a guide pointed out various paintings. There was no question that the paintings were there and that you could see them. But then you heard your teacher or guide try to explain what the artists were attempting to convey through their works. That explanation sounded a whole lot more like opinion. In fact, you may have wondered what would happen if you came back with another teacher or guide. Would you hear a different explanation?

The question of whether or not the painting exists is easy to answer. What gave rise to the painting is much more mysterious. The same thing can be said about the relationship between design and intention. Design can be observed and measured; intention cannot. If we go back to our earlier statement that our *faith* emerges from a combination of facts, assumptions, and beliefs, we could differentiate design and intention in this manner:

- *Faith* related to design derives from facts and the assumptions we make about those facts.
- *Faith* related to intention, while incorporating some observable facts, relies much more on assumptions, intuition, and beliefs.

So does belief or faith in an intentional design correlate directly to the existence of God? Once again the answer is "not necessarily," although it is moving more strongly in that direction. The range of philosophies and religions based on intentional design is nearly as broad as our earlier discussion concerning design itself. On one end would be faith in a self-contained intelligence within the universal matter that imprints an intentional design on the evolution of the universe. On the other end would be faith in an anthropomorphic God who systematically plans and implements a specific design as he creates the universe.

Where we fall on this philosophical spectrum depends on several factors. In many cases it has a strong basis in what we have been told by the culture and subculture in which we have grown up. Very few of us start off life with a clean slate. A second factor relates to the conclusions we have drawn from our own observations. This combines both an objective and subjective approach to the interpretations that lead to these conclusions. Finally, our conclusions about intentional design will be impacted by personal encounters with mystical experiences that take place beyond the realm of objective observation and explanation.

So what can we do to enhance the processes forming our *faith* related to intentional design? Here are two faith actions we should take:

NOUN-ACTION

Describe as clearly as you can what you believe concerning how intentional the design of the universe is. Again, be careful to describe what is truly your belief rather than someone else's.

VERB-ACTION

Explore why you believe what you believe. Engage in activities of exploration that will answer this. Here are some suggested actions that can help you:

- Enroll in a philosophy class that can help you explore this realm. It will help you learn how to develop conclusions based on what you encounter in life.
- Take a religion class that can help you explore these deeper questions from a more mystical approach. As pointed out earlier, they can also help you explore how others have worked through this subject.
- Talk to other people about these issues, especially people you respect. Don't be afraid, however, to include people who disagree with you.
- Pursue spirituality on a mystical as well as rational level.

What do I believe about the intentionality of my personal place in the universe?

The true exploration of an individual Life Calling really takes shape as we answer this third question. Everything prior to this is for the most part general; now it becomes personal. In this whole discussion of design, is there a particular place for me? Was I specifically meant to be here? If so, why was I meant to be here? As those questions are answered, the sense of purpose and calling starts to emerge. The greater my assumption that I am intentionally meant to be here, the greater will be the potential for me to discover a purpose for my life. Richard Leider (1997) calls this the *Power of Purpose*. This assumption that there is an intentional place for me in the universe becomes a spiritual magnet drawing me to something greater than mere existence.

The question of my place in the universe, however, produces a greater challenge than the previous questions about intent. It relies much more on a transcendent level in forming our *faith*. Once my exploration leads me to the assumption that there is a particular intentional place for me in the universe, I enter into the spiritual realm of a cause-and-effect relationship. And there I will encounter the need for an ultimate reality who is the cause of my intentional place in the universe—God. The "who" and "what" of God, however, will be an ongoing exploration as we continue to develop our personal *faith* that will become our guiding mind-set. So here are two faith actions we should take at this level as we continue to form our *mind-set*:

NOUN-ACTION

Describe as clearly as you can what you believe concerning how intentional your place is in the design of the universe. Again, be careful to describe what is truly your belief rather than someone else's.

VERB-ACTION

Continually pursue activities of exploration that will increasingly uncover how intentional your place is in the design of the universe. Here are some suggested actions that can help you:

- Take philosophy and religion classes that can help you explore this realm.
- Enroll in classes studying the classics. Here you can learn how some of the greatest minds in history have struggled with uncertainty about their personal place in the universe.
- Continue to talk with other people about these issues. Seek out people who you believe have strong traits of wisdom.
- Pursue mystical spirituality on a very personal level.
- Additionally, continue to explore who and what the ultimate reality is that has specifically intended for you to have a place in the universe. The same actions suggested above will likely help you in this exploration as well.

Faith and Worldviews

The three fundamental questions we have explored exist at some level in the hearts and minds of every person. Is there a design to the universe? If so, is there intention to this design? If there is an intentional design, am I personally a part of it? As our answers to these three questions begin to emerge, they will shape our worldview. James Sire (1997), a noted scholar who has studied worldviews, defines a worldview as a set of pre-conceived ideas that we hold about the basic makeup of our world (or universe). Our worldview has a very strong impact on our Life Calling because the nature of a Life Calling in our

SUPERNATURALIST		NATURALIST
Intentional creation	< Origins >	Random chance
Deliberate design	< Blueprint >	Accidental pattern
Unique purpose	< Guidance >	Chaotic possibilities
Permanent place	< Results >	Temporary niche
Response to a Life Calling	< Choices >	Best guess

TABLE 2-1
Supernaturalist vs. Naturalist Understanding of Life Calling

SUPERNATURALIST		NATURALIST
Biblical point of view		Pop-culture point of view
Created in God's image/heart	< Beauty >	Models, Celebrities, etc.
Comes from omniscient God	< Intelligence >	Seeks as status symbol
Glory to God /God-given	< Success >	Gratification of self
Role model - witness	< Fame >	Opportunity for money /possessions
Enjoy God's creation /don't sin	< Fun >	Instant gratification
Glory to God	< Glory >	Revel in your power
Child of God	< Dignity >	Impress others

TABLE 2-2
Supernaturalist vs. Naturalist Understanding of Ourselves

lives is dependent on the basic assumptions of our worldview. Consider the table in Table 2-2. It contrasts the understanding of Life Calling coming from a worldview based on a "naturalist" and a "supernaturalist" assumption. The "naturalist" worldview is formed around the belief that nature contains all there is, and all basic truths are truths of nature. The "supernaturalist" world-view is formed around the belief that there is an order of existence beyond the scientifically visible universe and there is spiritual or mystical truth from this realm that is just as important and reliable as that derived from the visible or natural realm.

Our worldview will begin to have a shaping effect on the way we begin to view ourselves because one will be informed by biblical concepts and the other will be informed by popular culture. Consider the contrasts suggested in Table 2-2. How would you fill in the differing views? We will explore this more in depth in Exercise 3 later in this chapter.

Concepts Summary

Faith: everybody has it…it's just a matter of who or what it is in. As we rely on both noun-actions and verb-actions to clarify our faith, we will begin to develop a better sense of reality and our place in it, and our faith will become a clearer mind-set that can also become a stronger guide to our Life Calling.

Insight

Scripture supplies valuable insight that directly relates to the three important questions of faith related to our origin:

1. What do I believe about the design of the universe?
2. What do I believe about the intentionality of the universe?
3. What do I believe about the intentionality of my place in the universe?

SCRIPTURAL INSIGHT 1 ▸ *Faith Is at the Heart of Understanding*

Now faith is being sure of what we hope for and certain of what we do not see. This is what the ancients were commended for. By faith we understand that the universe was formed at God's command, so that what is seen was not made out of what was visible. HEBREWS 11:1-3

The words at the beginning of Hebrews 11 clearly describe the role of faith when it comes to understanding a Life Calling. There is a great deal of evidence concerning the design of the universe and our place in it, but in the end there will always be an element of things that are not seen that will require a degree of hope and faith.

This passage regarding faith shows three important dimensions. First, faith correlates to what we hope for. That dimension of faith is about the future—we hope something is going to happen. Second, faith correlates to our certainty about what has already happened. That dimension of faith is about the past—we are certain that something happened even though we did not see it. Third, faith is active in what we are trying to understand right now. That dimension of faith is about the present—we engage faith as an active verb to discover meaning in our lives on an ongoing basis.

This 3-dimensional aspect of faith is a very important dynamic in our search for a Life Calling. Faith about the past is foundational in answering the three main questions related to our origins. None of these questions can be answered either "yes" or "no" without relying on faith. Ironic, isn't it? The most devoutly religious person and the dyed-in-the-wool atheist both rely on faith because neither of them can see what happened at the beginning of the universe. The difference between the two is that most religious people openly embrace being persons of faith, while most atheists delude themselves into believing that faith has no place in their thinking.

When Jesus, Peter, James, and John came down from the mountain where Jesus was transfigured, they encountered a crowd in an uproar. A man had brought his son to be healed; the son was possessed by an evil spirit. The other disciples who did not go up the mountain were unable to heal the son, and a great controversy had erupted. Now Jesus was back and the father came to him and pleaded for help in words prefaced with "if you can." Jesus told him if he could believe, all things would be possible. The father answered with one of the most authentic and open responses in the Bible—"I do believe; help me overcome my unbelief!"

Most of us are right there with the father. We want to have faith, and yet our lives are full of doubt as well. We want to believe that we are intentionally here for some greater purpose that God has. Yet when our path is not clear and things go wrong, it so easy for us to give up and start doubting that there is any real meaning, significance, or hope for our lives. The only solution for that dilemma is to hang on to our faith—being sure of what we hope for and certain of what we don't see.

> **PERSONAL REFLECTION** 〉 Do you believe there is a divine design to the universe and that you have an intentional place in that design? What is it that you are hoping for in your life right now? What is keeping you from being certain about things you cannot see?

SCRIPTURAL INSIGHT 2 〉 *Believing Is Not Necessarily Seeing*

We live by faith, not by sight. 2 Corinthians 5:7

An old saying says that "seeing is believing." These words come from the concept that if you can't show me the evidence or proof, then I will remain skeptical and withhold my belief. On the surface that seems like a good practice that could keep us from being misled and ending up on paths we really did not want to travel. The problem is that if we build our belief about reality on only that which we can see, we will greatly limit our input of information that can help form our faith.

Think about this example. While I am writing this section of the book, I am in a room with an open window. I can hear through that window the sound of water falling into a pond. From where I am writing, however, I cannot see the waterfall. So does it exist or not? You're probably saying, "Of course it exists! Get up and go look out the window." You are probably also wondering if I am crazy. Knowing something exists is not reliant on sight alone. In my example, sound was just a good a source of information.

You might be tempted to counter my example with the notion that "sensory intake is believing." In other words, as long at the senses can take in some measurable input, then you can use that to establish your beliefs; it doesn't have to be just sight. An experience Jesus had during the familiar event we call the Triumphal Entry provides an interesting insight concerning that argument. The story recorded in John 12 describes Jesus coming into Jerusalem riding on a donkey with crowds of people waving palm branches and shouting "Hosanna!" Many people wanted to see Jesus and talk with him; among these were some people of Grecian descent who followed the Jewish faith. A series of conversations went on among these Greeks, Jesus' disciples, and Jesus. At one point Jesus called on God to glorify his name. Immediately a voice called out from heaven, "I have glorified it, and will glorify it again." The interesting thing is that while some people heard the voice, others heard only thunder.

So then, the data we take in through our senses is not necessarily the basis for belief because sometimes it is interpreted differently by different people. As a result of this, it is just as valid to start with faith and let that faith inform our interpretation of data, as it is to gather data and let it inform our faith. That is what Paul meant when he said we live by faith rather than by sight. These words were spoken in the context of a discussion about whether he would rather live in his mortal body in his present situation, or leave this life and live in the life to come in heaven. His conclusion was that he would live by faith in the hope for a better life to come, not by being bound to the hardships that seem so real in the present life.

When we think about the reality of which we are a part and from which we have come, there is evidence within nature itself to provide a rational belief in a divine design to the universe and to our lives. In Romans 1:20 Paul concluded that "since the creation of the world God's invisible qualities—his eternal power and divine nature—have been clearly seen, being understood from what has been made, so that people are without excuse." Our faith, then, is better termed vision-limited rather than totally blind. The data is there if we know how to correctly interpret it.

As devout Christians we may differ in how we interpret the data regarding the manner or length of time in which our creation took place, but our faith can look beyond our sight and be anchored in the belief that there is a design to the universe. This will guide our discovery of a Life Calling.

> **PERSONAL REFLECTION** What do you hear in your life right now—the voice of God or thunder? Do you wait to form your faith on what you see, or do you interpret what you see on the basis of your faith? Are you looking for your Life Calling in your faith or in your sight?

SCRIPTURAL INSIGHT 3 *The First Word about Our Life Calling*

By the word of the LORD were the heavens made, their starry host by the breath of his mouth. He gathers the waters of the sea into jars; he puts the deep into storehouses. Let all the earth fear the LORD; let all the people of the world revere him. For he spoke, and it came to be; he commanded, and it stood firm. PSALM 33:6-9

As we search for our Life Calling, we can be confident that not only is there a design and Designer behind the universe in which we exist, but that there is also intentionality to that design. The inspirational words of King David reinforce this in another Psalm: "The heavens declare the glory of God; the skies proclaim the work of his hands. Day after day they pour forth speech; night after night they display knowledge. There is no speech or language where their voice is not heard. Their voice goes out into all the earth, their words to the ends of the world" (Psalm 19:1-4). So it is with both faith and reason that we can open the Bible, read and agree with Moses' words in the very first verse: "In the beginning God created the heavens and the earth" (Genesis 1:1).

This is foundational to the concept of a Life Calling because it starts our faith with confidence that our present reality began with a word spoken by God. Without that confidence, everything else that we say about Life Calling will always be doubted. But with that first word of creation, we have hope that God will finish his speech. In other words, he will keep speaking into our creation and our lives. I don't know about you, but that gives me a great sense of assurance.

What is the personal implication for us of God's creative word? Paul gives this illustration in Romans 9. A potter takes a lump of clay and decides to make some pottery. With some of the clay, he decides to make some fancy vases used by high-class people to decorate their houses. But with another lump of the same clay, the potter chooses to form a larger container that can be used to collect trash. When you think about it carefully, both pieces of pottery have a valuable use. Now you might think how much nicer it would be if you were the fancy vase rather than the trash pot, but aren't you glad we have receptacles for trash? Paul's main point in the story, however, is that it is the potter's rightful decision to choose which type of pot the clay will become. And that takes us back to our main verse, "By the word of the Lord were the heavens made." By that same word you and I came into existence. By that word some of us may attain lofty positions in life, and by that word others of us will fill common places of labor. But in the end, it is the same God and the same word that makes each. Therefore, we can accept our Life Calling— wherever it takes us—with faith that God not only spoke it to be, but also commanded it, so that whatever it is, it will stand firm.

> **PERSONAL REFLECTION** > Is God speaking your Life Calling into existence or are you bringing it about by your own word? What keeps you from hearing the word of the Lord concerning your life and then trusting it?

SCRIPTURAL INSIGHT 4 > *Something You Can Personally Believe In*

In the beginning was the Word, and the Word was with God, and the Word was God. He was with God in the beginning. Through him all things were made; without him nothing was made that has been made. JOHN 1:1-3

The Greek work translated as "Word" in English versions of the Bible is "Logos." This is the root from which our word "logic" has come to us. John, by his choice of the Greek "Logos," saw Jesus as the personification of all knowledge and logic. He then contends that this "Logos" first of all is eternal, second of all is God, and third of all is the Creator of all things. There was no doubt in John's mind as to the intentionality behind the design of the universe.

The question that arises next is, Do I believe that there is an intentional place for me in the universe? In our search for a Life Calling, this is the question that strikes closest to our hearts. As wondrous and intricate as the universe is, and as clear as its intentional design is manifested, it is all empty and hollow if there is not a personal place for each of us in it.

We can move one step beyond this in our confidence as reflected in Psalm 8:3, 4. "When I consider your heavens, the work of your fingers, the moon and the stars, which you have set in place, what are mere mortals that you are mindful of them, human beings that you care for them?" God, by very nature and definition in the Judeo- Christian tradition, works with intention in designing the universe. And that design includes a personal place and Life Calling for each one of us. Notice those words at the end of the passage. The writer is surprised that God does care for us. That truly is something to believe in!

A favorite parable told by Jesus describes a shepherd who had 100 sheep. At the end of the day, the shepherd brought his sheep together into a tight flock where he could keep them safe during the darkness. However, when the sheep were all together, the shepherd realized that there were only ninety-nine. One sheep had not made it back and was out, lost in the night. The shepherd left the ninety-nine sheep in the safety of the flock and went out in search of the one lost sheep. When he found the sheep he placed it on his shoulders and carried it back to the others.

INSIGHT

That parable has multiple applications of meaning, but one that is especially important to our discussion of Life Calling is that the shepherd had great concern for one individual sheep. God created the universe and as part of that creation, he intentionally made each one of us. Our individual lives matter. Can we prove that with hard data from the creation? No. It is something we ultimately have to accept by faith. That is why faith is a foundational value; it may be the most basic of foundational values. Remember, though, no matter which side you're on in these philosophical issues, it takes faith—faith in God or faith that there is no God. Atheists only delude themselves that they are not religious. In reality they just have their own form of religion.

What about your faith? Are you confident that God cares about you and has a plan for you? More importantly, are you living your life according to that faith and confidence?

> **PERSONAL REFLECTION** > Have you taken time lately to think about the fact that God is mindful of you and cares about you personally? How does this impact your search for your Life Calling?

SCRIPTURAL INSIGHT 5 > *God Has a Plan for You*

This is what the LORD says: "When seventy years are completed for Babylon, I will come to you and fulfill my good promise to bring you back to this place. For I know the plans I have for you," declares the LORD, "plans to prosper you and not to harm you, plans to give you hope and a future. Then you will call on me and come and pray to me, and I will listen to you. You will seek me and find me when you seek me with all your heart. I will be found by you," declares the LORD, "and will bring you back from captivity. I will gather you from all the nations and places where I have banished you," declares the LORD, "and will bring you back to the place from which I carried you into exile." JEREMIAH 29:10-14

While the first and foremost application of this message is specifically to the people of Israel held in captivity by the Babylonians, there is a general principle that can be gleaned from this message regarding God's way of dealing with all of his people down through the ages. God knows the plans he has for each of us, and there are four important elements to each plan.

First, God plans to prosper us. Be careful with the word "prosper," though, because you might think that means to make us financially wealthy. That is not what is meant here. What this means is that God intends for us to be successful in carrying out his plans for us. In other words, God does not call any of us to a Life Calling in order to fail. Failure in our lives comes when we stray from his plans and purpose.

Second, God's plans will not harm us. I was born near Waikiki Beach in Hawaii and spent a good share of the rest of my life living along the beaches of California. A few years ago I responded to what I believe was God's plan for me to leave those beaches and come to live and work in the middle of a cornfield in Indiana. When my wife and I went through the first winter, we were tempted to believe that God's plan was bringing us harm. But over the succeeding years we have seen how his plans did not harm us but actually brought us great blessing and fruitfulness.

Third, God's plans give us hope. We all want hope, but what exactly does that mean? It means that we can look forward to what lies ahead of us with desire and confidence. Wouldn't you like to wake up each morning and look ahead to that day with such feelings? By faith you can.

Finally, God's plans guarantee us a future, and a good one at that. That future helps us to keep everything else about our Life Calling in context. No matter what happens along the path we follow, if we are traveling on God's path, the destination will be good. This can be a source of great encouragement with every step we take as we pursue our Life Calling.

> **PERSONAL REFLECTION** ⟩ Have you lost hope in your search for a Life Calling? Could that be because you are not searching with all your heart? How can the passage in Jeremiah help you regain that hope?

INSIGHT

Discovery

How can the Discovery Guides help you identify, understand, and establish a *faith* that can become a guiding mindset for your life?

T **THEORY**	Study of biblical, philosophical and scientific theories is essential to establish good principles within your mind-set. This study can be pursued in formal classes, but you can also pursue it in your own personal reading. Start creating a list of books that will aid your exploration. Ask others for recommendations.
E **EXAMPLES**	You can learn a great deal about how to explore the deep questions concerning reality by talking with wise people in your life. Find such people and ask them if they would be willing to mentor you for a semester or school year.
A **ASSESSMENT**	Formal assessments do not really play a major role in helping you understand and establish faith in your life.
C **COUNSEL**	Whether you are attending a secular or faith-based institution, there are likely pastors or spiritual counselors on or near your campus who would be willing to give you guidance in how to explore deep questions related to your life and existence.
H **HISTORY**	The Concepts section of this chapter already recommended study of the Classics. These great minds in history struggled with the deep questions related to life, and you can learn from their observations. A good place to start would be to read works of St. Augustine, Martin Luther and C.S. Lewis.
E **EXPERIENCE**	As you develop principles within your faith, you will make assumptions that really are the equivalent of hypotheses as one step in the scientific method. In that methodology, experimentation with a hypothesis is the next step in testing its reliability. Similarly, assumptions of faith and philosophy can be tested in your life experiences, and from these experiences you will modify and solidify them.
R **RREFLECTION**	In the long run, your *faith* has to be your own. Once you have studied, read, and listened to others, you will need to reflect on what you have learned and heard. Take time for quiet meditation where your own spirit can speak to you. If you don't do this, what you gain will remain theory and likely will not enter into practice in your life.

DISCOVERY

Story

It had been a long drive across the desert of Southern California, then crossing the Colorado River into Arizona and on to Williams, where they turned north toward the Grand Canyon. It was late in the evening as Ken Neimon, Diana's father, pulled his large RV into Trailer Village and maneuvered into their reserved campsite.

The six high school graduates were glad to disembark from the motor home, newly christened the *Nautilus*. *Twenty Thousand Leagues Under the Sea* had been one of their favorite books in English class. It seemed appropriate that for a long trip such as theirs (though it would be only two, not twenty, thousand leagues), their "ship" should be named the "Nautilus" after the famed submarine of that tale. The large RV made long trips like the one they had just completed a lot more comfortable than a car … but still, it had been a long trip.

Lorena could hardly contain her excitement. Seeing the Grand Canyon had been a dream of hers for a long time. She had read all she could about the park and had secured maps before they had left on their great expedition. Furthermore, she had lectured the rest on the Canyon's wonders for nearly the entire trip across the desert. The others were quite glad to get outside.

"Okay, guys, no sleeping in late tomorrow," Lorena urged. "We'll eat breakfast and then get going. We'll walk to Mather Point. That's traditionally the first view of the canyon because the road from the south entrance leads directly to this overview. We turned into Trailer Village before we went by it, so we'll see it tomorrow."

The others were used to Lorena instructing them, so they just grunted their agreement. They were just as interested in getting to sleep—after a quick snack, of course.

"I'm not done!" Lorena insisted, seeing that she had begun to lose her audience. "We'll ride the shuttle along the West Rim Drive to Hermit's Rest. From there we'll pick up the Hermit Trail and hike a ways down into the canyon. Don't worry. It's no big deal; we're not going to the bottom!"

"Geez, Lor, you're so generous," Ryan responded with a less-than-subtle mocking tone.

The sun was already well above the horizon by the time the travelers woke the next morning. Ground rules had been agreed to concerning the length of time that could be spent getting ready each morning. Adam had been firm on that issue. He had two sisters and more than enough experience! He was concerned that a good part of their day could be wasted if too much time was allowed for getting ready. After all, there were three girls plus a mother on board the *Nautilus*. Everyone cooperated, and after a good breakfast, the adventurers were on their way to Mather Point.

The six stood at the rail looking down into one of the most spectacular sights on earth. Below them lay a very colorful, steep-sided gorge with a dark green river at the bottom.

"Okay, Lor, it's definitely more than a big ditch." Justin was ready to apologize for his disparaging remark made a month earlier. "How do you get something this—as they say—grand?"

Lorena stared down into the canyon as she answered, "Weathering and a whole lot of erosion. That's what Mr. Johnson told us in class."

"Lorena, do you think God created this canyon?" Diana asked.

"Yeah, I do." Lorena looked back up and caught Diana's eyes. "I believe he designed the processes of the universe, and this canyon is a result of those processes."

"The sign here says it took millions of years. My youth pastor said all the earth is less than six thousand years old. Which do you think it is?" Adam asked.

"You know what, Adam? That might not be the most important place to start." Lorena looked over toward him. "There are some who see God as a Force permeating all aspects of the universe—sort of like in *Star Wars*. Many religions, on the other hand, see God as a very personal being who painstakingly created all features of the earth. And as you said, some believe it was in a short amount of time. You know what is remarkable? At either extreme, or all that is in between, it shows faith in a design to the universe exists, even though the philosophy of the people holding that faith may vary widely. When you are looking at this canyon, the rest of the earth, or your life specifically, I think that's the place to begin—faith that there *is* a God and a design behind the reality we're looking at. Don't worry so much about the years."

"Hey, you philosophers, isn't that the shuttle we're supposed to be on?" Abriella pointed back to the top of the stairs, and they all started running.

The ride to Hermit's Rest was filled with more impressive vistas of red, pink, gray, and white rock layers carved into an elaborate network of canyons and chasms. After arriving at their destination, the six began their descent down Hermit Trail. The plan was to hike a couple of miles—enough to get a feel for being in the canyon. The challenge would be that a couple of miles also meant a vertical drop of a thousand feet. The climb back out would test their physical fitness.

They had been hiking for about an hour when Adam called, "Hey, take a look at this!" He pointed to a large sheet of sandstone. Everyone crowded around to see a pattern running down the sandstone

that clearly looked like the tracks of a large, lizard-like creature. Footprints bordered what surely was a dragging tail. What was even more remarkable was the fact that the tracks looked like they could have been made yesterday, yet they were solidified in a piece of rock a lot older than that.

After spending some time looking at the fossil tracks and finding some more around the area, the six continued on down the trail a short distance more to an overhang formed in the limestone creating a cave that afforded some relief from the hot, glaring rays of the noonday sun. It also provided a good place to eat the lunch they had brought with them in daypacks.

"You think God cared about that giant lizard or whatever made those tracks?" Ryan asked as he bit off a piece from his sandwich. "Lorena may think that God designed the processes of the universe, but it still makes you wonder if any of the actual parts were intentional—like that lizard, or more important, any of us."

"Yeah, and if that intention includes a plan for what I'm supposed to do with my life," Adam chimed in. "Then maybe I could figure out what to study in college."

"Did it ever occur to you that maybe God's intentional design for you is that you're equipped to explore and figure out your place in that design on your own?" Lorena's question to Adam and the others carried a certain level of intensity.

"I'd rather have it spelled out in one of those rocks on the way back up the trail, like the lizard tracks," Adam answered. "Then I wouldn't have to wonder."

"I'm with you, man," Ryan echoed.

"Yeah, Lorena. Not all of us can figure things out like you can," Diana added.

"Maybe we just don't look in the right places," Lorena responded.

"What do you mean?" Abriella asked.

"I don't know for sure," Lorena answered. "I just think it starts by having faith that we all are part of God's larger design and then using whatever gifts and abilities we have to start exploring what that means. You guys all think that I have it all together because I know where I'm going to college and what I'm going to study. But you know what? There are plenty of times when I'm not sure I'm doing the right thing, so I'm still exploring too. But I have faith that there's something to find."

The looks on the faces of the others indicated that they had just learned a startling new fact about their longtime friend. It would not be the last startling new discovery they would make on their transcontinental adventure.

▶ Exercises

All of us have values we hold about reality; these form the mindset with which we approach our lives. Sometimes, though we have lived with a mindset for many years, it still is hard for us to define what reality is for us specifically. Use the following exercise to help you understand your concept about reality.

Clarifying Your Faith Using Noun-Actions

EXERCISE 1

In the columns below, statements are made in the left-hand and right-hand columns that for the most part contradict each other. The middle column provides an "I don't know" option. In each case, choose the option that best describes where you are in your thinking at this point in your life, and then explain why you selected that option.

In the beginning God…	In the beginning a god…	I don't know	In the beginning something…	In the beginning nothing…
Why I believe this:	Why I believe this:	Why I don't know:	Why I believe this:	Why I believe this:

The universe originally unfolded and continues to unfold from an intentional intelligent design established by God.	The universe originally unfolded and continues to unfold from some sort of intentional design.	I don't know	The universe originally unfolded and continues to unfold from some sort of design, though intention is uncertain.	The universe originally unfolded from an unintentional, chance event and continues to unfold from random events.
Why I believe this:	Why I believe this:	Why I don't know:	Why I believe this:	Why I believe this:

EXERCISES

I am an intentional part of God's universal plan.	I am an intentional part of some god's (or gods') universal plan.	I don't know	I am an important part of some universal design.	I am a result of human desire, passion or an accident.
Why I believe this:	Why I believe this:	Why I don't know:	Why I believe this:	Why I believe this:

▶ Summarizing Your Assumptions

1. In one sentence describe your assumption about reality and your place in it based on your answers given in the preceding answers in this exercise. This is the "noun" aspect of your current *faith*.

_____

_____

_____

_____

2. What kind of framework does this place on your search for a Life Calling?

_____

_____

_____

_____

_____

_____

EXERCISES

Strengthening Your Mindset Using Verb-Actions

It is not enough to clearly describe what your *faith* is right now. You need to take actions that continue to clarify and deepen this *faith*. The cycle depicted in Figure 2-3 gives us a good guideline for developing a faith-strengthening exercise program by recommending four main activities that lead from one to another in a continuous cycle.

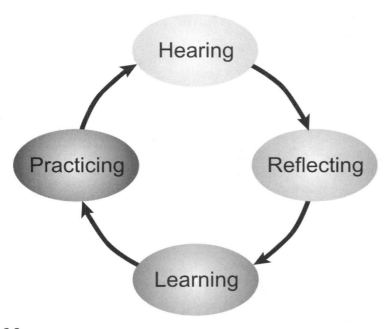

FIGURE 2-3
Strengthening Your Faith

1. Hearing

You might think that we all hear the same way. Actually that is not the case. There are at least three different ways to hear, and each person has a preference.

1. *Ears*: This is what most of us think of when we try to define hearing. It involves actually listening to a message that is audibly delivered to you. Some examples of this might include:
   • Listening to sounds around you
   • Spoken words
   • Sermons
   • Lectures
   • Discussions
   • Conversations
   • Debates
   • Songs

2. *Eyes*: You may not have thought about it in this way, but you not only "see" with your eyes, you also "hear" with your eyes. When you read something or see something happen, it often conveys some level of meaning (a message) to you. Some examples of this might include:
   • Observation of events around you
   • Printed words
   • Pictures

- Paintings
- Television
- Movies
- Plays
- Internet
- Power Point slides

3. *Thoughts*: When you enter the realm of reflective thought, you will often "hear" ideas emerge from these thoughts—messages.
   - Contemplation of ideas presented to you
   - Personal reaction to things you have seen or heard
   - Intentional times of meditation
   - Creative imagination
   - Conscience
   - Inner struggle with issues or problems

Think back on your life. When you have been successful at hearing a "message," which of the three ways (ears, eyes, thoughts) was usually the most effective one in helping you "hear" the message? Which way was next in effectiveness? Which was third? List them in order below:

1. First most effective way to hear: _____

2. Second most effective way to hear: _____

3. Third most effective way to hear: _____

---

2. Reflecting

Once you hear something, what do you do with it? Probably the worst mistake is to react immediately without even thinking about it. The better choice is to take time and reflect on what you heard. During this reflection you need to ask important questions related to four key areas:

1. *Knowledge* – Does what I've heard match with established information and truth?
   - This does not mean that what you heard might be some discovery never before encountered. But even when that is the case, that discovery still should be examined through the lens of what is already known to be true. For example, a pronouncement that gravity will discontinue as a force in two years should be looked at with a healthy degree of skepticism. Too much current knowledge argues against that prediction.
   - While this Body of Knowledge includes scientific and historical knowledge, it also includes philosophical and religious knowledge.

2. *Wisdom* – Does what I've heard coincide with the understanding of mainstream society throughout ancient and recent history?
   - This does not mean that all new ideas are unacceptable. It basically means the past is a key to interpreting the present and predicting the future. For instance, a sudden contention that murder is now an acceptable premise would be rejected based on the long-standing traditions of most civilized societies to the contrary.
   - Again, the role of religion would come into play.

3. *Reason* – Does what I've heard make sense?
   - Sometimes you don't need to check something out against knowledge or traditions. Sometimes it just plain illogical and doesn't make sense. You don't need to waste your time trying to evaluate the wisdom of someone trying to establish a cult on the new idea that up is down and down is up.

EXERCISES

- The same thing holds true in the world of religion. It is illogical to establish a faith on the claim that evil is good and good is evil.

4. *Experience* – Does what I've heard work?
   - You might consider this the laboratory factor. Try it out. Sometimes things sound reasonable, fit with tradition, and seem to be based on solid theory, but in the end they just plain don't work.
   - Put religious ideas to the same test. Somewhere along the way they need to work if they are truly valid.

Does an idea need to correctly answer all four questions? Not necessarily. For instance, an idea based on solid theory that also makes good sense and works might be worth considering even if it doesn't follow established tradition. However, if it doesn't match any of the four, beware!

Now let's give reflection a trial run. Choose some premise you hold in your faith or have heard. For example, a premise might be that if you go to college, you will have a better job after college. Whatever you choose, write in the appropriate blank below. Continue to evaluate it using the questions given.

PREMISE REFLECTION	
Premise:	
Does the premise match with established information and truth?	☐ Yes ☐ No
Explain your conclusion:	
Does the premise coincide with the understanding of mainstream society throughout ancient and recent history?	☐ Yes ☐ No
Explain your conclusion:	
Does the premise make sense?	☐ Yes ☐ No
Explain your conclusion:	
Does the premise actually work if it is put into action?	☐ Yes ☐ No
Explain your conclusion:	

EXERCISES

3. Learning

As you reflect on a proposed idea or concept and put it through the rigor of your reflection evaluation using the four questions, you will begin to see patterns and information emerge out of this evaluation. Collect these and begin to learn in such a way that you can apply what you learn to other situations that might arise in the future.

To test this out, go back and evaluate the explanations you gave for your answers in the Premise Reflection you just completed. List below three or four concepts you observe that can help you evaluate future ideas proposed to you.

_____

_____

_____

_____

4. Practicing

The final stage in the Faith-Strengthening Cycle involves putting what you have learned into practice. A good way to start is by reviewing some of the premises you currently hold and then running them through the cycle. List below several principles you might evaluate using the cycle. Then find time over the next few weeks to do this.

_____

_____

_____

_____

_____

_____

EXERCISES

What Difference Does Your Worldview Make?

In the Concepts section of this chapter, we proposed that our worldview will begin to have a shaping effect on the way we begin to view ourselves because one will be informed by biblical concepts and the other will be informed by popular culture. Several areas were outlined for consideration as to the contrasting differences a "naturalist" and "supernaturalist" worldview would produce. The table is repeated below. Answer the following questions as a process to develop contrasting views of each area outlined based on that worldview.

1. Describe a "supernaturalist" view of each area based on biblical concepts. Include at least one passage from scripture to support your conclusion.

2. Describe a "naturalist" view of each area based on concepts from popular cultural sources. Include at least one quote or specific example from the popular media to support your conclusion.

3. How can the view you end up adopting impact your understanding of your Life Calling?

SUPERNATURALIST		NATURALIST
Biblical point of view		Pop-culture point of view © Art Explosion
	< Beauty >	
	< Intelligence >	
	< Success >	
	< Fame >	
	< Fun >	
	< Glory >	
	< Dignity >	

TABLE 2-2
Supernaturalist vs. Naturalist Understanding of Ourselves

Expanding Your Worldview through Liberation Learning

Formation of our Foundational Values and our ultimate worldview does not take place in a vacuum of ignorance. Discovery of our Life Calling includes the need to study and integrate faith, virtue, wisdom and service into a path that leads to intellectual and character development. This is what Paul referred to as transformation by the renewing of your minds in Christ. This then forms the context for pursuing majors and careers in a way designed to prepare you to realize your human potential in Christ. Your transformation also sets the context for living your life to its fullest extent as faithful stewards of the unique gifts God has entrusted to you.

This kind of learning occurs best when we have minds that have experienced "liberation learning." What does this mean? This kind of liberation is not only freeing us from something, it is also freeing us to something. "Liberation learning" liberates students from the captivity of ignorance, closed minds and delusion by revealing to them different ways of looking at the universe. "Liberation learning" liberates students to pursue, engage, and apply truth through a lifelong process of growth that will help them fulfill their full God-given human potential—a Life Calling.

Figure 2-4 depicts eight pillars of study as forming the primary structure of "liberation learning." To accomplish "liberation learning," you need to explore classes within each of these pillars of study to accomplish specified learning outcomes. These learning outcomes may be imbedded in courses related to your major or other majors, or in separate courses developed to provide a learning experience directly related to the specific area of liberation learning. A look at each of the pillars will help you understand this more clearly. You should complete one or more classes in the following subject areas to accomplish specified outcomes that will liberate your learning.

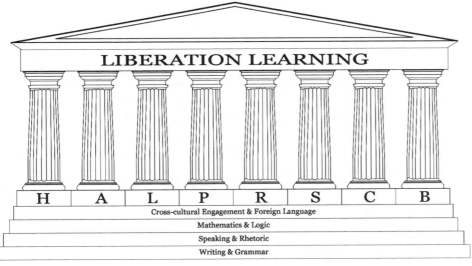

FIGURE 2-4
Liberation Learning

H – *History*

You should be able to:

- Recognize the prominent world civilizations, periods, events, personalities, and developments.
- Identify the basic techniques of historiography (the methods of studying history).
- Analyze a period of the history of a selected civilization.
- Explain how the historical period analyzed contributed to the development of the selected civilization.
- Apply insights gained from analysis to an understanding of foundational issues related to human existence.
- Demonstrate personal value of the civilizing role of knowing and understanding history in personal and societal direction, purpose, growth and improvement.
- Evaluate history through the lens of your faith and worldview, and evaluate your faith and worldview through the lens of history.
- Integrate a knowledge and understanding of history as a framework for investigating all other areas of liberation learning.

A – *Aesthetics*

You should be able to:

- Recognize prominent visual and musical artists and their works across a historical framework.
- Summarize classic theories in the philosophy of art and aesthetics.
- Understand the nature of art and aesthetic experience and the ability of this experience to stimulate your imagination, inspire great thoughts, and provoke profound feelings.
- Generate questions of wonder about the nature of the creative process, the work of art, and aesthetic experience.
- Display creative thinking and expression by personally producing visual and musical works of art.
- Differentiate between prominent art forms in both the visual and musical medium.
- Demonstrate personal value of the civilizing role of art and aesthetic experience in personal and societal direction, purpose, growth and improvement.
- Evaluate aesthetics as an expression of God's creativity.
- Integrate a knowledge and understanding of art and the aesthetic experience into the investigation of all other areas of liberation learning.

L – *Literature*

You should be able to:

- Recognize prominent literary authors and their works across a historical framework.
- Compare and contrast the ideas that have shaped literary works and historical events.
- Understand the nature of literature and its ability to stimulate one's imagination, stir great thoughts, provoke critical thinking, and inspire well-lived lives.
- Write critical analyses that reflect the student's ability to synthesize ideas and themes from selected original texts and secondary sources.
- Explain how the ideas of selected literary works analyzed contributed to the intellectual and social thought of that period as well as to the present.
- Differentiate between prominent literary forms.
- Display critical and creative thinking and expression by personally producing literary pieces.
- Demonstrate personal value of the civilizing role of literature in personal and societal direction, purpose, growth and improvement.
- Evaluate literature through the lens of your faith and worldview, and evaluate your faith and worldview through the lens of literature.
- Integrate a knowledge and understanding of art literature into the investigation of all other areas of liberation learning.

P – Philosophy

You should be able to:
- Recognize and understand at an introductory level a range of prominent philosophers and philosophical problems across a historical framework.
- Analyze selected philosophers and problems with independence of thought and a critical and analytical approach to the theories and concepts, as well as the assumptions on which they are based.
- Explain how the ideas of selected philosophers and philosophies have contributed to the intellectual and social thought of that period as well as to the present.
- Demonstrate skills in careful reading; in comprehension and compression of textual material; in careful analysis; in critical reflection; in rational argument; in sympathetic interpretation and understanding.
- Write and explain your own personal philosophy in a way that demonstrates clear thinking, sound argumentation, the clear and well-organized expression of ideas, impartial pursuit of truth, and a high degree of intellectual autonomy.
- Understand the role of philosophy in shaping intellectual and religious thought.
- Demonstrate personal value of the civilizing role of philosophy in personal and societal direction, purpose, growth and improvement.
- Evaluate philosophy through the lens of your faith and worldview, and evaluate your faith and worldview through the lens of philosophy.
- Integrate a knowledge and understanding of philosophy into the investigation of all other areas of liberation learning.

R – Religion

You should be able to:
- Recognize the major world religions and their basic teachings.
- Summarize the basic themes and beliefs of the religious tradition you personally adopt.
- Analyze the foundational sacred documents of the religious tradition you personally adopt.
- Apply insights gained from the analysis to a reasoned understanding of a worldview.
- Justify how your religious tradition answers the major ontological questions of existence and meaning.
- Outline the relationship between religion-based and moral social responsibility.
- Explain how religion has contributed to the development of civilization.
- Demonstrate personal value of the civilizing role of religion in personal and societal direction, purpose, growth and improvement.
- Integrate a knowledge and understanding of religion into the investigation of all other areas of liberation learning.

S – Science

You should be able to:
- Recognize the major fields of scientific investigation.
- Articulate the steps used in the scientific method for investigating phenomena, acquiring new knowledge, or correcting and integrating previous knowledge.
- Appraise the strengths and weaknesses of scientific inquiry.
- Practice hands-on applications of a selected sub-discipline of science.
- Gather and analyze scientific data through observations.
- Draw conclusions based on observations.
- Hypothesize and design an experiment to test the hypothesis.
- Evaluate sources of information for scientific validity.
- Articulate what is meant by a scientific world-view.
- Value the natural world through the paradigm of stewardship of God's creation.

EXERCISES

- Explain how science has contributed to the development of civilization.
- Demonstrate personal value of the civilizing role of science in personal and societal direction, purpose, growth and improvement.
- Integrate a knowledge and understanding of science into the investigation of all other areas of liberation learning.

C – Civitas (citizenship that imparts shared responsibility, a common purpose, and sense of community)

You should be able to:

- Recognize prominent theories and theorists related to civic culture throughout history.
- Understand the basic values of the civic culture in your nation and compare and contrast these with the basic values of other international civic cultures.
- Identify and explain the fundamental roles of government and institutional, political, legal, economic, and educational concepts, policies and processes that work to create a "civilized" society.
- Relate civic theory and concepts to personal responsibility and stewardship.
- Explain how the ideas of selected civic theories have contributed to the intellectual and social thought of that period as well as to the present.
- Value civic culture, including government, through the paradigm of God's ordination.
- Demonstrate personal value of the civilizing role of government, economics and education in personal and societal direction, purpose, growth and improvement.
- Integrate a knowledge and understanding of civics into the investigation of all other areas of liberation learning.

B – Human Behavior

You should be able to:

- Recognize prominent theories and theorists in the fields of sociology, psychology and anthropology.
- Describe the physical and cultural development, biological characteristics, and social customs and beliefs of humankind.
- Understand the nature of culture and social structure.
- Analyze the reciprocal relationship between the individual and society.
- Understand the thought processes and behavior of humans in their interaction with the environment.
- Apply psychological principles to personal, social, and organizational issues.
- Recognize, understand, and respect the complexity of your country's socio-cultural and international diversity.
- Value human dynamics through the paradigm of human beings as temples of God.
- Demonstrate personal value of the civilizing role of the human behavior in personal and societal direction, purpose, growth and improvement.
- Integrate a knowledge and understanding of human behavior into the investigation of all other areas of liberation learning.

▶ Competencies to Support Liberation Learning

You will need basic competencies that will support you in your pursuit of liberation learning, in development within a major area of study, and in life after college. There are four competencies that should be included in any education experience in order for that experience to be complete and successful in liberating the learner. These competencies could be developed through learning experiences that occurred prior to college; are imbedded in the courses related to liberation learning outlined above; are in the courses related to a student's major; or are in separate courses developed to support competency development.

EXERCISES

Smith, C.S., and Denton, M.L. (2005). S*oul Searching: The Religious and Spiritual Lives of American Teenagers*. New York: Oxford University Press.

Smith, C.S., and Snell, P. (2009). *Soul in Transition: The Religious and Spiritual Lives of Emerging Adults*. New York: Oxford University Press.

Tozer, A.W. (1957). *The Pursuit of God*. Camp Hill, Pennsylvania: Christian Publications.

Wilkens, S., and Sanford, M. (2009). *Hidden Worldviews*. Downers Grove, Illinois: Intervarsity Press.

REFERENCES

Living with Character

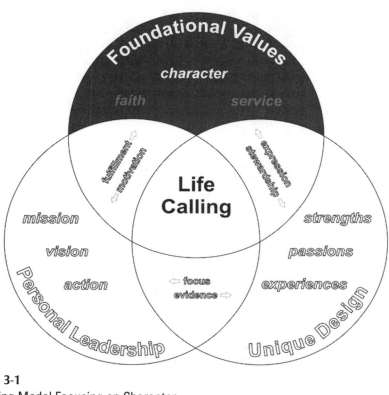

FIGURE 3-1
Life Calling Model Focusing on Character

The first main component of the Life Calling Model is *Foundational Values.* The second of these values is ***character.***

A man is but the product of his thoughts...what he thinks, he becomes.

MOHANDAS GANDHI

CHAPTER OBJECTIVES

1. Explain the concept of life congruence
2. Understand the relationship between faith and character
3. Examine the nature of moral silos in your own life
4. Begin explaining the role character plays in forming your own concept of a Life Calling

KEY TERMS

Character = the moral and ethical quality of people demonstrated in the actions taken in life consistent with the *mind-set* they establish for their lives

Congruence = quality of coinciding exactly when superimposed

Ethical = being in accordance with the accepted principles of right and wrong that govern conduct

Moral = of, pertaining to, or concerned with the principles or rules of right conduct or the distinction between right and wrong

Silo = a cylindrical tower used for storing something (usually coarse food for livestock) so as to keep it separate from other contaminating elements

Concepts

There is a well-known saying, "Practice what you preach." The thought behind the saying encourages people to act out in their lives what they claim with their words. This concept leads us to the next element of the Life Calling Model. As we establish foundational values for ourselves, we start by discovering what we hold to be true about reality and our place in it. These become the *mind-set* on which our lives are built—our faith. The question that naturally arises out of this process is how then will we live in response to this *faith*? The answer to that question becomes the value we hold about ourselves. In other words, do we value our own lives enough to live what we believe according to our *faith*? This value of ourselves is observed far more in our actions than in our statements. This is why we look at *character* to determine this. We define character as *Life Congruence*—the moral and ethical quality of people which is demonstrated through their actions and is consistent with the faith they establish for themselves.

Let's examine in more detail what we mean by "life congruence." The morals and ethics we live by come from the standards of what is right, or are just emerging from our discovery of our own foundational values. Character-based logic dictates that we should live our lives consistent with these standards. That is what we mean by "life congruence."

Let's go back to the world of science and math to help us clarify this. In geometry, congruent triangles are triangles that coincide exactly when superimposed. If we take that concept and apply it to our characters, it implies that the way we live should coincide exactly with the beliefs we hold for our lives (Figure 3-2). When we don't live in *life congruence*, we can end up in a condition that psychologists refer to as cognitive dissonance. That's just an elaborate way of saying "disagreement within our mind." What it means is that we will have a perception or awareness that there is an incompatibility between two patterns of thought in our lives. In the case where we are not living in *life congruence*, the incompatibility is between the way we perceive the reality in which we live and the way we perceive how to actually live in that reality.

FIGURE 3-2
Life Congruence

Life that is congruent

The principles we claim to believe for our lives = The way we actually live our lives.

The principles we claim to believe for our lives ≠ The way we actually live our lives.

Life that is not congruent

This incompatibility or disagreement within our minds often leads to a strange condition. Often, this incompatibility drives us to acquire or invent new thoughts or beliefs that can help reduce the amount of disagreement between the two perceptions. Sometimes we just modify our existing beliefs to accomplish this. In other words, we allow our actions to determine our beliefs instead of the other way around. The far easier solution would be to live our lives congruent with our beliefs!

Another way people attempt to deal with the disagreements within their minds is to use separation. I have termed this phenomenon as "moral silos." Figures 3-3 a and b illustrate this. A typical farm would have a single silo by the barn where food for livestock is stored to keep it separate from other contaminating elements (Figure 3-3a). If we lived in life congruence, we would have one moral silo with one set of life guidelines that enable us to live our lives consistently with our personal credo (system of principles) based on our *faith*.

In practice, however, we rarely find that the case. Instead, we have multiple silos by our barn (Figure 3-3b illustrates what some of those could be) that each has a different set of moral guidelines. The "Driving" silo to the far right has been included to help illustrate this. Very few of us could honestly say that we always drive the speed limit. More likely we would say that when the speed limit on the interstate highway is 65, we drive 70. If asked why, we would likely

FIGURE 3-3A
Single Moral Silo

FIGURE 3-3B
Multiple Moral Silos

explain that we're pretty sure we would not be stopped by a state trooper for driving an extra five miles per hour (and we would probably be right from what many troopers have told me). When we examine our moral guidelines for that driving silo, we would have to conclude that the main guideline is if we don't get caught, it's okay. If we move to the other silos, however, we likely would not want to think that same main guideline was in place. But if we took time to look carefully at each one, we probably wouldn't find consistent guidelines for those, either.

Why is this important when it comes to finding a Life Calling? The net effect of this approach tends to lead us away from life congruence and toward a life where we *say* one thing with our mouth and *do* something different with our actions. This disconnect leads to inconsistency in our lives and is often a source of great confusion when it comes to finding direction.

Let's look at this more closely in relationship to our model for discovering a Life Calling. In the last chapter we looked at the *faith* we establish for our lives. We explained this *faith* in the context of our model as the foundational value we hold about reality. We further said that there were three important questions to be answered about reality in establishing our *faith*:

1. What do I believe about the nature and pattern of the universe?
2. What do I believe about the plan behind the universe?
3. What do I believe about the intentionality of my personal place in the universe?

How we answer each of these questions and the actions we live out once we've reached those conclusions directly relates to our understanding of the "character" element in this model.

If my answer to Question #1 leads me to believe that there is some level of design to the overall universe, then in trying to understand my Life Calling, I would want to understand the nature of that design and then live my life *congruent* with it. That is nothing more than a simple principle of universal *harmony*. If, on the other hand, I believe there is some level of design to the overall universe, but I then live my life totally ignoring this while hoping to find a Life Calling, I am pursuing senseless *disharmony*.

If my answer to Question #2 leads me to believe that there is some level of intentionality to the design of the universe, then in trying to understand my Life Calling, I would want to determine the level of intentionality as best I could with the realization that this intentionality begins to build a sense of reason for my existence. This would encourage me even more to live my life *congruent* with that design. That is nothing more than a simple principle of universal *purpose*. If, on the other hand, I believe there is some level of intentionality to the design to the universe, but I then take actions that reflect an attitude that there is no intention for my life, my actions lead me down a path of *purposelessness*.

If my answer to Question #3 leads me to believe that there is a particular intentionality to me personally being a part of the design to the overall universe, then in trying to understand my Life Calling, I would want to understand as best I could what my particular place in the design is with the realization that this particular intentionality begins to build a sense of meaning for my existence. With a greater sense of both purpose and meaning beginning to emerge in my *faith*, the need to live my life *congruent* with the universal design is even greater. That is nothing more than a simple principle of universal *significance*. If, on the other hand, I believe there is a particular intentionality to me personally being a part of the design to the overall universe, but I make all my decisions about life as if there was no personal place for me in the universe, my life would seem to be totally *insignificant* as if I didn't matter.

Concepts Summary

What happens when we do not pursue life congruence in the search for a Life Calling and end up in a state of disharmony, purposelessness, and insignificance? Almost always we will fall into the "mind disagreement" condition described earlier and illustrated in the discussion of moral silos. When we are in this state, we will try to find ways to lessen the distress caused by this unsettled circumstance. The most common way is to invent new patterns of thought or revise current ones in such a way that we can convince ourselves that we are pursuing a Life Calling when in actuality we are not, or we tell ourselves that there is no such thing as a Life Calling or that it isn't important. Many people have fallen into this trap, and at the end of their lives, they often look back with remorse, feeling that they have not achieved what they were meant to accomplish. The way to keep this from happening is to develop a life of character that pursues life congruence—where the premises we believe guide the way we act.

CONCEPTS

Insight

The Concepts section introduced the need for life congruency. This was defined as living our lives in such a way that they coincide exactly with the faith we hold. In this section we will look more closely at what the Bible says about life congruency.

SCRIPTURAL INSIGHT 1   *Faith Needs to Be Followed by Action*

What good is it, my brothers and sisters, if people claim to have faith but have no deeds? Can such faith save them? JAMES 2:14

Have you ever seen a slab poured to become the foundation for a house, but then for whatever reason, the builder was unable to build any structure on the foundation? It just sits there for months or years with no one able to live on it or to take any advantage of it. That is what our lives are like, according to James, when we develop a faith but it does not have any impact on the way we live our lives.

The people who find great effectiveness in pursuing their Life Calling are those who live in a totally opposite manner from what we just described. These are people whose faith moves directly into a life of character. They live their lives in such a way that actions taken coincide exactly with the faith they hold. We can call that concept life congruency. James' questions clearly reveal the strong belief that faith must be accompanied by corresponding actions if the faith is to serve any useful purpose.

The Apostle Paul called for something similar in Galatians 5:25 with these words: "Since we live by the Spirit, let us keep in step with the Spirit." A person can have faith in something and not be spiritual in any way. But that is not the kind of faith that will lead us to find our Life Calling. Such a purpose results from God's call on our lives, and is powered by a faith that can come only by God's Spirit working on our spirit. Paul likens this to walking in step with the Spirit. What does this mean? It means the spiritual life we claim should be matched by the spiritual walk we take. So then, Galatians 5 introduces the Spirit's power as the key to success in the call to action found in James 2.

Israel's first king, Saul, had a struggle with this concept. He claimed to be a follower of God but really lived his life following his own direction rather than God's. On one occasion Israel was going to war with one of its many enemies and the prophet Samuel delivered a message from God to the king telling him to destroy everything in the battle and not to bring back any spoils. Saul decided he did not need to live according to God's word even though he claimed to be a follower of God, so when he saw livestock of the enemy that was strong, he decided to capture it and take it with him. This was a direct violation of God's instructions. When Samuel scolded Saul for his disobedience, Saul made a lame excuse that he had brought the animals back to sacrifice to God. Samuel did not buy this excuse at all. Instead he rebuked Saul with these well-known words found in 1 Samuel 15:22: "Does the LORD delight in burnt offerings and sacrifices as much as in obeying the LORD? To obey is better than sacrifice, and to heed is better than the fat of rams." As a result of this God rejected Saul as king and turned instead to David.

What is the implication for us as we pursue our Life Calling? It means that when we find out God's direction for our lives, God expects us to live accordingly. For instance, in the last chapter we examined passages that assured us that God was our Creator and that he has plans for our future that are meant to give us hope. If we then go out and live as if there were no plans or hope and make decisions for our lives accordingly, then we are no better off than Saul. The key to keep this from happening is to maintain a steady process, moving our faith directly into the actions of our lives—just as James advised.

> **PERSONAL REFLECTION** > Where are you at right now? Are you walking in step with the Spirit as your Life Calling is being revealed to you, matching the actions in your life with direction being revealed? Or are you talking as if you had a Life Calling but living as if it doesn't exist or doesn't matter?

SCRIPTURAL INSIGHT 2 > *Build Your Life Calling on a Solid Foundation*

Therefore everyone who hears these words of mine and puts them into practice is like a wise man who built his house on the rock. The rain came down, the streams rose, and the winds blew and beat against that house; yet it did not fall, because it had its foundation on the rock. But everyone who hears these words of mine and does not put them into practice is like a foolish man who built his house on sand. The rain came down, the streams rose, and the winds blew and beat against that house, and it fell with a great crash. MATTHEW 7:24-27

Matthew 7 gives us a good contrast between people who live their lives in consistent with their faith and those who don't. One has a Life Calling built on rock; the other has a Life Calling built on sand. If you feel like you are stumbling along in life with no idea of where you are going, no sense of a Life Calling, no clear direction, no voice of God calling you, then one good place to begin looking for an answer is life congruence. Are you putting God's words into action? If you claim faith that God has a purpose for your life, yet you take action as if the faith made no difference, then you are living on sand and you will not find a Life Calling guiding you. Let's look at this in relationship to three points of faith we gained from Chapter 2.

Point of Faith: God created the entire universe.

- *Living in the light* = Realizing that my Life Calling is best understood in a universal context created by God.
- *Living in the darkness* = Making decisions for my life that are based only on my own interests for the present situation.

Point of Faith: God cares about each one of us individually.

- *Living on rock* = Seeking to understand my Life Calling from a sense that I have personal meaning, significance and hope.
- *Living on sand* = Making decisions for my life as if God had no part in my being here and has no interest in what happens to me.

INSIGHT

Point of Faith: God has plans to prosper you and not to harm you, plans to give you hope and a future.

- *Living in rock* = Pursuing my Life Calling from a sense that I have one and that it is good.
- *Living on sand* = Making decisions for my life as if I had no purpose and that most everything that has or will happen to me has not been very good.

When we consider those contrasts, we begin to realize why a life not lived consistently with our faith ends up in confusion without any knowledge of where we are going. If we want to know where we are going, we need to start by living consistently with our faith.

One of the most dramatic illustrations of this can be found in the tragic story of Judas Iscariot. Here was a man who spent three years living very close to Jesus as one of the Twelve Disciples. He was a man of great talent and leadership, even among the other eleven disciples. Yet somewhere in this whole process he never made his actions subject to what he claimed was his faith. When confronted about this by Jesus, rather than changing his way he instead turned against Jesus and betrayed him. In the end Judas' life was one built on sand and he had no knowledge of where he was going, so he took his own life.

Peter denied Jesus publicly and Thomas doubted him after the resurrection. What was the difference between them and Judas? When they were confronted by the inconsistency of their proclaimed faith and their actions, they chose to change their actions and make them consistent with their faith. And in the end they were able to progress along a fruitful life path with a sense of Life Calling.

If you desire to have a clear understanding of your Life Calling and live a life built on a foundation of rock, matching your faith with your actions is a good place to start.

> **PERSONAL REFLECTION** ⟩ Do you feel like your life is built on a solid foundation of rock, or do you feel like it is shaky and built on sand? If you feel like you are on sand, is there an area of your life where you are living in a manner inconsistent with your faith about how God would like you to live? What would it take to get you to change that practice today?

SCRIPTURAL INSIGHT 3 ▶ *Actions Speak Louder Than Words*

Jesus told this parable: "There was a man who had two sons. He went to the first and said, 'Son, go and work today in the vineyard.' "I will not,' he answered, but later he changed his mind and went. "Then the father went to the other son and said the same thing. He answered, 'I will, sir,' but he did not go. Jesus then asked: "Which of the two did what his father wanted?" MATTHEW 21:28-31

This passage ended prior to the answer being given so that you as the reader could have the chance to think in your own mind what answer you would give. The first son seems so defiant. How could he be the correct one? The second son seems so much more respectful. But even the hostile crowd challenging Jesus was able to figure out the best answer.

"The first," they answered.

And Jesus agreed.

So what can we learn about character and life congruency from this story. Looking at all the elements in the faith-character equation, words are the least important. What that means is that saying something is not enough. Saying you will do the right thing and then not doing it is worse than saying you won't do the right thing and then changing your mind and doing it. Of course the best thing would be to say you will do the right thing and then do it!

The bottom line is that actions better reflect the heart than words do, and that is consistent with what we have been reading in the earlier passages. Life congruency begins with what we believe in our heart and then finds fruition in how those beliefs play out in our actions, not just in our words.

When I was a young boy, my father had a saying that he constantly reminded me of in many situations: "Your word is as good as your bond." Here's the explanation of what he meant by that saying. The term "bond" in this saying means a binding security or firm assurance. So if I say something with my words, it should be binding and provide others with an assurance that they can rely on these words. They should have no doubt that I will follow up my word with corresponding action. My father was constantly encouraging me to pursue life congruence (though he never used those words). He wanted me to be a person of character. And even now, so many years later when he has passed on from this earth, I can still hear that advice.

Have you decided to live in such a way that you maintain three-fold congruence—words, faith, and action? If not, your life will be in confusion because you will not know which path to follow. Life congruency is an important key to Life Calling and to living a truly effective life.

> **PERSONAL REFLECTION** > What is more important to you, to sound good or to have good actions? Is your word your bond, where others can always depend on you to do what you say? How can you increase this in your life?

SCRIPTURAL INSIGHT 4 > *Nobody Said a Life of Character Would Be Easy*

So I find this law at work: Although I want to do good, evil is right there with me. For in my inner being I delight in God's law; but I see another law at work in me, waging war against the law of my mind and making me a prisoner of the law of sin at work within me. What a wretched man I am! Who will rescue me from this body of death? Thanks be to God, who delivers me through Jesus Christ our Lord! ROMANS 7:21-25

Engaging our faith into a life of action and character is not necessarily an easy thing to do. Paul's description in Romans 7 clearly describes the struggle related with the attempt for such life congruency. What compounds this problem even more is the tendency to be living with strong moral actions of character in one area of our life while wrestling or even failing with morals in another area.

When we live in total life congruence according to our faith, as described in the first insight concerning James 2, we have one set of life guidelines that enables us to live our lives consistently according to our faith no matter what issue we confront. In practice, however, we find some areas of our faith a real struggle and set our standards lower, resulting in a multiple set of faith guidelines for our lives. These were called "moral silos" in the Concepts section. The problem with this approach is that it causes confusion in our search for a Life Calling. We begin to see a purpose in some areas of our lives and not in others. The problem is that the lowest level of morals and character begins to tear down all the others as well, and in the end we begin to doubt that we have any purpose for our lives at all.

Is there any hope? Look at Paul's last words in the passage for today. Our hope is in the deliverance that can come only through Jesus.

When David was chosen by God to become king of Israel, the prophet Samuel described him as a man after God's own heart (1 Samuel 13:14). But wait a minute; how can this be true about David? This is the same David who saw Bathsheba taking a bath on her roof, and arranged to have a sexual affair with her even though she was married to one of his trusted military leaders, Uriah. When she became pregnant from this act of moral failure, David compounded the moral breakdown even further by arranging to place Uriah directly in the line of fire during battle where he was killed. David then took Bathsheba to be his own wife. You talk about conflicting moral silos—David had some pretty strong ones! Yet he is described as a man after God's own heart. How can that be? It is seen in David's response when confronted by Nathan the prophet about David's failure. Listen to a few of David's contrite words from the powerful Psalm 51.

Have mercy on me, O God, according to your unfailing love; according to your great compassion blot out my transgressions. Wash away all my iniquity and cleanse me from my sin…Create in me a pure heart, O God, and renew a steadfast spirit within me. Do not cast me from your presence or take your Holy Spirit from me. Restore to me the joy of your salvation and grant me a willing spirit, to sustain me. (VERSES 1, 2, 10-12)

When we struggle with living a life of character marked by moral inconsistency, and we *will*, according to Romans 7, we need to be quick to look to Jesus as our hope of deliverance and confess openly to him and ask for his help as David did in his times of moral failure. That's what it means to be people after God's own heart. John the disciple of Jesus assures us that when we confess like this, God will forgive us and cleanse our failures (1 John 1:9). This is what will continually keep us coming back to a path of Life Calling.

> **PERSONAL REFLECTION** ⟩ What are you struggling with right now that is making it difficult to see a Life Calling? What is keeping you from going in prayer to God right now and openly confessing and asking for his help to deliver you?

SCRIPTURAL INSIGHT 5 ▶ *God Doesn't Give Up Even When We Do*

I thank my God every time I remember you. In all my prayers for all of you, I always pray with joy because of your partnership in the gospel from the first day until now, being confident of this, that he who began a good work in you will carry it on to completion until the day of Christ Jesus. PHILIPPIANS 1:3-6

Scriptural Insight #4 presented a perplexing struggle in the process of turning faith into consistent actions of character. But as perplexing as that struggle is, the promise in Philippians 1 is just as encouraging. *The key phrase in this passage is* "being confident of this, that he who began a good work in you will carry it on to completion." It is easy for us to get discouraged about our Life Calling when we evaluate it right now as if today was the end of the story. But the fact of the matter is that our lives and our Life Calling continue to unfold each day, and we need to have confidence that God will carry his good work in us through to completion. This confidence becomes a very important part of life congruency. Our inconsistency is constantly being worked on by God's consistency.

One of the best Bible stories to illustrate this is found in the life of Peter. In one moment he was walking on the water to join Jesus; in the next moment he was sinking because of fear. In one moment he was declaring Jesus to be the Messiah, and Jesus was conferring on him the keys to the kingdom of heaven; in the next moment Peter was rebuking Jesus, who in return, equated Peter's words with those of Satan. In one moment Peter claimed that he would never disown Jesus even if all the other disciples fell away; the next moment he was denying Jesus in the courtyard, cursing to help make his point. Peter lived a very inconsistent life during his time with Jesus. Yet at the end of this period after Jesus' resurrection, Jesus walked with Peter along the northern shores of Galilee and called Peter to feed Jesus' sheep; by this he meant to help those who would follow Jesus to grow in that life. In other words, Jesus consistently worked with Peter to call him back from his inconsistent life.

That should be a source of great hope to each of us. We don't want those conflicting moral silos in our lives. We don't want to live with inconsistent characters. But try as we might, we find that although we want to do good, evil is right there with us, just like Paul describes in Romans 7. Our hope is not that we will be able to turn this around and deliver ourselves from this struggle. Our hope is in a consistent God who not only begins a good work in us, but stays at that good work until he has carried it clear through to completion.

When we explore the term "Life Calling," we can discover two important implications. First, a calling has a caller. It is God who calls us to his purpose, not us calling ourselves. Second, it is a calling, not a call. In other words, it is ongoing, not just a one-time event. Our verse today assures us that God started the work in us and will keep at it every day until it is done at the coming of Jesus. That is good news!

PERSONAL REFLECTION ⟩ Is God the primary voice in your life, calling you to a Life Calling right now? Are you proceeding in your life with the belief that God is constantly working for your good? How can you keep that thought uppermost in your mind as you face the challenges in your life right now?

INSIGHT

 Discovery

How can the Discovery Guides help you identify and understand *character-*based living and develop life congruence?

T **THEORY**	Study of philosophical theories, especially those established within the context of your religion, can help you begin to understand your own moral and ethical premises. This study can also help you develop practices that can lead to greater consistency between your stated *faith* and your lived-out actions. This will lead to stronger life congruence and a more discernable purpose for your life. This study can be pursued in formal classes, but you can also pursue it in your own personal reading as well. Start creating a list of books that will aid your exploration. Ask others for recommendations.
E **EXAMPLES**	The lives of other wise and devout persons provide one of the best sources for learning how to live a consistent life. Observe them and find time to talk. Keep a constant search for such people. Many times you will find them in positions you may not have thought of, such as food servers, groundskeepers, janitors, secretaries, and other positions that may not be in the limelight of your institution.
A **ASSESSMENT**	Formal assessments are not the main tool in developing character. There are some self-assessments that can help you explore this area of your life. *CHARACTER COUNTS!* is one of the most widely used approaches to character education in public education.
C **COUNSEL**	People speaking into your life can be powerful sources of guidance and strength in character development. Finding someone who can serve as a mentor to you during your college years can make a great difference in your success.
H **HISTORY**	The classics are full of stories dealing with the struggle to live out one's life with character. Select some of these and learn from their experiences.
E **EXPERIENCE**	As you develop principles within your mindset, you will make assumptions that really are the equivalent of hypotheses as one step in the scientific method. In that methodology, experimentation with a hypothesis is the next step in testing its reliability. Similarly, assumptions of faith and philosophy can be tested in your life experiences, and from these experiences you will modify and solidify them.
R **REFLECTION**	Keep a personal journal and then take time to reflect on what is happening in your life. This will help you see what level of character is at work and whether or not you are living with moral silos or with a consolidated life.

▶ Story

The *Nautilus* and its voyagers had left the Grand Canyon taking the East Rim Drive to Desert View. By that time, Lorena had certainly not been shortchanged of spectacular views. Traveling on they passed through the Painted Desert, where they were again dazzled by stunning colors. This led to Flagstaff, where they rejoined Interstate 40. I-40 would be their route for a long time as they traversed the country. As they started eastward, an afternoon thunderstorm washed the *Nautilus* with a downpour.

"I've got a question for you, Lor." Adam's voice broke into the steady hum of the road. "You said there is definitely a design to the universe, and each of us is a unique part of that design. How do you know that going to UCLA is part of that design? Did you check it out?"

Abriella broke in before Lorena could respond. "That's crazy, Adam. How could she figure that out?"

"What do you mean, Abi?" Justin asked.

"I mean, what's she suppose to do? Check out to see if UCLA is mentioned in the Bible?" Abriella replied.

"Come on, Abriella, you know that's not what I meant." Adam was frustrated. "We can all talk about faith or design or God or whatever. But it seems like when it comes to life, we all just take whatever comes our way every day and play it by ear. Isn't that more or less how you chose UCLA, Lor?" Adam turned back toward Lorena.

"I wouldn't say I played it by ear," Lorena answered in a somewhat sarcastic tone. "I chose a top-rated school and worked hard to get in. That's hardly playing it by ear."

"You just made my point!" Adam shot back.

"Your point being…?" Diana broke in.

"Faith or God didn't have anything to do with her going to UCLA." Adam's voice grew more intense.

"She wanted a good school…pure and simple."

There was a brief period of dead silence.

"Lorena…?" Diana asked.

"I'm thinking!" Lorena growled.

"Adam's right," Ryan jumped in. "Life is like surfing."

The others all laughed because they knew this was Ryan's passion.

"You paddle your board out. You lie there and wait. And when you see a good wave, you start paddling hard and try to catch it." Ryan was definitely in his element as he flailed his arms. "You don't think about design. You don't think about faith. You don't even think about God, to be honest. You just ride it!"

"I don't know if I buy that, Ryan." Abriella shook her head as she spoke.

"Why not?" Ryan countered.

"Well, it just seems like if we are part of some larger plan for the universe," Abriella explained, "we ought to be able to find out what our part is. Remember Mr. Powell's trig class?" Abriella asked. All the others except Lorena groaned. It had not been an easy class. "He taught us that when all the corresponding sides of two different triangles are equal they are congruent. In other words, they are the same."

"I'm lost," Ryan sighed.

"It's simple." Abriella's brow wrinkled with frustration. "We should live our lives consistent with what we believe about reality. If we believe God made us with a purpose, then we should live our lives according to that purpose—you know, congruency."

"I'm not sure I understand," Diana said.

"I know I don't understand!" Ryan agreed. "Old Powell was weird, and I never understood a thing he said."

The others laughed as they recalled Ryan's struggle to get through school.

"So what about UCLA?" Diana steered them back on track.

"If Lorena believes it's her calling to be a doctor, then she should choose the school that can best prepare her," Abriella said, and then added, "That's congruency."

"And what if you're lost like Adam?" Justin asked. "Or me?"

"Start with what you know and live up to that," Abriella replied. "That's all any of us can do."

"Sometimes that's kind of hard," Adam said.

"No one ever said congruency was easy." Abriella's voice held a hint of resignation. "It's just the right thing to do. It's really a matter of character."

Ken Neimon looked over from the driver's seat to his wife Kim, who was sitting in the front right passenger seat, and winked. High school graduates did not have this level of discussions in their day. They were both proud of the six.

"This is pretty heavy," Ryan sighed. "I think I need to rest my brain." The others agreed, and again the hum of the road dominated the sound.

Their journey took them on through New Mexico and then across the Texas panhandle. They stayed overnight in Amarillo, and then on through Oklahoma. As they traveled eastward toward Little Rock, Arkansas, they began to encounter the Ozark Mountains.

From Little Rock, they continued on to Memphis, Tennessee, their first encounter with the Mississippi River. But it was not the river they stopped to explore in Memphis—rather, it was Graceland Mansion.

"Who can be sure?" Abriella laughed. "Maybe Elvis isn't dead and will be there!"

The next day the journey continued on across Tennessee through Nashville and Knoxville and over the Great Smokey Mountains.

"I think I could be happy living here," Adam observed. "Rivers with water, trees that are green, awesome mountains–mm, I can handle it." The others agreed.

"Do you have to like country music if you live here?" Lorena asked, pointing to a sign that read *Dollywood*.

"Good question," Adam replied. "We'll need to check that out first."

One hour later they arrived in Asheville, North Carolina, with a definite planned stop. A friend of the Neimons had recommended the Salsa Restaurant as one of his favorite places to eat. None of them went away disappointed or hungry. They continued on across North Carolina, then to Virginia, and finally, four days after leaving the Grand Canyon, the explorers arrived in Washington, DC.

Washington, DC. is a city perfectly designed for exploration. The capitol is loaded with history and current events. There is art and architecture, and of course there is the Smithsonian Institution. The six found plenty of things to explore within the various museums.

On their last day in the nation's capitol, they walked along the mall. They had been to the Lincoln Monument, through the Roosevelt Monument, past the Jefferson Monument, around the Tidal Basin, over to the World War II monument, and now to the Washington Monument. They began an ascent up the 897 steps to the top. Lorena was in far better mental shape than she was in physical shape, and she began to lag behind the others. Adam hung back to stay with her, even though she insisted he go on with the others. He had done the same thing on the hike back up the Hermit Trail. *How could such a decent person*, she wondered, *be so confused about his life?* "

Lor, what do you think about Abi's speech on congruence back in Flagstaff?" Adam looked back at Lorena, who was still a few steps behind. "How can it help make a difference in my life?"

"What is it that you want in your life most of all?" Lorena asked, panting as she struggled to keep up.

"Some sort of purpose," Adam answered. "I don't want to choose some college major for a specific job and then find out that I screwed up the rest of my life because it was a wrong decision."

"Okay, so it's purpose you want in your life." They kept climbing as Lorena talked. "Here's what I think Abi meant when she was talking about congruency. You and I both believe that God has a place for us in this life. But that's just a first step."

"What's the next step?" Adam asked.

"Well, we not only believe there's a place," Lorena continued, "but that place begins to make us believe there is a reason for our existence. That should encourage you even more to want to live your life according to God's design because that's what gives you the purpose you are looking for."

"Maybe you're right." Adam stopped for a moment and turned around.

"There's one more thing," Lorena answered, glad for a short break in the climbing. "I also believe that when you and I find our special place in this world, that is where we can find meaning for our existence. That will give our life significance."

"You know what, Lor?" Adam placed his hand on her shoulder. "That's exactly what I want—significance. I don't want to just be nothing, an afterthought in an accidental universe."

"Neither do I, Adam. Neither does anyone else." Lorena gave him a nudge and added, "We'd better keep climbing."

By the time they reached the top, the others had already spent several minutes enjoying the view.

"What do you guys see?" Adam asked.

"There are a lot of other monuments all around us," Ryan answered.

"So what does that mean, Lor?" Adam asked as he and Lorena both moved to the small windows to take a look.

"It means these leaders were people of character—congruence, as Abi called it." Lorena was looking directly at the Lincoln Memorial. "They all believed in something and then took actions in their lives to live according to what they believed."

"I wonder if there are any more of those types of leaders left," Adam mused, addressing no one in particular.

STORY

▶ Exercises

Character is the value we hold about ourselves that is observed in moral and ethical actions taken in our lives consistent with the principles we have developed for our lives—what we described as *Life Congruence*.

Philosophers and theologians from the earliest civilizations to the present have suggested different forces at work in all people affecting the formation of character. Modern psychologists have done the same. Though the terms vary, they can all be summarized into three main categories. The first is a *self-centered* force that affects character formation—what do I care about and what brings me the greatest benefit? The second is a *legalistic* force that affects character formation—a set of rules formed by well-meaning people trying to interpret what is righteous or virtuous living and then imposing it on people who say they want to be righteous or virtuous. The third is a *principle-centered* approach to character—what is the right thing to do based on universal self-evident truths?

Whenever legitimate human needs arise within us, these three powers go to war, and how we respond determines the level of character-based life congruency that will develop in our lives:

If we respond with a *self-centered* approach that focuses on "what's in it for me," we will end up doing what is contrary to *principle-centered* values. This is not character-based life congruency.

If we respond with a *legalistic* approach, our wants are still congruent with a self-centered approach. Though we may end up doing what appears to be consistent with *principle-centered* values in our outward actions, our inward desires are still consistent with a *self-centered* approach. This is not character-based life congruency either.

If we respond with a *principle-centered* approach that is congruent with universal truths, we will end up not gratifying the desires of self-centeredness nor will we be bound by an arbitrary set of rules. Instead we will have life alignment with universal values and principles. This is true character-based life congruency.

Moral Silos

EXERCISE 1

This exercise can help you start to see what level of congruency takes place in your life.

Directions: Honestly rate yourself for each of the areas listed below. You will rate yourself on a "sliding scale." This means the numbers in between the statements represent a range, and you can choose where you feel you fit in the range by circling the appropriate number. If you read the statement and feel your answer is "always" or "never" still choose "1" or "5" depending on what end of the scale you more closely agree with. After completing a subject area, total your score by adding together the numbers you have circled.

This exercise is for your personal use only and will not been seen by your instructor or others unless you choose to share it with them You are encouraged to share this with someone you trust in order to gain the most benefit from this exercise through accountability.

EXERCISES

Area 1: School/Homework

When prohibited to leave the campus during the school day or because of curfew, I:	Rarely sneak away	①—②—③—④—⑤	Frequently sneak away
When struggling with a question on a test, I:	Rarely cheat	①—②—③—④—⑤	Frequently cheat
When talking to my teacher about a late assignment, I would:	Rarely lie	①—②—③—④—⑤	Usually lie
When using the Internet to gather other people's information for my work, I would:	Rarely present their work as my own	①—②—③—④—⑤	Frequently present their work as my own
If my classmate needs help with an assignment and I know the teacher would consider it cheating, I would:	Rarely help them cheat	①—②—③—④—⑤	Frequently help them cheat
If I don't feel like I am prepared for the work due that day at class, I would:	Go anyways	①—②—③—④—⑤	Pretend to be sick and not go.

My total points for Area 1: _____

Area 2: Driving

When I am driving, I:	Rarely exceed the speed limit	①—②—③—④—⑤	Usually exceed the speed limit
Because the law requires it, I:	Usually wear a seat belt	①—②—③—④—⑤	Frequently do not wear a seat belt
If pulled over by a policeman, I:	Rarely try to talk my way out of a ticket	①—②—③—④—⑤	Frequently try to talk my way out of a ticket
Before getting my regular license, I:	Usually followed the probationary license law	①—②—③—④—⑤	Rarely followed the probationary license laws
When coming to a stop sign, I:	Usually come to a complete stop	①—②—③—④—⑤	Rarely come to a complete stop
When approaching a yellow light and I am not already in the intersection, I:	Rarely speed up to go through it	①—②—③—④—⑤	Frequently speed up to go through it

My total points for Area 2: _____

EXERCISES

Area 3: Work

When working a job with required hours, I:	Usually show up on time	①—②—③—④—⑤	Frequently show up late
When working at a job where I am paid by the hour, I:	Rarely sit in the back and talk to other workers when I know I should be working	①—②—③—④—⑤	Frequently sit in the back and talk to other workers when I know I should be working
When dealing with an employer about something I am accused of, I:	Rarely lie	①—②—③—④—⑤	Frequently lie
My behavior around my co-workers compared to my behavior around my church or school friends is:	Rarely any different	①—②—③—④—⑤	Frequently very different
When working a job to a fixed time, I:	Rarely leave work early	①—②—③—④—⑤	Frequently leave work early
When working a job, I:	Rarely talk negatively about co-workers or employers behind their backs	①—②—③—④—⑤	Frequently talk negatively about co-workers or employers behind their backs

My total points for Area 3: _____

Area 4: Media

My personal music and/or videos were:	Mostly bought through a legitimate vendor	①—②—③—④—⑤	Mostly downloaded illegally or acquired without payment
When viewing materials on the web, in magazines, videos, etc. I:	Usually only view wholesome and appropriate materials	①—②—③—④—⑤	Frequently view inappropriate materials
When posting pictures or information about myself on my personal websites, I:	Usually only post items I would not mind my parents or teachers to see	①—②—③—④—⑤	Frequently post items I would not want my parents or teachers to see
During class, church or chapel, I:	Rarely send and receive text	①—②—③—④—⑤	Frequently send and receive text
When using school computers on school time, I:	Usually stay only on school - approved websites	①—②—③—④—⑤	Frequently access non-school approved websites

(Continued)

EXERCISES

When watching television or movies, I:	Usually watch media that has only good values	①—②—③—④—⑤	Usually watch media that has questionable values

My total points for Area 4: _____

Area 5: Relationships

When I am talking to a friend about sensitive matters, I:	Rarely lie even if the truth may hurt them	①—②—③—④—⑤	Frequently lie in order not to hurt them
When talking with authorities in my life (parents, teachers, etc.), I:	Usually show them respect	①—②—③—④—⑤	Frequently show them disrespect
When wanting a desired result in a situation with another person(s), I:	Rarely manipulate it to get what I want	①—②—③—④—⑤	Frequently manipulate it to get what I want
When romantically involved with someone and we have the opportunity to cross physical boundaries inappropriate to pre-marriage, I:	Rarely cross these physical boundaries	①—②—③—④—⑤	Frequently cross these physical boundaries+
In a serious dating relationship, I:	Rarely cheated (emotional or physically) on the individual	①—②—③—④—⑤	Frequently cheat (emotional, physically) on the individual
In dealing with a sibling or another person, I:	Rarely harass him/her either verbally, emotionally or physically	①—②—③—④—⑤	Frequently harass him/her either verbally, emotionally or physically

Area 6: Faith

When considering my relationship with God, I am:	Concerned about commitment and growth	①—②—③—④—⑤	Rarely think about commitment and growth
When considering my relationship with God, I:	Usually spend meaningful time in prayer	①—②—③—④—⑤	Rarely spend any time in prayer
When I am talking to new people about the idea of faith, I:	Usually want to share what I believe about my faith	①—②—③—④—⑤	Usually prefer to not share anything about my faith
When dealing with people different from myself, I:	Usually can see God's creation in them and seek understanding	①—②—③—④—⑤	Frequently judge them and get frustrated with the differences

EXERCISES

When talking with "Christian" adults, about my personal faith, I:	Usually am open and honest about my struggles	①—②—③—④—⑤	Usually just tell them what they are looking to hear
When thinking about my life, I:	Usually feel that I need to rely on something greater than myself to help me	①—②—③—④—⑤	Usually feel that I need to rely on myself rather than something greater than me

My total points for Area 5: _____

My total points for Area 6: _____

Place your totals for each of the areas inside the top of the appropriate silo below.

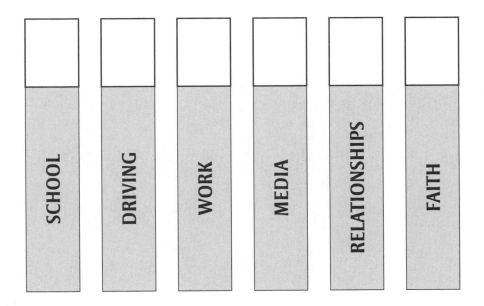

▶ **Reflection Questions**

1. Are there one or more areas that have a much higher score compared to other areas? If so, why do you believe that is the case?

2. Were there a lot of statements in which you assigned yourself middle range scores (3's)? If so, what do you believe this says about your ethics and value system?

3. Did question #1 reveal that you have moral silos in your life? How does this affect how you live your life?

EXERCISES

Mentoring and Accountability

The hectic pace of your social life and the heavy demands of your academic studies can often lead to placing the development of your character on hold during your college experience.

Many times in the transition from high school to college, a sense of community is often lost. When this happens, there are fewer people around you who can help keep you accountable to live the congruent life you have intended for yourself. One of the best ways to fill this loss is to seek out a relationship with a mentor.

Mentors are individuals who can serve in many different capacities, such as spiritual guides, life coaches, counselors, teachers, accountability partners, or sponsors. A mentor might be a teacher, staff member, or older student. Whoever it might be, this mentor has traveled the path before you and can help you as you make difficult transitions when starting your college journey.

MENTORING
Step 1: Does my school have a formal mentoring program? (If the answer is no, move on to Step 2.)
What is the location of the mentoring office?   Who is the contact person?
Step 2: What kind(s) of mentor do I need?
❑ Spiritual Guide ❑ Life Coach ❑ Counselor ❑ Teacher ❑ Accountability Partner ❑ Sponsor
Step 3: Who do I know who might fill that desired role? (If you have a formal mentoring office, they can help you find this type of person.)
Step 4: Based on my time management plan, what times do I have available to meet with my mentor?

MENTORING
Step 5: When will I set up time to meet with this person to ask if they will mentor me?

You may also wish to establish a network of peer accountability in addition to a mentoring relationship or as a substitute relationship if mentoring is not available. This approach creates an environment that allows for intentional connections between you and other peers who are going through the same experience. However, it is more than just a way for you to connect with other students. It challenges both you and other students to become more accountable to each other for your actions, as you begin to explore Life Calling.

ACCOUNTABILITY
Step 1: Who do I know who might want to join with me in this type of relationship? (If you have a formal mentoring office, they can help you find this type of person.)
Step 2: Based on my time management plan, what times do I have available to meet with my accountability peers?
Step 3: When will I set up time to meet with these persons to ask them if they will join with me?

◗ References

The following resources have been used in this chapter.

Gandhi, M.K., and Attenborough, R. (2000). *The Words of Gandhi*. New York: Newmarket Press

Palmer, P.J. (2000). *Let Your Life Speak*. San Francisco: Jossey-Bass.

The following resources may be useful as you explore the development of *character* in your exploration of Life Calling.

Albion, M.S. (2000). *Making a Life, Making a Living: Reclaiming Your Purpose and Passion in Business and in Life*. New York: Warner Books.

Bennet, W.J., ed. (2008). *The Moral Compass: Stories for a Life's Journey*. New York: Touchstone.

Schuurman, D.J. (2004). *Vocation: Discerning Our Callings in Life*. Grand Rapids, Michigan: Erdmans Publishing Co.

Smith, G.T. (2011). *Courage and Calling: Embracing Your God-given Potential*. Downers Grove, Illinois: Intervarsity Press.

Schwen, M.R., and Bass, D.C., Eds. (2006). *Leading Lives That Matter: What We Should Do and Who We Should Be*. Grand Rapids, Michigan: Erdmans Publishing Co.

Belmonte, K. (2002). *Hero for Humanity: A Biography of William Wilberforce*, Colorado Springs, Colorado: Navpress Publishing Group.

A Life of Service

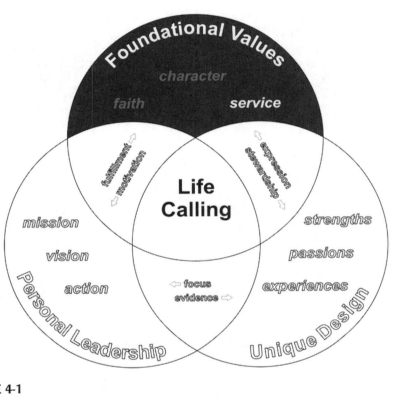

4

FIGURE 4-1
Life Calling Model Focusing on Service

The first main component of the Life Calling Model is *Foundational Values.*
The third of these values is ***service***.

CHAPTER OBJECTIVES

1. Understand the role of service in understanding your Life Calling
2. Begin clarifying your value of other people
3. Understand the value of servanthood as a deeper motivation for service

*All men are caught in
an inescapable
network of mutuality,
tied in a single
garment of destiny ...
I can never be what
I ought to be until you
are what you ought to
be, and you can never
be what you ought
to be until I am what
I ought to be. This is
the inter-related
structure of reality.*

MARTIN LUTHER KING, JR.

KEY TERMS

Action = an exertion of energy, power, or force to accomplish a desired end

Community = a group sharing common characteristics, interests, and heritage

Concern = a matter that engages a person's close attention, deep interest, or significant care

Connection = linking relationship and association that joins, unites, and binds

Respect = a feeling of appreciative, often deferential, regard and esteem

Responsibility = answerable or accountable for something or someone within our ability, power, or control to care for

Servanthood = the noblest form of love carried out in life's relationships

Concepts

Our foundational values about reality become clearer in the formation of the *faith* on which our lives are built. We also understand our personal place in that reality and live a life of *character* in response to this. However, our faith and character take us further than just ourselves. As we begin to understand our personal place in reality, it leads us to realize that our personal place is in a context of everyone else on earth as well. We realize that our life of character is meant to be lived in a commitment of *service* to others. We can also see this as *Life Connection*—the value I hold about others that respects them and seeks to understand them in a spirit of community and the need to take actions of character that are carried out with a sense of concern and responsibility for others.

How does this play out in the search for a Life Calling? There are five key concepts in our understanding of *service* that can help us see this.

The first concept involves our **respect** for others. As we begin to understand our personal place in reality, it leads us to realize that every person on earth has a similar personal place in reality and must be given the same respect that we hold for ourselves based on the premises established in our mind-set. Respect also means that we serve others in a way that does not rob them of their dignity. We will seek to honor, rather than demean, those we serve.

The second concept leading to service is **community**. The discovery of our Life Calling takes place in the environment of a community. What we mean by community is an interacting body of individuals with common characteristics or interests. A Life Calling cannot be discovered or pursued in isolation from other people. Actually, the less connected a person is from others in society, the less capable that person will be to discover a Life Calling. So we seek to be a part of those we serve, rather than staying apart from those we serve.

The third concept leading to service is **concern**. This is simply a regard for or interest in someone. Common characteristics or interests in a community may commingle with each other and not necessarily lead to service. It is rather when that regard for an interest in someone arises to a state of concern that a commitment to service starts to emerge. We need to be careful, however, that the concerns that rise within us are truly fulfilling a need of those we serve rather than just addressing problems that bother us.

Understanding and experiencing concern are very important to the discovery of a Life Calling. Every Life Calling includes a significant component of concern which forms the drawing power that gives Life Calling its calling aspect. When people stifle the attitude of concern in their lives, they begin to pursue a pseudo calling, which in reality turns out to be a pursuit of selfishness. Selfishness is the antithesis of Life Calling. When we pursue a selfish path, we are almost always traveling in the exact opposite direction of our Life Calling.

The fourth concept leading to service is ***responsibility***. As concerns arise in us for others in our world community, an internal social force will develop that will create in us a sense of obligation, and this social force will demand courses of action. This is what we mean by responsibility. It can be ignored, but it cannot be avoided. It will confront us just as surely as the force of gravity will. How we respond will determine at what level service is realized in our life and whether or not we will truly experience the drawing force of a Life Calling. Everyone's Life Calling involves a call to service. If this call to service is avoided, then our Life Calling will be avoided as well, and we will not experience a sense of purpose in our lives.

The fifth concept leading to service is ***action***. Serving communities interact. They do or perform something for each other. Service is not just a state of mind or attitude. Service is never fully realized until action has been taken. Life Calling is far more often found in action than it is in inaction. Some have said it is like a car. It is easier to steer a moving car than a parked car. Hence, action is important in searching for a Life Calling. When we fail to take action, we tend to stay in one place in our lives, and we are always trying to determine where we are going from the same vantage point. The problem is that when we are frozen in place by inaction, the vantage point is more of a blind spot, and we are not really able to see what lies ahead and in what direction we should be going. The better choice is to take action and begin moving. And the most productive action for discovering a Life Calling is action arising from compassionate service to others in our world community.

The following table shows us how service can develop into an integral part of our character.

3 LEVELS OF SERVING

Level of Serving	Description	Level of Operation
Servitude	*Forced Act of Serving Another Person*	Body
Service	*Decided Act of Serving Another Person*	Mind
Servanthood	*Attitudinal Act of Serving Another Person*	Spirit

TABLE 4-1
3 Levels of Serving

When we are forced to serve others, we comply with our bodies, but our minds and spirits resist. This is what could be referred to as "servitude." Let's use the Thanksgiving holiday as an example. Your mother tells you that you will be going with your family to serve meals at the local rescue mission. You, on the other hand, were looking forward to a relaxing day off from school along with a good meal. You go with your family because you respect your parents' authority, but deep down you feel like you are being forced to do this. That is service coming from "servitude."

It is only when we begin to voluntarily offer service that it is elevated to a nobler level in our lives. This starts with individual acts of service where we make a conscience decision to serve. Let's go back to our example. Your mother comes to you and asks if you think it would be a worthy action for your family to serve meals at the local rescue mission. You think about it and decide that this really is the spirit of Thanksgiving, so you say yes and go with your family. This is a service done truly in the spirit of service.

However, for service to reach the highest level where it is an integral part of our character, it must develop to the point where it is an ongoing, continuous attitude within us so that we serve whenever we detect a legitimate need. This is what is meant by the term "servanthood"– love acted out in life's relationship in a way that places the needs of others before one's own self interests. However, this should be carried out without burning yourself out, otherwise you would have nothing left to offer in service. Let's go to our example one more time. This time you go to your mother and suggest to her that you think your family should serve meals at the local rescue mission on Thanksgiving because you believe this is the true spirit of the holiday. This is the highest level of service because it comes from a continuous attitude in your spirit of caring about others and always being on the lookout for their needs.

This concept is illustrated clearly in the *Mutual Influence Model* developed by Chris Clum, the executive director of Experience Mission, a nonprofit international community service and development organization. This model (Figure 4-2) examines attitudes that exist when we interact with others who are different from us. The model characterizes the natural tendencies of people–to judge and control in an attempt to force change on others.

The better way to bring about change is through an attitude of servanthood that leads to mutual influence. Here you must push beyond your natural tendencies and develop a spirit that loves and accepts others, learning from and about them, and truly partnering with them. Read carefully the brief description of these attitudes at the bottom of the model and ask yourself if the mutual influence role comes easily to you, or if it is something that will require significant effort for you to understand.

Based on the model above, we could define Mutual Influence as a set of attitudes and actions that will provide the best approach to the important issues of establishing respect and trust in relationships with others, especially those we serve. Our goal in service should be to reach this state of mutual influence. Only at this level can growth occur that will lead to the "inescapable network of mutuality" and the "inter-related structure of reality" that Martin Luther King, Jr. identified in the opening quote of this chapter. He said we must reach this mutual influence if we are ever going to truly discover who we ought to be and fulfill our Life Calling.

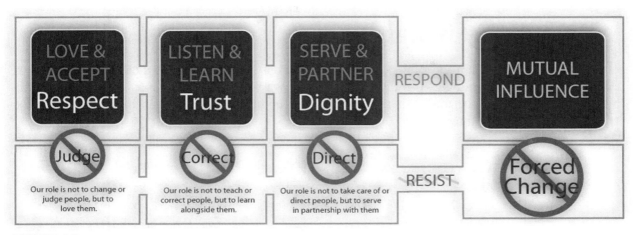

FIGURE 4-2
Mutual Influence Model

Concepts Summary

What happens when we do not engage in service as we search for a Life Calling? Earlier we said that *service* could be thought of as *Life Connection*. When we do not engage in service as we search for a Life Calling, the search will be greatly limited because we will fail to connect with other people. Without that connection, a valuable source of information will be lost—information about ourselves, information about the world around us, and information about the universal design of which we are a part. Without those elements, it will be impossible to discover a Life Calling.

Insight

When the Bible is studied as a whole, serving others is a common theme that dominates throughout scripture. We will find that as our foundational value concerning others increases, our ability to discover our Life Calling will be enhanced.

SCRIPTURAL INSIGHT 1 ▶ *True Service Begins with Respect*

About noon the following day as they were on their journey and approaching the city, Peter went up on the roof to pray. He became hungry and wanted something to eat, and while the meal was being prepared, he fell into a trance. He saw heaven opened and something like a large sheet being let down to earth by its four corners. It contained all kinds of four-footed animals, as well as reptiles and birds. Then a voice told him, "Get up, Peter. Kill and eat."

"Surely not, Lord!" Peter replied. "I have never eaten anything impure or unclean." The voice spoke to him a second time, "Do not call anything impure that God has made clean." This happened three times, and immediately the sheet was taken back to heaven. Acts 10:9-16

Peter's vision in Acts 10 is immediately followed by the arrival of a contingent from a centurion named Cornelius. He was an officer in the Italian Regiment seeking spiritual help. In that society, people from Peter's background did not associate with people from Cornelius' background. However, God did not care about their petty rules and wanted Peter to go to Cornelius' house and work with him. That's why God sent Peter the vision. Peter learned from the vision and went to Cornelius' home. He began his teaching with these words: "I now realize how true it is that God does not show favoritism but accepts those from every nation who fear him and do what is right" (Acts 10:34-35).

Too often people render service to others with an attitude that looks down on those being served. This condescending spirit does not lead to the spirit of service that can help reveal your Life Calling. The Life Calling Model that is the basis for this book starts with faith that we have been created in this universe by God for a reason. It then calls us to live lives of character consistent with our faith. We do not live out our faith in isolation. Our faith moves us toward a life of service to others. This service is based on the same attitude that we have toward ourselves.

The Mutual Influence Model characterizes respect in these terms: "Out of love we are able to resist our natural tendency to judge and try to change others. When we give respect to another person—as a genuine act of love—it allows us to simply accept them as they are: unique creations of a loving God" (Clum, 2005). By incorporating the Life Calling Model, we could add to this that others are not only unique creations of a loving God, but that they are created for a reason. Because of this, they deserve our utmost respect.

Such an attitude of respect can completely change the way we look at service. It becomes a matter of mutuality where people help each other based on a match of provision and needs. Those who have the provision share with those who have the needs. But those whose needs may require your provision in one area may have provisions that you need in another area—the concept of mutuality. Too many times service is seen in a one-way manner—the noble helper here to serve the less-noble needy person. When service arises out of this attitude, it completely ignores the intentionality of God's creation of that other person, and it leads those so-called helpers to have a distorted view of their own value and importance. Such a distorted view completely blocks the ability to see God's true Life Calling and leads people into a confused life.

The better approach is to see service as an opportunity to stand beside others as equals and try to find answers and solutions based on varying circumstances. When we do this, we will start to discover information about our Life Calling.

> **PERSONAL REFLECTION** ⟩ Do you see those who are in need of your help as your equals, or do you look down on them? How can you start to view others as intentional creations of God just like you are? How can this make a difference in your attitude of service?

SCRIPTURAL INSIGHT 2 ▶ *Serving Others Is Best Accomplished in a Community of Mutual Influence*

There was a man all alone; he had neither son nor brother. There was no end to his toil, yet his eyes were not content with his wealth. "For whom am I toiling," he asked, "and why am I depriving myself of enjoyment?" This too is meaningless—a miserable business! Two are better than one, because they have a good return for their labor: If they fall down, they can help each other up. But pity those who fall and have no one to help them up! Also, if two lie down together, they will keep warm. But how can one keep warm alone? Though one may be overpowered, two can defend themselves. A cord of three strands is not quickly broken. ECCLESIASTES 4:8-12

When members of the human race have respect for each other, they can join forces to mutually help each other. This is the best way to approach the concept of service. Solomon paints a bleak picture for the person who is all alone in life. A community, or the three-strand-cord, is in his opinion the strongest approach to society. It is interesting to look deeper at Solomon's analogy of the cord of three strands. When you look at such a cord or rope, you quickly discover that these strands do not run parallel but independent of each other. Instead, you see that they are interwoven and braided together in a way that is quite collaborative. That is what we mean when we say that service needs to be based on a framework of community.

An important basic concept is found in the Creation story in Genesis where God observed Adam and concluded, "It is not good for the man to be alone. I will make a helper suitable for him" (Genesis 2:18). Of course God then creates Eve and the two become the parents of civilization. This is often used in marriage ceremonies to validate marriage as an institution. While not disagreeing with that, the case can be made, however, that the problem with "aloneness" was not just an issue of marriage. The stories that follow the Genesis account throughout the rest of the Bible all take place in the context of a community of people. It is fair to conclude that God created human beings to need each other. Our ability, and indeed call, to serve each other in community is a central part of our Life Calling.

In the *Mutual Influence Model*, referred to in Scriptural Insight #1, three important actions are identified that can lead to building the kind of community attitude necessary for true service. First, love and accept others as they are, not as we think they should be. Second, listen and learn from others by centering our attention on their world rather than our own personal interests, values, and faith. Third, serve and partner with others by recognizing what they have to contribute and how our collaboration will bring a better, longer lasting result while maintaining the dignity and sense of worth of all involved. Our job is not to take care of people, but to serve in partnership with them. As we interact with others and demonstrate respect for them, the diversity of our lives creates opportunities for reciprocal learning, growth and life change.

A *community* is an interacting body of individuals with common characteristics or interests. In the story of the Good Samaritan, everybody involved was a human being. In fact, they were all of an ethnic background that had far more similarities than differences, so their characteristics as humans were much more in common than were the religious or philosophical differences they might have had. Furthermore, they really all should have had the same interests: attendance to physical needs. The conveyor of compassion in this story, the Good Samaritan, understood this nature of common unity—community—and made decisions based on that understanding. The priest and the Levite did not.

We have something to learn from everyone once we set aside our personal judgments and cultural prejudices—things we may have previously used to determine a person's worth. Our job is not to change others, but to change ourselves.

> **PERSONAL REFLECTION** ⟩ When you serve others, is your focus primarily on changing them based on your personal judgment of what they need? Or is your focus on changing yourself based on what you learn from others as you serve alongside of them? How can you start to partner with those you serve rather than "help" those you serve?

SCRIPTURAL INSIGHT 3 ⟩ *Respond to Others with Concern and Compassion*

When Jesus heard what had happened, he withdrew by boat privately to a solitary place. Hearing of this, the crowds followed him on foot from the towns. When Jesus landed and saw a large crowd, he had compassion on them and healed their sick. MATTHEW 14:13&14

The call to service rises out of *concern* for others. Concern can be defined as a matter that engages our close attention, deep interest, and/or significant care. It is the driving force in the attitude of compassion.

After the death of John the Baptist, Jesus was sorrowing because John was a relative, a supporter, and a colleague in building the kingdom of heaven. Jesus withdrew by boat privately to a solitary place. He wanted to be alone with his thoughts where he could reflect on what had happened. He also wanted to work through his feelings. Everybody needs that kind of alone time when traumatic events take place. Unfortunately, the needs of people do not always allow for this. The crowds followed Jesus on foot around the Sea of Galilee. When Jesus landed and saw all the people, he had compassion on them and healed their sick.

Verses 15 through 21 tell the rest of this well-known story of compassion. Jesus miraculously fed five thousand men plus as many or more women and children using five small barley loaves and two fish.

One chapter later in Matthew a similar incident takes place all over again. Jesus had been teaching and ministering for three days to four thousand men plus as many or more women and children. Matthew 15:32 describes what happened at that point: "Jesus called his disciples to him and said, 'I have compassion for these people; they have already been with me three days and have nothing to eat. I do not want to send them away hungry, or they may collapse on the way.'"

As in the earlier incident, Jesus responded by taking a few barley loaves and fish and breaking them into thousands of pieces that ended up feeding everybody with quite a bit to spare. In both of these incidents, compassion was given as the motivating force that resulted in the miracles.

An important concept that compassionate concern brings to service is the realization that the focus is others-centered rather than self-centered. This was clearly the case in the story of the Good Samaritan. The safest and easiest decision would have been to ignore the man who had been beaten and robbed, and continue on the trip with no responsibilities or liabilities. Instead, the Samaritan had a regard for the suffering condition of the man attacked by robbers and put the needs of the man before his own self-interests. When we take that same attitude into our realm of service, we will find that it opens a unique portal to the discovery of Life Calling that can really not be found in any other way.

> **PERSONAL REFLECTION** ⟩ When you serve others, is your focus others-centered or self-centered? Do you avoid becoming involved with others in need if you feel it was not your fault that they are in such a situation? How can you begin to put the needs of others before your own self-interests without being exploited by others?

SCRIPTURAL INSIGHT 4 ⟩ *Service Is a Responsibility, Not a Choice*

They devoted themselves to the apostles' teaching and to fellowship, to the breaking of bread and to prayer. Everyone was filled with awe at the many wonders and signs performed by the apostles. All the believers were together and had everything in common. They sold property and possessions to give to anyone who had need. Every day they continued to meet together in the temple courts. They broke bread in their homes and ate together with glad and sincere hearts, praising God and enjoying the favor of all the people. And the Lord added to their number daily those who were being saved. ACTS 2:42-47

Service never really becomes a regular practice in our lives until we begin to accept it as a *responsibility*. In the two stories describing Jesus' feeding of the masses, the disciples working with Jesus wanted to send the people away so they would not have to take care of them. But Jesus felt a responsibility for them and did not want the people to suffer harm because of the failure to meet this responsibility.

The same was true in the story of the Good Samaritan. The priest and the Levite felt no responsibility for bringing aid to a bad situation and just ignored it. In fact the story points out that they took drastic measures to avoid the situation. How drastic? I have been to the site where this took place. The path parallels a narrow canyon between Jericho and Jerusalem. The path, or more correctly, paths, were so tight on the canyon walls that there was a path on each side of the canyon with traffic traveling in opposite directions on the respective sides—sort of like our present day divided highways. So the priest and Levite did not just take a step to the other side of the same path; they descended clear down the canyon, climbed back up to the other side and then walked against traffic to avoid the man.

But the Good Samaritan had decided in his heart long before arriving on the scene of the crime that wherever it was in his power, it was his responsibility to bring goodness into a situation where evil was prevailing.

The attitude taken by the early-forming Christian church is impressive when it comes to serving each other. They did not view their own possessions as actually theirs; rather they saw them as resources given to all of them by God. So when anyone had a need, those who had provision to address this need saw it as their responsibility and took action to do it. The status of being in need and being the provider changed back and forth as circumstances varied.

Responsibility means being answerable or accountable for something or someone within our ability, power, or control to care for. This means that service is not really something that is optional. It is, rather, something that we should do when we have the ability, power, or control to give such service.

People often complain about confusion concerning what they should be doing in life, their struggle with discovering their Life Calling, or having a sense of calling. When this is the case, one of the best places to begin gathering information to clear up the confusion is in the act of service. Life Calling is directly tied to the concept of responsibility, and service is one of the best places to learn the lesson of responsibility.

> **PERSONAL REFLECTION** ▷ Do you believe that it is your responsibility to bring goodness into a situation where brokenness, need, or evil is prevailing? How can you work on establishing or strengthening your willingness to take responsibility in situations where needs arise?

SCRIPTURAL INSIGHT 5 ▶ *It All Comes Together in Action*

"A man was going down from Jerusalem to Jericho, when he fell into the hands of robbers. They stripped him of his clothes, beat him and went away, leaving him half dead...A Samaritan, as he traveled, came where the man was; and when he saw him, he took pity on him. He went to him and bandaged his wounds, pouring on oil and wine. Then he put the man on his own donkey, took him to an inn and took care of him. The next day he took out two silver coins and gave them to the innkeeper. 'Look after him,' he said, 'and when I return, I will reimburse you for any extra expense you may have.'" Luke 10:30-35

Prior to a football game, it is common for the coach to work with the team during the week ahead of the game developing theory, strategy and plans for how they should play the game. Even the day of the game, there is often a pep talk in the locker room to inspire the players to give their all to the game. While all of this is good and helps prepare the players for the game, the fact of the matter is that the game does not take place until the kick-off. Furthermore, the players can stand around in the huddle and talk about what they hope to do, but until they actually hike the ball and execute the play, it is all talk.

The same is true for service. We can talk about the reason for service and the best way to do it. But until we finally take action, no service will actually be given.

The story of the Good Samaritan is one of the greatest stories of compassionate service. The story came about in response to a question asked of Jesus by a man who considered himself very religious—an expert in the law. The man wanted to know what he could do to secure eternal life for himself. When Jesus confirmed that he needed to love God and to love his neighbor, the man asked, "Who is my neighbor?" Jesus answered this question with the well-known story of the Good Samaritan—which, incidentally, he was telling to a man and the crowd around the man who didn't like Samaritans at all.

Based on his understanding of respect, community, concern, and responsibility, the Good Samaritan took actions that brought both provision and healing to desperate situations. Again, it is interesting to note in the story of the Good Samaritan that the priest and Levite took action as well, based on their incorrect understanding that led them to shirk any spirit of compassion. This same spirit likely tempted the man of the law who asked Jesus the question that led to the telling of the story of the Good Samaritan. He lacked an understanding of the value of service, and this likely contributed greatly to his inability to determine what led to eternal life (his Life Calling).

And that leads us to an important application in our own lives concerning these reflections regarding service. When we find ourselves following the attitudes of the priest and Levite more than that of the Good Samaritan, we tend to turn away from the community of people around us and avoid taking responsibility for others and showing compassionate actions. If we fall into this trap, we will find it very difficult to discover the true nature of Life Calling because a significant aspect of Life Calling arises from compassionate service that is required in a spirit of community. So here are five important steps we can take to make sure that compassion is part of our experience:

1. Keep your eyes out for the plight of others in your communities just as much as you do for yourself.

2. Always approach situations with others in a positive spirit of respect for them as unique creations of God.

3. Maintain compassionate concern and regard for or interest in their situation rather than a negative critical attitude about their situation.

4. Determine in your heart before you encounter situations that whenever it is in your power to do it, you will take responsibility to bring goodness into a situation where evil is prevailing.

5. Commit yourself to taking your compassion to the stage of action. Don't be caught in the misconception that an attitude of pity or sympathy is enough to demonstrate compassion. The final test of compassion is found in action.

As we take these five steps in our lives, we will find that our foundational value concerning others increases, and this will greatly enhance our ability to discover our Life Calling.

PERSONAL REFLECTION ⟩ How can you develop or strengthen the five attitudes outlined above? How can this help you discover your Life Calling?

INSIGHT

▶ Discovery

How can the Discovery Guides help you understand and commit to a life of *service*?

T THEORY	Study of social sciences can help inform your service to others. Although this study is often pursued in formal classes, you can also pursue it in your own personal reading as well. Start creating a list of books that will aid your exploration. Ask others for recommendations.
E EXAMPLES	Service in the lives of other persons is a very good place to learn about it in your own life. Observe them and find time to talk to them. Keep a constant search for such people. Many times you will find them in positions you may not have thought of, such as food servers, groundskeepers, janitors, secretaries, and other positions that may not be in the limelight of your institution.
A ASSESSMENT	There are quite a few assessments that measure skills, attitudes, and motivations related to service. You might want to use some of these to help you direct your service in an effective manner.
C COUNSEL	People speaking into your life can be powerful sources of guidance and strength in service. Finding someone who can serve as a mentor to you during your college years can make a great difference in your success. Many colleges and universities have an office coordinating community service. You might want to check this out and talk with someone in that office if your institution has one.
H HISTORY	The classics and historical biographies are full of stories dealing with notable people who have lived lives of service to others. Select some of these and learn from their experiences.
E EXPERIENCE	Get involved with service activities going on in your college or university. You can find these in your residence life, in your classes, in your student clubs and governments. You will discover where your heart is for service by experiencing it.
R REFLECTION	Take time to reflect on what you have learned about your *physical strengths* in the other six activities of discovery. Consider what you agree with and why.

DISCOVERY

▶ Story

New York City is not a place where a first-time visitor particularly wants to drive. It's difficult enough in a car, but in a 42-foot motorhome—forget it. Because there are no RV parks in New York City itself, the *Nautilus* and its shipload of adventurers headed for Liberty Harbor RV Park in Jersey City, New Jersey. They could actually see the Statue of Liberty from the park, and it was close to a station where they could catch public transportation to Manhattan. The six explorers from California looked forward to traveling on these famed subways.

The trip from Washington, D.C., had taken the travelers through Baltimore and Philadelphia. There had been a brief stop in Philadelphia to see Independence Hall and the Liberty Bell, and to grab a quick Philly Cheesesteak at Pat's King of Steaks, the original home of this famous, less-than-healthful sandwich.

The next three days were marked by a whirlwind of activity and emotion. They had been exhilarated by the view from the top of the Empire State Building. They had been inspired by their visit to the Statue of Liberty and Ellis Island. They had been deeply moved by their visit to the National September 11 Memorial. But when it came to excitement, their visit to Broadway could not be matched. It was a marvelous mixture of glamour, glitz, hype, bright lights, and chaos. They took in the smash hit *Men are from Mars, Women are from Venus*, the somewhat irreverent and loose adaptation of psychologist John Gray's twentieth-century classic work on opposite sex relationships.

Their last afternoon in New York was drawing to a close. The six assembled in Grand Central Station to begin the subway trip back to Jersey City. The buzz reminded them of an angry beehive, and the not-so-pleasant smell of hundreds of sweating people filled the air. The hectic scene at the station began to intimidate them; Seahaven seemed so far away, and homesickness seemed a lot nearer.

"I've never seen so many different types of people," Diana observed. "I mean, we're not exactly from Kansas, but even California isn't this diverse."

"Yeah," Ryan agreed. "It kind of makes me uncomfortable. I kind of feel out of place."

"Welcome to my world!" Abriella said in a soft voice. Her comment caught the others off guard. "And my world," Lorena echoed.

"That's weird," Ryan said. "We've hung out together most of our lives, and so I have never thought about us having any differences."

"That's because you've always been in the majority," Abriella responded. "And I don't say that to put you down. It's just that when you are always surrounded by plenty of people who look and seem a lot like you, you never feel out of place. But when you're a person whose color automatically sets you apart as a minority, you always feel in some sense you are out of place."

"Wow! I never thought of it that way, Abi," Adam said. "I've always thought of you as a best friend since as long as I can remember."

"And that's the way I feel about you and all of us," Abriella replied. "But it doesn't change the fact that I am treated differently by other people."

"I think I know what you mean," Lorena joined in. "In most people's minds, I'm a Mexican. A few might say 'Latino,' but I know what's in most of their minds. I'm not ashamed that I was born in Mexico. We go back and visit my relatives there every year. But now I'm an American, and I'm proud of it. The problem is that some others are not proud that I am. In fact they'd like me to go back to Mexico."

"Think about me, Lorena," Abriella responded. "You were actually born in another country and then came to the United States But my relatives have been in this country as long as anybody's. And yet I am not thought of as totally American. I am called African American, as if to indicate I am only half entitled to my citizenship. No one who is white can know what it is like to live like that."

"You know what's weird?" Justin asked the question of nobody in particular. "I know what it is like to feel I don't fit in with everyone else. But I think a lot of times I'm treated in a different way. I think stereotypes play a part."

"What do you mean, Justin?" Adam asked.

"For some reason or another, people who like to lump ethnic groups together decided that Asians are smart," Justin replied. "And so I probably haven't felt looked down on as much as Abi or Lorena. But that's crazy. Over 60 percent of the population of the world could be called Asian. Some are smart; some are not. But think of it: that number is made up of hundreds of subgroups. My family came from Korea. In our minds, we're just as different from the Japanese as any of you who are white. Why try to lump us all together?"

"Hey, guys, it's not just race," Ryan spoke up. "See the man over there sitting on the floor to the right of the drinking fountain? My guess is that he doesn't have a lot of money … probably is homeless. Look at the expression on people's faces when they walk by him. Many try to avoid him. My mom and dad were like that for a while before I was born. Even now we still don't have much money. It's no fun to use food stamps when you go to the store. People look at you and might as well say 'loser' out loud."

"That word has never entered my mind about you," Diana responded emphatically.

"That's cool, Diana, and I appreciate it," Ryan answered. "But you've never seen life from my side of the tracks. Captain Nemo and the misses seem to be doing pretty well." (Ryan had coined the nickname for Diana's father from the combination of the motorhome's adopted name *Nautilus* and an alteration of the last name of its driver "Neimon" … though Ryan couldn't be sure whether "Nemo" came from Jules Verne's novel or from the lost fish in Pixar's animated film—nor did he care.)

"Yea, but it works both ways. I think it's like what Justin said," Diana responded strongly. "I think you stereotype people with money just as much as you do anybody else."

"I'd take my chances," Ryan replied. "Hey, I'm not putting you down or anything, Diana. You've been the nicest rich person I've ever known, and your parents have certainly helped me and my family a lot."

"There's the problem," Diana said as she pointed at Ryan. "Why can't I just be a nice person you know, not a nice rich person you know?"

"Well, give me all your money, and you can be!" Ryan laughed.

Diana mockingly hit him on his shoulder.

"But we like stereotypes," Adam said. "It's the lazy way to observe people, and we all do it. For instance, that lady over by the third bench in a wheelchair, what do you think when you see her?"

"I'm trying to figure out who it is over there that is with her to take care of her," Lorena answered.

"So you don't think she is traveling alone?" Adam asked further.

"Of course not; how could she?" Lorena replied.

"Isn't it interesting how quick you can assume that she is dissatisfied with her situation and wants or needs our help or at least someone's help," Adam continued. "I mean, I'll be honest. That's what I thought when I first saw her."

"Yeah, but she might have been in that wheelchair since she was a little kid," Justin broke in. "And she might be just as comfortable getting around on her own as you or I am. The point is that when we are standing over here, we really don't know her situation and shouldn't be coming to conclusions about her without getting to know her."

"There's quite a lot of differences in this place," Lorena observed. "But did you notice how quickly and easily we fit them all into groups—groups, incidentally, that we concoct. Who knows whether or not we were right? The problem is that as soon as we do that, we quit thinking of them as individuals."

"You are right, Lor," Adam responded. "It makes me kind of ashamed of myself."

"To be honest with you, I feel a little bit uneasy in this place … almost threatened," Diana said in a timid voice.

"Why, Diana?" Lorena asked.

"I don't know." Diana looked back at all of the people as she spoke. "I guess because it's so different than home. There's part of me that just wants to be back in my safe, upper-middle-class, white environment of Seahaven."

"Hey, Seahaven isn't that safe," Justin countered.

"It isn't that white either," Lorena laughed. "There's a lot of us there."

"I know," Diana agreed. "I guess I'm just more comfortable with what I'm used to."

"But don't you think God meant for us to be with other people? You know, sort of like that idea of the world as a village?" Adam challenged.

"I suppose," Diana responded. "But it isn't always easy or comfortable."

"I agree with Adam," Lorena said. "We've all been talking the last few days about how to find out our purpose or calling in life. I don't think you can find it if you don't have some concern for others."

"Exactly!" Adam was glad for the support. "Our Life Calling is mostly about serving others; that's what I believe. And you won't serve others if you're always looking down on them with some stereotype and don't have a sense of respect and responsibility."

"So you're saying that if I don't serve others, I won't be able to figure out what I should do in life?" Justin was puzzled.

"Yep. That's what I believe," Adam answered confidently. "I think that's what the parable of the Good Samaritan was all about."

"Wow! That's heavy." Justin leaned back on the bench. "Maybe that's why I've had such a tough time figuring out what to do with my life."

The sound of metal wheels clattering on steel tracks filled the air accompanied by the screech of brakes.

"Hey guys, I think our train is coming in. We'd better get ready to load." Abriella began to marshal the troops. "We don't want to spend the night here in Grand Central Station."

"I know *I* don't," Diana added.

The others murmured their agreement and began to make their way to the loading ramp.

STORY

 # Exercises

Understanding and Appreciating Diversity

From *Life Skills for college: A Curriculum for Life* by Earl J. Ginter and Ann Shanks Glauser. Copyright © 2002 by Earl J. Ginter and Ann Shanks Glauser.

We know that our attitudes and beliefs influence our perceptions. We assimilate attitudes and beliefs throughout our lives, forming assumptions about the way things are and are not, including judgments about people. Unfortunately, we tend to filter out information that does not affirm, or align with, our perception of the world, so we tend to rely on many biased assumptions to guide us through life. Biased assumptions distort the truth and give rise to prejudices that keep us confined in narrowly defined spaces. Is there any way for us to get out of our own little boxes to see what is truly going on around us? The answer is, emphatically, yes! Biases can be intentional or unintentional. They might be based on cultural isolation or ignorance. When you form a belief about an entire group of people without recognizing individual differences among members of the group, you are engaging in stereotyping.

We are all guilty of stereotyping because of the way in which the mind stores, organizes, and recalls information to reduce complexity and help us make quick decisions (Johnson & Johnson, 2000). Johnson and Johnson report that the term *stereotype* was initially used in the eighteenth century to describe a printing process that duplicated pages of type. According to Johnson and Johnson (2000) it was not until 1922 that Walter Lippman used the term to describe the process by which people gloss over details to simplify social perceptions. We tend to stereotype people to whom we do not pay much attention. The practice of stereotyping can lead to prejudice, which can lead to discrimination. Why does it endure? Read over the reasons given in the box below.

Reasons Why Stereotypes Endure

1. People tend to overestimate the association between variables that are only slightly correlated or not correlated at all, creating an **illusionary correlation**. Many people, for example, perceive that being poor and being lazy are associated. Any poor person who is not hard at work at the very moment you notice him or her may be perceived to be lazy. Low-power groups can easily acquire negative traits in this way, and once acquired, the stereotype is hard to shed.

2. Having a prejudice makes people notice the negative traits they ascribe to the groups they are prejudiced against, and they more readily believe information that confirms the stereotypes than evidence that challenges them. People tend to process information in ways that verify existing beliefs. This tendency to seek, interpret, and create information that verifies existing beliefs is known as the **confirmation bias**.

3. People have a **false consensus bias** when they believe that most other people share their stereotypes. They tend to see their own behaviors and judgments as quite common and appropriate, and to view alternative responses as uncommon and often inappropriate.

4. Stereotypes tend to be **self-fulfilling**. Stereotypes can subtly influence intergroup interactions in such a way that the stereotype is behaviorally confirmed. People may behave in ways that elicit the actions they expect from out-group members, thus confirming the stereotype.

5. People often dismiss individuals who do not match a stereotype as exceptions to the rule or representatives of a subcategory.

6. Stereotypes often operate at an implicit level below people's conscious awareness.

7. People often develop a rationale and explanation to justify their stereotypes and prejudices.

From Johnson, Frank P. *Joining Together: Group Theory and Group Skills*, 7/E. Copyright © 2000 by Pearson Education. Reprinted by permission of Pearson Education, Inc., Upper Saddle River, NJ.

What can you do to overcome biases that cloud your perceptions and create distortions? How do you move beyond intolerance and prejudice? These are questions that have no easy answers. Examining your own attitudes, becoming more aware of other cultures, and developing a multicultural view that will help you communicate, appreciate, and respect people from diverse backgrounds are steps in the right direction.

▶ Examine Your Attitudes

Your culture surrounds you. Culture influences the way you think, feel, and behave. Identities are forged within the cultural context in which you live. Society, the larger culture in which you live, sends both positive and negative messages about the self. Unconscious or conscious beliefs about the way you are supposed to be can create a great deal of pain for those who are excluded and marginalized by the majority members of society. If while you were growing up you received a constant stream of negative messages that you were not okay because your cultural rules were different from those in the dominant culture, you may have internalized feelings that you are not okay. Prejudice has a negative impact on the process of identity formation. Examine some of your own prejudices by answering the following questions.

Name:_____ Date:_____ Class:_____ Section: _____

▶ Assessing Cultural Influences

1. When were you first aware of differences among people?

2. When did you become aware of your own racial/ethnic heritage?

3. When did you first experience some sort of prejudice? Do you remember your thoughts and feelings?

4. When did you first become aware that you had privileges or were denied privileges, based on your physical characteristics, socioeconomic background, or ability level?

5. How have others stereotyped you or members of your family?

6. What kind of messages did you receive as a child that you were inferior or superior to others? Who or what sent these messages?

Attitudes can create barriers to interacting with people from diverse backgrounds. When you see someone walking toward you, what do you tend to notice? Gender? Weight? Skin color? Clothing? Hair? What kinds of assumptions do you make based on your observations? Student? Sorority girl? Nontraditional student? Professor? Athlete? Foreigner? Finally, what assumptions do you make about each kind of person? We all assume things about people. Just remember that your assumptions are often incorrect. Prejudice is a learned habit, and it takes a conscious effort to break it.

Sources of Prejudice

Where do these prejudices come from? They come from a variety of sources.

Economic competitiveness and scapegoating. Scapegoating is the process of displacing aggression or projecting guilt onto a group of people. When the economy is bad, accusations like, "Those immigrants are taking away all our jobs," increase in frequency. Political candidates sometimes appeal to prejudices among voters. They may scapegoat immigrants, for example, in an effort to win votes from those who feel disempowered or frustrated with the economy.

Parents and Relatives.   What messages did your parents send about other people? When you were young and found yourself near a person in a wheelchair, what messages did you receive about how to behave? Did you observe the adult, look away, or maybe address the person accompanying the person with the disability rather than communicating directly with the person who was disabled? What about when you asked a parent if a friend who was from another socioeconomic or cultural group could come home with you or if you could go to his or her house? Messages can be overt or covert. The effect is the same. When negative messages are attached to differences between people, prejudice takes root.

Institutions.   Prejudice is learned through living in a society where prejudices are sustained. Who received the most privileges in your school? Did the gifted students get to engage in more creative learning situations than the other students? What about overweight children in your school? How were they treated? Who participated in sports and organizations with you? Were accommodations made for someone who was mentally or physically disabled? As a child, were you ever conscious of the fact all U.S. presidents have been white males?

Media.   What kinds of messages do you receive from magazines, movies, and television? What prejudices are perpetuated in the media? What groups of people are stereotyped? What types of misinformation about certain groups of people are broadcast? When you watch television or go to a movie, how are women depicted? How often are they depicted as sex symbols? Stereotyping is based on ignorance. Have you heard any disparaging remarks about others lately through the media? What about jokes about religion, sexual orientation, skin color, or weight?

Social Fragmentation.   Levine and Cureton (1998) found that undergraduate students across the country described themselves more in terms of differences than similarities. Their study also revealed that students today are more socially isolated than previous generations; increasingly, they voluntarily segregate themselves to form small self-interest groups. Look around you. Gaps between socioeconomic groups in this country seem to be widening. The sources that fuel prejudice come together to create a powerful, destructive force that can lead to discrimination and even violence.

EXERCISES

Name: _____ Date: _____ Class: _____ Section: _____

Responding to Differences

In our study of Concepts, we identified *service* as *Life Connection*—the value I hold about others that respects them and seeks to understand them in a spirit of community and the need to take actions of character that are carried out with a sense of concern and responsibility for others. A good illustration of this is found in one of the most familiar stories told to children growing up—the story of the Good Samaritan.

A man was going down a dangerous road, when he fell into the hands of robbers. They stripped him of his clothes, beat him, and went away, leaving him half dead. A religious leader happened to be going down the same road, and when he saw the man who had been beaten, he passed by on the other side. Not long after that a political leader came to the same place. After he had stopped and looked at the man who had been beaten, he too passed by on the other side.

But a Samaritan (which in the story represented a foreigner who was despised by the people of that country) traveling the road came to the place where the man was who had been beaten. When the Samaritan saw him, he took pity on the man who had been beaten. He put ointment on the wounds and bandaged them. Then he took the man to an inn and took care of him. The next day he gave money to the innkeeper. "Look after him," he said, "and when I return, I will reimburse you for any extra expense you may have."

The story ends by asking "Which of these three do you think was a neighbor to the man who fell into the hands of robbers?" Everyone who has heard this story always gives the answer "The Samaritan who had mercy on the man."

The moral of the story is service is not a matter of title or status but of compassion and action.

As you encounter people who are different than you, what is your reaction to them? Look at the list of differences below and then indicate what kind of actions you usually take based on the scale given derived from the three characters in the story.

After you have indicated your reaction, reflect on your openness to others with these differences. Also reflect on the biases and prejudices you might have, especially the ones you found that you didn't know were there in your attitude.

R = *Avoid before you engage (like the religious leader in the story)*

P = *Avoid after first contact (like the political leader in the story)*

S = *Engage in a spirit of respect, community, concern, responsibility, and action despite differences (like the Samaritan in the story)*

Category	R	C	S
Ethnic differences Reflections:			
Economic differences Reflections:			
Lifestyle differences Reflections:			
Apparel differences Reflections:			
Language differences Reflections:			
Religion differences Reflections:			
Personality differences Reflections:			

EXERCISES

Follow-up Questions

1. How can "R" and "P" responses hinder your ability to discover your Life Calling?

2. What steps in your life do you need to take to move your reactions more from an "R" or "P" response to an "S" response?

References

The following resources have been used in this chapter.

Buechner, F. (1992). *Listening to Your Life*. San Francisco: Harper San Francisco.

Clum, C. (2005). *Mutual Influence Model*. Port Townsend, Washington: Experience Mission, Inc.

Ginter, E.J., & Glauser, A. S. (2002). *Life skills for college: A curriculum for life*. Dubuque, IA: Kendall/Hunt Publishing Company.

Johnson, D., & Johnson, F. (2000). Joining *together: Group theory and group skills*, 7/e. Boston: Allyn and Bacon.

King, M.L., and Washington, J.M. (1990). *A Testament of Hope: The Essential Writings and Speeches of Martin Luther King, Jr.* New York: Harpercollins Publishers.

Levine, A., & Cureton, J. S. (1998). *When hope and fear collide*. San Francisco: Jossey-Bass.

Mutascio, P. (2004). *Essential resources for campus-based service, service-learning and civic engagement*. Providence, RI: National Campus Compact.

The following resources may be useful as you explore the development of service in your exploration of Life Calling.

Blaikie, W.G. (1881). *The Personal Life of David Livingstone*. New York: Harper and Brothers. Reprinted by BiblioLife Reproduction Service.

Bonaventure, Saint, Cardinal. (1898). *The Life of St. Francis of Assisi*, 4th ed. London, R. Washbourne; New York, Benziger Bros.

Chawla, N. (1992) *Mother Teresa: The Authorized Biography*, Darby, Pennsylvania: Diana Pub Co.

Miller, M.R. (Ed.). (2007). *Doing more with life: Connecting Christian higher education to a call to service*. Waco, TX: Baylor University Press.

Nouwen, H.J.M. (1989). *In the Name of Jesus: Reflections on Christian Leadership*. New York: Crossroad.

Placher, W.C. Ed. (2005). *Callings: Twenty Centuries of Christian Wisdom on Vocation*. Grand Rapids, Michigan: Erdmans Publishing Co.

Schwen, M.R., and Bass, D.C., Eds. (2006). *Leading Lives That Matter: What We Should Do and Who We Should Be*. Grand Rapids, Michigan: Erdmans Publishing Co.

Section I Conclusion

Foundational Values

In Section One we found that at the core of our lives, there exists a set of foundational values that we hold about reality, ourselves and others. We have a personal creed that attempts to explain the reality of the universe, and then we develop attitudes of self-worth and worth of others based on this explanation.

We establish a mindset that leads to character, and character gives rise to service. This foundational dynamic based on values permeates all other aspects of our lives.

As we search to discover our Life Calling, the clearer we understand and engage these foundational values, the clearer our search for that Life Calling will be. This really is where the exploration for a Life Calling should begin because foundational values form the "ground rules" for conducting our search. They also give us the meaning in our lives that are part of the universal need experienced by all humans.

Unique Design

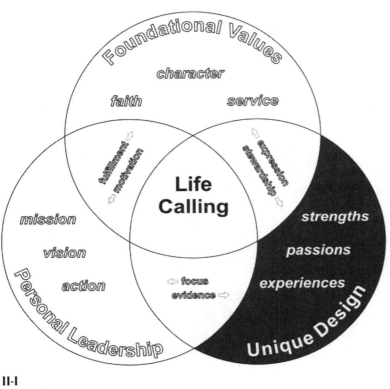

FIGURE II-I
Life Calling Model Focusing on Unique Design

Section II deals with the second main component of the Life Calling Model—
Unique Design.

Foundational values may have universal application, but they have individual expression as they are conveyed through our *unique design*. People are like the proverbial snowflake—no two are completely alike. This distinctiveness found in each person reflects the design of the universe. In Chapter 1, we explored the concept that there is an intentional place for each of us in the universe. We said this concept is foundational to our *faith*, the mindset we hold about reality. In Section II, we add to this concept that not only is our place in the universe intentional, but it is also unique. In other words, it is not by accident that we are here and that we are who we are. We are meant to be!

This unique design can best be observed in the distinct characteristics that combine to make us who we are, the things we deeply care about, and how all of these are shaped by what we encounter throughout life. As we search for our Life Calling, our unique design is the most fundamental place to look when seeking to discern the unique nature of this calling as it applies to us as individuals.

In this section we will examine the three major elements of our unique design—strengths, passion, and experiences—and discover their roles in determining our Life Calling.

Empowered by Strengths

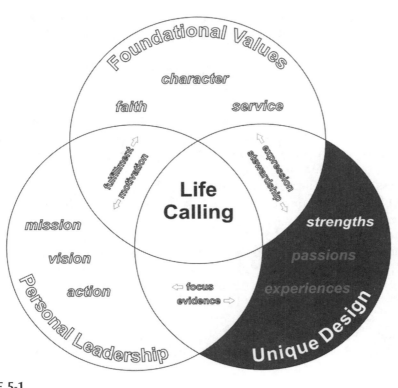

5

FIGURE 5-1
Life Calling Model Focusing on Strengths

The second main component of the Life Calling Model is *Unique Design.* **Strengths** comprise the first element of this design.

CHAPTER OBJECTIVES

1. Understand the nature and value of strengths in your life
2. Explain why focusing on strengths is a better path to understanding your Life Calling than focusing on weaknesses
3. Identify the five main strengths categories in the Strength Matrix that empower you as an individual
4. Begin identifying strengths in your life

CONCEPTS

KEY TERMS

Asset = useful or valuable quality or thing that is an advantage or resource

Design = combination of plans, organization, details, features, and structure of an entity

Failure = act or condition of not achieving something desired, planned, or attempted

Feelings = sensations experienced when one is stirred internally from non-physical sources

Holistic = of or relating to holism (a theory that the universe and especially living nature is correctly seen in terms of interacting wholes)

Matrix = a multidimensional arrangement that correlates two or more qualities to a single item

Mediocrity = condition of being only ordinary or of moderate quality; neither good nor bad; barely adequate

Sensibility = capacity to respond to or be susceptible to sensory stimuli

Strengths = qualities or features that bring power, force, vigor, or sustenance

Success = achievement of something desired, planned, or attempted

Synergistic = the interaction of elements in such a way that when they combine, they produce a total effect that is greater than the sum of the contributions made by the individual elements

Transcendental = beyond ordinary or common experience, thought, or belief; existing above and independent of the ordinary range of perception in the material universe and space-time continuum

Uniqueness = state of being the only one or the sole example; single; solitary in type; having no like or equal

Weakness = quality or feature that is inadequate or defective

Will = the power of control that the mind has over choosing one's own actions

▶ Concepts

One of the more difficult things for people to do is to discover their own uniqueness and to accept it. We live in a society that gives a lot more emphasis to conformity than to uniqueness. You don't have to see very many advertisements to realize conformity is the main goal. Education is no different. The loftiest goals of education should be to help people discover their uniqueness and then develop that uniqueness to its fullest potential in whatever direction it goes. Instead, our educational systems are more like assembly lines turning out plastic widgets, trying to make each widget like the others. Businesses and organizations exhibit the same pattern. They fit people to their plans, requiring them to conform, rather than adapting their plans to their people by making full use of the talents and skills the people have to offer. Unfortunately, churches tend to follow this same pattern. A certain type of person in the church is identified as "good," and everybody else is encouraged, if not expected, to conform to this "good" type.

The frustrating thing about these situations is that this is not the way we are created. We are each very much unique individuals, and each of us has very distinct characteristics that combine to make us who we are. In the Life Calling Model, we have labeled this component as our Unique Design, and the first element of this component we identified as *strengths*. *Strengths* are the capacities in our lives that are (or have the potential to be) the most fruitful—definitely considered our top assets above our liabilities or even our middle-of-the-road features. *Strengths* need to be examined from two perspectives: first, from an assets-based perspective and second, from a holistic perspective.

Assets-Based Perspective

Concentrating on strengths as assets in the Life Calling Model gives the model far greater effectiveness. At the beginning of this section, we said that organizations of all types tend to concentrate on conformity more than uniqueness in individuals. Unfortunately, the same thing is true about strengths.

In many cases the focus is more on the remediation of weaknesses than it is on the leveraging of strengths. We are not saying that there is no value in shoring up our weaknesses to a level where they will not be detrimental to our lives. We all want to do that. But beyond that, focusing on the areas of our weaknesses will never make us effective or successful. This is a liabilities-based perspective that really does not lead to effective outcomes.

Let's examine this with the illustration in Figure 5-2. We have a road running across a plain in front of the mountains. At the left-hand extreme of the road we will put "failure," and on the right-hand extreme we will put "success." At the top, two arrows extend in opposite directions from the center of the mountains. The arrow pointed to the left indicates that "weaknesses" lead to failure, whereas the arrow pointing to the right indicates that "strengths" lead to success. Now let's put a car to the left end of the road. This car will represent us as individuals dealing with weaknesses and strengths in an attempt to drive away from failure toward success.

Many organizations and institutions follow a mistaken belief that eliminating weaknesses in people will produce a direct move clear to success located at the right-hand side of the picture. What happens in reality, however, is depicted

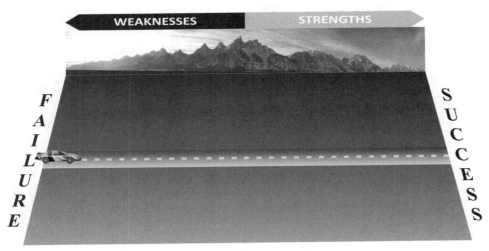

FIGURE 5-2
Failure vs. Success

CONCEPTS

in Figure 5-3. People who do nothing more than eliminate weaknesses in their lives, while certainly "driving" away from weaknesses, never move beyond a middle zone of non-failure/non-success—a zone best understood as a "zone of mediocrity." The left-pointing "weaknesses" arrow only makes it back to the middle.

This is good in that it is better than being stuck on the left-hand side of the picture in life—failure. However, it is not great. Have you ever met anyone whose primary goal in life is to be mediocre? Probably not. Earlier in this book we pointed out that a common desire among almost all people is for meaning, significance, and hope. Mediocrity is certainly not the path to satisfying these needs. How do we "drive" to the right-hand side of the picture to achieve success? How can we accomplish those things in life we desire, plan for, and attempt? The right-pointing "strengths" arrow in Figure 5-4 shows the answer— by using our strengths. In other words, as we focus on identifying, developing, and using our strengths, we will greatly increase our likelihood of success.

In many ways what we accomplish when we do this is leveraging our strengths. Leveraging is a term borrowed from the financial world. In that

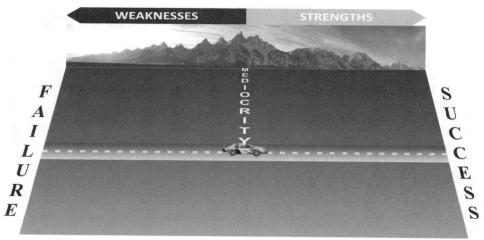

FIGURE 5-3
Eliminating Weaknesses

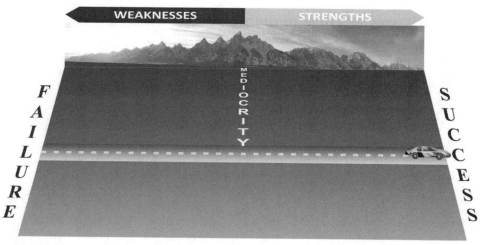

FIGURE 5-4
Leveraging Strengths

world it refers to the use of various financial instruments or borrowed capital to increase the potential return on an investment. If we apply this concept to our discussion, we are employing our strengths to increase the potential for our success. In fact, this is the best way to deal with weaknesses as well. We can leverage our strengths to make up for areas of weakness in our lives.

Let's look at a simple example to illustrate how this works. When I was in elementary school, students were evaluated in handwriting. I didn't have good handwriting. This was in part due to the fact that I was not born with excellence in what we call fine-motor skills—working precisely with my hands. But it was probably impacted more by the fact that I was not born with patience to work diligently on developing fine-motor skills. And so I always received bad grades in handwriting and handwritten assignments. My mind, however, is good at picking up patterns and learning procedures, so I found that learning to type on a keyboard came very easily to me. I quickly learned to leverage this strength to produce my written assignments in school, and my grades went up because the teachers could easily read my assignments. This had not been the case when I turned them in as handwritten assignments.

It should not surprise us, then, that people who concentrate on strengths like this in all areas of their lives are the most successful. You may hear stories of how they struggle to overcome their weaknesses, but if you listen carefully, you will discover that they did this by finding ways to use their strengths. You will also find that people who concentrate on identifying and developing their strengths find it far easier to discover their Life Calling because our strengths form one of the best pointers toward our Life Calling.

Holistic Perspective

A strengths-based approach to uniqueness will produce greater clarity and effectiveness if it encompasses a holistic perspective. A common problem among many strengths-based approaches to human uniqueness is that they employ a narrow, often singular focus looking at one aspect of uniqueness. A far more effective approach is to include as many areas of strengths as possible in looking at uniqueness.

Howard Gardner, a psychologist at Harvard University, proposed a theory he called multiple intelligences. He advocated the idea that human capacities need to be evaluated across a broad spectrum, and he placed them in seven categories summarized in Table 5-1. (Gardner, 1983).

Linguistic	Words and language
Logical-Mathematical	Logic and numbers
Musical	Music, sound, rhythm
Bodily-Kinesthetic	Body movement control
Spatial-Visual	Images and space
Interpersonal	Other people's feelings
Intrapersonal	Self-awareness

TABLE 5-1
Gardner's Seven Intelligences

Though Gardner is not ready to expand his list, he has considered adding four other intelligences (Smith, 2002). They are shown in Table 5-2.

Naturalist	Environmental concern
Spiritual	Truth and values
Existential	Ultimate issues
Moral	Sanctity of life

TABLE 5-2
Four Other Possible Intelligences

The Gallup organization is another strong proponent of a strength-based approach to individuality. Gallup's *StrengthsQuest* focuses students on strengths rather than weaknesses, believing that top achievers understand their talents and strengths and build their lives on them. *StrengthsQuest* leads students in a discovery of their natural talents and to unique and valuable insights into developing those talents into strengths.

In *Explorer's Guide* we will take an even broader approach to the concept of strengths. We will look at this concept in what is called the *Strengths Matrix™* (Figure 5-5).

Strengths MATRIX ™		DIMENSIONS				
		Gifts	Knowledge	Skills	Attitude	TOTAL
D O M A I N S	Physical					
	Emotional					
	Intellectual					
	Psychological					
	Spiritual					

FIGURE 5-5
Strengths Matrix™

Five important domains are identified in the *Strengths Matrix*.

Physical strengths.   The capacity of your life that gives your body distinct features and enables you to perform actions with your body.

Emotional strengths.   The capacity of your life that enables you to correctly experience and use feelings and sensibility.

Intellectual strengths.   The capacity of your life that enables you to acquire knowledge and develop an ever-expanding understanding of this knowledge in a manner that produces wisdom.

Psychological strengths.   The capacity of your life that enables you to exercise your will in deciding on courses of action.

Spiritual strengths.   The capacity of your life that enables you to discern and respond in service to transcendental supernatural inner leading of God.

There is a second important axis on the *Strengths Matrix*. This axis, running across the top, identifies four crucial dimensions in each of the five strengths domains.

Gifts.   Capabilities and features in a strength dimension that came into your life without your own doing. You were basically born with these.

Knowledge.   Information and understanding you gain by learning about a strength dimension and how to incorporate it into your life.

Skills.   Abilities you develop in a strength dimension by repeated practice of the disciplines and actions associated with the dimension.

Attitude.   Frame of mind that you develop and adopt reflecting your beliefs and values concerning a strengths domain.

Total.   Your overall strength in a domain is determined by the synergistic combination of all four dimensions.

The search for a Life Calling needs to not only explore all five strengths domains, but it also needs to take into consideration all four dimensions. This is why we have described this as a holistic approach to strengths. How does this work? Let's consider four examples:

Example 1.   A girl is born with a high level of giftedness in one of the strength domains. She identifies this early in life with the help of her parents and others. She has a positive disposition or attitude about this area of her life, and so she studies as much as she can about it and works hard at developing her skills in this area. As a result, this becomes a very strong overall area of strength in her life, and the strength takes a leading role in guiding her toward her Life Calling.

Example 2.   A boy is born with a moderate level of giftedness in one of the strength domains. This becomes clearer during the early-teen years. When he begins to see this clearly, he develops a very positive disposition or attitude about this area of his life, and he begins to study as much as he can about it. He also works hard to develop his skills in this area. As a result, this becomes a strong overall area of strength in his life. It may not be quite as strong as the girl in Example 1, but it is still strong enough that he is able to find guidance from it toward his Life Calling.

Example 3.   A girl is born with a low level of giftedness in one of the strength domains. As she grows up, she realizes this and develops a realistic disposition about this area of her life. She studies about and even works to develop adequate skills in this area. In the long run, however, this area will probably never

CONCEPTS

be more than a supporting area in her life, and she should look to other areas to find guidance toward her Life Calling.

Example 4.   A boy is born with a high level of giftedness in one of the strength domains. Even though he suspects this, he has a bad attitude about this strength domain, and this grows into a very negative disposition. As a result, he avoids this area of his life as much as he can. He does not study about it and never engages in skills development in this area. As a result, although this strength domain has a great potential to help guide him toward his Life Calling, it will not do so until his disposition changes. It will remain an unrealized potential. He will likely try to pursue other areas and may end up confused about his Life Calling.

Blended Perspective

A problem can arise when analyzing strengths in a matrix if we begin to view the strengths domains as completely separate from each other. There is a great deal of interaction and interdependence from one domain to another. Figure 5-6 illustrates the better view of the domains where aspects of a

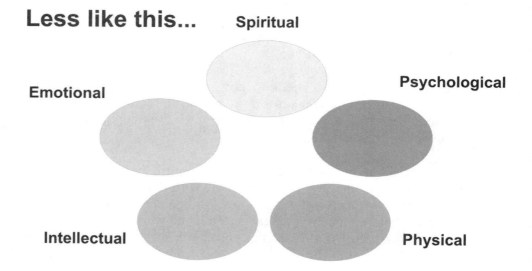

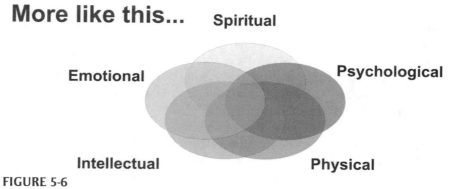

FIGURE 5-6
Blend of the Strengths Domains

domain overlap anywhere from one to all of the other domains. Some of the most productive areas of our lives will be in that central zone where all the domains overlap.

Concepts Summary

A major problem with our society is that it tends to place its focus only on the physical and intellectual strengths. As a result, many people tend to restrict their search to these areas when looking for a sense of purpose or calling. In reality, the search for a Life Calling needs to explore all five strengths domains. Understanding all these strengths domains is so important that the next five chapters will examine each.

 Insight

The Bible contains numerous passages about the gifts God gives us to make us strong in his power. These can become a great source of guidance concerning our Life Calling.

SCRIPTURAL INSIGHT 1 ▶ *You Are Fearfully and Wonderfully Made*

For you created my inmost being; you knit me together in my mother's womb. I praise you because I am fearfully and wonderfully made; your works are wonderful, I know that full well. My frame was not hidden from you when I was made in the secret place. When I was woven together in the depths of the earth, your eyes saw my unformed body. All the days ordained for me were written in your book before one of them came to be. PSALM 139:13-16

This is one of the most encouraging passages in scripture related to who we are as individuals and the purpose and calling we have for our lives. Three ideas stand out in particular.

First, God was and continues to be intensely involved in your creation as a person. The analogy of being knit or woven together suggests that this involvement is on an intricate level. It is tempting to wonder at times if anyone cares about the particulars of our lives. Psalm 139 gives us the answer that yes, God does.

Second, God made us to be awesome creatures. David praised God because he was "fearfully and wonderfully made." When was the last time you looked in the mirror and said "Praise God; I am fearfully and wonderfully made?" That really is how you should start of each day because it is true. We tend to avoid such statements because we think it would display pride. Our false conceptions of humility lead us to instead put ourselves down. When we do that, in reality we are not truly displaying humility. Instead, we are criticizing God for what he made. And that is the key to this passage. We are not bragging about our fearfulness or wonderfulness. David did not praise God because he was "fearful and wonderful." He instead praised God because he was "fearfully and wonderfully made." The praise went to God for God's work, not David's work.

Third, God's involvement in our lives began before we showed up and continues on throughout all of our days. Have you ever heard parents talk about their son or daughter as being "their accident?" Psalm 139 directly challenges that idea. There are no accidents with God. You can have confidence that God knew you were coming before you got here and worked to put you together just as you are. Furthermore, he knows about all the days of your life that will continue coming and is a work in those days as well. God's got you "covered" from start to finish.

It is no wonder that David praised God for all of this. It gave him tremendous hope that he truly did have a Life Calling.

PERSONAL REFLECTION ▷ When was the last time (if ever) that you praised God for how fearfully and wonderfully he made you? What keeps you from doing that right now?

SCRIPTURAL INSIGHT 2 *Love God with All That You Have*

Hear, O Israel: The LORD our God, the LORD is one. Love the LORD your God with all your heart and with all your soul and with all your strength. DEUTERONOMY 6:5

In the Jewish tradition coming out of the teaching of Moses, there was one commandment considered to be the "Great Commandment." In other words, this commandment superseded all others. When asked by a Jewish expert in the law as to which was the greatest commandment, Jesus quickly replied: "Love the Lord your God with all your heart and with all your soul and with all your mind." Jesus was referring to Deuteronomy 6:5 when Moses had given this command to the Israelites during their wilderness journey from Egypt to Canaan.

What is interesting is that the passage in Deuteronomy lists heart, soul and strength as the dimensions with which to love God in totality. The passage quoting Jesus in Matthew 22:37 lists heart, soul and mind. If we combine these two, then, what makes these two passages important to our exploration for a Life Calling is the fact that two passages identify four different domains in our lives that give us capacity to love God: heart, soul, mind and strength. In Jesus' dialogue with the Jewish leader Nicodemus, recorded in John 3, Jesus told him that "no one can enter the kingdom of God without being born of water and the Spirit. Flesh gives birth to flesh, but the Spirit gives birth to spirit." Jesus identifies one more capacity with which we can love and serve God. This is a spiritual dynamic that operates within the human nature that is separate from all the other capacities (those others he referred to as "flesh").

In the Concepts section of this chapter, these five capacities are referred to as "domains" within a Strengths Matrix. What is the ultimate use of all five of these strength domains? Both Jesus and Moses were clear in their answer to this question—"Love the Lord your God" with all of them. This is the first and foremost element in your Life Calling. If you are willing to look at and dedicate all five domains of your strengths to God and the pursuit of your Life Calling, you will likely find your life complete and your direction clear. If you are unwilling, however, you will likely find your life incomplete and confusing.

PERSONAL REFLECTION Is your love for God manifested in all five strength domains of your life—body, heart, mind, soul, and spirit? Or are you holding back in one or more domains? How can you incorporate all areas of your life in your love for God? How can this give you a clearer Life Calling?

SCRIPTURAL INSIGHT 3 *God Has a Sizeable Investment in You and Expects You to Use It*

"Again, it will be like a man going on a journey, who called his servants and entrusted his wealth to them. To one he gave five bags of gold, to another two bags, and to another one bag, each according to his ability. Then he went on his journey. The man who had received five bags of gold went at once and put his money to work and gained five bags more. So also, the one with two bags of gold gained two more. But the man who had received one bag went off, dug a hole in the ground and hid his master's money.

"After a long time the master of those servants returned and settled accounts with them. The man who had received five bags of gold brought the other five. 'Master,' he said, 'you entrusted me with five bags of gold. See, I have gained five more.'

"His master replied, 'Well done, good and faithful servant! You have been faithful with a few things; I will put you in charge of many things. Come and share your master's happiness!'

"The man with two bags of gold also came. 'Master,' he said, 'you entrusted me with two bags of gold; see, I have gained two more.'

"His master replied, 'Well done, good and faithful servant! You have been faithful with a few things; I will put you in charge of many things. Come and share your master's happiness!'

"Then the man who had received one bag of gold came. 'Master,' he said, 'I knew that you are a hard man, harvesting where you have not sown and gathering where you have not scattered seed. So I was afraid and went out and hid your gold in the ground. See, here is what belongs to you.'

"His master replied, 'You wicked, lazy servant! So you knew that I harvest where I have not sown and gather where I have not scattered seed? Well then, you should have put my money on deposit with the bankers, so that when I returned I would have received it back with interest.

"'Take the bag of gold from him and give it to the one who has ten bags. For those who have will be given more, and they will have an abundance. As for those who do not have, even what they have will be taken from them. And throw that worthless servant outside, into the darkness, where there will be weeping and gnashing of teeth.'" MATTHEW 25:14-30

And he expects us to put them to good use.

As we continue on in this story, we can make a third observation—that the three servants did not receive equal numbers of bags of gold. The master determined their ability to handle this wealth and distributed the wealth accordingly. From this we can learn that God determines what our capacity is and then gives us strengths as he deems appropriate. One person may seem to have strengths in all five dimensions while another seems to have them in just two. Now, we can spend the rest of our lives resentful if we have fewer than another person, but that is not going to accomplish good in our lives and will deter our search for our Life Calling.

This is one of those places where the interactive nature of all three components in the Life Calling Model comes into play. Our Foundational Values start with *faith* that there is a God who created the universe with an intentional plan that includes each one of us. We have to exercise this same faith that God knows what he is doing and knows our capacity for strengths better than we know ourselves.

In 1 Corinthians 6:19&29, the apostle Paul says, "Do you not know that your bodies are temples of the Holy Spirit, who is in you, whom you have received from God? You are not your own; you were bought at a price. Therefore honor God with your bodies." It is very easy to start thinking that what we have in our lives belongs to us or is our own doing. When we take this view, it becomes easier to start looking at others and wondering why some of them have more than we do. When we see our strengths as investments in us from God according to his wisdom and plan, then we can concentrate more on being good stewards of what he has placed in us, and our Life Calling will be much clearer.

A fourth observation, and one of the most important observations that can be made from this story, is that the master's reward of the servants was based on what each of them did with what each had been given. No servant was challenged to do something with bags of gold not given to him. Too many people worry more about working on what they don't have rather than expanding what they do have. We can learn from the Parable of the Talents that God's blessing of our Life Calling comes based on what we do with the strengths we have, not the ones we do not have!

As we conclude our look at the Parable of the Talents, let's look at the master's words to the first two servants who invested their gold; the commendation is exactly the same. He did not say "Great job!" to the servant with five bags and "Pretty good job" to the one with two. He said "Well done!" to both of them because they had both doubled their gold. From this, we can learn that God expects us to work with what we have been given and to know that when we do, he is pleased.

Our final observation comes from the ending of this story. Few who read the story of the talents like how it ends. The punishment that was meted out to the servant that did nothing with the one bag of gold seems so severe. What he had was taken from him, and he was banished to a place that sounds pretty bad. As harsh as it sounds in the story, the important truth that we can glean from this is that ignoring and neglecting the strengths that God has given us is a serious failure in God's eyes. And when it comes to the discovery of our Life Calling, failure to use our strengths will make it difficult—if not impossible—to discern our Life Calling or to be blessed by God in our pursuit of it. The moral of the story: take God's gifts seriously and do something with them!

> **PERSONAL REFLECTION** ⟩ Do you recognize the strengths God has placed in your life as investments? Do you express gratitude and care for what God has given you, or do you look at what others have with envy? How can you increase your gratitude for what God has given you on a regular basis? What are you doing right now in your life with what God has given you? How will this help reveal more clearly your purpose and calling?

SCRIPTURAL INSIGHT 4 ⟩ *God Has a Sizeable Investment in You*

"Again, it will be like a man going on a journey, who called his servants and entrusted his wealth to them. To one he gave five bags of gold, to another two bags, and to another one bag, each according to his ability. Then he went on his journey. MATTHEW 25:14-15

For the next three insights, we are going to look at Jesus' Parable of the Talents found in Matthew 25. When using this parable to help us understand strengths, we can begin to understand how God distributes strengths, and what he expects us to do with these gifts. The first two verses we are looking at set the story up. A master gets ready to leave on a long trip and puts his wealth in the hands of servants with the intent that they do something with it to increase its value. He left quite a bit of wealth. Each of these bags weighed 1200 ounces. When this edition of *Explorer's Guide* was written, gold was valued at $1,600 (US dollars) per ounce and headed higher. If we use that rate, each bag would be worth $1,920,000. Let's list some observations from this powerful story.

The first observation is that the master put something very valuable into the hands of all three servants. From this we can safely conclude that everyone has been entrusted with strengths from God. Think about it—the servant given just one bag of gold still was entrusted with nearly two million dollars of wealth. That's a lot, and is what makes this story so powerful. God entrusts every one of us with a great deal of strengths, even at a bare minimum. Our problem is not that we don't have strengths; it is, instead, that we don't take time or have the ability to identify them. I was speaking about this once to a group of young women who were in troubled situations. One of them confronted me right in front of the others claiming that she had no strengths. In response, I challenged her to give me twenty minutes with her, and in that time I would identify at least five strengths of hers. She wanted it done right there in front of the others, so I obliged and told her to start talking. Within five minutes we had identified six strengths. I have yet to find anyone who does not have some strengths.

The second observation that we can find in the first two verses of this story is that each of the servants received his bags of gold from the Master. We learn from this that all of our strengths are gifts ultimately from God. In fact, the Apostle James concludes in James 1:17 that EVERY good and perfect gift comes from God. The importance of this concept is that our strengths should be dealt with in our lives with a sense of stewardship. They are not ours, but rather they are investments placed in us by God.

> **PERSONAL REFLECTION** > Do you recognize the great value of the strengths God has invested in your life? Do you express gratitude and care for what God has given you? How can you increase your gratitude for what God has given you on a regular basis?

SCRIPTURAL INSIGHT 5 > *God Determines Your Capacity*

"To one he gave five bags of gold, to another two bags, and to another one bag, each according to his ability. Then he went on his journey. The man who had received five bags of gold went at once and put his money to work and gained five bags more. So also, the one with two bags of gold gained two more. But the man who had received one bag went off, dug a hole in the ground and hid his master's money. Matthew 25:15-18

As we continue on in this story, we can make a third observation—that the three servants did not receive equal amounts of gold. The master determined their ability to handle this wealth and distributed the wealth accordingly. From this we can learn that God determines what our capacity is and then gives us strengths as he deems appropriate. One person may seem to have strengths in all five dimensions while another seems to have them in just two. Now, we can spend the rest of our lives resentful if we have fewer than another person, but that is not going to accomplish good in our lives and will deter our search for our Life Calling.

This is one of those places where the interactive nature of all three components in the Life Calling Model comes into play. Our Foundational Values start with *faith* that there is a God who created the universe with an intentional plan that includes each one of us. We have to exercise this same faith that God knows what he is doing and knows our capacity for strengths better than we know ourselves.

The Apostle Paul says in 1 Corinthians 16:19&29, "Do you not know that your bodies are temples of the Holy Spirit, who is in you, whom you have received from God? You are not your own; you were bought at a price. Therefore honor God with your bodies." It is very easy to start thinking that what we have in our lives belongs to us or is a result of our own doing. When we take this view, it becomes easier to start looking at others and wondering why some of them have more than we do. When we see our strengths as investments in us from God according to his wisdom and plan, then we can concentrate more on being good stewards of what he has placed in us, and our Life Calling will be much clearer.

> **PERSONAL REFLECTION** ⟩ Do you focus your gratitude on the gifts God has given you, or do you look at what others have with envy? How can you learn to praise God for what you have received and also praise God for what others have received—even when it looks like they have received more than you?

SCRIPTURAL INSIGHT 6 ⟩ *God Expects You to Use the Sizeable Investment He Places in You*

"After a long time the master of those servants returned and settled accounts with them. The man who had received five bags of gold brought the other five. 'Master,' he said, 'you entrusted me with five bags of gold. See, I have gained five more.'

"His master replied, 'Well done, good and faithful servant! You have been faithful with a few things; I will put you in charge of many things. Come and share your master's happiness!'

"The man with two bags of gold also came. 'Master,' he said, 'you entrusted me with two bags of gold; see, I have gained two more.'

"His master replied, 'Well done, good and faithful servant! You have been faithful with a few things; I will put you in charge of many things. Come and share your master's happiness!'

"Then the man who had received one bag of gold came. 'Master,' he said, 'I knew that you are a hard man, harvesting where you have not sown and gathering where you have not scattered seed. So I was afraid and went out and hid your gold in the ground. See, here is what belongs to you.'

"His master replied, 'You wicked, lazy servant! So you knew that I harvest where I have not sown and gather where I have not scattered seed? Well then, you should have put my money on deposit with the bankers, so that when I returned I would have received it back with interest.

"'Take the bag of gold from him and give it to the one who has ten bags. For those who have will be given more, and they will have an abundance. As for those who do not have, even what they have will be taken from them. And throw that worthless servant outside, into the darkness, where there will be weeping and gnashing of teeth.'" MATTHEW 25:19-30

A fourth observation, and one of the most important observations that can be made from this story, is that the master's reward of the servants was based on what each of them did with what each had been given. No servant was challenged to do something with bags of gold not given to him. Too many people worry more about working on what they don't have rather than expanding what they do have. We can learn from the Parable of the Talents that God's blessing comes based on what we do with the strengths we have, not the ones we do not have!

As we conclude our look at the Parable of the Talents, let's look at the master's words to the first two servants who invested their gold; the commendation is exactly the same. He did not say "Great job!" to the servant with five bags and "Pretty good job" to the one with two. He said "Well done!" to both of them because they had both doubled their gold. From this we can learn that God expects us to work with what we have been given, and when we do, he is pleased.

Our final observation comes from the ending of this story. Nobody who reads the story of the talents comes away liking the end of the story. The punishment that was handed out to the servant that did nothing with the one bag of gold seems so severe. What he had was taken from him, and he was banished to a place that sounds pretty bad. As harsh as it sounds in the story, the important truth that we can glean from this is that ignoring and doing nothing with the strengths that God has given us makes it a serious failure in God's eyes. And when it comes to the discovery of our Life Calling, failure to use our strengths will make it difficult—if not impossible—to discern our Life Calling or to be blessed by God in our pursuit of it. The moral of the story: take God's gifts seriously and do something with them!

> **PERSONAL REFLECTION** > What are you doing right now in your life with what God has given you? How will this help to more clearly reveal your purpose and calling?

 Discovery

How can the Discovery Guides help you identify and understand your strengths?

T **THEORY**	You can increase your knowledge about the five strengths domains in various departments and classes at your college or university. Introductory classes are often a good place to start. Here are some suggestions for each of the five domains.Physical—Physical Education, Music, Art, Speech classes and programsEmotional—Behavioral Science classes and programs Intellectual—Most of your majors and classes, but education and psychology classes can help you with learning theory Psychological—Behavioral Science classes and programs Spiritual—Religion and Philosophy classes and programs The writings of D. O. Clifton, E. C. Anderson, L. A. Schreiner, M. Buckingham, and M. E. Seligman are good sources for understanding a strengths approach to human uniqueness.
E **EXAMPLES**	Find people who excel in these various strengths domains. Observe them and find time to talk to them. Ask them to share with you how they discovered and developed these strengths.
A **ASSESSMENT**	*StrengthsFinder* and the *StrengthsQuest* approach form the leading assessment for looking at an overall strengths approach to human uniqueness and potential. Check with your Student Development office to see if this program is in operation at your campus.
C **COUNSEL**	Professional counselors and life coaches are trained to help you in the exploration of strengths. Your college and university will likely have a center where you can find such help. Additionally, family members, teachers, pastors, and friends know you well and can help you assess your strengths. Their counsel should not be ignored.
H **HISTORY**	Search for historical biographies of notable people who have exhibited these strengths. Select some of these and learn from their experiences. Also study the developmental history of positive psychology and strengths theory.
E **EXPERIENCE**	Get involved with activities where you can test your strengths in the five domains. You will learn quickly whether or not you have skills in a domain.
R **REFLECTION**	Take time to reflect on what you have learned about strengths. Pay special attention to analyzing your attitude and disposition toward each of the strengths domains. A negative attitude would hinder your ability to develop in these domains.

DISCOVERY

▶ Story

The visit to New York City had left the explorers exhausted, so it was not surprising when they assumed sleeping positions in the motorhome as the *Nautilus* left the RV park and reconnected with Interstate 95. However, they opened their eyes occasionally for a glance out the windows because there was still so much to see. They crossed the Hudson River on the famed George Washington Bridge. Everyone was excited to see it—with the possible exception of Ken Neimon, whose stress levels had risen several notches as he struggled to maneuver the motorhome through the heavy traffic.

The travelers fell back into a state of semi-sleep as the journey continued on toward Connecticut. As they passed through New Haven, Lorena woke the others excitedly.

"Hey, guys, we're in New Haven!" she exclaimed.

"Fabulous," Ryan mumbled groggily. "Do you want us to let you out?"

"Get a life, Ryan," Lorena retorted. "This is the home of Yale University. You don't get much better than that!"

"You know what, Lor? You take your books and your classes and your Yale University, and you have a good life," Ryan shot back. "Give me a good wave and my board, and I'll have just as good a ride." The thoughts of surfing back at Seahaven seemed a lot more appealing to him than studying in college.

"Ryan, you can sound so much like a loser at times." Lorena's tone was loaded with frustration. "Don't you have *any* desire to succeed in life?"

"Don't be so quick to define success for another person, Lorena." Diana came to Ryan's defense.

"Yeah, Lor." Ryan appreciated the support.

The rest of the explorers began to stir. They smelled the possibility of a delicious argument, and no one wanted to miss out.

"You're both crazy!" Lorena insisted. "The only thing that will get you ahead in this world is your brain. The intelligent rule the world, and college is where you develop that intelligence."

"That's bull, Lor," Justin replied sarcastically. "Half the people ruling the world never even saw a college. It looks to me like the strong rule the world, not the smart. And no offense, Lor, but Ryan has you beat in that department by quite a long shot." Ryan's physique was well developed from his many years of surfing.

"Hey, you guys, don't you think there are more strengths in life than brains and brawn?" Adam asked quickly, trying to hold back a possible flood of nasty retorts.

"Beside looks, like Diana's, what did you have in mind, Adam?" Abriella asked. Diana blushed at her question. Her good looks could not be ignored, but she wanted to be known for more than just a pretty face.

Everybody looked at Adam.

"I'm not sure." Adam answered. "Sometimes when I'm down and I talk to my mom, she doesn't have great intellectual thoughts, but instead she just knows I'm down and knows the right words to change my mood. It seems like her feelings are just as much a strength as Lorena's intellect or Ryan's muscles."

"Diana's like that," Abriella said. "She can always tell where our feelings are at. I've always felt that's one of her greatest strengths."

"Yeah, and her looks," Ryan added. Diana grew even redder.

"Diana and Ryan—Beauty and the Beast," Lorena added sarcastically.

"Be nice, Lorena!" Abriella chided.

Adam continued, "I think emotions can be a strength; so can a person's spiritual life."

"Oh boy." Lorena rolled her eyes. "Sounds like one of those warm, fuzzy psychobabblers. You know, the kind that couldn't make it intellectually, so they start creating categories to make themselves look good."

"Geez, Lorena. You really are stuck on your brains." Abriella's observation was blunt—though correct.

"Yeah, and if your brains are so great," Ryan joined in, "how come Abriella was the valedictorian?"

If the others were not paying total attention before, they were now.

"That's not fair, Ryan." Adam, the ever-leader, felt the need to defuse the situation as he saw the anger and hurt in Lorena's eyes. "Being smart is not just about grades or IQ tests."

"So what are emotional strengths?" Justin asked. "Is that like when a guy breaks up with a girl, for a good reason, no doubt, and the girl doesn't get all mushy and cry?"

"Sounds like you've had experience, Justin." Lorena was not finished with taking shots.

"No, Lor. I was just summarizing your diary," Justin shot back.

Ken Neimon shot a quick glance at his wife. They were starting to have second thoughts about how mature these six were after all.

"Why don't you all shut up and let Adam talk? After all, he's the only one that has made sense in this conversation." Diana was frustrated with the quarreling among Lorena, Ryan, and Justin.

"I don't know, but I just think we have a lot more types of strengths in our lives than we give ourselves credit for," Adam explained.

"You mean like Lorena being able to decide on pre-med for her college major while all the rest of us are totally lost?" Diana asked.

"Speak for yourself, Diana," Ryan responded. "I'm not lost. I exercised that strength and decided not to go to college."

"That was your stupidity, not your strength!" Lorena said hotly.

"Lorena's always able to make decisions quickly, and for the most part they're right," Abriella tried to redirect the conversation before total war broke out.

"At least she tells us they are," Ryan responded.

Before long, almost everyone was in the fray at some point, throwing barbs, dodging them, or getting hit by them. It showed no sign of letting up for the next half hour. Then Ken Neimon interrupted.

"I hate to break in on your fun, but the sign up ahead says we're about to enter Rhode Island."

The fight ceased, and everyone looked out the windows. They were ready for a break in the action and were glad to take in the scenery for the next twenty minutes. They all laughed when in that short amount of time they saw a sign welcoming them to Massachusetts.

"I swear," Ryan spoke, "that state was smaller than most of the counties back in California. So how much longer 'til we get to Boston, Captain Nemo?"

"Less than an hour would be my guess," Ken Neimon answered.

"Fabulous," Ryan responded, "because I don't know how much more of this petty bickering I can take. It's hard when you're an older, more mature man like me." A big smile spread across his face.

"Oh, give me a break." Lorena's scorn was deep. "I'd say you were getting in your punches pretty good there, Mr. Maturity."

Boston could not come soon enough.

STORY

 **Exercises**

Understanding Your Strengths through *StrengthsFinder*

If it is possible for your school or institution to participate, we highly recommend that you take the *StrengthsFinder 2.0* from the Gallup Organization (http://strengths.gallup.com/110440/About-StrengthsFinder-2.aspx) as the primary exercise in Chapter 5. If you are able to complete this online assessment, you will receive a comprehensive *Strengths Discovery and Action-Planning Guide* that is based on your *StrengthsFinder 2.0* results. This guide will provide you with:

* Your top five theme report
* 50 Ideas for Action (10 for each of your top five themes)
* A Strengths Discovery Activity that helps you think about how your talents, investment, experience, skills, and knowledge work together to build strengths
* A Strength-Based Action Plan for setting specific goals for building and applying your strengths in the next week, month, and year

Work with your class instructor who will facilitate you in your understanding of the results and how to use them in your life.

EXERCISE 2

Expanding Your Understanding of Your Strengths Using the *StrengthsMatrix 360*

1. Identify four different people who know you and who love and care for you. Choose the four so that they represent each of the following categories:
   • Parent _____
   • Teacher (present or former) _____
   • Friend _____
   • Sibling or relative who is younger than you _____

2. Provide all of the people you have identified with a copy of the *StrengthsMatrix 360* (not the Mirror) chart below and ask them to answer the questions for each of the five domains. Let them know that it is okay if they answer that they have not seen a domain as being strong in your life. Tell them this will help you better understand yourself. Encourage them to give an example if they answer that a domain is strong in you.

Strengths MATRIX 360		Definition	How strong do you see this domain in me (weak, moderate, strong, very strong)?	Can you give me an example of when you have seen this domain in me?
D O M A I N S	**Physical**	My capacity to perform physical actions with my body		
	Emotional	My capacity to correctly experience and use feelings and emotions		
	Intellectual	My capacity to acquire knowledge and effectively understand it		
	Psychological	My capacity to exercise my will in deciding on courses of action		
	Spiritual	My capacity to discern and respond in service to the inner leading of God		

EXERCISES

3. Now you personally answer the questions for each of the five domains using your perception.

Strengths MATRIX Mirror		Definition	How strong do I see this domain in myself (weak, moderate, strong, very strong)?	What has been my most fulfilling experience in this domain?
D O M A I N S	*Physical*	My capacity to perform physical actions with my body		
	Emotional	My capacity to correctly experience and use feelings and emotions		
	Intellectual	My capacity to acquire knowledge and effectively understand it		
	Psychological	My capacity to exercise my will in deciding on courses of action		
	Spiritual	My capacity to discern and respond in service to the inner leading of God		

4. Reflect on the answers from both activities in this exercise and summarize below what they have revealed to you about yourself.

EXERCISES

 References

The following resources have been used in this chapter.

Gardner, H. (1983). *Frames of Mind: The Theory of Multiple Intelligences*. New York: Basic Books.

Palmer, P. J. (2008). "Creating 'Circles of Trust' in Academic Life. Preconference Workshop. 27th Annual Conference on the First-Year Experience. February 16, 2008.

Smith, M.K. (2002). "Howard Gardner and Multiple Intelligences." *The Encyclopedia of Informal Education*. Retrieved January 28, 2005, from http://www.infed.org/thinkers/gardner.htm

Strengths Matrix™ taken from Millard, B. (2004). "Discover Your Uniqueness." Retrieved March 15, 2008, from the Life Discovery Interactive website: http://www.ldinteractive.com/Display.asp?Page=fldMotivations

The following resources may be useful to you in your continuing exploration of Life Calling as you look at your Unique Design and your overall *strengths*.

Buckingham, M., and Clifton, D.O. (2001). *Now, Discover Your Strengths*. New York: The Free Press.

Clifton, D.O., and Anderson, E. (2001). *StrengthsQuest: Discover and Develop Your Strengths in Academics, Career, and Beyond*. Washington, DC: Gallup.

Schwen, M.R., and Bass, D.C., Eds. (2006). *Leading Lives That Matter: What We Should Do and Who We Should Be*. Grand Rapids, Michigan: Erdmans Publishing Co.

Empowered by Physical Strengths

Strengths MATRIX™	DIMENSIONS				TOTAL
	Gifts	Knowledge	Skills	Attitude	
Physical					
Emotional					
Intellectual					
Psychological					
Spiritual					

(DOMAINS label appears vertically along the left side of the table)

FIGURE 6-1
Physical Domain of the **Strengths Matrix™**

The *Strengths Matrix* is comprised of five strengths domains. In this chapter we will explore **Physical Strengths**.

CHAPTER OBJECTIVES

1. Understand the nature and value of physical strengths
2. Identify eight different categories of physical strengths
3. Begin identifying physical strengths in your life

KEY TERMS

Brute = entirely physical
Culture = predominating attitudes, values, and behavior that characterize the functioning of a group of people
Elusive = difficult to detect, grasp by the mind, analyze, define, or describe
Physical = features or actions pertaining to the body
Potential = possibility; capable of being or becoming

Concepts

As you visit a college campus or arrive there as a new student, you will probably notice athletes who are good at sports, musicians who excel at singing or playing instruments, artists who are creative and expressive, and student leaders who speak with eloquence. And you might be tempted to think, *Wow! Where do I fit in?* Part of your confusion might be that you are assessing your physical strengths in too restrictive a manner.

We defined the *physical strengths* domain as the capacity in our lives that gives our bodies distinct features and enables us to perform actions with our body. This is an area of our lives with which most of us are quite familiar. However, we often have too narrow a view concerning what constitutes our physical strengths. Let's look at a wide-ranging perspective that classifies these into eight broad categories.

1. *Brute force.* The muscular ability that enables people to excel at lifting great weights or exerting great pressure. This is often what people think of when they hear the term *physical strengths*; of course, there is much more to physical strengths than brute force. Interestingly when looked through the comprehensive filter of the *Strengths Matrix*, this rarely falls under the element of pure giftedness. Although some people are born with the tendency to develop such strength, it primarily comes from repeated practice. Bodybuilders, wrestlers, warriors, and football players are good examples of people who possess brute force.

2. *Artistry.* Bodily dexterity that enables a person to arrange colors, forms, materials, or other elements in a manner that affects the sense of beauty, specifically the production of the beautiful in some sort of manifestation. The hand-eye coordination of these people enables them to produce works of art that others of us just cannot do. Good artists rarely result from just having this physical strength. They usually possess emotional strengths as well. Painters, sculptors, photographers, and filmmakers are good examples of people who possess artistic strengths.

3. *Music.* The use of the body to produce or manipulate sounds and or rhythms. This ability can be exerted by the voice or the hands or even by the feet. Many times these individuals are born with voice capabilities or special hearing that makes them adept at musical endeavors. We often say they have an ear for music. However, if they do not complete the matrix and gain knowledge of music and pursue skills practice, they usually do not progress very far in the musical world. Singers and instrumentalists are good examples of people who possess musical strengths.

4. *Mechanics.* The use of the body to manipulate physical objects and machinery to accomplish tasks. This is usually done in a synergistic manner that combines the energy of the human with the efficiency of the machine to exceed the capability of either when working by itself. Auto mechanics, farmers, office workers, fast-food workers, heavy machinery operators, pilots, and soldiers are good examples of people who possess mechanical strengths.

5. *Craftsmanship*. Bodily dexterity that enables a person to work effectively with their hands or other parts of their body to create exquisite objects. In many cases, this is similar to mechanical strengths only on a finer scale. Good eye-hand coordination is essential to this strength. Carpentry, cooking, sewing, landscaping, and hairstyling are all good examples of people who possess craftsmanship.

6. *Oratory*. The use of the spoken voice to produce captivating tones and clear articulation. In other words, to speak clearly and sound good. Obviously oratory is more effective if a person possesses emotional and intellectual strengths to enhance what is being said. However, people with exceptional physical strengths in this area are often able to captivate others even when what they say doesn't make much sense! Politicians, lawyers, preachers, and teachers are good examples of people who often exhibit oratorical strengths.

7. *Kinesthetics*. The coordination and control of bodily positions, weight, muscles, or movement to achieve desired outcomes. We often refer to people who exhibit this strength as being athletic or graceful. Athletes, acrobats, and dancers are good examples of people with kinesthetic strengths. This strength is also often observed in a wide variety of recreational activities.

8. *Physical appearance*. The features of a person's body that we often refer to as good looks. For those of us who do not have this strength, we often are envious of those who do possess it. This is an interesting strength in that it varies by culture and by period. This is because society dictates what constitutes "good looks." In the Chapel section that follows, we will look at how God uses this strength, confirming that it rightfully should be considered a physical strength. Models and actors are good examples of people with strengths in physical appearance.

An important observation is that in the domain of physical strengths, contrary to popular opinion, few people excel by pure giftedness alone. For the most part people have to work across the matrix, even when they are gifted, developing their giftedness through knowledge acquisition and skills improvement.

Here is another observation we can make. Most cultures in our modern society place greater value on physical strengths than the other domains. As a result, we end up with a culture obsessed with performance and appearance. This often leads to feelings of inferiority and self-doubt in individuals who do not find their greatest distinction in this strength domain. Our society has done a poor job in dealing with this problem, and what has resulted is considerable confusion in the discovery of a Life Calling for those who struggle with this problem. This is why we believe it is so important to look at strengths across the entire Strengths Matrix without omitting the exploration of any of the strengths or their elements.

How do we identify physical strengths in our lives? Once they have been developed, it is usually not hard to recognize them. The more elusive aspect may be in identifying potential in the physical strengths domain. One effective way this takes place is by listening to what others who know us say about us. Another way is to complete exercises and assessments that test our physical abilities in a variety of areas. We will look closer at some examples of how to do this in the Exercises section of this chapter.

Concepts Summary

Physical strengths are much more than brute strength or strong muscles. Taking time to look over this broad spectrum can help us avoid discounting this area of strength too quickly in our lives.

Each of the strengths domains provides a bridge among the other dimensions. Physical strengths provide the bridge of *implementation* among the other strengths. What do we mean by this? It is through our bodily actions that we actually carry out ideas and initiatives that are generated by the other strengths.

▶ Insight

There are definitely endeavors in life that require certain physical strengths. Those have the physical strengths required for these endeavors will find more success than those who do not. It is a fact of life, and as such, should be used in evaluating where to maximize our strengths in pursuit of our Life Calling. No matter what the level of our physical strengths, however, we should use whatever we are given as an entrustment from God and use it to his glory. The following insights from the Bible help to illustrate this.

SCRIPTURAL INSIGHT 1 ▶ *It Makes a Difference When You Are Skilled*

Then the LORD said to Moses, "See, I have chosen Bezalel son of Uri, the son of Hur, of the tribe of Judah, and I have filled him with the Spirit of God, with wisdom, with understanding, with knowledge and with all kinds of skills—to make artistic designs for work in gold, silver and bronze, to cut and set stones, to work in wood, and to engage in all kinds of crafts. Moreover, I have appointed Oholiab son of Ahisamak, of the tribe of Dan, to help him. Also I have given ability to all the skilled workers to make everything I have commanded you. Exodus 31:1-6

The first of the strengths listed in the Strengths Matrix is physical strength. God gives to us and appreciates physical strengths. Consider the example given in Exodus 31.

The example is a man named Bezalel. During the long journey of the Israelites from Egypt to Canaan known as the Exodus, God directed Moses to build a tabernacle. God further directed Moses to employ a person with needed physical strengths to oversee the project and a team of physically gifted people to help him.

Bazalel, along with his colleagues Oholiab and Ahisamak, had physical strengths in the area of craftsmanship. According to the passage, these physical strengths had been developed across the matrix—ability (gifts), knowledge, skill and disposition. In other words, "these guys were good!"

A key concept from this conversation between God and Moses is that these physical strengths were a gift of God. We should never see our strengths as anything other than entrustments of God, and we should be diligent stewards over them.

A second concept is that these physical strengths were enhanced by the fact that God also filled Bazalel with the Spirit of God. The danger of physical strengths is that we begin to view them as our own doing and forget who they came from or that we need God's Spirit to effectively empower them. We need to remember Paul's words in 1 Corinthians 6:19 that our bodies are temples of the Holy Spirit.

Have you ever noticed the difference between an athlete, actor, speaker, or musician who obviously is sold on themselves and the athlete, actor, speaker, or musician who gives the credit to God? The difference is pretty obvious, and those sold on themselves are not very appealing. This is not to say that we do not need to work hard at developing our physical strengths. There are some people that think they can just pray to God and physical skills will develop miraculously. This doesn't work nor has it ever been God's plan. Just like we saw in the Parable of the Talents, God gives us gifts, but he then expects us to put forth effort to develop them to the fullest.

INSIGHT

> PERSONAL REFLECTION ⟩ Do you view your physical strengths as building blocks in God's temple? How are you using them to pursue your search for a Life Calling?

SCRIPTURAL INSIGHT 2 ⟩ *Good Speaking Takes More Than Eloquent Empty Words*

Meanwhile a Jew named Apollos, a native of Alexandria, came to Ephesus. He was a learned man, with a thorough knowledge of the Scriptures. He had been instructed in the way of the Lord, and he spoke with great fervor and taught about Jesus accurately, though he knew only the baptism of John. He began to speak boldly in the synagogue. When Priscilla and Aquila heard him, they invited him to their home and explained to him the way of God more adequately. When Apollos wanted to go to Achaia, the believers encouraged him and wrote to the disciples there to welcome him. When he arrived, he was a great help to those who by grace had believed. For he vigorously refuted the Jews in public debate, proving from the Scriptures that Jesus was the Christ. ACTS 18:24-28

Have you ever heard a motivational speaker who could speak really well, yet when you asked yourself what the speaker had said, you really didn't know? The person had great delivery but no substance. The ability to speak eloquently forms one area of physical strength. It is important, however, that the gift is supported by substance. Apollos is a good example from the Bible of someone possessing this strength and using it to carry out his Life Calling for God. We can learn a good lesson from Apollos concerning our strengths. He did not rely on the physical gift alone. He was obviously a captivating speaker as can be seen in his debating skills identified in this passage. This likely is also seen in Paul's first letter to the Corinthians where Christians in that city were dividing themselves as followers of various leaders and Apollos was one mentioned. But Apollos realized that eloquence by itself was not enough. He supported his eloquence with learning and a thorough knowledge of the Scriptures (which in his day was the Old Testament). When he discovered that his understanding of Jesus was not complete, he was open to learning more from Aquila and Priscilla.

One of the great challenges with any strength is to rely on our giftedness in that strength and not support it by developing our knowledge, skills, and disposition. Apollos provided us with a good example of how we should approach our strengths.

> PERSONAL REFLECTION ⟩ How can you support the physical strengths God has placed in you by learning more about them? If speaking is one of your strengths, how can you make sure you use this to God's glory?

SCRIPTURAL INSIGHT 3 ⟩ *Beauty Can Be More Than Skin-Deep*

Then the king's personal attendants proposed, "Let a search be made for beautiful young virgins for the king. Let the king appoint commissioners in every province of his realm to bring all these beautiful young women into the harem at the citadel of Susa. Let them be placed under the care of Hegai, the king's eunuch, who is in charge of the women; and let beauty treatments be given to them. Then let the young woman who pleases the king be queen instead of Vashti." This advice appealed to the king, and he followed it. Now there was in the citadel of Susa a Jew of the tribe of Benjamin, named Mordecai son of Jair, the son of Shimei, the son of Kish, who had been carried into exile from Jerusalem by Nebuchadnezzar king of Babylon, among those taken captive with Jehoiachin king of Judah. Mordecai had a cousin named Hadassah, whom he had brought up because she had neither father nor mother. This young woman, who was also known as Esther, had a lovely figure and was beautiful. Mordecai had taken her as his own daughter when her father and mother died.

When the king's order and edict had been proclaimed, many young women were brought to the citadel of Susa and put under the care of Hegai. Esther also was taken to the king's palace and entrusted to Hegai, who had charge of the harem. She pleased him and won his favor. Immediately he provided her with her beauty treatments and special food. He assigned to her seven female attendants selected from the king's palace and moved her and her attendants into the best place in the harem. ESTHER 2:2-9

This example of physical strength is a familiar character, Esther. Esther lived in the empire formed of the countries of Persia and Media. She was a young woman of Jewish decent living in Susa, the capital. The Jews had been taken as captives by the Persian Empire after the Persian conquest of the Babylonians who had first taken the Jews captive in their conquest of Israel. The king of Persia, Xerxes, had divorced his queen because she would not give in to his senseless, chauvinistic demands, and he was in the market for a new queen. He decided to choose a new queen by staging a beauty contest. Now God decided to use this opportunity to set things up for a later deliverance of the Jews from the sinister plots of a Persian named Haman. To do this, God needed someone who could win the contest. Here is where Esther enters the scene as described in the scripture passage for today.

Several points concerning physical strengths emerge from this story. First of all, Esther "had a lovely figure and was beautiful." Basically that means Esther was well-built and physically attractive. She probably would have been a supermodel if she lived in our time and culture. But Esther did not rely on her good looks alone, instead she did all she could to develop and enhance them. She got on the good side of Hegai, the eunuch in charge of all the young ladies, and they developed a regimen of beauty treatments and diet to make her a winner. She worked across the matrix to develop her knowledge and skills in the area of her physical strength of beauty.

The outcome of this story is well-known. Esther became queen by nature of her beauty. She was then able to use this position to plead with the king to spare the lives of the Jews who had come under an extermination sentence by the trickery of the evil Haman (who, incidentally, lost his life because of his tricks). To this day Jews celebrate Purim as one of the most joyous and fun holidays on the Jewish calendar. It commemorates this story of Esther, made possible in part by her physical strength of beauty.

You might be tempted, like me, to say that's great for Esther and others who have beauty like that. But what about plain old me? That takes us back to the Parable of the Talents. God determines what is best for us according to our capacity. This may not be an area in which we have capacity—I know in

INSIGHT

my case it is not! God does not expect us to do something like Esther did if we don't have beauty as one of those "bags of gold." If we do, however, he expects us to develop it and use it to his glory according to his plan.

> **PERSONAL REFLECTION** Do you have a hard time accepting your physical appearance? How can you start to see this as part of God's purpose in your life? If physical appearance is one of your strengths, how can you make sure you use this to God's glory?

SCRIPTURAL INSIGHT 4 *You Can Learn from a Person with the Complete Physical Package*

"I have seen a son of Jesse of Bethlehem who knows how to play the harp. He is a brave man and a warrior. He speaks well and is a fine-looking man. And the LORD is with him." 1 SAMUEL 16:18

Our fourth example of physical strengths comes from the life of the most beloved king of Israel, David. We pick up the story in 1 Samuel 16 where we find the current king of Israel, Saul, deserted by the Spirit of the Lord and fighting what was referred to as an evil spirit. This may have been a serious mental disorder. Whatever it was, it caused rage in Saul and fear in the heart of his attendants, so they wanted to get him some help. In verse 16 they advised Saul, "Let our Lord command his servants here to search for someone who can play the harp. He will play when the evil spirit…comes upon you, and you will feel better."

Saul agreed that this was a good plan and instructed the attendants to find such a person—someone with the physical strength of musical ability. No sooner was it said then, according to verse 18, one of the servants answered, "I have seen a son of Jesse of Bethlehem who knows how to play the harp. He is a brave man and a warrior. He speaks well and is a fine-looking man. And the LORD is with him."

Here was a comprehensive package of physical strengths: musical strengths, athletic strengths (warrior), oratory skills (speaks well), and good looks. Wow! It doesn't seem quite fair, does it? But the best part of that package for David was that the Lord was with him. David's athletic and warrior strengths came into play later in his confrontation with the giant Goliath recorded in 1 Samuel 17:34-50.

David said to Saul, "Your servant has been keeping his father's sheep. When a lion or a bear came and carried off a sheep from the flock, I went after it, struck it and rescued the sheep from its mouth. When it turned on me, I seized it by its hair, struck it and killed it. Your servant has killed both the lion and the bear; this uncircumcised Philistine [Goliath] will be like one of them, because he has defied the armies of the living God. The LORD who delivered me from the paw of the lion and the paw of the bear will deliver me from the hand of this Philistine." Saul said to David, "Go, and the LORD be with you…"

As the Philistine moved closer to attack him, David ran quickly toward the battle line to meet him. Reaching into his bag and taking out a stone, he slung it and struck the Philistine on the forehead. The stone sank into his forehead, and he fell facedown on the ground.

So David triumphed over the Philistine with a sling and a stone; without a sword in his hand he struck down the Philistine and killed him.

This famous victory would not have been possible if it had not been for David's physical strengths honed to perfection by years of practice as a shepherd. When we are willing to let him, God uses physical strengths for his glory.

PERSONAL REFLECTION > Personal Reflection: If you are physically gifted like David was, how can you keep from becoming conceited or ignoring the need for or value in the other domains of strengths? If physical strength is your greatest strength, how can you make sure you use this to God's glory?

SCRIPTURAL INSIGHT 5 > *The Inside Is as Important as the Outside*

But the LORD said to Samuel, "Do not consider his appearance or his height, for I have rejected him. The LORD does not look at the things human beings look at. People look at the outward appearance, but the LORD looks at the heart." 1 SAMUEL 16:7

In the Concepts section, we defined physical strength as the dimension of our lives that gives our bodies distinct features and enables us to perform actions with our body. We also observed that most cultures in our modern society place greater value on physical strengths than the other domains. Because of this, we end up with a culture obsessed with performance and appearance. This was just as much a problem in ancient cultures as well, as illustrated in the selection of David to succeed Saul as king of Israel. Saul had disobeyed God's instruction given to him through the prophet Samuel. God was not pleased with this and decided to remove Saul as king and replace him, so God sent Samuel to the home of Jesse where God told Samuel he would find the next king. We return to 1 Samuel 16 and find this story just ahead of where we were in our last insight. When Samuel arrived and told Jesse what was happening, Jesse brought his oldest son to meet Samuel. In that society the oldest son was always considered to be the most honored. When Samuel saw Eliab, the oldest son, according to verse 6 he thought, "Surely the LORD's anointed stands here before the LORD." However, Samuel and the Lord were not on the same page. Our text for this insight illustrates this with the words "the LORD does not look at the things human beings look at."

Whenever we look at physical strengths, we need to do so with the caution of this story. Physical strengths can easily deceive us into thinking that a person possesses strengths in all areas just because they possess physical strengths. Good-looking actors are thought to be worthy spokespersons for political or moral causes. Tall people find it easier to attain leadership than shorter people do. Professional athletes are looked up to as role models. However, in many of these cases, these people have not lived up to the esteem awarded to them on the basis of their physical strengths. We all would be better served if we followed the Lord's example and looked at the heart as well.

PERSONAL REFLECTION > Do you use physical strengths to honor God rather than yourself? How can you use your body to form a temple for the Holy Spirit? What can help you see your physical strengths as just one dimension among a combination of others?

INSIGHT

 # Discovery

How can the Discovery Guides help you identify and understand your *physical strengths?*

DISCOVERY

T THEORY	You can increase your knowledge about many of the *Physical Strengths* categories in departments and classes at your college or university. Introductory classes are often a good place to start. Here are some suggestions for each of the eight areas. *Brute force*—Physical education classes and sports programs. *Artistry*—Introductory classes in your art department that actually have you starting to enter into production of art; art theory classes will also help you see what kind of disposition you have toward the area of art. *Music*—Introductory applied classes in your music department and participation in musical groups; as with art, music theory classes will also help you see what kind of disposition you have toward the area of music. *Mechanics*—Many colleges will not have formal studies or programs that can help you explore this area; consider taking classes at a community or vocational college that might be more applicable to this area. *Craftsmanship*—You may find the same problem here as you would with mechanics; you may need to look at a different kind of school to learn about this area. *Oratory*—Nearly every college and university requires some kind of speech or communications course; this will provide you an opportunity to learn about your strength in oratory and to explore your disposition toward it. *Kinesthetics*—You can usually find opportunities to explore this area in two primary areas—physical education and dance; this is also an area to explore by participating with groups on your campus involved with kinesthetic activities. *Appearance*—If your institution has a program in fashion, that might be a place to explore; however, because this strength refers primarily to your own appearance, you will likely need to look toward other tools of discovery to explore this. Reading books about these various areas is another good way to learn more about the eight areas.
E EXAMPLES	Find people who excel in these various areas of physical strengths. Observe them and find time to talk to them. Ask them to share with you how they discovered and developed these physical strengths.
A ASSESSMENT	There are a wide variety of separate assessments that measure each of the eight categories of physical strengths. You might want to use some of these to help you assess your own physical strengths.
C COUNSEL	Professional counselors and life coaches are trained to help you in the exploration of physical strengths. Your college and university will likely have a center where you can find such help. Additionally, family members, teachers, pastors, and friends know you well and can help you assess your physical strengths. Their counsel should not be ignored.

H HISTORY	Search for historical biographies of notable people who have exhibited these physical strengths. Select some of these and learn from their experiences.
E EXPERIENCE	Get involved with activities where you can test your physical strengths in the eight categories. You will learn quickly whether or not you have an aptitude for each category.
R REFLECTION	Take time to reflect on what you have learned about your *physical strengths* in the other six activities of discovery. Consider what you agree with and why.

DISCOVERY

▶Story

It is interesting that the further people live away from a state, the greater their tendency is to lump all locations within that state under the label of the largest city. For instance, people from Ohio who are visiting friends in El Segundo, California, usually tell people that they are going to Los Angeles. Travelers headed to White Plains might say they are going to New York. This can even cross state lines. People who are really headed to Gary, Indiana, might instead say they are headed to Chicago, which, of course, is in Illinois. Even though the crew of the *Nautilus* kept talking about Boston, they were actually headed to Plymouth, Massachusetts.

Anyone who lives in or has traveled to Boston knows that driving there is a challenge for even the smallest of cars. Ken Neimon had heard the legends of one-way streets and narrow, twisting lanes long before their journey ever began and had decided there was no way the 42-foot *Nautilus* would make it. He had decided to find an RV park on the outskirts of the city and find other transportation into Boston properly.

Pinewood Lodge Campground was located in Plymouth, Massachusetts—the same Plymouth where Plymouth Rock was located. This made their Massachusetts landing point doubly valuable: it was near Boston, right at a historical spot the explorers wanted to visit.

"It isn't as big as I thought it would be." Justin seemed a little disappointed as he experienced the same reaction that first-time visitors often experience at Plymouth Rock.

"My guess is that the Pilgrims never set foot on this rock," the ever-skeptical Lorena muttered.

"Is 1620 the street address of the monument?" Diana asked. The others could not help themselves and burst out laughing.

"Don't be so dumb, Diana." Justin put his arm around her shoulders and gave her a squeeze. "1620 is the year that the Pilgrims landed."

Diana again turned red. She wanted so much to be respected for more than her looks, but sometimes she said things that did not help her case.

"Okay, Mr. Strengths." Abriella turned to Adam. "What kind of strengths did it take for the Pilgrims to survive once they got here?"

"Probably all of them, I would imagine," Adam answered. "But I imagine physical strength was right up there at the top. It was a real challenge to stay alive."

"When you say 'physical strength,' is there just one category?" Abriella asked.

"I don't think so," Adam replied. "It seems more like we have different types of physical strength."

"So if we were the Pilgrims," Justin asked, "which type of physical strength would each of us have, and would we survive?"

"Let's look at ourselves," Adam replied. "We can all decide who has which one and who would survive."

The group liked this approach. They were always ready to turn any activity into a game or a challenge.

"What about brute strength," Adam started. "You know, big muscles."

"That's easy," Lorena answered quickly. "Ryan. He puts the rest of us to shame."

"I resent that!" Justin protested, his tone slightly sarcastic. "Look at these specimens." He flexed his biceps, grunting like Tarzan. Both Justin and Adam were in good shape, but neither could come close to Ryan. Not only did Ryan surf, he was also an avid weight lifter.

"I still think Ryan wins that one. Does he survive?" Adam asked.

"I say he lives," Abriella answered. "He has strength to build a shelter, to defend himself, and to hunt for food. Definitely a survivor." The others agreed.

"Okay, okay." Lorena was always impatient. "Move on to another physical strength."

"What about painting or sculpture?" Adam said. "You have to have physical skills that help you arrange colors and shapes in some sense of beauty."

"Abriella," Lorena responded.

"Do you plan to answer all of these?" Ryan asked, his voice somewhat irritated.

"Don't you watch *Jeopardy*?" Lorena shot back. "You don't ring in, then you don't get any points!"

"No, I don't watch *Jeopardy*!" Ryan answered emphatically.

"Figures!" Lorena responded.

"Come on, you two," Adam interjected. "This is a game, not a fight." The way Lorena and Ryan glared at each other, however, did not seem to support this.

"I agree with Lorena," Diana said. "Abriella is definitely the artist among us."

"Yeah, and she's dead in two months," Justin added.

"You can't eat paintings or trade them for food. The Indians would have had no use for them."

"Aw!" Abriella staged a pout and thrust her bottom lip out.

"Sorry, Abi. You're dead." Ryan winked as he spoke.

"All right, what about musical ability like singing or playing an instrument?" Adam decided to move on before Lorena could push him to do so.

"That would have to be Lorena," Diana answered. "Anybody who wins as many competitions playing the piano as she does has got to be our representative in that category."

No one disagreed. Most of them played an instrument, but none of them came close to Lorena's accomplishments.

"Well, my guess is that if she can't play the war drums with the Indians, her piano will get her killed." Ryan seemed to enjoy his answer. "I say she's gone as quick as Abriella."

"Hey, what are you trying to do? Kill off all the women?" Abriella asked.

"Have to call 'em as I see 'em," Ryan responded. "In 1620, brute force was more important than all your frilly stuff. Sorry. Of course, *I'm* still alive."

"Heaven help our new nation!" Lorena mumbled.

"Moving right along," Adam continued. "What about working with tools?"

"That's Justin, man," Ryan answered. "The guy rebuilt his entire car!"

"I agree." Diana joined Ryan. "And I say he survives. He designs tools for growing crops and building shelters."

"Okay, what if working with tools is more like craftsmanship," Adam continued. "While it's sort of like the mechanical ability, it produces more exquisite products."

"I give in," Ryan said. "I admit it. What the heck does exquisite mean?"

No one laughed because none of them was very sure of the meaning of "exquisite products" either.

"I'm talking about producing something on a more delicate or more exacting level," Adam explained. "You know, kind of like framing the house would be mechanical. Building the cabinets would be craftsmanship."

"What about *craftwomanship*?" Abriella asked. The others laughed.

"Okay. I think we could include hairstyling in this category," Adam answered.

"Not all hairstylists are women!" Lorena shot back.

"Touché," Adam agreed. "So who fits this category?"

"I think it's Justin again," Diana answered. "The furniture he builds is beautiful."

"Yeah, but the Pilgrims don't need beautiful furniture. They need food, shelter, and safety," Lorena broke in. "I say he's down the tubes."

"Wait!" Justin protested. "You just let me live, and now you're killing me?"

"Justin's half alive and half dead," Lorena compromised. They all laughed.

"Too bad we don't have a hairstylist among us," Ryan added. "That person would live if they could do a Mohawk." Everybody else groaned.

"I think I've got three more." Adam held three fingers up as he spoke.

"What about being a good speaker?"

"That's you, Adam," Lorena again responded quickly. "There's no doubt about that." The others agreed.

"So do I live, or do I die?" Adam asked.

"I think you live," Abriella responded. "You'd find a way to communicate with the natives. You'd make peace, and then you'd get them to help you stay alive. Look at how you keep all of us at peace."

"Wait!" Diana broke in. "You just killed all the ladies and left all the men alive."

"Hey, I'm only half alive," Justin reminded her.

"So, what are our last two choices?" Lorena sounded anxious to bring this game to an end.

"The next one I think would be athleticism as in coordination of the body," Adam replied.

"We're all pretty athletic … except Lorena, of course," Ryan said.

Lorena glared at him, but she knew he was telling the truth. *I'm not that out of shape*, she told herself. *It just isn't that important to me.*

"And I bet being athletic would help us all stay alive," Justin added. "We could escape our enemies and chase our prey. So I guess that means we're all alive again … or at least *almost* all of us."

"What's our last category, Adam?" Abriella asked.

"Physical appearance—you know, good looks," Adam replied.

The other five all said "Diana" at the same time, and Diana once again flushed bright red.

"And I say it keeps her alive," Ryan injected quickly. "We use her looks to sell her to the chief as a squaw." He smiled, proud of himself.

"Awww." Abriella's voice carried empathy. "Poor Diana. We can't let her go."

"Thanks, Abriella." Diana laughed and gave Abriella a hug.

"Okay, now that we got that over with, where to now?" Lorena asked.

"Let's catch a shuttle to Plimouth Plantation museum," Adam answered, pointing to the location on a map he held open for the other to see.

"Why is it spelled weird like that?" Abriella asked.

"I read in a brochure that it's an old-fashioned spelling used by Governor Bradford in his original history of the colony. When they built the modern museum, this spelling was adopted to differentiate the museum from the modern town of Plymouth," Adam explained. "It kind of gives an extra sense of history. That's a big theme at the museum. In fact, I hear that the role players there don't break out of character. It should be fun. We can see how the Pilgrims lived."

"At least the ones that *did* live," Ryan added, smirking at Lorena. She glared back.

STORY

EXERCISE 2

Expanding Your Understanding of Your Physical Strengths Using the *Physical-Strengths 360*

1. Identify four different people who know you and who love and care for you. Choose the four so that they represent each of the following categories:

   • Parent _____

   • Teacher (present or former) _____

   • Friend _____

   • Sibling or relative who is younger than you _____

2. Provide all of the people you have identified with a copy of the *Physical-Strengths 360* (not the Mirror) chart below and ask them to answer the questions for each of the eight areas of physical strength. Let them know that it is okay if they answer that they have not seen as being strong in your life. Tell them this will help you better understand yourself. Encourage them to give an example if they answer that an area is strong in you.

Physical Strengths 360	Definition	How strong do you see this physical quality in me (weak, moderate, strong, very strong)?	Can you give me an example of when you have seen this physical strength in me?
Muscular Strength	The muscular ability that enables people to excel at lifting great weights or exerting great pressure.		
Artistry	Bodily dexterity that enables a person to arrange colors, forms, materials, or other elements in a manner that affects the sense of beauty, specifically the production of the beautiful in some sort of manifestation.		
Music	The use of the body to produce or manipulate sounds and or rhythms. This ability can be exerted by the voice or the hands or even by the feet.		
Mechanics	The use of the body to manipulate physical objects and machinery to accomplish tasks.		
Craftsmanship	Bodily dexterity that enables a person to work effectively with their hands or other parts of their body to create exquisite objects.		

(Continued)

EXERCISES

Physical Strengths 360	Definition	How strong do you see this physical quality in me (weak, moderate, strong, very strong)?	Can you give me an example of when you have seen this physical strength in me?
Oratory	The use of the spoken voice to produce captivating tones and clear articulation. In other words, to speak clearly and sound good.		
Flexible body movement	The coordination and control of bodily positions, weight, muscles, or movement to achieve desired outcomes. People who exhibit this strength are often referred to as being athletic or graceful.		
Physical appearance	The features of a person's body that are referred to as good looks. This varies by culture and by period because society dictates what constitutes "good looks."		

3. Now you personally answer the questions for each of the eight areas using the results from Exercise 1 and your perception.

Physical Strengths Mirror	Definition	How strong did I see this area in myself (weak, moderate, strong, very strong)?	What has been my most fulfilling experience in this physical strength?
Muscular Strength	The muscular ability that enables people to excel at lifting great weights or exerting great pressure.		
Artistry	Bodily dexterity that enables a person to arrange colors, forms, materials, or other elements in a manner that affects the sense of beauty, specifically the production of the beautiful in some sort of manifestation.		
Music	The use of the body to produce or manipulate sounds and or rhythms. This ability can be exerted by the voice or the hands or even by the feet.		

EXERCISES

Mechanics	The use of the body to manipulate physical objects and machinery to accomplish tasks.		
Craftsmanship	Bodily dexterity that enables a person to work effectively with their hands or other parts of their body to create exquisite objects.		
Oratory	The use of the spoken voice to produce captivating tones and clear articulation. In other words, to speak clearly and sound good.		
Flexible body movement	The coordination and control of bodily positions, weight, muscles, or movement to achieve desired outcomes. People who exhibit this strength are often referred to as being athletic or graceful.		
Physical appearance	The features of a person's body that referred to as good looks. This varies by culture and by period because society dictates what constitutes "good looks."		

4. Compare your scores to the evaluation from others in the Physical-Strengths 360. What do others see in you that you may not see in yourself? What can you learn about your perception of yourself?

5. Reflect on what you learned in both Exercise 1 and Exercise 2 and summarize below what they have revealed to you about yourself.

EXERCISES

Maintaining Physical Well-being

Discussing Physical strengths provides us with a good opportunity to discuss your physical well-being in general. The pressures of college life can tempt you to let this slip in your life. What can you do to keep this from happening?

▶ Nutrition: You are what you eat

That heading is not just a clever saying, it is a fact. Your body does not magically regenerate itself from some unknown source. The basic building blocks of every part of your body come from the things you eat and drink. Your brain is a part of your body and so good physical health greatly affects good mental health. You need to take ownership of providing good nutrition to your body. You cannot assume that your institution's food service will do that for you.

A good way to start is by understanding what a balanced diet looks like. There has been a lot of discussion about this over the last decade. The government tried using what they called "MyPyramid" with the intent to make a more individualized approach to diet and health. That didn't work so in 2011 USDA introduced the new "ChooseMyPlate" approach.

You can learn more about this approach at the following website: http://www.choosemyplate.gov. If you want to see how "ChooseMyPlate" relates more specifically to you, follow this link: http://www.choosemyplate.gov/myplate/index.aspx

One problem with all of the government's approaches is that they have had wide variety of influences in their creation. The obvious ones – USDA scientists, nutrition experts, staff members, and consultants—make sense. Others influencers on the government's dietary recommendations may not make as much sense. Intense lobbying efforts from a variety of food industries also helped shape the government's recommendations.

Experts from the Harvard School of Public Health wondered if the intent of the government "is to give us the best possible advice for healthy eating, then it should be grounded in the evidence and be independent of business." Instead of waiting for this to happen, they decided to create the Healthy Eating Pyramid based on their research. This has received support from sources such as *Men's Health* and is included in this book as another good source for nutritional guidance.

It is based on the best available scientific evidence about the links between diet and health. This new pyramid fixes fundamental flaws in the USDA pyramid and offers sound information to help people make better choices about what to eat.

The Healthy Eating Pyramid sits on a foundation of daily exercise and weight control. Why? These two related elements strongly influence your chances of staying healthy. They also affect what and how you eat and how your food affects you. The other components of the Healthy Eating Pyramid are described in the list that follows along with the servings per day in parentheses.

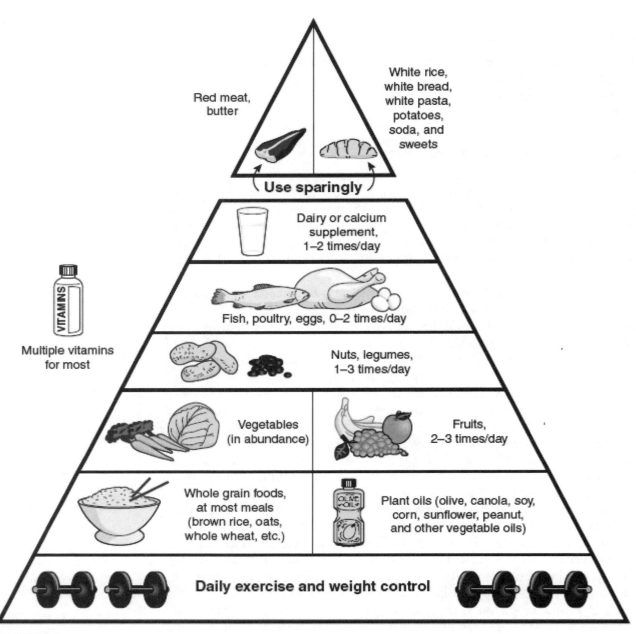

FIGURE 6-2
Healthy Eating Pyramid

Source: From *EAT, DRINK, AND BE HEALTHY* by Walter C. Willett, M.D. Copyright © 2001, 2005 by the President and Fellows of Harvard College.

- **Whole Grain Foods (at most meals)**. The body needs carbohydrates mainly for energy. The best sources of carbohydrates are whole grains such as oatmeal, whole-wheat bread, and brown rice. They deliver the outer (bran) and inner (germ) layers along with energy-rich starch.
- **Plant Oils**. American gets one third or more of their daily calories from fats. Eating the right type of fats is important. The Healthy

Pyramid specifically mentions plant oils, not all types of fat. Good sources of healthy unsaturated fats include olive, canola, soy, corn, sunflower, peanut, and other vegetable oils, as well as fatty fish such as salmon.

- **Vegetables (in abundance) and Fruits (2 to 3 times)**. A diet rich in fruits and vegetables can decrease the chances of having a heart attack or stroke; protect against a variety of cancers; lower blood pressure; help you avoid the painful intestinal ailment called diverticulitis; guard against cataract and macular degeneration, the major cause of vision loss among people over age 65; and add variety to your diet and wake up your palate.

- **Fish, Poultry, and Eggs (0 to 2 times)**. These are important sources of protein. A wealth of research suggests that eating fish can reduce the risk of heart disease. Chicken and turkey are also good sources of protein and can be low in saturated fat. Eggs, which have long been demonized because they contain fairly high levels of cholesterol, aren't as bad as they're cracked up to be. In fact, an egg is a much better breakfast than a doughnut cooked in an oil rich in trans fats or a bagel made from refined flour.

- **Nuts and Legumes (1 to 3 times)**. Nuts and legumes are excellent sources of protein, fiber, vitamins, and minerals. Legumes include black beans, navy beans, garbanzos, and other beans that are usually sold dried. Many kinds of nuts contain healthy fats.

- **Dairy or Calcium Supplement (1 to 2 times)**. Good bone strength takes calcium, vitamin D, exercise, and a whole lot more. Dairy products have traditionally been Americans' main source of calcium, but you need to be careful of saturated fat. Calcium supplements offer an easy and inexpensive way to get your daily calcium.

- **Red Meat and Butter (Use Sparingly)**: These sit at the top of the Healthy Eating Pyramid because they contain lots of saturated fat. You're better off if you can switch eating red meat every day, to fish or chicken. Also, try switching from butter to olive oil.

- **White Rice, White Bread, Potatoes, White Pasta, Soda, and Sweets (Use Sparingly)**: All of these foods can cause sudden increases in blood sugar that can lead to weight gain, diabetes, heart disease, and other chronic disorders. Whole-grain carbohydrates cause slower, steadier increases in blood sugar that don't overwhelm the body's ability to handle this much needed but potentially dangerous nutrient.

- **Multiple Vitamin**: A daily multivitamin, multimineral supplement offers a kind of nutritional backup. A standard, store-brand, RDA-level one is fine. Look for one that meets the requirements of the USP (U.S. Pharmacopeia), an organization that sets standards for drugs and supplements.

An increasing number of college students are pursuing a vegetarian life style. Because of this, we have included a vegetarian recommendation. This could be compared with the Harvard Healthy Eating Pyramid to guide you in your nutrition if this is a life style you follow.

EXERCISES

EXERCISES

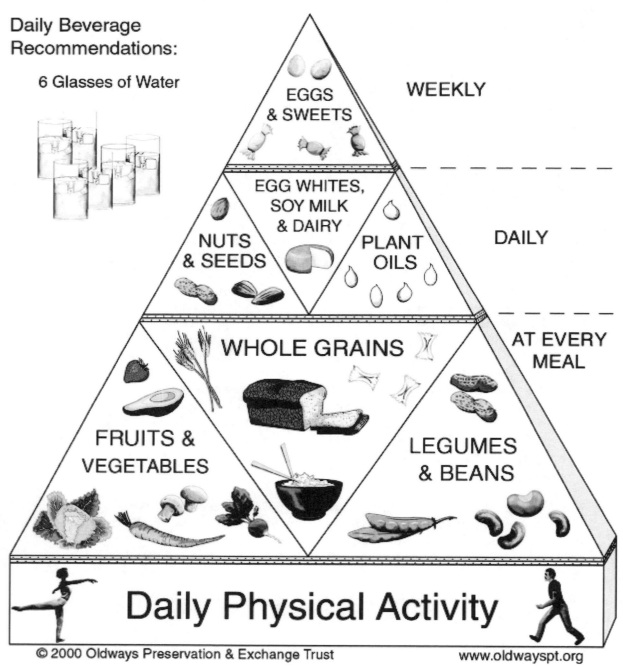

FIGURE 6-3
Vegetarian Diet Pyramid

▶ Weight Management: Focus on health more than appearance

(Adapted from *College & Career Success, 3/e* by Marsha Fralick. Copyright 2006, Kendall/Hunt Publishing Company.)

Maintaining a healthy weight is one of the keys to a long and healthy life. Being overweight increases the risk of high blood pressure, high blood cholesterol, heart disease, stroke, diabetes, cancer, arthritis, and breathing problems. Researchers believe that 55 percent of Americans are overweight and about 25 percent are obese. The problem of overweight children and adults is a major health concern today. The best way to lose weight is by establishing patterns of healthy eating and exercise.

Americans struggle with how to maintain a healthy weight. Some turn to crash diets that severely restrict calories and food choices. Crash diets are not recommended because the weight loss is temporary and the body can be deprived of important nutrients. Another serious problem is eating disorders such as anorexia that can lead to serious health problems, and even death in severe cases. Symptoms of an eating disorder include a preoccupation with food or body weight, dramatic weight loss, excessive exercise, self-induced vomiting, and abuse of laxatives. Anyone with these symptoms should consult a health care provider.

Body Mass Index (BMI) is a commonly used method of evaluating a person's weight. It is based on the ratio of weight to height. To calculate your BMI, first answer these two questions:

1. What is your height in inches? _____

2. What is your weight in pounds? _____

Calculate your BMI using the following formula:

$$\text{BMI} = (705 \times \text{body weight}) \div (\text{height} \times \text{height})$$

Example: A person who is 66 inches tall and weighs 155 pounds:

$$\text{BMI} = (705 \times 155) \div (66 \times 66) = 25$$

Body Mass Index Categories

BMI	Weight Characterization
Less than 18.5	Underweight
18.5-24.9	Normal weight
25-29.9	Overweight
30 and above	Obese

There are some exceptions to consider when using BMI to evaluate weight:
- Body builders and other athletes may have a higher BMI because muscle weighs more than fat.
- For the elderly, a BMI between 25 and 27 may be healthier and protect against osteoporosis.
- The BMI is not designed to be used with children.

EXERCISES

Another way to evaluate your weight is to simply measure around your waist. A measurement of over 35 inches for women or 40 inches for men places a person at greater risk of health problems. If your BMI is over 25 or your waist measurement increases, reduce calories and increase activity.

Here are some suggestions for managing your weight:
- Be physically active
- Choose healthy foods (see previous section)
- Eat sensible portions
- Lose weight slowly

▶ Physical Exercise

Eating right is not enough on its own; you need to put the nutrition to work so that the body can make good use of it. The way to do that is to combine healthy eating with healthy exercise. This is important for good health and for disease prevention. According to The Center for Disease Control (CDC), however, despite the proven benefits of physical activity, more than 50 percent of American adults do not get enough physical activity to provide health benefits, and 25 percent of adults are not active at all in their leisure time (www.cdc.gov/nccdphp/dnpa/physical/everyone/index.htm).

Physical activity is something that benefits everyone, and it does not necessarily have to be hard or challenging. According to the CDC, moderate-intensity physical activities will bring the health benefits you need to function optimally in life. Their current recommendations include physical activities such as cardio or aerobic activities and resistance, strength-building, and weight-bearing activities. For students trying hard to balance time and schedules, the questions of how much exercise is necessary becomes important. The CDC website provides the following recommendations.

- **Cardio or aerobic activities**. Achieve the aerobic activity recommendation through one of the following options:
    - A minimum of 30 minutes of moderate-intensity physical activity per day (such as brisk walking) most days of the week

    or

    - A minimum of 20 minutes of vigorous-intensity physical activity (such as jogging or running) 3 days a week

---

- **Resistance, strength-building, and weight-bearing activities**. Two days a week, incorporate strength training into your routine. Strength training activities, such as weight lifting, maintain and increase muscle strength and endurance. A goal to reach towards is completing 6-8 strength training exercises, with 8–12 repetitions per exercise.

Moderate-intensity exercises include activities such as:
- Dancing
- Riding a stationary bike
- Actively playing with children
- Taking Jazzercise
- Mowing lawn, general
- Frisbee playing, general
- Playing golf, walking the course

- Shoveling light snow
- Downhill skiing with light effort
- Raking leaves
- Hand washing/waxing a car
- Playing basketball, shooting hoops
- Walking, brisk pace (mall/around a track/treadmill)
- Doing water aerobics

Vigorous-intensity exercises include activities such as:
- Racewalking, jogging or running
- Swimming laps
- Tennis, singles
- Bicycling more than 10 mph, or on steep uphill terrain
- Circuit training – a combination of strength, endurance and aerobic exercises

Here are four suggestions that can help you get going with a physical fitness program:

1. Find a time in your schedule where you can exercise on a regular basis.

2. Choose activities that you will enjoy. This gives you a better chance of sticking to it

3. If possible, find someone else to join with you. This makes it a more enjoyable activity because of the shared experience.

4. Exercise within your capabilities. Many people try to do something that is too far beyond them right at the start and end up straining a muscle. They then are back out of action and do not develop the habit of exercising.

▶ Sleep: An often-ignored key to health and success in college

Have you ever sat down in an afternoon class and spent the entire class period trying not to fall asleep? In fact you might be one of those students who doesn't even try to fight it, but just goes ahead and sleeps through the whole class. Sleep is an important part of all aspects of health. Getting enough sleep can help you think more clearly, get your work done consistently and on time, and complete complex tasks and just plain have more enjoyment to life.

Unfortunately, the ages from 12 to 25 years are often a phase of your life when getting enough sleep at consistent times becomes a real struggle. In a research completed in 1997 by a Working Group on Problem Sleepiness at the National Institutes of Health (NIH), adolescents and young adults (the age bracket just mentioned) were identified as a population at high risk for problem sleepiness. Serious risks were identified with this problem, leading the group to recommend that steps must be taken to reduce the risks.

The National Sleep Foundation Research Report and Resource Guide on *Adolescent Sleep Needs and Patterns* (2000) has used this and other studies to base its findings and recommendations. It identified four risks with problem sleepiness:

1. Increased risk of unintentional injuries and death

2. Low grades and poor school performance

3. Negative moods

4. Increased likelihood of stimulant use

You don't have to look at that list very long to determine that sleep is an important element of physical health and a successful college experience. The National Sleep Foundation Report (2000) cites the work of Carskadon et al. (1980) as recommending 8.5 to 9.25 hours of sleep for this age bracket. The report points out that this age bracket, however, averages about 7 hours of sleep each night, with 6.5 hours being more typical of sleep on a school night. The conclusion that can be drawn is that students are not getting the amount of sleep they need to operate at an optimal level and to avoid the risks listed above.

So what can you do to improve this in your college experience? Cuseo, Fecas, and Thompson (2007) offer ten suggestions. Here is a brief summary of their list:

Increase awareness of your sleep habits by keeping a sleep log or sleep journal.

Make special note of nights when you slept well or poorly and note what you did before going to bed on those nights. Look for relationships between certain things you do (or don't do) during the day on nights that you sleep well.

Attempt to get into a regular sleep schedule by going to sleep and getting up at about the same time each day.

An irregular sleep schedule can disrupt the quality of sleep. If you can get your body into a regular sleep schedule or cycle, you're more likely to establish a biological rhythm that makes it easier for you to fall asleep, stay asleep, and awake naturally from sleep according to your own "internal" alarm clock. Try to preserve a somewhat stable sleep schedule even during midterms and finals. This will help you stay physically and mentally alert for those exams.

Sleep in the same place each night.

We are creatures of habit. By sleeping in the same environment, these sensations become repeatedly associated with sleep; and when they are encountered, our body is more likely to respond automatically by falling asleep.

Make sure the temperature of your sleep room is not too hot (no higher than 70 degrees).

For most people quality, uninterrupted sleep is more likely to take place at cooler, more comfortable room temperatures.

Attempt to get into a relaxing bedtime ritual each night.

Find some activity that is particularly relaxing for you and make it into a bedtime ritual. This can get you into a worry-free state and help you fall asleep sooner.

Avoid intense mental activity just before going to sleep.

Light mental work may serve as a relaxing pre-sleep ritual, but cramming intensely for a difficult exam or doing intensive writing before bedtime is likely

EXERCISES

to generate a state of mental arousal, which will interfere with your ability to "wind down" and fall asleep.

Avoid intense physical exercise before going to sleep.

Physical exercise tends to energize you and keeps you from falling asleep. If you're going to exercise in the evening, it should be done at least three hours before going to sleep.

Avoid consuming sleep-interfering foods, beverages, or drugs in the late afternoon or evening.

In particular, avoid stimulants like caffeine or any food that will activate your digestive system in a significant way.

Modify your environment.

If you are consistently awakened by noise or you are disturbed by light or brightness, consider wearing earplugs or eyeshades to bed.

When planning your daily work schedule, be aware of your natural biological rhythms—your peak periods and down times.

Studies show that humans prefer to go to sleep early and wake up early, and others prefer to stay up late at night and get up late in the morning. Be aware of your most productive hours of the day and schedule your highest priority work and most challenging tasks at times when you tend to work at peak effectiveness, and schedule lighter work at times when your energy level tends to be lower. Also, keep your natural peak and down time in mind when you schedule your courses. Attempt to arrange your class schedule in such a way that you experience your most challenging courses at times of the day when your body and mind are most ready to accept that challenge.

▶ Evaluating Your Physical Well-Being

Based on the information in the preceding discussion on physical well-being, answer the questions below to explore where your physical status is at right now.

1. How would you describe your eating habits as contrasted with the Healthy Eating Pyramid?

_____

_____

_____

_____

_____

_____

EXERCISES

2. What steps could you take to improve your diet and nutrition?

_____

_____

_____

_____

_____

3. In which category did your BMI place you?

_____

4. Based on this, what actions do you need to take in your life?

_____

_____

_____

_____

_____

5. What is the best time in your schedule when you can exercise on a regular basis?

_____

6. What moderate-intensity activity do you enjoy most?

_____

7. What facilities are at your school or near your school that could be used for this activity?

_____

_____

8. What vigorous-intensity activity do you enjoy most?

_____

9. What facilities are at your school or near your school that could be used for this activity?

_____

_____

EXERCISES

10. Identify a friend or friends who could join with you in this activity.

    _____

11. What did you learn about your sleep habits from your sleep log/journal?

    _____

    _____

    _____

    _____

    _____

    _____

12. What would be the best time for you to go to sleep and to get up?

    _____

    _____

13. Describe your favorite sleeping environment.

    _____

    _____

    _____

14. What can you do to create such an environment in your college room?

    _____

    _____

    _____

15. What nighttime activity is particularly relaxing for you?

    _____

16. How could you incorporate this into a bedtime ritual?

    _____

    _____

    _____

EXERCISES

▶ References

The following resources have been used in this chapter.

Fralick, M.F. (2006). *College & Career Success*, (3rd ed.), Dubuque, IA: Kendall/Hunt Publishing Company.

National Institutes of Health, National Center on Sleep Disorders Research and Office of Prevention, Education, and Control. (1997, August). Working group report on problem sleepiness. Washington, DC: U.S. Government Printing Office, (2000).

National Sleep Foundation Research Report and Resource Guide. (2000). *Adolescent Sleep Needs and Patterns*. Washington, DC: Author.

Willett, W.C. (2005). *Eat Drink and Be Healthy: The Harvard Medical School Guide to Healthy Eating*. New York: Free Press.

The following resources may be useful to you in your continuing exploration of Life Calling as you look at your Unique Design and your *physical strengths*.

Centers for Disease Control: www.cdc.gov

Millard, B. (1996). *LifeQuest: Planning Your Life Strategically*. Ventura, CA: Life Discovery Publications.

Schwen, M.R., and Bass, D.C., Eds. (2006). *Leading Lives That Matter: What We Should Do and Who We Should Be*. Grand Rapids, Michigan: Erdmans Publishing Co.

Empowered by Emotional Strengths

Strengths MATRIX ™	DIMENSIONS				TOTAL
	Gifts	**Knowledge**	**Skills**	**Attitude**	
D O M A I N S Physical					
Emotional					
Intellectual					
Psychological					
Spiritual					

FIGURE 7-1
Emotional Doman of the *Strength Matrix*™

The *Strengths Matrix* is comprised of five strengths domains. In this chapter we will explore ***Emotional Strengths***.

CHAPTER OBJECTIVES

1. Understand the nature and value of emotional strengths as expressed in the concept of Emotional Intelligence
2. Identify four abilities associated with Emotional Intelligence
3. Begin identifying emotional strengths in your life

KEY TERMS

Emotion = that part of the consciousness that involves feeling and the capacity to detect and respond to sensory stimuli
Environment = the totality of surrounding things, conditions, or influences
Feeling = extra-rational internal sensation not connected with sight, hearing, taste, smell, or what is classically correlated to touch

Concepts

What are the most important and significant experiences you will have during this school year? If you start to list them in your mind, you will find that they will likely be full of emotion. You may go to your first class and feel both excitement and apprehension. You may get your first "A" in college and feel pride and satisfaction. You may make a new friend and gain a real sense of belonging. You may give your first speech or class presentation and feel nervous. You may try out for the varsity basketball team, and if you don't make the cut, you may feel depressed or angry at what you see as rejection. Whether they are positive, negative, or neutral, emotions play an important role in our lives because they alert us to something important in ourselves or in our environment.

Successfully navigating your college experience will likely call into play your ability to effectively work with your emotions, and this takes us to the concept of *emotional strengths*. We defined the *emotional strengths* domain as the capacity in our lives that enables us to experience feelings and sensibility. What do we mean by these terms? When we talk about our feelings, we are describing an experiential state that builds within us in response to sensations, sentiments, or desires we encounter. Sensibility refers to our responsiveness toward other things or persons, such as the feelings of another person or changes in the environment.

If we were to collect all the words in the English language that express our emotions, they would probably number in the hundreds. The paradox, however, is that with all those words, we still have great difficulty describing our emotional experiences to others. Why is that? Perhaps it stems from the view of emotions throughout the history of Western civilization. Emotions have, for the most part, been seen as a disruption to rational thinking and a hindrance to making good decisions. But now that view is changing.

John Mayer, a psychologist at the University of New Hampshire, and Peter Salovey, a psychologist at Yale University (currently Dean of Yale College), proposed the concept of emotional intelligence, defining it as "the ability to monitor one's own and others' feelings and emotions, to discriminate among them, and to use this information to guide one's thinking and action" (Mayer & Salovey, 1993; Salovey & Mayer, 1990). Mayer and Salovey have been joined by another psychologist, David Caruso, in systematizing the study of emotional intelligence and developing a credible tool for measuring it (Mayer-Salovey-Caruso Emotional Intelligence Test, or MSCEIT, 2002). Daniel Goleman, a journalist specializing in the area of the brain and psychology, worked from the writings of Mayer and Salovey to popularize the concept of emotional intelligence in his international bestseller, *Emotional Intelligence* (Goleman, 1995).

Rather than seeing emotions as some sort of a primitive aberration in people that leads them to make mistakes and experience regrets, instead the findings show "that emotion is not just important but absolutely necessary for us to make good decisions, take optimal action to solve problems, cope with change, and succeed" (Caruso & Salovey, 2004). It is not hard to see, then, that emotional strengths play an important part in the discovery of a Life

Calling. The basis for emotional intelligence is made up of four skills or strengths:

1. **Identify and Express Emotions**. This is the fundamental ability to recognize feelings and emotions by (a) being aware of emotional clues in yourself and in people around you, (b) being able to discern between different types of emotion, (c) being able to identify the level of intensity to which the emotion is present, and (d) being able to identify what these emotional clues mean.

   People with strength in this ability are better pilots of their lives because they have a surer sense of how they really feel about personal decisions from whom to marry to what job to take. They are also tuned in to the emotions of others and as a result have healthier and stronger relationships.

2. **Use or Generate Emotions**. This is the ability to know which emotions or moods are best for different situations and to get yourself into the "right mood."

   People with strength in this ability employ their feelings to enhance their thinking and endeavors. They realize that emotions, when rightly used, can help them solve problems, make better decisions, reason out situations, and be more creative. They will be more self-motivated and will prioritize their thinking process based on emotional input.

3. **Understand Emotions**. This is the ability to recognize and grasp emotional information. This starts by gaining an emotional vocabulary—knowledge of simple and complex emotional terms. It then adds emotional comprehension—understanding how emotions combine to form another emotion, progress or intensify, or transition from one emotion to another. Finally, emotional analysis occurs—being able to understand possible causes of emotions and predict what kind of emotions people will have in different situations.

   People with strength in this ability have a solid grasp of emotional intelligence. They will tend to be more accurate in their interpretation of moods and emotional situations, and as a result will be more likely to deal correctly with such situations.

4. **Manage Emotions**. This is the ability to regulate emotions in yourself and in other people. This involves monitoring, observing and distinguishing differences, and accurately labeling emotions as they are encountered. This ability is based on the belief that feelings and moods can be improved or modified, with strategies being developed to accomplish this. This does not mean, however, the denial or suppression of your emotions or the emotions of others.

   People with strength in this ability can bounce back quickly from life's setbacks and upsets. They are also able to assess the effectiveness of how they recognize and handle emotions in various situations.

Concepts Summary

Ironically, emotional strengths may be confused in our modern society with weakness, and society responds by not placing as great a value on this strength domain. As a result, we end up with a culture where relationships are confused and people try to hide from each other. This inner turmoil often leads to feelings of inferiority and self-doubt and causes confusion in the search for a Life Calling.

Emotional strengths are harder to detect than physical strengths. Once again, one of the most effective ways is listening to what those who know us well say about us. Another way is to complete exercises and assessments of our emotional strengths. We will look more closely at some examples of how to do this in the Exercises section of this chapter.

Remember, each of the strength dimensions provides a bridge among the other dimensions. Emotional strengths provide the bridge of *feelings* among the other strengths. What do we mean by this? It is through our emotions that we actually sense and feel what is going on with the other strengths. This adds color and vitality to our lives.

▶ Insight

When the Bible addresses emotions, it most often uses the heart to identify the source of these emotions. Scriptures associated with the role of emotions provide abundant insight related to how these can affect our pursuit of a Life Calling.

SCRIPTURAL INSIGHT 1 ▷ *Who Do You See When You Look in the Mirror?*

If any of you think you are something when you are nothing, you deceive yourselves. Each of you should test your own actions. Then you can take pride in yourself, without comparing yourself to somebody else, for each of you should carry your own load. GALATIANS 6:3-5

Have you ever been around people who have a very unrealistic view of themselves? Sometimes it is seen in a very negative self-image, but many times it manifests itself in an image that is something quite a bit better than is warranted.

Consider the giant Goliath as an example. He had convinced himself that he was invincible. He failed to realize that adeptness was as important as size in combat. When he saw David (who, if you remember, was rather physically fit himself) come out to meet him, he ridiculed him. "'Am I a dog, that you come at me with sticks?' And the Philistine cursed David by his gods. 'Come here,' he said, 'and I'll give your flesh to the birds and the wild animals!'" (1 Samuel 17:43&44). Of course, you know the end of this story. David defeated Goliath.

Such a distorted view of self can hinder the discovery of a Life Calling. That's why the Apostle Paul was constantly exhorting those whom he taught to strive toward a more effective Christian life. He had a keen insight into the human condition, and that's why he cautioned in the passage in Galatians 6 that we need to have a realistic view of ourselves.

We need to take caution that we don't misread what Paul counseled in this passage. He is not saying that we should think of ourselves as nothing, in the sense of worthless. Instead, he is concerned about people who do not have good self-awareness. They either see themselves in a manner no one else does, or they fail to see themselves in a manner in which nearly everyone else does. In either case they lack self-awareness. The emotional strength Paul encourages is for each of us to look inside of ourselves and test ourselves so that we know who we are. He cautions not to try to be somebody else, but to know ourselves and to be ourselves. That is what he means by carrying our own load.

In the search for a Life Calling, those who have this emotional strength will find the search easier. They will avoid the confusion caused by copying someone else's self-identity rather than living their own identity.

> **PERSONAL REFLECTION** ▷ Who do you see when you look in the mirror? Have you learned to see yourself with a healthy reality and to praise God for who you are? What can help you have better self image?

SCRIPTURAL INSIGHT 2 ▷ *Learn to Know in Your Spirit as Well as in Your Mind*

Immediately Jesus knew in his spirit that this was what they were thinking in their hearts... MARK 2:8

For most of his years of ministry, Jesus lived in the town of Capernaum. One day when he was at the home where he stayed, some men brought a friend of theirs who was paralyzed to Jesus so that he could heal the man. There was such a crowd around Jesus that they could not get to him. Just a few months prior to writing this section of the book, I stood in the ruins of that house. It was not very big, so if a crowd was around Jesus, it would have been impossible to get a man on a stretcher through to Jesus. The friends were not deterred, however. They climbed to the roof, likely made of palm branches and mud, and made an opening through which they lowered their friend. We pick up the story in Mark 2:5-12.

When Jesus saw their faith, he said to the paralyzed man, "Son, your sins are forgiven."

Now some teachers of the law were sitting there, thinking to themselves, "Why does this fellow talk like that? He's blaspheming! Who can forgive sins but God alone?"

Immediately Jesus knew in his spirit that this was what they were thinking in their hearts, and he said to them, "Why are you thinking these things? Which is easier: to say to this paralyzed man, 'Your sins are forgiven,' or to say, 'Get up, take your mat and walk'? But I want you to know that the Son of Man has authority on earth to forgive sins." So he said to the man, "I tell you, get up, take your mat and go home." He got up, took his mat and walked out in full view of them all. This amazed everyone and they praised God, saying, "We have never seen anything like this!"

In our study of emotional strengths, the key phrase in this story is, "Immediately Jesus knew in his spirit that this was what they were thinking in their hearts." The mistake on our part would be to think that only Jesus could know this. As we learn to listen to the emotions of others more closely, we will find that we can develop the ability to recognize them even without any words being spoken.

Consider the example of King Artaxerxes and Nehemiah. Nehemiah was troubled about his fellow Jews in Jerusalem, and when he came before the king, Artaxerxes could recognize this. He asked Nehemiah, "Why does your face look so sad when you are not ill? This can be nothing but sadness of heart" (Nehemiah 2:2). This emotional sensitivity by the king led to a great initiative for the Jews leading to the rebuilding of Jerusalem.

Because of how they are "wired" internally, this is an emotional strength that is easier for some and more difficult for others. However, it is something all of us can learn to do at some level. Because our Life Calling is directly tied to service to others, we can be far more effective at discovering our purpose and carrying it out when we can recognize the emotions of others.

> **PERSONAL REFLECTION**   Do you take time to read the emotions of others, or do you just plunge on ahead in your life regardless of what is happening with others? What can you do to strengthen your ability to identify the emotions of others and to value them?

SCRIPTURAL INSIGHT 3   *Emotional Strength Can Help You Learn to Keep the Peace*

Blessed are the peacemakers, for they will be called children of God. MATTHEW 5:9

Not only did Jesus call peacemakers blessed in the Sermon on the Mount, but later he stated to the people: "You are the salt of the earth." (Matthew 5:13-14) What did he mean by that? The answer can be found in his later words recorded in Mark 9:50: *Salt is good, but if it loses its saltiness, how can you make it salty again? Have salt in yourselves, and be at peace with each other.*

To be "the salt of the earth," must mean to maintain relationships of peace with others—relationships characterized by combining the various elements of personality into a mosaic of pleasant interaction. The Apostle James asserted that "peacemakers who sow in peace raise a harvest of righteousness" (James 3:18).

In his 1989 speech accepting the Nobel Peace Prize, the Dalai Lama, the spiritual and political leader of the Tibetan people, shared this remarkable insight that identified the key to outward peace:

> Inner peace is the key: if you have inner peace, the external problems do not affect your deep sense of peace and tranquility. In that state of mind you can deal with situations with calmness and reason, while keeping your inner happiness. This is very important. Without this inner peace, no matter how comfortable your life is materially, you may still be worried, disturbed or unhappy because of circumstances.

And as we discovered in the earlier quote, it begins with an inner peace. This is a true emotional strength. Again, because of how they are "wired" internally, this is an emotional strength that is easier for some more than others. But it is available to all. The Apostle Paul informs us that the peace of God, which transcends all understanding, will guard your hearts and your minds in Christ Jesus (Philippians 4:7). So to gain a greater sense of peace and emotional strength, we should begin with the peace of God found in a relationship with Jesus.

What can we learn from all of these scriptures? We can learn that emotional strength exists and we should strive to develop this type of strength. We also need to realize that just like in any other strength domain, some of us will be stronger in certain areas while others of us will be stronger in the other areas. Knowing this will help us in our search for our Life Calling.

INSIGHT

PERSONAL REFLECTION ⟩ Does your emotional strength lead you to fully experience God and others? How can you help your emotions become salt, leading you to be at peace with others?

SCRIPTURAL INSIGHT 4 ⟩ *Sometimes You Need Something to Keep You Going*

All these people were still living by faith when they died. They did not receive the things promised; they only saw them and welcomed them from a distance. And they admitted that they were aliens and strangers on earth. People who say such things show that they are looking for a country of their own. If they had been thinking of the country they had left, they would have had opportunity to return. Instead, they were longing for a better country—a heavenly one. Therefore God is not ashamed to be called their God, for he has prepared a city for them. HEBREWS 11:13-16

INSIGHT

What is it that keeps somebody going when things go wrong or goals are not immediately met? We've all met people who have this kind of determination and we often wish we could catch a little bit of it from them. There is something inside of them driving this determination. Hebrews 11 provides a valuable insight to this inner quality. This chapter has often been called the Hall of Faith because it provides a list of people who achieved great things by the power of their inner faith. Faith can become a powerful bridge between our spirits and our emotions. The Bible characters honored in this chapter certainly exhibited a high degree of self-motivation, but it was based on their faith.

Now we might be tempted to argue that these people were not self-motivated but rather reward-motivated. After all, wasn't the hope for a heavenly home what kept them going? It would be a mistake for us to believe that self-motivation means a complete absence of sensitivity to rewards or consequences. But we rarely receive these immediately. They are often distant in the future. Emotional strength helps us to understand our feelings and inform them with our faith. Remember we started our search for a Life Calling by exploring our Foundational Values of faith and how this faith needs to be lived out in our character.

Emotional strength that becomes an internal self-motivator means that we respond to life's challenges and opportunities on our own as opposed to responding from the pressure of others. This will be an important capacity for distinguishing our own Life Calling from those that others try to impose upon us.

> **PERSONAL REFLECTION** > What is it that is inside of you motivating your life right now? Do you take time to listen to it? How are you allowing your faith to be a bridge between your spirit and your emotions?

SCRIPTURAL INSIGHT 5 > *Emotionally Strong Lives Produce Spiritual Fruit*

But the fruit of the Spirit is love, joy, peace, patience, kindness, goodness, faithfulness, gentleness and self-control. Against such things there is no law. Those who belong to Christ Jesus have crucified the sinful nature with its passions and desires. GALATIANS 5:22-24

The Apostle Paul's outline of the "Fruit of the Spirit" is one of the better-known passages in scripture. The final component of this fruit identified in the list is self-control. Paul expands on this concept with the statement on crucifying the sinful nature with its passions and desires. Is he saying that we should not have passions or desires—or emotions at all? No! Rather he is exhorting us to manage our emotions and control those that are sinful and would result in spiritual failure.

James, the early leader of the Christian church in Jerusalem, applied this same concept specifically to the emotion of anger. He says, "my dear brothers and sisters, take note of this: Everyone should be quick to listen, slow to speak and slow to become angry, because our anger does not produce the righteousness that God desires." (James 1:19, 20)

If you look back over the list of components in spiritual fruit, you will see many tied to emotions. It would be a mistake, then, to confuse self-control with stifling emotions. If we did this, we would in reality be stifling spiritual fruit.

One last thought on managing our emotions comes from Proverbs 25: 25-27. "It is not good to eat too much honey, nor is it honorable to seek one's own honor. Like a city whose walls are broken down is a man who lacks self-control."

Those who are strong in managing their emotions live a less-vulnerable life. Those who don't manage their emotions have no barriers, and they end up vulnerable to a variety of emotional attacks. This can often cause them confusion as they attempt to discover a Life Calling.

PERSONAL REFLECTION ▷ Are you sensitive to your emotions, determining when to use them and when to hold them in waiting? Do you use self-control or do you just stifle all emotions? What can help you see your emotional strengths as a strong asset in your life?

INSIGHT

Discovery

How can the Discovery Guides help you identify and understand your *emotional strengths*?

T **THEORY**	The best source of theory about emotional intelligence can be found in the research and writings of Drs. Jack Mayer, Peter Salovey, and David Caruso. The work of Dr. Reuven Bar-On is a good secondary source, and the writings of Ronald Goldman can be used as a popular summary of theory. You might also be able to increase your knowledge about Emotional Strengths in psychology classes at your college or university.
E **EXAMPLES**	Find people who excel in these various areas of emotional strengths. Observe them and find time to talk to them. Ask them to share with you how they discovered and developed these emotional strengths.
A **ASSESSMENT**	A variety of assessments claim to measure emotional intelligence and strengths. You might want to use some of these to help you assess your own emotional strengths. The *Mayer-Salovey-Caruso Emotional Intelligence Test (MSCEIT)* is the best assessment. This assessment should be used, however, only in conjunction with a professional administrator trained in how to use and debrief it with you.
C **COUNSEL**	Professional counselors and life coaches are trained to help you explore emotional strengths. Your college and university will likely have a counseling center, and they may have counselors trained in emotional intelligence. Make sure if they use tools like the *MSCEIT*, they have received training in how to use the tool. Additionally, family members, teachers, pastors, and friends know you well and can give you valuable insights about yourself.
H **HISTORY**	Search for historical biographies of notable people who have exhibited these emotional strengths. Select some of these and learn from their experience. Also study the developmental history of the theory of emotional intelligence.
E **EXPERIENCE**	Get involved with activities where your emotional strengths will be tested. This includes just about every relationship with others you might have. You will learn quickly whether or not you have skills in the four abilities.
R **REFLECTION**	Take time to listen to your emotions and reflect on what you hear. Reflect on how you could become more effective in listening to your emotions and using emotional information in guiding your life. Reflect on your disposition or attitude about emotional strengths in general and yours in particular.

DISCOVERY

Story

It had been a full day: First Plymouth Rock, then the Plimouth Plantation, and finally a trip to the Cranberry World Visitors Center to see how Ocean Spray actually grows and produces all their products. While there, they learned that the majority of cranberries were grown in Massachusetts. Then they had returned to the *Nautilus* to eat and crash for the rest of the evening.

"That stuff about physical strengths was really interesting, Adam," Abriella said as their conversation began to dwindle into silence. "We're all so different, but we're all good friends."

"Even Ryan and Lorena?" Diana asked teasingly.

"Aw, come on. We love each other." Ryan reached out his hand to Lorena and she grabbed it, laughing. The two of them had been at each other's throats since they were in kindergarten, but they were always there for each other as well. The other four never could completely understand the relationship.

"You learn a lot about yourself when you talk through things like that," Abriella continued. "It helps you see why you think the way you do and move in the directions you go. I'd like to explore the other strengths as well."

"Me too," Diana joined in. The others nodded their heads in agreement.

"What about emotional strengths?" Abriella asked.

"Ohhhhh boy!" Diana exclaimed. "If we were hoping to get to sleep early tonight, I think that just went out the window."

"What are you saying, Diana?" Justin laughed. "That we're a bunch of emotional wrecks?"

"You think?" Diana answered with a hint of sarcasm.

"What about Adam there—Mr. Rock of Gibraltar?" Justin quickly came back with the question.

"Hey, I have my moments and days," Adam broke in.

I think most of us would be glad to take any of your worst days, Adam," Lorena said. The others murmured in agreement. They loved him and valued his strength in their group. No one challenged it or resented it.

Adam was about to respond but then thought better of it. The others put a lot of pressure on him, but he had learned to accept his role.

STORY

"I find it really hard to read emotions sometimes," Abriella reflected. "Just look around at all of us right now. Can you tell what kind of mood we are in?"

"I think we'd better go back to physical strengths," Justin half-jokingly suggested. "I don't think I'm going to do too well in this area."

"It's so easy to just let life happen and never think about what's going on inside of you." Diana shifted in her chair. "But I guess you never have that problem, Adam."

"Don't be so sure, Diana," Adam replied. "Sometimes I can feel a lot of pressure from you guys, and it gets a little lonely. But I don't stop to recognize it, and I never talk about it." Adam's eyes were visibly moist. The motorhome grew very silent.

Abriella reached over and grabbed one of Adam's hands. Lorena placed her hand on his shoulder.

After a minute or two, Adam broke the silence. "I guess part of emotional strength is being able manage your emotions." He began to laugh, and the others all joined in. "It's a strength to know what emotions are appropriate at what time."

"Yeah, but that doesn't mean you should always stuff your emotions, does it?" Lorena asked.

"No, I don't think it does. I think the ability to manage emotions means you know when to let them out as well," Adam replied.

"Like you just did?" Diana asked.

"Like I just *almost* did," Adam corrected. His personal turmoil still needed to be dealt with, but he had stopped before this could happen. The others sensed this.

"Sometimes I feel that even when I recognize my emotions, I don't want to use them—like they're a weakness or something," Adam continued. "I think if I could get over this, I would be able to make better decisions and maybe even have more self-motivation."

"That counts Ryan out!" Lorena exclaimed. "He can't get enough motivation to even go to college."

"Give it a rest, Lor," Ryan sighed. "You'll be old by the time you finish all that doctor training stuff.

Besides, I'm self-motivated to do the things I care about. I'd like to see you swim out against the waves with your board."

"I'm not sure we really understand emotions or how they are a strength." Adam realized that he'd better move on quickly. "I think understanding them is important."

"Well that counts Lorena out," Ryan announced, returning Lorena's volley. She slapped him on the back.

"See? There's the evidence!" Ryan pointed out to the others. "I'm a very sensitive and fragile person, but Lor never lets up on me. Who knows how scarred I am in life?"

Lorena rolled her eyes and began playing an imaginary violin.

"We should just banish the two of them to a deserted tropical isle," Diana suggested.

Adam smiled, but in his own mind he was not so sure that the two of them would mind that as much as the others might think.

"So what does it all mean—to have emotional strength?" Abriella asked.

"I think it all boils down to working effectively with our own emotions and those of other people in relationships," Adam replied.

"Like Diana?" Justin asked.

"I would think so," Adam answered. "Diana gets along so well with all of us because she can recognize our emotions so easily, and she understands and appreciates them."

"But I think you do too, Adam," Diana replied. "You get along with us, and you help us get along with each other. I see that as a tremendous strength." The others agreed.

"Let's be careful." Lorena laughed and gave Adam a hug. "Or we'll get Adam crying again." Adam rolled his eyes, but he returned her hug.

"Hey, you philosophers. Are you going to keep on like this all night, or do you plan to sleep?" Ken asked from the other end of the motorhome.

"Good point, Captain Nemo," Ryan called. "I was just going to suggest the same thing."

And just like that the day ended.

Expanding Your Understanding of Your Emotional Abilities Using the *Emotional-Abilities 360*

1. Identify four different people who know you and who love and care for you. Choose the four so that they represent each of the following categories:
   • Parent _____
   • Teacher (present or former) _____
   • Friend _____
   • Sibling or relative who is younger than you _____

2. Provide all of the people you have identified with a copy of the *Emotional-Abilities 360* (not the Mirror) chart below and ask them to answer the questions for each of the four emotional abilities. Let them know that it is okay if they answer that they have not seen an ability as being strong in your life. Tell them this will help you better understand yourself. Encourage them to give an example if they answer that an ability is strong in you.

Emotional Abilities 360	Definition	How strong do you see this emotional ability in me (weak, moderate, strong, very strong)?	Can you give me an example of when you have seen this emotional ability in me?
Identify Emotions	This is the fundamental ability to recognize feelings and emotions by (a) being aware of emotional clues in yourself and in people around you, (b) being able to discern between different types of emotions, (c) being able to identify the level of intensity to which the emotion is present, and (d) being able to identify what these emotional clues mean.		
Use Emotions	This is the ability to know which emotions or moods are best for different situations and to get yourself into the "right mood."		
Understand Emotions	This is the ability to recognize and grasp emotional information by developing an emotional vocabulary, emotional comprehension, and emotional		

(Continued)

Emotional Abilities 360	Definition	How strong do you see this emotional ability in me (weak, moderate, strong, very strong)?	Can you give me an example of when you have seen this emotional ability in me?
	analysis that understands possible causes of emotions and predict what kind of emotions people will have in different situations.		
Manage Emotions	This is the ability to regulate emotions in yourself and in other people by monitoring, observing and distinguishing differences, and accurately labeling emotions as they are encountered. This does not mean, however, the denial or suppression of your emotions or the emotions of others.		

3. Now you personally answer the questions for each of four abilities using the results from Exercise 1 and your perception.

Emotional Abilities Mirror	Definition	How strong did I see this emotional ability in myself (weak, moderate, strong, very strong)?	What has been my most effective example of when I used this emotional ability?
Identify Emotions	This is the fundamental ability to recognize feelings and emotions by (a) being aware of emotional clues in yourself and in people around you, (b) being able to discern between different types of emotions, (c) being able to identify the level of intensity to which the emotion is present, and (d) being able to identify what these emotional clues mean.		
Use Emotions	This is the ability to know which emotions or moods are best for different situations and to get yourself into the "right mood."		

Emotional Abilities Mirror	Definition	How strong did I see this emotional ability in myself (weak, moderate, strong, very strong)?	What has been my most effective example of when I used this emotional ability?
Understand Emotions	This is the ability to recognize and grasp emotional information by developing an emotional vocabulary, emotional comprehension, and emotional analysis that understands possible causes of emotions and predict what kind of emotions people will have in different situations.		
Manage Emotions	This is the ability to regulate emotions in yourself and in other people by monitoring, observing and distinguishing differences, and accurately labeling emotions as they are encountered. This does not mean, however, the denial or suppression of your emotions or the emotions of others.		

4. Compare your scores to the evaluation from others in the Physical-Strengths 360. What do others see in you that you may not see in yourself? What can you learn about your perception of yourself?

5. Reflect on what you learned in both Exercise 1 and Exercise 2 and summarize below what they have revealed to you about yourself.

EXERCISES

4. Manage your stress

If you are experiencing high levels of stress, what can you do to keep this from overpowering you?

a. Monitor your emotions to gather important information about your state of emotional wellbeing. Use this information to make a decision, and adapt your behavior.

Use good self-talk. Apply the emotional strength of "what if" thinking to bring direction to chaotic emotions and thoughts. This will help you gain a better understanding of all the different scenarios possible in your situation. This often also has a calming influence.

c. Attend to your spiritual wellbeing. It has a direct relationship to your emotional wellbeing and your level of stress. You will learn more about how to do this in Chapter 10. Give special attention to meditational solitude and prayer.

d. Attend to your physical wellbeing. It also has a strong relationship to your emotional wellbeing and your level of stress. Give special attention to diet, aerobic exercise and sleep.

e. Practice breathing exercises to help calm your thoughts.

"Practicing regular, mindful breathing can be calming and energizing and can even help with stress-related health problems ranging from panic attacks to digestive disorders." Andrew Weil, M.D. (2008). For students this can include test anxieties as well.

f. Listen to soothing music that relaxes you rather than excites you.

g. Lie down in a comfortable place and tense and relax your muscles. Start with the muscles in your head and work your way down to your toes. Tense each muscle for five to ten seconds and then release the tension completely.

h. Talk to a friend who is a good listener.

i. Find something to make you laugh. Laughter actually releases endorphins that improve your mood and decrease levels of the stress-causing hormones.

j. Imagine yourself in a pleasant place. Choose a place that has good memories for you. Create a mind picture as you think about this place.

k. Keep things in perspective. Remind yourself of what is going well. Rationally think through best and worst case scenarios. Focus on the bigger picture rather than the immediate picture. Ask yourself how important this issue will be in the longrun.

▶ References

The following resources have been used in this chapter.

The following resources have either been used in this chapter or may be useful to you in your continuing exploration of Life Calling as you look at your Unique Design and your *emotional strengths*.

Caruso, D., Kornacki, S., & Brackett, M. (2006). *Teaching Emotional Intelligence Skills*. Stamford, CT: EI Skills Group.

Mayer, J.D., and Salovey, P. (1993). "The Intelligence of Emotional Intelligence." *Intelligence*, 17, 433–442.

Salovey, P., and Mayer, J.D. (1990). "Emotional intelligence." *Imagination, Cognition, and Personality*, 9, 185–211.

Weil, A. (2008). http://www.drweil.com/drw/u/id/ART00521

The following resources may be useful to you in your continuing exploration of Life Calling as you look at your Unique Design and your *emotional strengths*.

Caruso, D., & Salovey, P. (2004). *The Emotionally Intelligent Manager*. San Francisco, CA: Jossey-Bass.

Fralick, M.F. (2011). *College & Career Success*, 5/e. Dubuque, IA: Kendall/ Hunt Publishing Company.

Goleman, D. (1995). *Emotional Intelligence: Why It Can Matter More than IQ*. New York: Bantam Books.

Livermore, D. (2009). *Leading with Cultural Intelligence: The New Secret to Success*. New York, NY: AMACOM.

Saccone, S. (2009). *Relational Intelligence: How Leaders Can Expand Their Influence Through a New Way of Being Smart*. San Francisco, CA: Jossey-Bass Publishers.

Schwen, M.R., and Bass, D.C., Eds. (2006). *Leading Lives That Matter: What We Should Do and Who We Should Be*. Grand Rapids, Michigan: Erdmans Publishing Co.

REFERENCES

Empowered by Intellectual Strengths

Strengths MATRIX™	DIMENSIONS				
	Gifts	**Knowledge**	**Skills**	**Attitude**	**TOTAL**
D O M A I N S Physical					
Emotional					
Intellectual					
Psychological					
Spiritual					

FIGURE 8-1
Intellectual Domain of the ***Strengths Matrix™***

The *Strengths Matrix* is comprised of five strengths domains. In this chapter we will explore ***Intellectual Strengths***.

CHAPTER OBJECTIVES

1. Understand the nature and value of intellectual strengths
2. Identify the discovery, process, and application disciplines associated with intellectual strengths
3. Begin identifying intellectual strengths in yourself
4. Identify your own preferred learning style
5. Understand how to apply your own preferred learning style

CONCEPTS

> **KEY TERMS**
>
> **Discovery** = observing and learning about something for the first time in one's experience
>
> **Ever-expanding** = ongoing process that is constantly making progress in a positive manner
>
> **Understand** = perceive the meaning of something learned; grasp the idea of its significance; comprehend
>
> **Apply** = to make use of as relevant and important to a situation or action
>
> **Intelligence** = capacity for learning, reasoning, understanding, and similar forms of mental activity
>
> **Wisdom** = the power to discern and judge properly what is true or right or of moral value

▶ Concepts

Probably every student in high school asks, "Am I smart enough to go to college?" SAT or ACT scores may have given you one answer. GPA from high school has given you another. You may have even taken IQ tests to find the answer to your question. The problem is that you might be asking the wrong question. Maybe you need to focus less on "if" you're smart and more on "how" you are smart. What do we mean by that? We defined the *intellectual strengths* domain as the capacity in our lives that enables us to acquire knowledge and develop an ever-expanding understanding of this knowledge in a manner that produces wisdom. Let's examine how this takes place.

Intellectual Capacity

Throughout recent history, intellectual capacity has been correlated to what has been termed the "intelligence quotient," better known as IQ. This is determined by measuring an individual's ability to respond to visual imagery, to respond to verbal input, and to apply skills in both areas to the solution of problems. This ability is related to many different capacities. Ten of the more commonly recognized capacities are listed below:

- *Verbal Capacity* = the ability to read and write, remember, and think with words.
- *Quantitative Capacity* = the ability to recognize, manipulate, comprehend, remember and think with quantitative concepts and relationships represented by numerical symbols.
- *Image Capacity* = the ability to perceive, analyze, synthesize, remember, and think with visual patterns.
- *Auditory Capacity* = the ability to detect, analyze, synthesize, and discriminate auditory stimuli, especially those related to speech.

- *Short-Term Memory* = the ability to store and recall information within a few minutes.
- *Long-Term Memory* = the ability to store information and to efficiently retrieve it later in the process of thinking.
- *Reasoning Capacity* = the ability to form concepts and solve problems.
- *Processing Capacity* = the speed with which an individual can perform automatic cognitive tasks.
- *Reaction Capacity* = the immediacy with which an individual can react to stimuli or a task.
- *Informational Capacity* = the amount of specific information acquired and retained by an individual.

More recent studies have shown that equating intellectual strengths solely to intellectual capacity is too narrow a focus. Howard Gardner, who we referred to earlier in Chapter 4, has proposed the idea of multiple intelligences (1983). In other words, people might be "intelligent" or "smart" in different ways.

Learning Styles

One of the primary reasons that the intellect needs to be looked at with a broader perspective is that people learn in different ways or styles. One simplified approach to learning styles divides people into three primary groups of visual, auditory, or kinesthetic/tactile learners as illustrated in Figure 8-2.

- **Visual** learning occurs primarily through looking at *images*, such as pictures, diagrams, demonstrations, and body language.
- **Auditory** learning occurs primarily through hearing *words*—both spoken and written.
- **Kinesthetic/Tactile** learning occurs through *hands-on* doing and interacting.

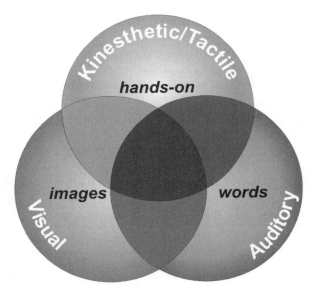

FIGURE 8-2
Learning Styles

You will notice that the spheres in Figure 8-2 overlap each other. This represents the true nature of learning styles. People rarely, if ever, learn only in one style. The reality is much more a preference in learning styles. However, it is important to understand what style you prefer. This can help you approach classes and studying in a more effective manner. Later in the Exercises section of this chapter you will have the opportunity to explore this more in depth and apply it to your own situation.

Learning Atmosphere

Another approach to learning that shows our distinctiveness as individuals was developed around our preferred atmosphere or setting for learning. This concept suggests that each person has unique strengths and preferences across a full spectrum of physiological, sociological, psychological, emotional, and environmental elements. The interaction of these elements occurs differently in everyone and will affect the way they concentrate on, process, absorb, and retain new and difficult information (Dunn & Dunn, 1992, 1998, 1999).

STIMULI	ELEMENTS
Environmental	Sound
	Light
	Temperature
	Design
Emotional	Motivation
	Persistence
	Responsibility
	Structure
Sociological	Self, Pair, or Team
	Feedback from Authority
	Variety vs. Routine
Physical	Perceptual
	Intake
	Time
	Mobility
Psychological	Global/Analytic
	Right/Left Hemisphere
	Impulsive/Reflective

TABLE 8-1
Learning Atmosphere

Knowing your own strengths and preferences in this learning atmosphere can be important to success in your college experience and in life after college. Later in the Exercises section of this chapter, you will have the opportunity to explore this more in depth and apply it to your own situation.

Intellectual Disciplines

A final approach to consider in understanding intellectual strengths centers on the disciplines of the mind that help us build the ability to discover, understand, and apply truth in an ever-expanding manner. Jay Wood (1998), a philosophy professor at Wheaton College, refers to these as intellectual virtues. James Sire (2000), a professor at the University of Missouri, considers these to be habits of the mind. Assessing your strengths in these disciplines and developing them will help you in your academic pursuits as you progress into college.

Our definition of intellectual strengths identifies three categories of intellectual disciplines: (1) those we use to discover knowledge; (2) those we use to process the knowledge into an understanding of truth; and (3) those we use to apply the truth after we understand it. Figure 8-3 illustrates the various disciplines that lead to intellectual strengths in each of these three categories.

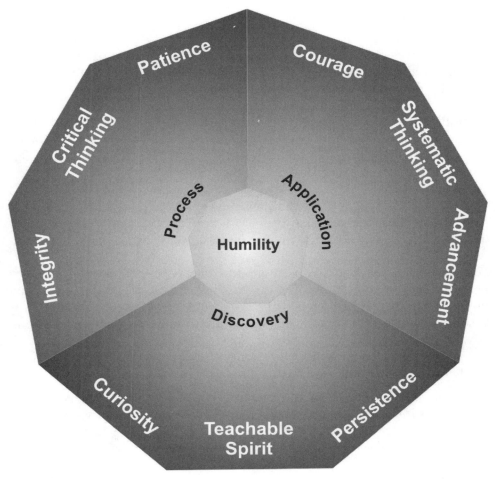

FIGURE 8-3
Intellectual Disciplines

1. Discovery disciplines

Curiosity. A strong desire to learn more about something. People who are curious have an excitement for knowledge and eagerness to search for truth. They openly inquire about why things are the way they are. They truly are explorers in the galaxy of information and comprehension.

Teachable spirit. A willingness and eagerness to learn. People who are teachable are characterized by an absence of a "know-it-all" attitude. They are not indifferent to knowledge. They are open to diverse views and forms of knowledge.

Persistence. A firm and steadfast continual search for knowledge and truth. People who are persistent keep on pursuing truth despite obstacles, warnings, or setbacks. They do not give up their quest even when data is inconsistent, obscure, or seemingly nonexistent.

Humility. Discovering humility is a modest view of one's own importance pertaining to the possession of knowledge. People who have intellectual humility always see themselves as a learner and are always willing to be taught by others.

2. Process disciplines

Integrity. The quality or condition of interpreting information collected with honesty. People who have intellectual integrity do not make data fit their preconceived ideas. Instead they collect data with an open mind and then allow this data to inform the conclusions they make.

Critical Thinking. The mental process of actively and skillfully conceptualizing, applying, analyzing, synthesizing, and evaluating information to reach an answer or conclusion. People who think critically ask "why" questions constantly. They rarely accept things at face value.

Patience. The capability of calmly awaiting an outcome or result even in the face of obstacles or challenges. People who are intellectually patient do not come to hasty conclusions and are not impulsive in their interpretations.

Humility. Process humility is a modest view of one's own importance pertaining to the possession of understanding. People who have intellectual humility do not see themselves as omniscient and hold very few "truths" as absolute. To them, the search for meaning and understanding is a lifelong adventure.

3. Application disciplines

Courage. The quality of spirit that enables a person to face the unknown or new ideas without fear of implications or repercussions. People who are intellectually courageous avoid being dogmatic. They are willing to take risks in proposing new ideas or relinquishing old ideas that no longer appear to be valid.

Systematic thinking. The mental process of formulating concepts into an organized set of interrelated ideas or principles that can be applied to life.

People who think systematically realize that knowledge and understanding are useful only if others can see how to interact with and use them.

Advancement.   The application of an understanding of knowledge to improve on what was already known. People who advance intellectually take forward steps in acquiring and understanding knowledge. Their desire is to see intellectual activity as a developmental process that leads to progress. They are not satisfied with the status quo.

Humility.   Application humility is a modest view of one's own importance pertaining to thrusting one's own understanding on others. People who have intellectual humility do not see themselves as a dogmatist whose duty it is to tell others how they should live. People with intellectual humility instead see their role as inspiring others to join the journey of discovering, understanding, and applying truth.

Concepts Summary

For the most part, when people talk about intellectual strengths, they are referring primarily to IQ. As a result of this, we end up with a culture where people think they are smart when they really aren't. This confusion often leads to feelings of inferiority and self-doubt related to IQ and causes uncertainty in the search for a Life Calling.

From our discussion we see that your true intellectual strengths are affected by your learning style and your preferred learning atmosphere. Further, we found that intellectual strengths are made up of disciplines that encompass a far greater spectrum than just IQ. This complexity, as with the other strengths, makes it harder to see when we have these strengths. Again, one of the most effective ways is listening to what others who know us well say about us. We will also look at another way to explore intellectual strengths in the Exercises section of this chapter.

Remember, each of the strength dimensions provides a bridge among the other dimensions. Intellectual strengths provide the bridge of *information* among the other strengths. What do we mean by this? It is through our intellect that we learn about what is going on with the other strengths. This adds the knowledge and understanding required to live our lives.

CONCEPTS

 # Insight

The Bible promises that we can have perfect peace in our lives if we have minds that are steadfast, and that this steadfastness comes from trust in God (see Isaiah 26:3). Scripture also provides insight on how we can develop the strength of mind.

SCRIPTURAL INSIGHT 1 *Strong Minds Are a Gift from God*

To these four young men God gave knowledge and understanding of all kinds of literature and learning. And Daniel could understand visions and dreams of all kinds. DANIEL 1:17

Do you ever look at some other person in one of your classes and wonder how they can know so much? They always seem to have the right answers. A few years ago on the television game show *Jeopardy*, a show that in part tests a person's accumulation of information, there was a contestant named Ken Jennings who won seventy-four games in a row—by far, a record. Everyone wondered how he could have so much information in his mind.

Intellectual strength, of course, is more than the accumulation of information. It is the capacity of our lives that enables us to discover, understand and apply truth in an ever-expanding manner. Daniel and his three companions were a good example of this. When Babylon's King Nebuchadnezzar put these four to the test, Daniel 1:20 records that, "in every matter of wisdom and understanding about which the king questioned them, he found them ten times better than all the magicians and enchanters in his whole kingdom." I think we can all admit—that's pretty good. We'd all be happy with half that level. Notice, though, in the original verse at the beginning of this devotion that at least some element of this was a gift from God.

There is a gift capacity in the *Strengths Matrix* and this applies to intellectual strengths, as well as the others. There is a component in our intellects that comes as a gift from God in the unique design of our lives. You can describe it as heredity or whatever else you want to call it, but it is in us because of the overall design of the human race. We can complain that we were not given enough, but that really takes us back to the Parable of the Talents in chapter 5. God gives us gifts each according to our capacity. And then it's a matter of what we do with what we have been given.

An interesting observation in life is that people who have the greatest mental capacity based on their gifts do not always end up with the greatest level of wisdom or practical understanding. In speaking of spiritual wisdom, Jesus said, "I praise you, Father, Lord of heaven and earth, because you have hidden these things from the wise and learned, and revealed them to little children" (Matthew 11:25).

> **PERSONAL REFLECTION** Are you using the intellectual strength that God has given you to its fullest potential? How are you using your mind to pursue your Life Calling?

SCRIPTURAL INSIGHT 2 *Seek, Store Up, and Apply Knowledge*

The heart of the discerning acquires knowledge; the ears of the wise seek it out. PROVERBS 18:15

When you read about Daniel and his three friends, it would be easy to say, "I might as well give up because I can never be that smart!" But there are also capacities of knowledge and skills that can be pursued by all of us. In fact, Proverbs 19:27 warns, "Stop listening to instruction, my child, and you will stray from the words of knowledge." We can all develop our intellectual strength, and it begins with listening to the wisdom of others and collecting good information. The book of Proverbs is filled with such advice. Here are three of them that can teach us important actions to take:

1. Proverbs 15:14 – *The discerning heart seeks knowledge, but the mouth of a fool feeds on folly*. Knowledge rarely falls on us. It more often comes when we intentionally choose to seek it out. Those who choose to do this will build intellectual strength. They will also increase their ability to discern or discover a Life Calling by actively searching for information to feed their minds.

2. Proverbs 10:14 – *The wise store up knowledge, but the mouth of a fool invites ruin*. Seeking knowledge is not enough. Intellectual strength is built by storing the knowledge in our minds. That way we will be able to use it when we need it.

3. Proverbs 23:12 – *Apply your heart to instruction and your ears to words of knowledge*. If the knowledge we seek and then store in our minds is never used, it is of no use to us. It ends up just taking up space in our brains. Instead we need to apply the knowledge we gain to all aspects of our lives. In fact, knowledge forms one of the important dimensions of all domains in the Strengths Matrix.

One last proverb provides us with one good way to find knowledge and to develop our intellectual strength. *Walk with the wise and become wise, for a companion of fools suffers harm* (Proverbs 13:20). If we hang around with people like Daniel and his friends, we will start to learn from them and benefit from their wisdom. When I was in college, I was a varsity tennis player. I discovered that my tennis game improved when I played with those who were better than me. This proverb teaches us that the same thing happens in the area of intellectual strength. When we associate with people that can pull us up, we will improve. When we hang out with those who can drag us down, that is what will likely happen.

> **PERSONAL REFLECTION** ⟩ Are you actively seeking, storing up and applying the kind of knowledge that can help you build intellectual strength? Are you walking with the "wise" or hanging out with the "fools"?

SCRIPTURAL INSIGHT 3 ▶ *Learn the Difference Between Knowledge That Puffs Up or Builds Up*

We know that "We all possess knowledge." But knowledge puffs up while love builds up. Those who think they know something do not yet know as they ought to know. But whoever loves God is known by God. 1 CORINTHIANS 8:1-3

It is important for us to take notice that intellectual strengths involve more than just amassing knowledge. Understanding and application are just as important. In fact, the Apostle Paul warned of people who think they have intellectual strengths but do not go beyond knowledge. In 2 Timothy 3, Paul describes a type of people who love themselves rather than God. He says they have a form of godliness but deny its power. And he warns Timothy to have nothing to do with them. Then in verse 7 he describes these people as "always learning but never able to acknowledge the truth."

In that same spirit Paul addressed this in a different passage found in 1 Corinthians 8:1-3. He warns about this self-contained knowledge that does not include understanding. Here is what we can learn from this passage.

1. We all possess some level of knowledge. We sometimes think that some people have knowledge, while others don't. But in reality, we all possess some kind of knowledge. The issue that relates to intellectual strengths is what kind of knowledge it is. Some kinds of knowledge build intellectual strengths, while other kinds work to weaken our intellect.

2. Knowledge by itself puffs up. In other words, it can lead to conceit if it is not grounded in love. Love leads us to build others up rather than promote ourselves. Intellectual strength comes from the kind of knowledge that is associated with love.

3. Those who think they know may not know as they ought to. There is a knowledge that leads to higher things, but there is also knowledge that is not useful and may even be harmful. This was the issue in the Garden of Eden with the Tree of the Knowledge of Good and Evil.

4. Knowledge rooted and grounded in the love of God is the kind of knowledge that can lead us to the higher levels we seek and help us to discover our Life Calling.

> **PERSONAL REFLECTION** Are you seeking the kind of knowledge that puffs up or builds up? Which tree draws you as you search for Life Calling—the Tree of Life or the Tree of the Knowledge of Good and Evil?

SCRIPTURAL INSIGHT 4 *Intellectual Strength Begins with Trust*

Trust in the LORD with all your heart and lean not on your own understanding; in all your ways acknowledge him, and he will make your paths straight. Do not be wise in your own eyes; fear the LORD and shun evil. This will bring health to your body and nourishment to your bones. PROVERBS 3:5-8

Proverbs 3:13&14 informs us of the value that occurs when we go beyond knowledge to understanding. *"Blessed are those who find wisdom, those who gain understanding, for she is more profitable than silver and yields better returns than gold."* Fortunately scripture also helps us to find out how to get the proper understanding to go along with the knowledge we collect. Proverbs 1:7 says, "the fear of the LORD is the beginning of knowledge, but fools despise wisdom and discipline." When we add to this the passage for today's devotions from Proverbs 3:5-8, we can begin to see the proper context for building intellectual strengths.

First of all, this does not mean that we should not try to understand things on our own. It does not mean that we should turn off our minds. It means that we should begin our search for knowledge with the fear of the Lord. This means that we acknowledge God as the source of all knowledge and wisdom and look to him to inspire our understanding.

Second of all, when we acknowledge the Lord in all our ways, he will make our paths straight. This goes back to that foundational value of faith we looked at earlier in our study. If we hope to find that straight path which is our Life Calling, we need to start by acknowledging that it comes from God, not our own cleverness.

Third of all, intellectual strength built upon our own estimate of ourselves is no real strength at all. True intellectual strength is built upon a rightful estimate of God and the role he plays in our minds.

Last of all, intellectual strength based on a relationship of trust in God builds physical strength as well. The body and the mind are connected.

> **PERSONAL REFLECTION** ▷ Does your knowledge begin with trust in God or trust in yourself? How can you increase your trust in God as the starting point for building your intellectual strength?

INSIGHT

SCRIPTURAL INSIGHT 5 ▷ *Live in the Wise Man's House*

Therefore everyone who hears these words of mine and puts them into practice is like a wise man who built his house on the rock. The rain came down, the streams rose, and the winds blew and beat against that house; yet it did not fall, because it had its foundation on the rock. But everyone who hears these words of mine and does not put them into practice is like a foolish man who built his house on sand. The rain came down, the streams rose, and the winds blew and beat against that house, and it fell with a great crash. MATTHEW 7:24-27

We define intellectual strength as the capacity of our lives that enables us to discover, understand and apply truth in an ever-expanding manner. That definition includes application. We need to properly apply godly knowledge and understanding to our lives. Jesus described this in his famous analogy of the wise man and the foolish man. Hearing words or gaining knowledge but doing nothing with them is not intellectual strength. In fact in Jesus' analogy, and also earlier in the proverbs we looked at, to hear words or gain knowledge and not apply it to our lives in our actions is foolishness.

When we take knowledge that has been gained in the context of trusting God, and we then apply it to the actions of our lives, this becomes true wisdom. This process of correctly applying God's wisdom is what Paul meant when he counseled in 2 Timothy 2:15, "Do your best to present yourself to God as one approved, a worker who does not need to be ashamed and who correctly handles the word of truth."

As we look back over all of the verses used in the insights dealing with intellectual strengths, we could combine them into a sequential development plan for intellectual strengths.

Step 1: Fear the Lord
Step 2: Listen to instruction
Step 3: Seek God's understanding
Step 4: Apply understanding to your life

> In all of this…work diligently to correctly handle truth

Unless we incorporate all of these elements into the way we handle knowledge and learning, we will likely not attain true wisdom nor develop real intellectual strengths.

PERSONAL REFLECTION > Are you putting God's words into action, living like a house built upon a rock? What can you do in your life to more correctly handle the word of truth and become an approved worker?

INSIGHT

Discovery

How can the Discovery Guides help you identify and understand your *emotional strengths*?

T THEORY	You can increase your knowledge about *Intellectual Strengths* in departments and classes at your college or university. Here are some suggestions. *Psychology classes* are a good place to explore the architecture and development of the brain and intellectual skills. *Educational classes* are a good place to explore learning styles and learning developmental theory. Art departments that actually have you starting to enter into production of art; art theory classes will also help you see what kind of disposition you have toward the area of art. Nearly all majors and departments address intellectual strengths as they relate to the department's particular discipline in some manner, usually in their introductory classes. There is also a great deal of research and writing about intellectual strengths. Search these out and learn from them.
E EXAMPLES	Find people who excel in intellectual strengths. Observe them and find time to talk to them. Ask them to share with you how they discovered and developed these intellectual strengths.
A ASSESSMENT	A variety of assessments have been used to measure various aspects of intellectual strengths. A great deal of controversy surrounds exactly what they measure. You might want to concentrate primarily on tools that can help you assess the way you learn and then develop learning strategies that can give you greater success in your educational experience.
C COUNSEL	Professional educational counselors, advisors, and life coaches are trained to help you explore intellectual strengths. Your college and university will likely have a center where you can find such help. Additionally, family members, teachers, pastors, and friends know you well and can give you valuable insights about your learning styles and intellectual strengths.
H HISTORY	Search for historical biographies of notable people who have exhibited these intellectual strengths. Select some of these and learn from their experience. Also study the developmental history of the intellectual and learning theory.
E EXPERIENCE	The college experience will automatically thrust you into activities where your intellectual strengths will be tested. You will learn quickly whether or not you have skills in this area and in what way you learn best.
R REFLECTION	Take time to reflect on what you learn in your classes. Reflect on what were the most effective ways in which you learned. Reflect on your disposition or attitude about intellectual strengths in general and yours in particular.

DISCOVERY

▶ Story

It was a special day for United States citizens: the Fourth of July, a day to celebrate the birth of the nation. The day began early with the travelers boarding an early morning train in Plymouth and traveling to South Station in downtown Boston, the best place to celebrate the nation's birth. They made their way to the Boston Commons, where their goal was to find the starting point for the Freedom Trail. This walking tour would take them along scenes of decisive events in the nation's struggle for freedom at the time of the American Revolution.

Although Ryan had been the one to suggest that they visit Boston on their trip several months earlier, it was Lorena who had convinced them to walk the Freedom Trail. She was excited to learn a thing or two about the origins of the United States. Though their enthusiasm for history varied, they all looked forward to the experience.

"Okay, Lor, start us off. What's the story on this park?" Justin asked.

"First of all, it's considered to be the oldest public park in the country," Lorena replied. "But beyond that, it's the site of many important gatherings. Martin Luther King spoke to a rally here during the struggle for civil rights. Pope John Paul held a large outdoor mass here. Of course, we'll start our walk on the Freedom Trail here."

They had all picked up walking guides for the Freedom Trail, so they already had some idea of what they would be seeing. They were still interested, however, in Lorena's take on things. When it came to intellectual knowledge, Lorena was their resident expert on most subjects. She seemed to have an insatiable desire for knowledge. They walked along the Freedom Trail, passing by the State House and then coming to the Old South Meeting House.

"What's the big deal here, oh wise one?" Ryan asked Lorena in his usual mocking way.

"Ever hear of the Boston Tea Party?" she asked him in return.

"Yeah. Isn't that where the founding fathers all came together and drank British tea?" Ryan responded.

Lorena thought it was likely a good decision on Ryan's part not to go to college. *Why waste the money?* she thought to herself, but she decided not to voice this opinion. "Right time period, Ryan, but your facts are a little off the mark. It wasn't a party to *drink* tea; it was a party to *destroy* tea. The revolutionaries dressed up as Indians, took the tea from boats, and threw it in the harbor."

"Why did they do that?" Diana asked.

"They were protesting. They didn't like the fact that the king of England had levied heavy taxes on them without their having any representation," Lorena explained. "And the Old South Meeting House is where they met and planned the Tea Party."

"So the guys that started our country were like terrorists?" Ryan asked.

"Sort of," Lorena answered.

"Kind of funny, isn't it?" Abriella observed. "We think of them as heroes, not terrorists."

"That's pretty much the case with any revolution," Lorena replied.

"One side sees the revolutionaries as heroes, and the other side sees them as threats."

The discussion continued as they walked on to the Paul Revere House, where he lived and started his famous "midnight ride." All of the explorers were aware of this part of history, and they were fascinated to see where it began.

"So, Adam. What kind of strengths do you think Paul Revere had?" Abriella returned to the discussion from the previous day.

"Well, he was a silversmith, so he must have had the physical strength of craftsmanship," Adam said. "But I think he also demonstrated intellectual strength."

"You mean like Lorena has?" Diana asked.

"Or like Lor *thinks* she has?" Ryan added.

"At least I have some reason to think it," Lorena shot back.

The others had given up on any cease-fire between the two.

"It's interesting," Adam continued. "We always equate intelligence with the accumulation of knowledge, GPA, or test scores. I'm not sure that what's it all about...I'm not saying that's all Lorena excels in," he was quick to add.

"Thanks," Lorena sulked.

"What do you think it is?" Diana persisted.

"Think about it, why are we on this walk?" Adam asked.

"It's Lorena's fault!" Ryan quickly answered. "She always wants to know more about everything."

"I agree," Adam replied. "And maybe that's why we all think of her as intellectually strong. She's curious—always eager to learn more about things. I wish I was more that way."

"Kind of like this walk?" Justin asked.

"I think this would qualify," Adam answered.

"Yeah, but what about the problem that she thinks she knows everything?" Ryan interrupted. "Don't you have to be willing to learn? If you think you know everything, how can this supposed intellectual strength grow?" He looked at Lorena as he spoke.

Lorena glared back at him.

"You're right, Ryan," Adam responded. "You can't be curious and think you have all the answers at the same time. They would cancel each other out."

"I don't think I have all the answers!" Lorena spoke with an emphatic voice. "But it's better to have some answers than none, Ryan." Her voice hinted of a put-down.

"*Persistence* is the third intellectual strength. This is when you keep on searching for answers even when faced by formidable obstacles," Adam continued.

"What about the forefathers here? They didn't have all the answers," Justin observed. "It seems like they were constantly looking for ways that they could change the status quo in the colonies. Don't you think you've got to keep at it if you're going to discover truth?"

"Couldn't agree more," Adam replied. "Again, I think that's what sets Lorena apart from the rest of us. She is so darn persistent in learning new stuff."

"Hey, we're at the Old North Church where Paul Revere received his signal for his ride." Diana interrupted the discussion.

"One if by land, two if by sea," Justin commented. "Or was it two if by land, one if by sea?"

"It's a good thing you weren't the one riding that horse," Abriella laughed. "We might still be colonies."

"What do you think it was that made these people willing to put their lives on the line like this?" Lorena asked. "Why not just give the king what he wanted and be happy?"

"I think it was because they were willing to ask the 'why' questions and not be satisfied with just the 'what' questions," Adam answered. "You remember how Mr. Anderson was always telling us in history class that we needed to be critical thinkers and not accept things at face value? That's the way the forefathers were."

"That's why I think Lorena outshines me intellectually," Abriella commented. "I may have beat her with my GPA—and that was only by a tenth of a point—but she always asks those 'why' questions. She's never satisfied with the first answer."

"She's just plain never satisfied," Ryan added.

"We've got to be careful that we don't just try to make the facts fit into what we already think is true," Adam continued. "If we want to expand our intellect, we have to approach the study of subjects with an open mind, allowing what we learn to inform the conclusions we might come to."

"Anybody understand what he just said?" Ryan asked.

"Yes," Lorena responded. "Everybody but you."

"And we have to be patient with the process." Adam ignored the diversion.

"Sort of like you have to be when you constantly have Ryan and Lorena at each other's throats?" Diana asked.

Adam laughed. "That's a different kind of patience. I think intellectual patience is not jumping to conclusions or being impulsive in making interpretations."

By now, they had arrived at Bunker Hill Monument on their walk.

"What's this monument, Lorena?" Abriella asked.

"This is the site of the first major battle of the American Revolution," Lorena answered. "The start of our nation."

"I thought the first shot was fired at that bridge we're visiting tomorrow. Did I miss something?" Diana asked.

"That was the first shot, but it didn't result in a major battle," Lorena explained. "This was the first full-scale battle."

"And it's a good location to bring up another point about intellectual strength," Adam observed. "*Courage.* You've got to be willing to face the unknown or new ideas without fear of what will happen to you. The revolutionary leaders certainly were willing to do that."

"For sure," Justin agreed. "I don't know if I would have been willing to take that kind of risk."

"No one really knows that until they're faced with it," Lorena replied. "You might have been willing to do far more than you think if you'd been there."

Justin frowned and then smiled, unsure whether that was a criticism or a compliment. He decided to receive it as a compliment. Criticism Lorena usually reserved for Ryan.

They continued to walk on from Bunker Hill and ended up at the berth of the USS *Constitution*, the oldest commissioned ship still active and in service in the U.S. Navy.

"Why is it called 'Old Ironsides'?" Justin asked.

"It developed the reputation that cannonballs would bounce off its sides," Lorena explained.

"Would they really do that?" Abriella wondered.

"The ship's still here, isn't it?" Lorena countered.

"Okay, work that into your scheme of intellectual strengths, Adam," Diana laughed.

"You're pressing me, Diana," Adam answered, smiling. "I'll give it my best. Maybe it has to do with thinking that is useful. People who are smart in that matter recognize that knowledge and understanding are useful only if they can be used by others. So if you discover that oak is a good deterrent for cannonballs, you incorporate this thinking into the science of shipbuilding."

"You're stretching that a little," Lorena laughed.

"I told Diana she was pressing me," Adam protested, but he laughed too.

"Hey, we're almost done with the walk, so keep on going," Diana demanded.

"If you insist," Adam laughed. "I think a very important part of intellectual strength is to always want to keep moving forward…like our walk here. Always searching for a greater understanding of knowledge so we can improve on what's already known. I think truly intelligent people don't want to maintain an intellectual status quo."

"That is so you, Adam," Diana observed. The others nodded in agreement.

They walked from the USS *Constitution* to the subway station and caught a train that would take them to their next adventure. It had been everyone's desire from the first moment they decided to visit the Boston area to be there for the Fourth of July. Their plan was to take in the Boston Pops and the Fireworks Spectacular! at the Hatch Shell on the borders of the Charles River. "If you know anything about Fourth of July celebrations, you know this is as good as it gets," Lorena had informed them. "And you don't want to be short-changed, do you?"

As they sat on the lawn along the Charles River, Lorena pointed northwest across the river to the campus of the Massachusetts Institute of Technology.

"You want to talk about intellectual strength? Well, there it is!" she said emphatically. "And if you keep looking a mile past that in the same direction, you'll come to Harvard University. There you have it. The intellectual capital of the world." She had tried to interest the others to visit the campuses earlier in the day, but to no avail.

"I thought you said it was that Yale school back in Connecticut," Ryan argued.

"Well, that's part of it too," Lorena replied.

"So basically you have no idea where this so-called capitol really is," Ryan scoffed. "Well, let me help you. It's in every seventh wave coming in on a good surfing day."

Lorena rolled her eyes. "You're beyond hope."

Fortunately, the others were spared the continuing battle by the start of the concert.

By the time it was over, they had not been disappointed. They had never seen such a dazzling display of fireworks. And of course the Boston Pops' rendition of the *1812 Overture* in sync with the fireworks was the highlight of the evening.

They made their way back to the subways and then caught the train back to Plymouth. It was nearly midnight when they returned to the *Nautilus*.

"Did we ever finish with your lecture on intellectual strength, Adam?" Diana observed with a smile.

"One more point, and I'll be quick because we're all tired," Adam replied.

"Fabulous," Ryan yawned. "Short and sweet, my good friend."

"And I think it might be the most important— *humility*," Adam said.

"Hmm," Lorena mused thoughtfully. "I might need to work on that one." The others were surprised. If Ryan had made that comment, they would have understood. Lorena's authentic self-disclosure caught them off guard.

"Oh, I don't know, Lor," Adam finally responded. "I think all of us struggle with this. We all think we know everything and that it is our duty to tell everybody else how they should live. I think that's hard for all of us."

Ryan put his arm around Lorena's shoulders and gave her a squeeze.

"It's a hard struggle for me too."

Have the planets aligned? the others wondered.

STORY

Music	Technical
Mechanics	Utilized
Craftsmanship	(Improved)
Oratory	(Commanded)
Flexible body movement	Ignored
Physical appearance	Strengthened

HIGHLIGHTS OF WHAT I WAS PHYSICALLY GOOD AT OR DID *IN MY COLLEGE YEARS*	
AREA	**OBSERVATIONS**
Muscular Strength	Continue Building
Artistry	Unused
Music	(Explored)
Mechanics	(Desire)
Craftsmanship	Question
Oratory	Manipulate
Flexible body movement	Working
Physical appearance	Bettering

EXERCISES

2. Go back through your lists and circle the verbs or key phrases. Then use these verbs to summarizing below your perceived physical abilities in the different areas indicated.

I think the words that describe me are:

Inquisitive, Building, Improving, Commanding, Exploring, and desiring

Exercises

Caleb Ostrander

ur Physical Strengths Inventory

ood way to assess your physical abilities is to look at what you have already
e. The eight physical strengths categories are: *brute force* (muscular
ength), *artistry, music, mechanics, craftsmanship, oratory, kinesthetics*
xible body movement), and *physical appearance*. Use these categories or
hers you might think of to complete the assignment that follows.

1. Reflect on your life and then use brief or one-word statements to fill in the chart below.

HIGHLIGHTS OF WHAT I WAS PHYSICALLY GOOD AT OR DID *IN MY CHILDHOOD*	
AREA	**OBSERVATIONS**
Muscular Strength	Strong for age
Artistry	Creative
Music	Natural
Mechanics	Inquisitive
Craftsmanship	Unique
Oratory	Expansive
Flexible body movement	Average
Physical appearance	Cute?
HIGHLIGHTS OF WHAT I WAS PHYSICALLY GOOD AT OR DID *DURING MY HIGH SCHOOL YEARS*	
AREA	**OBSERVATIONS**
Muscular Strength	Building
Artistry	Developed

(Continued)

D. Life cannot be shaped to meet all of your unique needs. Some of your instructors will teach their classes in a manner that does not particularly fit your learning style, and you will have to learn how to adapt to this. However, there are some strategies you can use to help make this process easier. The three sections below present strategies that you might find useful in learning within your preferred style.

Kinesthetic/Tactile Learners

Kinesthetic/Tactile Learners will find these strategies helpful:

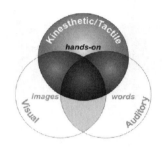

- You learn best by doing, so find ways to become actively involved in what is going on in your class.
- You tend to be easily distracted, so find a place to sit in your classes that minimizes those distractions and helps keep you focused on what the instructor is doing.
- You remember best by direct involvement in what you are learning, so create your own learning activities that correspond to information you are trying to memorize.
- You like to attack problems physically, so think of ways to turn all problems in a class into a physical activity.
- You like to read stories with a lot of action, especially at the beginning, so ask your instructor to help you find these kinds of stories related to the subject you are learning.
- You like writing and drawing, so use your iPad or paper and writing instrument to constantly engage in this activity while you listen to material being taught.
- You like hands-on activities with real objects that can be touched, so use Play-Doh or something similar to create objects related to material you are learning.
- You like interaction with others, so join small-group discussions or learning-teams.
- You like creating things with your hands, so make charts, models, diagrams, etc. to help you connect to what you are learning.
- You tend to learn best when your body is active, so try reading while working out on an exercise machine.

Visual Learners

Visual Learners will find these strategies helpful:

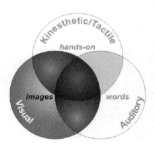

learn best by seeing, so find a place to sit in your classes that allows o see the instructor, whiteboard, and projection screen or monitor y.

end to be quiet and become impatient when extensive listening is for, so follow along in your text book or hand-outs during a lecture entation to help you stay involved.

e to take notes, so do this during lectures and make sure to also draw s to represent concepts.

e greater immediate recall of information that is presented visually, te flash cards with pictures on them to review things you need to ber.

EXERCISES

- You tend to solve problems deliberately, planning in advance and organizing your thoughts by writing them down, so make sure you allow yourself time to do this during a test or in preparation for a test.
- You like to read stories with a lot of descriptions and narratives, so ask your instructor to help you find these kinds of stories related to the subject you are learning.
- When you read something, you often like to stop and stare into space, imagining the scene, so take time to do this as you read rather than just "plowing" through the material.
- You like to view DVDs, *YouTube* clips, pictures, or anything else you can see, so ask your instructor to help you find these kinds of visual sources related to the subject you are learning.
- You tend to benefit from visual emphasis as you read, so highlight important information as you read.
- You tend to be easily distracted by visual stimuli, so avoid surfing the Internet, engaging in social networking, or looking at pictures other students have on their cell phones, iPads, or computers during class.

Auditory Learners

Auditor Learners will find these strategies helpful:

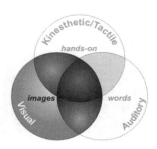

- You learn best by hearing everything that is going on, so find a place to sit in your classes that allows you to hear the instructor well and to participate in class discussions.
- You tend to like talking about the pros and cons of a situation, so don't be afraid to challenge ideas presented in class in an acceptable manner.
- You enjoy listening but also cannot wait to get a chance to talk, so make sure you participate in class discussion.
- You learn best by hearing things, so repeat words or descriptions out loud over and over when learning them.
- You tend to move your lips or speak under your breath while reading, so don't be afraid of this as you read.
- You learn best by hearing things, so discuss class material with a friend or fellow student.
- You acquire information better when it is presented orally, so make sure you attend lectures and presentations and do not rely solely on reading a textbook.
- You respond best to information that is presented to you orally, so when you miss a class, try to get a hold of a podcast or recording rather than just getting someone else's notes.
- There is some evidence of left-ear or right-ear advantage in listening tasks.
- You tend to process verbal information more efficiently and accurately with your right ear than with your left ear, so in class, sit so that your instructor will be located to your right.

Expanding Your Understanding of Your Learning Styles Using the *Learning-Styles 360*

1. Identify four different people who know you and who love and care for you. Choose the four so that they represent each of the following categories:
   - Parent _____
   - Teacher (present or former) _____
   - Friend _____
   - Sibling or relative who is younger than you _____
2. Provide all of the people you have identified with a copy of the *Learning-Styles 360* (not the Mirror) chart below and ask them to answer the questions for each of the three learning styles. Let them know that it is okay if they answer that they have not seen a style as being in your life. Tell them this will help you better understand yourself. Encourage them to give an example if they answer that a learning style is strong in you.

Learning Styles 360	Definition	How strong do you see this style of learning in me (weak, moderate, strong, very strong)?	Can you give me an example of when you have seen this learning style in me?
Visual	Visual learning occurs primarily through looking at images, such as pictures, diagrams, demonstrations, and body language		
Kinesthetic	Kinesthetic/Tactile learning occurs through hands-on doing and interacting		
Auditory	Auditory learning occurs primarily through hearing words—both spoken and written		

3. Now you personally answer the questions for each of the three learning styles using the results from Exercise 1 and your perception.

Learning Styles Mirror	Definition	What was my score in this learning style?	What has been my most effective example of when I used this style to learn?
Visual	Visual learning occurs primarily through looking at images, such as pictures, diagrams, demonstrations, and body language		
Kinesthetic	Kinesthetic/Tactile learning occurs through hands-on doing and interacting		
Auditory	Auditory learning occurs primarily through hearing words—both spoken and written		

4. Compare your scores to the evaluation from others in the Learning-Styles 360. What do others see in you that you may not see in yourself? What can you learn about your perception of yourself?
5. Reflect on what you learned in both Exercise 1 and Exercise 2 and summarize below what they have revealed to you about yourself.

▶ References

The following resources have been used in this chapter.

Aguilar, L.S., Hopper, S.J., & Kuzlik, T.M. (2001). *The Community College: a New Beginning*, (3rd ed.). Dubuque, Iowa: Kendall/Hunt Publishing Company.

Dunn, R.S., & Dunn, K.J. (1998). *The Complete Guide to the Learning Styles Inservice Dsystem*. Boston, Massachusetts: Allyn & Bacon.

Fralick, M.F. (2006). *College & Career Success*, (3rd ed.) Dubuque, Iowa: Kendall/Hunt Publishing Company.

Sire, J.W. (2000). *Habits of the Mind*. Downers Grove, Illinois: InterVarsityPress.

Wood, J.W. (1998). *Epistemology: Becoming Intellectually Virtuous*. Downers Grove, Illinois: InterVarsityPress.

The following resources may be useful to you in your continuing exploration of Life Calling as you look at your Unique Design and your *intellectual strengths*.

Schwen, M.R., and Bass, D.C., Eds. (2006). *Leading Lives That Matter: What We Should Do and Who We Should Be*. Grand Rapids, Michigan: Erdmans Publishing Co.

Empowered by Psychological Strengths

9

Strengths MATRIX™	DIMENSIONS				TOTAL
DOMAINS	Gifts	Knowledge	Skills	Attitude	
Physical					
Emotional					
Intellectual					
Psychological					
Spiritual					

FIGURE 9-1
Psychological Domain of the ***Strengths Matrix™***

The *Strengths Matrix* is comprised of five strengths domains. In this chapter we will explore ***Psychological Strengths***.

CHAPTER OBJECTIVES

1. Understand the nature, scope, and value of psychological strengths
2. Understand the appropriate processes for identifying psychological strengths
3. Begin identifying psychological strengths and preferences in yourself

KEY TERMS

Decision = the act of or need for making up one's mind
Information = important or useful knowledge or facts obtained in some manner as input from some source
Preference = feel more comfortable with, select, give priority to, or hold above other choices or things in estimation
Process = a continuous, systematic series of actions taking place in a definite manner directed to some end
Will = higher nature in human beings that enables them to reason critically and make moral judgments

 Concepts

From the time in high school when you start thinking about whether or not to go to college, to the time you graduate from college and move into the next phase of your life, your entire experience will be a constant process of making choices. The choices include what classes to take and when to take them, whether or not to go to class or buy the books for the class, how much to be involved in co-curricular activities, when and what to eat, who to hang out with or date, whether or not to go home at breaks, how many hours to work while going to college, and the list goes on and on. This can often produce a great deal of anxiety and concern for students, who ask themselves "How can I make the best decisions when confronted by these choices?" Understanding *psychological strengths* can help you begin to answer this question because it can help you see how you make decisions.

Many classic definitions of *psychological strengths* would characterize them as arising from the science that deals with all mental processes and behavior. Often emotional behavior is included in this. However, in the *Strengths Matrix*, we have chosen to consider emotional strengths as a separate category. As a result of this, in looking at *psychological strengths*, we have chosen to define a narrower spectrum of mental processes and behavior and have defined the *psychological strength* domain as the capacity in our lives that enables us to exercise our will in deciding on courses of action. What does "exercise our will" mean? The term *will* used here refers to the higher nature in human beings that enables them to reason critically and make moral judgements—that is, deciding what is right and wrong based on our value system.

Psychologists are behavioral scientists who study this dimension of the *Strengths Matrix* trying to figure out how the dimension works. One of these psychologists, Carl Jung, outlined a simplified theory. He proposed that this psychological process, as we have narrowly defined it, functions primarily with two activities: first, we take in information, and second, we evaluate the information and come to conclusions. Observations of this psychological process indicate that when our minds are active, we are involved with one or the other of these activities (Figure 9-2).

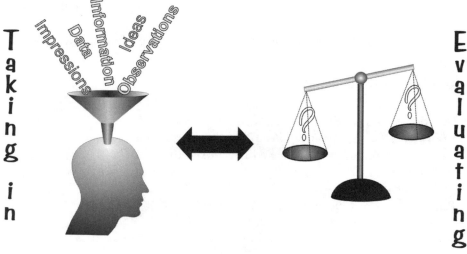

FIGURE 9-2
Psychological Process

When we approach these activities, we tend to come at them in different ways. Observations show that these differences can be determined along a scale measuring preference toward two end values. It is important to note, however, that both ways of taking in information are used by everyone, but one is usually preferred, and as a result, we feel more comfortable in activities associated with that preference and will develop it in our own lives more effectively. This can be an important concept to understand for students entering college because it has a definite impact on how they learn and how they will make judgments concerning what they learn.

Gathering Information

The first of the two scales measures our preferences in how we take in information in the process of deciding on courses of action. This intake of information is a process called "perceiving." Figure 9-3 illustrates that we have a preference in how we perceive. Some people have a perceiving preference that relies primarily on the process of observing facts or events through one or more of the five senses. Not surprisingly, this preference is referred to as "sensing." Other people have a perceiving preference that relies primarily on the less obvious process of observing meanings, relationships, and possibilities in an instinctive manner that operates beyond the normal mechanics of the conscious mind. This preference is referred to as "intuition."

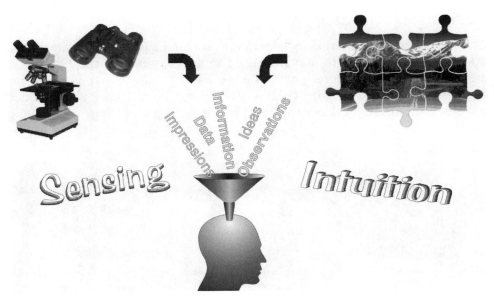

FIGURE 9-3
How do we prefer to take in information?

Our distinct preferences in the way we handle information operate quite differently for sensing or intuition. Table 9-1 outlines some of these distinctions.

It is important to note that one way is not better than the other. People with either preference will effectively gather information in their own way. It is also important to realize that both approaches are used by everyone, but one is usually preferred and better developed.

Sensing	Intuition
See information in specific parts and pieces	See information in patterns and relationships
Concentrate on information related to the present, enjoying what is there	Concentrate on information related to the future, anticipating what might be
Prefer working with practical information that solves immediate issues	Prefer imaginative information that leads to possibilities
Like information that is definite and measurable	Like information related to opportunities for being inventive
Start at the beginning, and evaluate information one step at a time	Jump in anywhere in looking at information, and may leap over steps
Work hands-on with parts to understand overall design	Study overall design to see how parts fit together
Enjoy using and refining information that is known and familiar	Enjoys experimenting with information that is new and different

TABLE 9-1
Sensing-Intuition Contrast

Making Decisions

Once we gather information by whichever process we prefer, we evaluate the information and come to conclusions. The second scale of the two scales mentioned earlier measures people's preferences in how they come to conclusions and make decisions (Figure 9-4). Some people have a preference toward coming to conclusions and making their decisions by relying

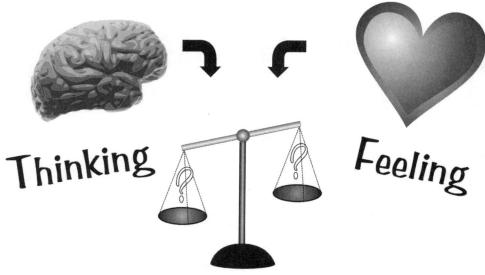

FIGURE 9-4
Preferred Basis for Making Decisions

primarily on an impersonal basis of rational consequences. This preference is referred to as "thinking" and relies heavily on a logical approach. Other people have a preference toward coming to conclusions and making their decisions by relying primarily on a personal basis of social values. This preference is referred to as "feeling" and relies heavily on a relational approach.

Our distinct preferences in the way we come to conclusions and make decisions also operate quite differently based on our preference for a logical-oriented *thinking* approach or relational-oriented *feeling* approach. Table 9-2 outlines some of these distinctions.

Thinking	Feeling
Comes to conclusions primarily with the head	Comes to conclusions primarily with the heart
Relies on logic to come to make decisions	Relies on personal convictions to make decisions
Gives priority to principles such as truth and justice	Gives priority to values such as relationships and harmony
Evaluates information as an onlooker from outside a situation	Evaluates information as a participant from within a situation
Starts with a critique that may lead afterwards to appreciation	Starts with appreciation that may lead afterwards to a critique
More comfortable at analyzing plans	More comfortable at understanding people
May seem distant or condescending to others in the decision-making process	May seem too involved or emotional to others in the decision-making process

TABLE 9-2
Thinking-Feeling Contrast

Remember, one way is not better than the other. People with either preference will effectively come to conclusions in their own way. And as we observed with the sensing-intuition difference, both the *thinking* and *feeling* approaches are used by everyone, but one is usually preferred and better developed.

Further Factors Impacting the Two Scales

While understanding the two scales discussed previously provides the primary explanation of psychological strengths, two other factors affect how these operate in our lives.

First impacting factor: which activity we prefer

The first of these influencing factors arises from the observation that we tend to operate in one of the psychological activities—judging of perceiving—more than the other one (Figure 9-5). It is important to understand what is meant by *judging*. It simply refers to the process of coming to a conclusion and making a decision. It **does not** refer to the negative connotation often associated with this term that suggests the formation of a critical or negative opinion.

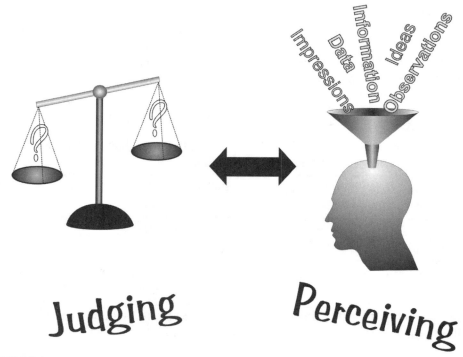

FIGURE 9-5
Preferred Activity

Table 9-3 outlines distinctions between people who prefer operating primarily in the *judging* psychological process and people who prefer operating primarily in the *perceiving* psychological process.

Judging	Perceiving
Characterized by others as an organized person	Characterized by others as a flexible person
Appear to need definite order and structure	Appear to be able to go with the flow
Prefer to have life under control	Prefer to experience life as it happens
Seem to find fulfillment in being decisive	Seem to find fulfillment in being curious, discovering surprises
Like clear limits and categories	Like freedom to explore without limits
Feel need to establish closure	Feel need to maintain openness
Meet deadlines by planning in advance	Meet deadlines by last minute pressure

TABLE 9-3
Judging-Perceiving Contrast

As we have stated before, it is important to remember that one way is not better than the other. People with either preference will effectively reach their objectives in life by following their own preferred way. And as we observed with the other two differences we have already looked at, both the *judging* and *perceiving* approaches are used by everyone, but one is usually preferred and better developed.

Second impacting factor: which activity we prefer

The other factor that affects the two main psychological processes emerges from the observation that our mental process is greatly influenced by where we get our energy in life for these processes (Figure 9-6). Some of us find that when we are taking in information and making decisions about it, we gain the greatest energy by interacting with the external world of people, experiences, and activities. We call this preference "extraversion." Others find that we gain more energy by interacting with the internal world of ideas, memories, and emotions when we are taking in information and making decisions about it. We call this preference "introversion." When we use that term, it is important to understand that this is **not** the typical use of that word that refers to a shy person who has some sort of social phobia and avoids other people. Instead, we refer to a person who prefers to process and make decisions internally.

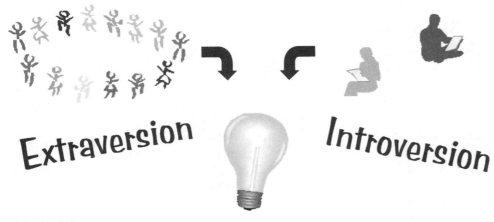

FIGURE 9-6
Preferred Environment

Table 9-4 outlines distinctions between people who prefer taking in information and making decisions primarily in an environment of *extraversion* and people who prefer taking in information and making decisions primarily in an environment of *introversion*.

Extraversion	Introversion
Act, then (maybe) reflect	Reflect, then (maybe) act
Talk thoughts out while formulating them	Formulate thoughts before speaking them out
Inclined to talk often regardless of whether or not it is necessary, usually using many words	Inclined to talk only when necessary, usually using few words

(Continued)

Extraversion	Introversion
Animated and exuberant	Quiet and reserved
Take the lead in initiating relationships	Wait for others to initiate a relationship
Energized by high level of social interaction	Drained by high level of social interaction
Seek relationships with many people at the same time	Seek very private; closely personal relationships with a few people

TABLE 9-4
Extraversion-Introversion Contrast

We will repeat one last time: it is important to remember that one way is not better than the other. People with either preference will effectively be energized as they take in information and make decisions in their own preferred way. And as we observed with the other three differences we have already looked at, both the *extraversion* and *introversion* approaches are used by everyone, but one is usually preferred and better developed.

Concepts Summary

Why is it important to understand this psychological process and its centrality to psychological strengths? The importance is obvious when we realize that this affects the way we will come to conclusions about our Life Calling and how we will make ultimate decisions concerning our life calling. Psychological strengths, like emotional strengths, are harder to detect than physical strengths. Once again, one of the most effective ways is listening to what others who know us well say about us. Another way is to complete exercises and assessments of our psychological strengths. We will look at some examples of how to do this in the Exercises section of this chapter.

Unfortunately, our modern society tends to value certain preferences in the psychological process more than others. Consequently, we end up with a culture where people are often trying to be someone they are not. This often leads to frustration and self-doubt and causes confusion in the search for a Life Calling.

Remember, each of the strength dimensions provides a bridge among the other dimensions. Psychological strengths provide the bridge of *reason* among the other strengths. What do we mean by this? It is through the psychological process of taking in information, organizing it, and then coming to conclusions about this information that we provide a rational approach to what is going on with the other strengths. This establishes a moral framework for our lives.

▶ Insight

The Bible presents quite a few choices for individuals to make as they pursue a Life Calling. For instance, at the end of his life as leader of Israel, Moses challenged the Israelites with these words:

> This day I call heaven and earth as witnesses against you that I have set before you life and death, blessings and curses. Now choose life, so that you and your children may live and that you may love the LORD your God, listen to his voice, and hold fast to him. DEUTERONOMY 30:19&20

The need for each of us to use our wills to make right choices is a constant theme of the Bible. This need lies at the very heart of the existence of our souls.

SCRIPTURAL INSIGHT 1 ▶ *You Have to Make the Choice Yourself*

"Now fear the LORD and serve him with all faithfulness. Throw away the gods your forefathers worshiped beyond the River and in Egypt, and serve the LORD. But if serving the LORD seems undesirable to you, then choose for yourselves this day whom you will serve, whether the gods your forefathers served beyond the River, or the gods of the Amorites, in whose land you are living. But as for me and my household, we will serve the LORD." JOSHUA 24:14-15

Joshua not only followed Moses as the leader of Israel, but also followed Moses' example in challenging the Israelites to make right choices. At the end of his tenure as their leader, Joshua was frustrated by the increasing trend of some of the Israelites turning away from God and worshiping other gods. In Joshua 24:14-15, he calls on them to exercise their wills and decide upon a course of action.

In our study and characterization of strengths, we defined psychological strength as the dimension of our lives that enables us to exercise our will in deciding upon courses of action. When it comes to our search for a Life Calling, this is incredibly important because the pursuit of a Life Calling will come down to an ability to decide upon courses of action.

Joshua had gathered his facts and was obviously convinced that the right choice was to serve the Lord. However, he tells the Israelites to gather their own facts concerning the desirability of serving the Lord. He also advises them to consider their options and then make their own choices.

You will need to follow that same advice as you consider your Life Calling. You cannot follow someone else's path. If you do, you will just be living their life. Instead, you are going to have to gather your own information and facts and then exercise your will and make decisions and choices.

It is clear that our strengths do not act independently of each other. Psychological strengths are greatly affected by the way we have used our intellectual strengths. If we have "correctly handled the word of truth," we will have better information with which to make decisions using our psychological strengths.

> **PERSONAL REFLECTION** ▷ Do you have a hard time making decisions? Are you tempted to just follow someone else's path? What could help you make better decisions on your own in life?

INSIGHT

SCRIPTURAL INSIGHT 2 ▶ *You Need to Become a Person Who Sees the Promised Land Rather Than Giants*

Then Caleb silenced the people before Moses and said, "We should go up and take possession of the land, for we can certainly do it." NUMBERS 13:30

Let's look at some examples in the Bible of this psychological decision-making process in action. We start with a story from the latter part of the Exodus era. The Israelites had been traveling through the desert on their way from Egypt to Canaan, the Promised Land. They arrived at an oasis known as Kadesh, a location about ninety miles south-southwest of Jerusalem. Moses decided to send spies up into Canaan to check out the land before taking the entire group. He chose twelve who went throughout the southern areas of what is now the nation of Israel. The twelve all saw the same sights; they collected the same data. But they processed the data quite differently.

Two of the spies, Joshua and Caleb, saw the fruitfulness of the land and combined this with data they had earlier collected related to God's miraculous actions in bringing the people of Israel out of Egypt, across the Red Sea, feeding them with manna, and giving them water from a rock. Based on this, they were convinced that God would deliver Canaan into the hands of the Israelites, and so they made this decision and advocated it to Moses and the people, as we read in our passage for today: "We should go up and take possession of the land, for we can certainly do it."

The other ten spies also saw the fruitfulness of the land. They, too, had seen the miraculous actions of God, but they did not give current credence to these acts. Instead, they were worried about the people of Anak who were reported to be descendants of the Nephilim. There are quite a few different speculative ideas about who these Nephilim are, but one thing seems to be common among all ideas—the Nephilim were giants among giants. So the ten were afraid and made their choice based on this fear. In Numbers 13:31-33, they strongly contended that no attempt be made to enter the land of Canaan.

But the men who had gone up with him said, "We can't attack those people; they are stronger than we are." And they spread among the Israelites a bad report about the land they had explored. They said, "The land we explored devours those living in it. All the people we saw there are of great size. We saw the Nephilim there (the descendants of Anak come from the Nephilim). We seemed like grasshoppers in our own eyes, and we looked the same to them."

The report of fear captivated the Israelites more than the message of optimism and faith delivered by Joshua and Caleb. The people complained bitterly against Moses, and in the end they did not go into Canaan, but instead wandered in the desert for forty years. The adults all died and it was their children who actually entered the Promised Land. Two adults did not die but did enter along with the children—Joshua and Caleb. They had psychological strengths that were much greater than the other Israelites. They were able to take in and process all the relevant data and then make a sounder choice.

If we are going to find and follow a Life Calling, we will need to be like Joshua and Caleb. Our decisions will need to be guided by relevant data leading to sound choices rather than by fear.

> **PERSONAL REFLECTION** > Are you following a path of sound choices in your life
> or are you guided by your fears? What could help you find more relevant data in your
> life on which to base your decisions?

SCRIPTURAL INSIGHT 3 > *Set the Right Priorities in Your Life in Making*
the Right Choice

*When Jesus heard this, he said to him, "You still lack one thing. Sell everything you
have and give to the poor, and you will have treasure in heaven. Then come, follow
me."* LUKE 18:22

The second example we will look at in the Bible of the psychological
decision-making process in action comes from the story of a person often
referred to as the rich young ruler. The story is important to our understanding of decision-making because it shows us how external factors can keep us
from making good internal decisions. Let's expand our text for today and pick
up the whole context in Luke 18:18-25.

> A certain ruler [Matthew refers to him as young in his account; hence, the
> nickname—rich young ruler] asked him, "Good teacher, what must I do to
> inherit eternal life?"

> "Why do you call me good?" Jesus answered. "No one is good—except God
> alone. You know the commandments: 'You shall not commit adultery, you
> shall not murder, you shall not steal, you shall not give false testimony, honor
> your father and mother.'"

> "All these I have kept since I was a boy," he said.

> When Jesus heard this, he said to him, "You still lack one thing. Sell every-
> thing you have and give to the poor, and you will have treasure in heaven.
> Then come, follow me."

> When he heard this, he became very sad, because he was very wealthy. Jesus
> looked at him and said, "How hard it is for the rich to enter the kingdom
> of God! Indeed, it is easier for a camel to go through the eye of a needle
> than for the rich to enter the kingdom of God."

You may not be rich, and because of this you are tempted to think that
this story does not apply to you. That would be a mistake. While this story
certainly has an application to the understanding of wealth and material possessions, what is even more important to learn from this story is the ability of
anything we possess externally to keep us from making good internal decisions. This could be relationships or activities just as easily as it could be
material possessions.

The rich young ruler's problem was that he cared more for his possessions
than he did for making the right decision and following after Jesus. As we
begin to discover our Life Calling, we will constantly be confronted with similar decisions. Our temptation will be to allow our current circumstances and
possessions to dictate our choices. When we give in to those temptations, we
will be in danger of making wrong decisions. We need to be directed by what
is right rather than what is comfortable.

INSIGHT

> **PERSONAL REFLECTION** What "possessions" might keep you from making good choices in your life? Are you guided more by what is right or by what is comfortable in your life?

SCRIPTURAL INSIGHT 4 *Accept the Good and the Bad That Accompany the Choices You Make*

His [Job's] wife said to him, "Are you still maintaining your integrity? Curse God and die!" He replied, "You are talking like a foolish woman. Shall we accept good from God, and not trouble?" In all this, Job did not sin in what he said. JOB 2:9-10

The next example we will look at in the Bible of the psychological decision-making process in action comes from the story of Job. Job was an extremely wealthy man who lived in the age of the patriarchs long before the time of Moses. He feared God and lived a righteous life. According to the story, on the supernatural level Satan challenged Job's integrity before God and was given permission to test Job. Satan brought a series of tragedies into Job's life, including the loss of his children, his wealth and his health. Things were so bad for Job that his wife suggested that he give up, curse God and die. But Job rebuked her and said, "Shall we accept good from God, and not trouble?"

Job's story is one of the more difficult ones to understand in the Bible. Why would God allow such a thing to be done to one of his faithful followers? This is one of those dynamics that occurs on a universal level that we will likely never understand in this life. The rebellion of Satan and his angels obviously had an impact across the universe that created some level of doubt that was not cleared up until the death and resurrection of Jesus. In that era of uncertainty, Satan may have had greater ability to challenge God and Job became an innocent victim. Whatever it was, Job's response is the lesson we can learn for decision-making. "Shall we accept good from God, and not trouble?"

If we try to make decisions about our Life Calling based only on those experiences in our lives that we deem good, we may miss some of the most important lessons. Those things we might consider trouble can provide us great insight into ourselves and into reality. Job knew that and maintained his steadfast trust in God. His decisions were based on that trust, not on a shallow misinterpretation of events in his life. This lesson leads us back to the foundational value of faith in the Life Calling Model. Our decision-making should be based on our trust in God—in good times and in bad times. This is the path that will lead us to our Life Calling

> **PERSONAL REFLECTION** Do you follow God only when things are going well, or do you also trust him when things are going poorly? What could help you to live more with the attitude that Job had and make your decisions based on trust rather than on what feels good?

SCRIPTURAL INSIGHT 5 *Make Sure You Know the Difference Between Your Will and God's Will*

He went away a second time and prayed, "My Father, if it is not possible for this cup to be taken away unless I drink it, may your will be done." MATTHEW 26:46

The final example we will look at in the Bible of the psychological decision-making process in action comes from the life of Jesus. Matthew 26:36-46 recounts Jesus' visit to the Garden of Gethsemane on the night he was betrayed by Judas and arrested. Verses 36-42 contain his experience of prayer and decision-making.

> Then Jesus went with his disciples to a place called Gethsemane, and he said to them, "Sit here while I go over there and pray." He took Peter and the two sons of Zebedee along with him, and he began to be sorrowful and troubled. Then he said to them, "My soul is overwhelmed with sorrow to the point of death. Stay here and keep watch with me."
>
> Going a little farther, he fell with his face to the ground and prayed, "My Father, if it is possible, may this cup be taken from me. Yet not as I will, but as you will."
>
> Then he returned to his disciples and found them sleeping. "Could you men not keep watch with me for one hour?" he asked Peter. "Watch and pray so that you will not fall into temptation. The spirit is willing, but the body is weak."

We can learn some important points about psychological strengths from this story.

First, Jesus was in a state of deep emotional stress and realized his need of support from his disciples. When making decisions under stress, the support of others is a valuable asset. As Ecclesiastes 4:10 remarks, "Pity those who fall and have no one to help them up!"

Second, Jesus' emotional decision was a desire for God to take the cup of suffering from him. His psychological decision, however, was to yield to the Father's will. The second and third time Jesus prayed, he moved the decision-making more and more into the Father's will. In the final words from our passage today, he says, " ... if it is not possible for this cup to be taken away unless I drink it, may your will be done."

Psychological strengths do not mean we should move ahead on our own with a disregard for God's will. When exercising our wills and making important decisions, we always need to make them in the larger context of God's will.

PERSONAL REFLECTION ⟩ Are you making decisions for your life that are formed in the larger context of God's will? What could help you make sure that you are looking at God's will?

INSIGHT

Discovery

How can the Discovery Guides help you identify and understand your *psychological strengths?*

T THEORY	The best source of theory about *Psychological Strengths* (as focused and defined in the Strengths Matrix and this study as related to using the will to make decisions) begins by looking at the concepts of Carl Jung. Subsequent research conducted by the mother-daughter team of Katherine Briggs and Isabella Myers is also a rich source of information about *Psychological Strengths*. You will also be able to increase your knowledge about *Psychological Strengths* in psychology classes at your college or university.
E EXAMPLES	Find people who excel at understanding their preferences in making good decisions. Observe them and find time to talk to them. Ask them to share with you how they discovered and developed these psychological strengths.
A ASSESSMENT	A variety of assessments claim to measure psychological strengths. As we have defined psychological strengths in this study, the best assessment for examining this is the *Myers-Briggs Type Indicator* (*MBTI*). The Step II interpretation of this assessment is very valuable in understanding how we operate in the decision-making process. Although this assessment can be used by a counselor without *MBTI* training, but who is trained in tests and measurements, it is much better understood when administered and debriefed by someone trained in how to use it.
C COUNSEL	Professional counselors and life coaches are trained to help you explore psychological strengths. Your college and university will likely have a counseling center with counselors trained in the use of MBTI and other psychological assessments. Additionally, family members, teachers, pastors, and friends know you well and can give you valuable insights about your psychological preferences.
H HISTORY	Search for historical biographies of notable people who have exhibited different psychological profiles in decision-making. Select some of these and learn from their experience. Also study the developmental history of the theory of psychological type and strengths.
E EXPERIENCE	Interact with people who have different psychological preferences than you. These experiences will help you understand yourself better and at the same time learn to appreciate and celebrate diversity in others.
R REFLECTION	Take time to reflect on what you learn about your psychological preferences from assessments and classes. Reflect on what this teaches you about how you will approach different aspects of life. Reflect on your disposition or attitude about psychological strengths in general and yours in particular.

▶ Story

Bunker Hill may have been the scene of the first major battle in the Revolutionary War, but the first gunshot was fired further to the west at Lexington and Concord, which was the *Nautilus*'s next destination. The Old North Bridge across the Concord River is known as the place where "once the embattled farmers stood, and fired the shot heard 'round the world." A statue of a Minuteman stands at one end of the bridge to honor this event.

The explorers plodded across the wooden planks of the bridge, marveling at how different the setting seemed from the battles of the Revolution. Concord River is a slow stream, and the gardens and trees surrounding the bridge seem to memorialize serenity more than violence.

"I wonder how the colonists ever decided to stage such a revolt," Abriella wondered as they paused to lean on the handrail of the bridge.

"How does anybody come to any decision?" Justin replied. "Look at us. We can't even make a decision about college, let alone revolution."

"Speak for yourself," Lorena interjected. "I had no trouble making my decision."

"Lor, do you really feel like you're better than the rest of us because you did that?" Ryan asked seriously—an unexpected change from his usual argumentative approach reserved for Lorena. "I mean, what if I don't go to college? Does that make me less of a person?"

"Are you going philosophical on me?" Lorena snapped, but then her face softened, and she placed her hand on top of Ryan's on the handrail. "I'm sorry, Ryan. You're right. I make it sound like that's what I think. I won't deny that I like studying and that I'm looking forward to college. But college or intellectual pursuit isn't what makes anybody greater or lesser of a person."

Abriella looked at Diana and raised her eyebrows, and Diana nodded back. The planets must still be aligned.

Diana turned to Adam. "So how do we make decisions? Is that one of our strengths?"

"I've got an idea," Adam replied. "Let's go over to Walden Pond. It's not too far from here. Remember when we read about Henry David Thoreau in English class? Walden Pond is where he used to go and think. Let's do the same and talk. Maybe we'll even end up making some decisions about our lives."

"I hope it helps me as much as it did Thoreau," Abriella commented. "I feel like I need to stop and think about all these decisions coming up so quickly. That sounds like the perfect place to do it."

STORY

They piled back into the *Nautilus*, and Ken drove the short mile through the center of Concord and on to Walden Pond, where the motorhome was parked at the headquarters. Then the explorers slowly walked down the path that ran alongside the small lake.

"It's bigger than what I thought of," Justin observed, "when I heard the word *pond*." When they came to Thoreau Cove and the site of his original house, they sat down on the leaves and pine needles and continued their discussion. It was almost as if Thoreau was there, listening to their conversation.

"Anybody remember their MBTI scores from Mrs. Wilson's class?" Adam asked.

They all answered that they did, except Ryan, who wasn't sure, but thought he did.

"Let's compare our results," Adam continued. "Decisions start by how we take in information," Adam explained. "Remember, some people primarily take in information through their five senses. Other people rely mostly on intuition. They can see patterns emerging from just a few facts."

"I'm one of those 'five-senses' people," Diana said confidently. "I need all the facts I can get with my senses. That other stuff doesn't seem real. I need to be able to see it or touch it."

"I know what you mean," Justin agreed. "Not some pie-in-the-sky pattern or hallucination that somebody says they have a hunch is real. Just give me the facts—step-by-step—and I'm happy."

"Do you know how boring you guys sound?" Ryan asked. "When I'm out there on the board, I can just feel when that right wave is coming. I can just feel it."

"Hard though it may be, I agree with Ryan," Lorena said.

"Fabulous. I knew we were soul mates," Ryan said, elbowing her.

"Well, I don't know if I'd go that far," Lorena laughed. "But I do like patterns. In history class, when we would just learn a bunch of dates, I was so bored. It's when all the events came together in a pattern to shape the future that interested me. It developed so many possibilities. I love that. I don't even care if we study the events in order."

"Oh my goodness! You really are messed up!" Diana exclaimed. "How can you study historical dates out of order? It makes no sense!"

Adam laughed. "See? We *are* different. What works for one person doesn't always work for another. You have to know your strength in that area."

"So after we collect the information, we're suppose to make some decision, right?" Lorena asked.

"That's right," Adam answered. "Evaluate your information and then come to some conclusion or judgment about it."

"And if I remember correctly, we do that in a different way as well," Abriella said.

"As a matter of fact, we do," Adam replied. "Some people make their judgments by relying on an impersonal basis of logical consequences. That's called objective thinking."

"That sounds like you, Adam," Diana commented.

"You're probably right, Diana," Adam said. "But I think Lorena makes her judgments in the same way."

"I think I agree," Lorena said. "But remind me of what the other way is before I commit to it."

"Other people make their judgments by relying on relationships or feelings," Adam continued. "They depend mostly on their personal social values."

"I'm definitely on the thinking side," Lorena decided. "That touchy-feely stuff is no way to make a decision."

"Wrong! Wrong! Wrong! My former soul mate!" Ryan cried in mock horror. "Peace and harmony are where it's all at. We just gotta love each other."

"Are we supposed to hum now, or hold hands and chant?" Lorena asked, raising an eyebrow at him.

"I don't know if I'm as far down the road as Ryan," Diana said, "but I do think I rely more on my feelings to make decisions than on—how did you describe it, Adam—objective thinking? That sounds so cold."

"Cold, but right!" Lorena added.

"Remember, Lor, what works for you and me may not work for Diana or Ryan," Adam cautioned.

"Yeah, Lor, give us a break," Ryan said, pretending to be deeply hurt.

Evidently the planets were not aligned anymore.

"So is that the end of it?" Abriella asked. "Is that how we make decisions?"

"No," Adam answered. "Remember, there were two other contrasts. The first is which process you prefer to engage in—taking in information, which is called perceiving, or making decisions, what MBTI called 'judging.' People who prefer perceiving tend to always keep things open and have a hard time coming to conclusions or decisions."

"Oh dear, that's me," Abriella sighed.

"So what's the problem, here?" Ryan asked. "Who needs the decisions? You've got the patterns and the feelings. Why not just keep them coming?"

"Oh brother!" Lorena sighed, exasperated. "You guys are such a mess. You can't make decisions. That's the trouble with all of you. You need to just choose a major and go to college and pursue it. Then you wouldn't be so lost like you are now."

"Let's make a decision now!" Ryan announced quickly. "Let's throw Lorena in the pond!" The others laughed as Lorena picked up a stick and swung it at Ryan, who dodged it easily.

"I don't think I agree with you, Lor," Justin said, breaking up the fight. "I may not have decided on a major, but I did make a decision about college. I think I'm one of those people who likes to bring closure to the information and make a decision."

"So what's the last contrast?" Diana asked Adam.

"Some people are more oriented in the psychological process toward interacting with the external world of other people, experiences, and activities," Adam explained. "Others are more oriented toward interacting with the internal world of ideas, memories, and emotions."

"Dude, I say give me that external world," Ryan said.

"Oh, yes," Lorena responded sarcastically. "There is no inner world of ideas in that empty head."

"Hey, be careful," Diana interrupted. "I think I'm an external world person too."

"I'm pretty sure I'm an internal person," Justin said.

"I think you're right," Adam agreed. "I think Abriella is too."

"I agree," Abriella said.

"I don't know which one I am," Lorena said with a puzzled frown on her face. "Sometimes I'm in my head, and other times I'm out with other people."

"Whichever one has a loud mouth, that's you," Ryan said. Lorena just glared at him.

"What about you, Adam?" Diana asked. "All of this talk about strengths and you apply it all to us, but we haven't heard much about you."

"I just lead the discussion," Adam replied. And it appeared that he had no intention of any further explanation. Even though they respected him more than anyone else, in many ways, Adam was a mystery to the others. Maybe Thoreau was there with them after all.

STORY

 **Exercises**

Understanding Your Psychological Strengths through *MBTI*

The best assessment related to *Psychological Strengths* was developed by the mother-daughter team of Katherine Briggs and Isabella Myers. This assessment is called the *Myers-Briggs Type Indicator (MBTI)*. It is quite likely that you will encounter this tool sometime in your college experience.

If it is possible for your school or institution to participate, we highly recommend that you take the *MBTI* from CPP, Inc. If you are able to complete this online assessment, you will receive a comprehensive report. This guide will provide you with:

- The MBTI Interpretive Report which will include your profile and an explanation of your results
- Workplace Report which will help you understand your MBTI results in your daily interactions in a work environment.

Work with your class instructor, or someone else in your institution, who is qualified to interpret MBTI results, and this person will facilitate you in your understanding of the results and how to use them in your life.

How Do You Make Decisions?

If you are unable to complete Exercise 1, complete this exercise as an alternative introduction to understanding your psychological strengths and how you use these strengths in making decisions.

Answer the four questions below. Evaluate each of the choices in the unshaded lines one line at a time. Then choose EITHER the right-hand response or the left-hand response. Place a checkmark in the box on either the left-hand or right-hand side of the chart. Total up the number of checkmarks in each set of answers, and place the sum for each side in the shaded box at the bottom of each set of answers.

How do you gather *most of the information for your life?*

Sensing		⇦or⇨	Intuition	
	Primarily on the concrete present	⇦focus⇨	Primarily on the abstract future	
	From concrete realities	⇦source⇨	From imaginative possibilities	
	Primarily to support practical solutions	⇦purpose⇨	Primarily to develop abstract concepts	
	Data gathered step-by-step	⇦path⇨	Data gathered in random directions	
	Present day experiences	⇦context⇨	Emerging theories	
	Traditional approaches preferred	⇦methods⇨	Original approaches preferred	
	← total number chosen →			

Once you have gathered the information, what is your primary basis for coming to conclusions and making most of the decisions about this information?

Thinking		⇦or⇨	Feeling	
	Rational thoughts	⇦context⇨	Empathetic feelings	
	How reasonable it is	⇦value⇨	How compassionate it is	
	Probing with questions	⇦method⇨	Accommodating with understanding	
	Critical thinking	⇦approach⇨	Compassionate consideration	
	Impartial toughness	⇦quality⇨	Sympathetic tenderness	
	Doing what is right	⇦goal⇨	Keeping harmony	
	← total number chosen →			

EXERCISES

Most people prefer to either bring the decision-making process to a decisive conclusion or to remain in the process of gathering information as long as they can. The two lists below describe what people in each of these categories are like. Which of the following describes what others see predominantly in you?

	Judging	⇦or⇨	Perceiving	
	Systematically move toward conclusions	⇦approach⇨	Move with flexibility toward conclusions	
	Plan out by setting goals	⇦method⇨	Maintain an openness to new information	
	Reach conclusion by starting early	⇦prompt⇨	Pressured toward conclusion by deadlines	
	Choice of actions determined by schedule	⇦pattern⇨	Play by ear in choice of actions	
	Decisions arrived at by set method	⇦endgame⇨	Decisions emerge out of unplanned insight	
	Predictably consistent	⇦summary⇨	Spontaneously unpredictable	
	⬅ total number chosen ➡			

In the decision-making process, where do you prefer to direct your attention and behavior, and in so doing find more energy?

	Extraversion	⇦or⇨	Introversion	
	Initiate interaction with others	⇦contact⇨	Wait for others to interact with you	
	Talk thoughts out as decisions are formed	⇦method⇨	Keep thoughts in until decision are formed	
	Interact gregariously with many people	⇦interaction⇨	Interact intimately with a few people	
	Take action in experiential learning	⇦analysis⇨	Contemplate in reflective learning	
	Often share your ideas with others	⇦discussion⇨	Mainly listen to the ideas of others	
	Act first and then evaluate the actions	⇦pattern⇨	Think first and then act accordingly	
	⬅ total number chosen ➡			

Look over your choices in Exercise 2 and then think about the direction this might give you in various situations.

1. The majority of the information I collect comes from _____ (sensing or intuition).
   a. Because of this, when I make decisions:
      • I will tend to concentrate on…
      • I might tend to neglect…
   b. Students with a *Sensing* preference…
      • Favor gathering a lot of facts and details. If this is your preference, you will likely need to take more notes in class and underline key points in your textbooks.
      • Have a tendency may be to postpone decisions until they have more facts or information. If this is your preference, begin your data collection early in any project in which you are involved.
      • Should pick instructors who provide detailed information and clear instructions. Avoid instructors who are random in their thoughts and don't follow a sequence in the class.

- Can sometimes miss the bigger picture. Bringing together all of your details into an outline of a concept map can help you overcome this.
   c. Students with an *Intuition* preference…
   - Favor looking at bigger concepts and ideas. If this is your preference, you may get bored in classes that focus on details rather than concepts. Don't be afraid to ask questions in class about the meaning of what you are learning.
   - Have a tendency to make decisions quickly on a premonition or hunch. If this is your preference, make sure that you take time to gather information that could help you in your decision.
   - Should pick instructors who explore big concepts and challenge students to dream. Avoid instructors who predominantly give lectures characterized by detailed lists of information.
   - Can sometimes ignore important information. Discipline yourself into taking notes or making lists as part of your learning and decision-making strategies.

2. The majority of my decisions are made on the basis of _____ (logic or relationships).
   a. Because of this, when I make decisions related to my college experience:
   - I will tend to rely on…
   - I might tend to ignore…
   b. Students with a *Thinking* preference…
   - Favor critically analyzing anything they are studying, and often take a leading role in class discussions and don't hesitate to ask challenging questions. If this is your preference, don't hesitate to debate issues with fellow students with a similar preference.
   - Have a tendency to make decisions based on rational arguments that ignore valuable emotional information. If this is your preference, make sure that you take time to reflect on the emotional and relational impact of your decision.
   - Should pick instructors who they respect and who can challenge them intellectually. Avoid instructors who don't respect the ideas or contributions of the students or who don't have a clear understanding of the area in which they are teaching.
   - Can sometimes be over confident and closed to the ideas of others. Force yourself to jot down good ideas others have when you are in a discussion, treat others respectfully even when you disagree.
   c. Students with a *Feeling* preference…
   - Favor social interaction in classes and in studying. If this is your preference, you need to see personal meaning to what you are learning. Find others who are like you to study together in a group.
   - Have a tendency to avoid decisions for fear of bringing pain to another person. If this is your preference, take time to talk to another person about a decision you need to make. They might help you see that short-term discomfort can lead to long-term benefit.
   - Should pick instructors who like group work, discussions, and relating to students. Avoid instructors who predominantly give logical lectures and leave no time for class interaction.
   - Can sometimes ignore doing the right thing because it is a painful choice. Find a friend who can hold you accountable in such situations and encourage you.

3. When others observe me, they will for the most part see me _____ (*judging* or *perceiving*).
   a. This gives me a benefit at…
   b. Students with a *Judging* preference…
   - Favor classes and studies that come to clear conclusions. If this is your preference, you need to see closure to what you are studying. You also will want clear expectations and guidelines.
   - Have a tendency to believe that making the decision is the most important part of the decision-making process, at the risk of doing so without all the information necessary. If this is your preference, take time to make out a list of pros and cons before make a decision to make sure that you have clearly thought it through and gathered sufficient information
   - Should pick instructors and classes that are structured and lead to a clear conclusion. Avoid instructors who are random dreamers with no clear lesson plan.

EXERCISES

- Can sometimes be too rigid and inflexible in their approach to school, life and others. If this is your preference, take time to engage in activities that are purely creative and don't necessarily have time limit.

c. Students with a *Perceiving* preference...
- Favor constantly exploring new ideas related to what they are studying, and don't like it when instructors jump to quick conclusions. If this is your preference, don't be afraid to explore on your own alternate concepts to what was presented in class.
- Have a tendency to postpone or change decisions whenever any new information comes to light. If this is your preference, make sure that you take into account the need to move forward with decisions even at the risk of it not necessarily being the ideal.
- Should pick instructors and classes that lend themselves to open-ended self-explanation. Avoid instructors whose primary concern seems to be "covering the material" or finishing the book.
- Can sometimes be disorganized in their approach to life. If this is the case, you will need to force yourself at times to make a schedule or budget if you are going to be successful. Find others who can help you get started on doing this.

4. The majority of my energy comes from _____ (*extraversion* characterized by external interaction or *introversion* characterized by internal reflection).
   a. This gives me a benefit at...
   - If I answered "external interaction," my answer to #3 is what will be dominant in my decision-making.
   - If I answered "internal reflection," the option I did not select in #3 will be dominant in my decision-making.
   b. Students with an *Extraversion* preference...
   - Favor classes that give plenty of opportunity for them to talk and discuss ideas. If this is your preference, you should form study groups to discuss ideas with others.
   - Have a tendency to take action before decisions are clearly thought through. If this is your preference, set an arbitrary length of time before you take action in order to force yourself to think through all the alternatives.
   - Should pick instructors who give students plenty of time to talk in class. Avoid instructors who predominantly lecture and leave no time for class interaction.
   - Can sometimes dominate discussions and ignore the ideas of others. If you fall into this trap, try keeping a log of the times you talk in a class and set a limit so as to allow others to participate.
   c. Students with an *Introversion* preference...
   - Favor classes that give plenty of opportunity for reflection and deep thought. If this is your preference, take time out of class to think through the topics that were addressed in class and comments made by the instructor or other students.
   - Have a tendency to make decisions through the internal thought process, and in so doing, leave others out of the process. If this is your preference, make sure that you share your ideas with others before locking them into mind.
   - Should pick instructors who ask reflective questions and are gentle in their approach to a class. Avoid instructors who are over-dominant in class or who put down students for their ideas.
   - Can sometimes never share an idea until they have clearly thought it through and made sure it is correct. If this is your preference, the problem is that by the time you are ready, the class has already moved on to some other topic, and you end up never taking part in the class discussions.

> Based on your responses in Exercise 1, how will this affect the way you make decisions in college, e.g. classes to take, when to study, which major to pursue, etc.?

EXERCISES

Expanding Your Understanding of Your Psychological Type by Using the *Psychological-Type 360*

1. Identify four different people who know you and who love and care for you. Choose the four so that they represent each of the following categories:
   - Parent _____
   - Teacher (present or former) _____
   - Friend _____
   - Sibling or relative who is younger than you _____

2. Provide all of the people you have identified with a copy of the *Psychological-Type 360* (not the Mirror) chart below and ask them to identify what they see as my preference in each of six contrasts in the four sections. Let them know that it is okay if they answer that they are not sure. Encourage them to give an example if they answer that a learning style is strong in you.

▶ **Psychological-Type 360**

How do you perceive that I gather information in my life?

	Sensing	⇦or⇨	Intuition	Can you give me an example of when you have seen this in me?
	Primarily on the concrete present	⇦focus⇨	Primarily on the abstract future	
	From concrete realities	⇦source⇨	From imaginative possibilities	
	Primarily to support practical solutions	⇦purpose⇨	Primarily to develop abstract concepts	
	Data gathered step-by-step	⇦path⇨	Data gathered in random directions	
	Present day experiences	⇦context⇨	Emerging theories	
	Traditional approaches preferred	⇦methods⇨	Original approaches preferred	
	← total number chosen →			

Once I have gathered information, what do you see me using as my primary basis for coming to conclusions and making most of the decisions about this information?

	Thinking	⇦or⇨	Feeling	Can you give me an example of when you have seen this in me?
	Rational thoughts	⇦context⇨	Empathetic feelings	
	How reasonable it is	⇦value⇨	How compassionate it is	

(Continued)

	Thinking	⇦or⇨	Feeling		Can you give me an example of when you have seen this in me?
	Probing with questions	⇦method⇨	Accommodating with understanding		
	Critical thinking	⇦approach⇨	Compassionate consideration		
	Impartial toughness	⇦quality⇨	Sympathetic tenderness		
	Doing what is right	⇦goal⇨	Keeping harmony		
	⇦ total number chosen ⇨				

Which of the following activities do you see me predominantly operating in?

	Judging	⇦or⇨	Perceiving		Can you give me an example of when you have seen this in me?
	Move systematically toward conclusions	⇦approach⇨	Move with flexibility toward conclusions		
	Plan out by setting goals	⇦method⇨	Maintain an openness to new information		
	Reach conclusion by starting early	⇦prompt⇨	Pressured toward conclusion by deadlines		
	Choice of actions determined by schedule	⇦pattern⇨	Choice of actions played by ear		
	Decisions arrived at by set method	⇦endgame⇨	Decisions emerge out of unplanned insight		
	Appear to be predictably consistent	⇦summary⇨	Appear to be spontaneously unpredictable		
	⇦ total number chosen ⇨				

In the decision-making process, where do you see me directing my attention and behavior, and in so doing finding more energy?

	Extraversion	⇦or⇨	Introversion		Can you give me an example of when you have seen this in me?
	Initiate interaction with others	⇦contact⇨	Wait for others to interact with you		
	Talk thoughts out as decisions are formed	⇦method⇨	Keep thoughts in until decision are formed		

Interact gregariously with many people	⇦interaction⇨	Interact intimately with a few people	
Take action in experiential learning	⇦analysis⇨	Contemplate in reflective learning	
Often share your ideas with others	⇦discussion⇨	Mainly listen to the ideas of others	
Act first and then evaluate the actions	⇦pattern⇨	Think first and then act accordingly	
← total number chosen →			

3. Now you personally answer the questions for each of the three learning styles using the results from Exercise 1 or 2 and your perception.

Psychological Type Mirror	Definition	What was my preference in this category?	What has been my most effective example demonstrating my preference?
Sensing-Intuition	How you gather most of the information for your life		
Thinking-Feeling	Your primary basis for coming to conclusions and making decisions about information you gather		
Judging-Perceiving	The process in which you prefer to remain dealing with information		
Extraversion-Introversion	Where you direct your attention and find more energy in the decision-making process		

4. Compare your preference to the evaluation from others in the Psychological-Type 360. What do others see in you that you may not see in yourself? What can you learn about your perception of yourself?

EXERCISES

5. Reflect on what you learned in Exercise 1 or 2 and Exercise 3 and summarize below what they have revealed to you about yourself.

Name: _____ Date: _____ Class: _____ Section: _____

Stranded in the Desert

From Johnson, Frank P. *Joining Together: Group Theory and Group Skills,* *7/e.* Copyright © 2000 by Pearson Education. Reprinted by permission of Pearson Education, Inc., Upper Saddle River, NJ.

Read the following description of a problem situation. Then answer the questions that follow.

You are one of the members of a geology club that is on a field trip to study unusual formations in the New Mexico desert. It is the last week in July. You have been driving over old trails, far from any road, in order to see out-of-the-way formations. At about 10:00 A.M. the specially equipped minibus in which your club is riding overturns, rolls into a 22-foot ravine, and burns. The driver and professional adviser to the club are killed. The rest of you are relatively uninjured.

You know that the nearest ranch is approximately 45 miles east of where you are. There is no closer habitation. When your club does not report to its motel that evening, you will be missed. Several persons know generally where you are, but because of the nature of your outing they will not be able to pinpoint your whereabouts.

The area around you is rather rugged and very dry. There is a shallow water hole nearby, but the water is contaminated by worms, animal feces and urine, and several dead mice. You heard from a weather report before you left that the temperature would reach 108 degrees, making the surface temperature 128 degrees. You are all dressed in lightweight summer clothing and you all have hats and sunglasses.

While escaping from the minibus each member of your group salvaged a couple of items; there are twelve in all. Your task is to rank these items according to their importance to your survival, with 1 being most important and 12 least important. Assume that the group has decided to stick together. How will you and your group survive?

___ magnetic compass

___ book, *Plants of the Desert*

___ rearview mirror

___ large knife

___ flashlight (four-battery size)

___ .38-caliber pistol

___ one transparent plastic ground cloth (6 ft by 4 ft) per person

___ piece of heavy-duty, light-blue canvas (20 ft by 20 ft)

___ one jacket per person

___ one 2-quart plastic canteen full of water per person

___ accurate map of the area

___ large box of kitchen matches

1. Look over the top five items you selected as being most important. Why did you select these particular five? What is your reasoning?

2. Form groups of about five people. You may assume that the number of club members is the same as the number of persons in your group. Read over the description of the situation again. What are the first decisions your group will need to make? As a group, come to a consensus of how you and your group will survive. What are some of the major problems that your group will have to overcome? Pay close attention to your reasons (premises) and your conclusions.

(After completing this exercise, turn to Appendix A to find what the experts have to say.)

3. If you are completing this exercise as part of a group, compare the psychological type preferences for each person in the group with the decisions that person made in this exercise. Can you detect any pattern in the decision making process of this exercise?

EXERCISES

References

The following resources have been used in this chapter.

Briggs-Myers, I., McCalulley, M.H., Quenk, N.L., & Hammer, A.L. (1998). *MBTI Manual: A Guide to the Development and Use of the Myers-Briggs Type Indicator* (3rd ed.). Palo Alto, CA: Consulting Psychologists Press, Inc.

Johnson, D., & Johnson, F. (2000). *Joining Together: Group Theory and Group Skills* (7th ed.). Boston: Allyn and Bacon.

The following resources may be useful to you in your continuing exploration of Life Calling as you look at your Unique Design and your *psychological strengths.*

Harbaugh, G.L. (1990). *God's Gifted People: Discovering Your Personality as a Gift.* Minneapolis, Minnesota: Augsburg Fortress.

Kise, J.A.G., Stark, D., and Hirsh, S.K. (2005). *Lifekeys: Discover Who You Are.* Bloomington, Minnesota: Bethany House Publishers.

Schwen, M.R., and Bass, D.C., Eds. (2006). *Leading Lives That Matter: What We Should Do and Who We Should Be.* Grand Rapids, Michigan: Erdmans Publishing Co.

Smith, G.T. (2011). *Courage and Calling: Embracing Your God-given Potential.* Downers Grove, Illinois: Intervarsity Press.

Empowered by Spiritual Strengths

Strengths MATRIX™	DIMENSIONS				
	Gifts	Knowledge	Skills	Attitude	TOTAL
D O M A I N S — Physical					
Emotional					
Intellectual					
Psychological					
Spiritual					

FIGURE 10-1
Spiritual Domain of the *Strengths Matrix™*

The *Strengths Matrix* is comprised of five strengths domains. In this chapter we will explore *Spiritual Strengths*.

CHAPTER OBJECTIVES

1. Understand the nature and value of spiritual strengths
2. Explain the transcendental nature of spiritual strengths in relationship to the other strengths
3. Identify the various levels of spiritual guidance that can occur in your life
4. Understand the identity and nature of intrinsic motivations of service and their relationship to spiritual strengths
5. Begin identifying spiritual strengths and intrinsic motivations in your life

CONCEPTS

Concepts

You could study and examine physical, emotional, intellectual, and psychological strengths from a purely human point of view. If you did, however, you would overlook the greatest domain of the Strengths Matrix, spiritual strengths. You can assess yourself, study theory, engage in personal development, and all the other valuable activities available to you in college, but in the long run, if you truly have a Life Calling, then you need to recognize that there is a power outside yourself greater than you who is calling you. It is no mistake that one of the twelve steps learned by persons working to overcome addictions is "recognizing a greater power that can give strength." This power comes from a dimension that transcends those connected to the other four strengths. To a great extent, this brings us back to the discussion in Chapter 2 regarding intentional existence in the universe. In most cultures this spirituality is attributed to a divine source or God.

We defined the *spiritual strengths* domain as the capacity in our lives that enables us to discern and respond in service to transcendental influences that are encountered above or beyond what is explainable by natural law or phenomena. What does that mean? There is level of interaction that occurs in our lives that cannot be explained by the processes we observe in the natural world. This can be referred to as God's inner leading, yet it would be incorrect to define this as if it was the only strength in which God leads. God works in all five of the dimensions in the Strengths Matrix and, consequently, leads us through all of these dimensions. However, because the spiritual dimension functions outside the natural realm, it often makes it easier to allow God's influence to occur in this dimension.

The definition of *spiritual strengths* identifies two primary areas of spiritual interaction—discerning and responding. Discernment focuses more on the receptive interaction where we listen and gain direction for our lives. Responding focuses more on the active part of the spiritual domain where we carry out the directions we have gained through discernment.

Spiritual Discernment

In all students there is an almost universal desire for meaning, significance, and hope. Yet many times the fast pace of college life can leave you feeling that none of these exist in your life. One of the most important things you can do to address this problem is to take time in your life to develop spiritual well-being. This can lead you to discern the spiritual influences at work in your life.

It is easy to get caught up in the intellectual and emotional challenges of college and forget that there is an abstract level of interaction that occurs in your life that cannot be explained by the processes you observe in the natural world. It is a dimension that exists apart from concrete existence. In fact it transcends dynamics associated with the other physical, emotional, intellectual, or psychological strengths.

When your spiritual wellness is neglected, often all other areas of your life begin to encounter problems, and you feel like you have no spiritual direction. This makes it very difficult to discover a Life Calling. So what spiritual habits can you develop that can help keep this spiritual neglect from happening and help promote spiritual well-being? Figure 10-2 shows eight important spiritual disciplines we can develop that will increase our spiritual strength.

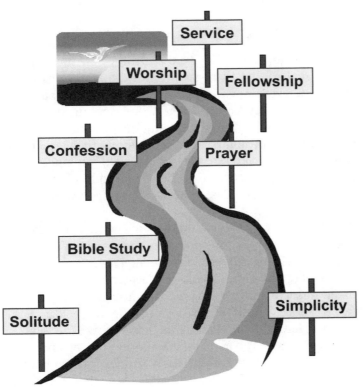

FIGURE 10-2
Spiritual Disciplines

Meditational Solitude.   Spend time by yourself so that you can listen to God's voice in your spirit.

Simplicity.   Reduce the distractions in your life that keep you from hearing God.

Bible Study.   Read passages in the Bible and seek to understand them and then apply the principles learned to your life.

Prayer.   Dialogue with God about both God's concerns and yours.

Confession.   Admit it to other people and to God when you have done something wrong to them and seek forgiveness.

Fellowship.   Join with other people in small groups and in large gatherings to pursue spiritual growth.

Worship.   Offer reverent honor and homage to God.

Service.   Develop a decided pattern of engaging with others to solve problems or needs encountered by these others.

A good way to start your spiritual wellness is to assess your current spiritual well-being. In the Exercises section of this chapter, you will have the opportunity to complete such an assessment.

Spiritual Response

As you begin to develop the ability to discern the spiritual influences in your life, you need to realize that these supernatural interactions take place on at least three different levels in your life. Most dramatic, of course, would be the phenomenal level. This level would involve miraculous events that guide or enable your path with no rational explanation. Second is the informational level. Here you receive thoughts and impressions that clearly do not come from your own mind, but provide you with crucial guidance. Third would be the motivational level. These are inner forces placed in your life to compel and guide how you serve others. This is the virtue of *servanthood*, a concept that was introduced in Chapter 4.

Central to the meaning of servanthood is the word *serve*. *Serve* is most often defined as "carrying out duties for another person; giving aid, assistance, or help to another person." As you will recall from Chapter 4, serving occurs from three different degrees of motivation. The lowest degree is *servitude*. This is where a person is forced to serve another person. The motivation is self-protection. The middle degree is *service*. This is where a person offers a decided act of serving to another person. Here the motivation is generosity. The highest degree is *servanthood*. This is where a person serves another out of an attitudinal act of serving. In other words, it just automatically springs forth in situations where it is called for out of an attitude of love. It is at this level that spiritual strengths can truly flourish in your life. As people move toward a spiritual response of servanthood in their lives that can lead them to flourish, they will encounter three primary components: spiritual gifts, spiritual fruit, and spiritual development.

Spiritual Gifts

One of the clearest discussions of spiritual gifts comes from the first-century writings of Paul of Tarsus, a keen observer of human nature, a leading theologian of that time, and an early leader of Christianity. Table 10-1 outlines the four most widely acknowledged lists, all from first century letters of Paul.

Paul starts his discussion in the Corinthian letter with the exhortation, "Now about spiritual gifts … I do not want you to be uninformed." He goes on to say that "there are different kinds of gifts, but the same Spirit distributes them. There are different kinds of service, but the same Lord. There are different kinds of working, but in all of them and in everyone it is the same God at work."

In trying to understand spiritual gifts, here is what we can extract from Paul. First, these operate in the spiritual dimension of our lives as gifts brought into that dimension by God. Second, the primary (and possibly only) context of spiritual gifts in our lives is service to others. Third, the power that operates spiritual gifts is directly from God. Finally, spiritual gifts occur in all people at some level of God's empowerment. With that understanding, let's look at the four lists.

The Romans letter lists seven gifts that are tied to the Greek word that means gift of grace. This implies that these different gifts come into our lives according to the grace given to us by God, not by our own doing. The context also suggests that these gifts should be allowed to motivate us from within to serve others in a particular way.

The Corinthians letter contains two lists. The first list outlines nine gifts as manifestations, or expressions, of God's Spirit in our lives. These are given to us for the common good, in other words, to benefit all of us in service to each other, not just for a person to use in isolation from other people. God gives these gifts to each person, just as God determines, not as the person seeks or chooses.

Romans 12:3-9	1 Corinthians 12:7-11	1 Corinthians 12:28	Ephesians 4:11-13
1. Prophesying	1. Wisdom	1. Apostles	1. Apostles
2. Serving	2. Knowledge	2. Prophets	2. Prophets
3. Teaching	3. Faith	3. Teachers	3. Evangelists
4. Exhorting	4. Healing	4. Miracles	4. Pastors
5. Giving	5. Miracles	5. Healers	5. Teachers
6. Governing	6. Prophecy	6. Helpers	
7. Mercy	7. Discernment	7. Administrators	
	8. Tongues	8. Tongues	
	9. Interpretations		

TABLE 10-1
Spiritual Gifts

The second Corinthians list identifies eight gifts as appointments by God of service to the church.

In the Ephesians letter, Paul again speaks of spiritual gifts, specifically mentioning five as given to some that they might prepare God's people for service. Three of these five match similar appointments in the second Corinthians list.

What can we learn from spiritual gifts that we can apply to our search for a Life Calling? First of all, they are very important elements in the dimension of our spiritual strengths that help to prepare us to carry out a distinct Life Calling. Second, because of this distinctiveness, we will each find particular roles in our Life Calling that better suit us than other roles. Finally, our Life Calling will best be discovered in the larger context of service to others rather than a career search. In fact, even our career searches should be conducted in a larger context of how we can best serve others—the concept of *servanthood* discussed earlier in this chapter.

Servanthood can best be described as love acting in life's relationships. *Servanthood* will express itself in a variety of ways, as we will serve each other differently based on the differing inner motivations that have been placed within us. These intrinsic motivations provide one of the best areas of study when looking at the spiritual strengths domain in the Strengths Matrix. The concept of intrinsic motivation can be traced back as far as classical Greek philosophy. However, one of the best classifications of intrinsic motivations in the context of spiritual gifts can be patterned after seven identified in the Romans letter written by Paul.

Based on historical context, plus assessing how they occur in thousands of individuals, the seven intrinsic motivations can best be labeled and defined as follows (Millard, 2012):

Proclaiming.   The inward motivation and capacity to:
- discern what is morally right and wrong in situations
- respond in service by publicly speaking out from internal convictions concerning what has been discerned

Helping.   The inward motivation and capacity to:
- discern legitimate needs or tasks others have
- respond in service by finding practical ways to provide physical assistance to help them fulfill these needs and tasks

Teaching.   The inward motivation and capacity to:
- discern truth through careful research
- respond in service by clearly presenting this truth to others in such a way that it will be easy to learn

Exhorting.   The inward motivation and capacity to:
- discern encouragement and practical solutions needed for life problems
- respond in service by outlining practical steps of actions others should take to overcome problems

Giving.   The inward motivation and capacity to:
- discern financial needs others have in their lives or efforts
- respond in service by financially investing in and supporting other worthwhile people and projects

Managing.   The inward motivation and capacity to:
- discern the organizational needs others have when working collectively together
- respond in service by organizing, coordinating and guiding their activities and setting goals for their endeavors

Comforting.   The inward motivation and capacity to:
- discern the emotions of others
- respond in service by providing mercy to those who are in emotional distress

These motivations will strongly influence the way you respond to people, situations, and problems in the world. The patterns of your inner motivations also help determine the roles you will adopt as a result of these spiritual strengths. Because of this, they also form good guidelines for your Life Calling.

Spiritual Fruit

In Paul's letter to the Galatians, he provides a list of virtues self-titled as fruit of the Spirit (Figure 10-3): *love, joy, peace, patience, kindness, goodness, faithfulness, gentleness*, and *self-control*.

An important observation can be made that distinguishes this segment of spiritual strengths from that found in spiritual gifts. First, the singular "fruit" is used in the title rather than the plural "fruits." Unlike spiritual gifts, where different gifts are given to different people, the nine elements of spiritual fruit

FIGURE 10-3
Spiritual Fruit

are all present in all people who freely allow spiritual power to work in their lives. In other words, this is not a list where we choose which fruit we want and disregard those we don't want. Because of this, we should not focus on high-lighting the strength of one element in relationship to the others. For example, it would be wrong to say I have the spiritual strength of peace. We should, rather, focus on measuring the presence of all elements of fruit in assessing levels of spiritual strength. The more complete the package of the nine elements develops in our lives, the greater will be the spiritual strength that leads to freedom in us, and the greater it will serve us as an asset in discovering and pursuing our Life Calling.

Spiritual Development

In the writings of Peter, like Paul a leader of the early Christian church, Peter outlined a list of eight spiritual qualities that we should include as part of our character development plan in maximizing our spiritual strengths. "Make every effort to add to your faith goodness; and to goodness, knowledge; and to knowledge, self-control; and to self-control, perseverance; and to persever-ance, godliness; and to godliness, brotherly kindness; and to brotherly kind-ness, love." (2 Peter 1:5–7)

The need for totality of these spiritual efforts in character development is more similar to spiritual fruit than it is to spiritual gifts. In other words, we don't receive a few of these qualities and forget about the others. To the con-trary, a case could be made in Peter's presentation that these qualities form in a sequence (illustrated in Figure 10-4), and that the spiritual strength of

FIGURE 10-4
Peter's Ladder

character is not achieved until all the qualities are present. Whether or not that is the case, the one thing we can conclude is that the total sequence can be used, similar to spiritual fruit, as evaluation criteria for the effectiveness of all our strengths in the *Strengths Matrix*.

Concepts Summary

When a comparison is made of the three categories—gifts, fruit, development—only one element shows up in all three categories—*faith. Faith* is a gift, a fruit, and a quality to be developed. That should be an indication of how important the element of *faith* is in the search for a Life Calling. It is not surprising to see that *faith* is the first element of the first component in the Life Calling Model.

As with the other strengths, one of the most effective ways to discover your spiritual strengths is listening to what others who know you well say about you. Another way is to complete exercises and assessments of our spiritual strengths. We will look at some examples of how to do this in the Exercises section of this chapter.

Our modern society tends to value strengths that can be explained in a rational or natural framework. When we follow this tendency, we end up with a culture where people often ignore spiritual strengths and the virtue of servanthood. This often leads to misdirection and a self-centered life and clouds the search for a Life Calling.

Remember, each of the strength dimensions provides a bridge among the other dimensions. Spiritual strength provides the bridge of *conviction* among the other strengths. What do we mean by this? It is through the spiritual strengths, especially the virtue of servanthood, that we gain a driving force from a source outside ourselves to guide what is going on with the other strengths. This establishes an inspirational framework for our lives.

CONCEPTS

Insight

Jesus taught us that there is a spiritual dynamic that operates within the human nature that is separate from all the other strengths. In speaking to the Jewish leader Nicodemus, Jesus referred to the other strengths as "flesh." "Jesus answered, 'Very truly I tell you, no one can enter the kingdom of God without being born of water and the Spirit. Flesh gives birth to flesh, but the Spirit gives birth to spirit.'" John 3:5&6. The Bible has much to say about this area of strength in our lives.

SCRIPTURAL INSIGHT 1 ▸ *Seeing Should Not Always Be Believing*

There is a way that appears to be right, but in the end it leads to death. PROVERBS 14:12

We defined *spiritual strength* as the domain in our lives that enables us to discern and respond in service to transcendental influences that are encountered above or beyond what is explainable by natural law or phenomena. We discovered that there is a level of interaction that operates in our lives that cannot be accounted for by natural explanations. This can be referred to as God's inner leading, yet it would be incorrect to define this as if it was the only strength domain in which God leads. God works in all five of the domains in the Strengths Matrix and, consequently, leads us through all of these domains.

However, because the spiritual domain functions outside of the natural realm, it often makes it easier to allow God's influence to occur in this domain. Why is this? The proverb that provides our text for today helps us understand the answer to this question. When we rely only on the other four strengths domains (physical, emotional, intellectual, and psychological), we will end up seeing things in our life path that appear to be "right." But when we travel down that path, we may end up encountering destruction. There are many aspects of our Life Calling that can only be "seen" with spiritual eyes.

At the beginning of the story of Paul's second great missionary journey recorded in Acts 16, he was traveling with Silas and Timothy. Paul wanted to travel into the region of Bithynia. It appeared to him to be the right thing to do. But verse 7 states, "...the Spirit of Jesus would not allow them to." In fact, a few nights later, Paul received a vision of a man in Macedonia begging him to come and help them. So that is where Paul and his companions went. Some very dramatic events took place because of this and a great work was accomplished.

Can you imagine Paul trying to explain his decision to others? They probably shook their heads and rolled their eyes. God expects us to use our physical, emotional, intellectual, and psychological strengths in making decisions about life. For the most part, that's where we should begin—just like Paul did in this story. And in most cases that will be the best path to follow. However, we should always be open and ready for God to block our path and take us in a different direction that makes little or no sense to us. When that happens, we will need to rely on that first foundational value of faith, knowing that God has a bigger plan that we can't see.

> **PERSONAL REFLECTION** > Do you follow only those ways that seem right to you, or are you open to God's leading in a direction that might not make sense to you? Do you take time to listen in your spirit to hear God's Spirit speaking to you?

SCRIPTURAL INSIGHT 2 > *Start First by Seeking the Right Things*

But seek first his kingdom and his righteousness, and all these things will be given to you as well. MATTHEW 6:33

The mistake that many people make when it comes to the domain of spiritual strengths and input in their lives is to believe that they should just sit back and wait for visions like Paul had, or a burning bush like Moses encountered, or a talking donkey like Balaam heard. They may even try to set up such miraculous events like Gideon did with his two fleece experiments. But Matthew 6:33 helps us to see that this is the wrong place to start in the area of the spiritual and supernatural domain. Instead, we should begin with God's kingdom and his righteousness. And there is nothing hidden or secret about these two. Ninety-nine percent of what you need to know about God's kingdom and righteousness is revealed in the Bible. So when we are confronted about decisions to make in life, that is the best place to start.

The problem that many of us have is that we wait until a decision is upon us before we start seeking God's kingdom and his righteousness. I have heard all sorts of interesting stories about people frantically searching for information in times like this. Some just let the Bible fall open and whatever page appears, they believe they will find the guidance they need on that page. This seems closer to a magical approach than a spiritual approach to seeking God's will. I have heard that others start reading the Bible from Genesis 1:1 every time they need some guidance. While this may result in many good opportunities to read the Bible, it is not an efficient way to work with God. A far more efficient and effective approach to God's kingdom and his righteousness is to be constantly studying the Bible. That's what Matthew 6:33 means when it says to seek first. When we have made that effort earlier in our lives, we will be prepared to hear and discern God's Spirit when critical times arise in our lives demanding decisions. Paul had studied God's Word thoroughly prior to his vision of the Macedonian man. Hence, he was not thrown off guard when the vision came.

In Matthew 7:7 & 8, not too far removed from our devotional verse for today, Jesus reiterates the need to take action in seeking God's will with these words: "Ask and it will be given to you; seek and you will find; knock and the door will be opened to you. For everyone who asks receives; those who seek find; and to those who knock, the door will be opened."

When we are not willing to put forth the effort of seeking, we will find it difficult to find God, his kingdom and righteousness, or our Life Calling.

> **PERSONAL REFLECTION** > Are you regularly seeking God's will for your life as revealed in his Word and by doing this, preparing ahead of time for crucial decisions? How can you make this a higher priority in your life?

INSIGHT

SCRIPTURAL INSIGHT 3   *Turn On the Lights*

Your word is a lamp to my feet and a light for my path. PSALM 119:105

Psalm 119 is the longest of the Psalms and also the longest chapter in the Bible. The basic theme of Psalm 119 is centered on what it refers to as God's word. At the time this psalm was written, this word consisted of the five books of Moses (Genesis through Deuteronomy). As God's written word continued to expand with the addition of the rest of the Old Testament and then the New Testament, the counsel contained in Psalm 119 still seems to apply and is useful for our study three thousand years later.

Psalm 119:105 is a useful continuation of the discussion we had in the previous devotion concerning Matthew 6:33 about seeking first God's kingdom and righteousness. We ended that discussion with the idea that the Bible was the place to start that seeking, and Psalm 119:105 lets us know why. God's word provides both a lamp to our feet and a light for our path. At first you might be tempted to think those are just two different ways to say the same thing, but when you look deeper, you find that two separate ideas are contained in this statement that are very valuable to our search for a Life Calling and in knowing God's will.

First, God's word is a lamp for our feet. This means that as we take each step of our lives, we can and should look to the Bible for enlightenment related to that individual step. In other words, we can seek first God's kingdom and righteousness as found in his word for each and every decision we take. Hopefully we have stored up his word in our memory so that we will have it immediately when we need it rather than having to start from Genesis 1 every time we make a decision!

Second, God's word is a light for our path. This means that as we make longer-term plans for our lives, we can and should again look to the Bible for guidance. That's why regular Bible study is so important to the process of discovering a Life Calling. It greatly illuminates the plans we should form and becomes the guiding principle for our lives.

The pursuit of our Life Calling is a balance between taking individual steps and making plans for those steps. Psalm 119:105 lets us know that the Bible plays a crucial part in both actions.

> **PERSONAL REFLECTION**   Are you using God's Word to guide your individual steps in your life? Are you using God's Word to make the long-range plans for your life?

SCRIPTURAL INSIGHT 4   *Put on the Full Armor of God*

Finally, be strong in the Lord and in his mighty power. Put on the full armor of God, so that you can take your stand against the devil's schemes. For our struggle is not against flesh and blood, but against the rulers, against the authorities, against the powers of this dark world and against the spiritual forces of evil in the heavenly realms. Therefore put on the full armor of God, so that when the day of evil comes, you may be able to stand your ground, and after you have done everything, to stand. Stand firm then, with the belt of truth buckled around your waist, with the breastplate of righteousness in place, and with your feet fitted with the readiness that comes from the gospel of peace. In addition to all this, take up the shield of faith, with which you can extinguish all the flaming arrows of the evil one. Take the helmet of salvation and the sword of the Spirit, which is the word of God. And pray in the Spirit on all occasions with all kinds of prayers and requests. EPHESIANS 6:10-18

In the Concepts section of this chapter, three elements of spiritual strengths were outlined: spiritual gifts, spiritual habits, and spiritual fruit. Ephesians 6 informs us that there is a fourth element—spiritual armor. In pursuing our Life Calling, spiritual armor can protect us from erroneous information or evil attempts to lure us away from our purpose. Ephesians 6 warns us that there is an entire supernatural network of evil formed to mislead and destroy us. But God provides us armor so that we can stand against this evil network. Let's look at the individual pieces of the "full armor" and see how this works.

Belt of Truth: In the full armor, a belt serves two purposes. It holds everything together, and it provides a basis on which to hang the rest of the armor. Truth provides that same function for our Life Calling. Everything related to our Life Calling must be held together by truth. And every aspect of our Life Calling must hang on truth. Otherwise we will be following a false path and end in destruction.

Breastplate of Righteousness: A breastplate covers and protects the heart. In the Strengths Matrix the heart corresponds to our emotional strengths. Guilt is one of the greatest enemies of emotional strength. The best armor against guilt is living our lives in the path of righteousness. When we seek this first and live according to it, we will find the emotional strength to discern our Life Calling and follow it no matter the cost.

Shoes of Peace: Shoes protect our feet so that we can take the necessary steps in battle. How does that relate to peace? Peace corresponds to our relationship with others. It is rooted in the attitude of servanthood. When our Life Calling is grounded in service to others, it will be protected from attacks of selfishness which can confuse and ultimately defeat us.

Shield of Faith: A shield protects us from the weapons brought against us by an enemy. Our faith in God and his Word protects us from any fiery weapon that the forces of evil would launch against us because it is tied back to our Belt of Truth. Remember, when it comes to our Life Calling, Satan's favorite weapons to use against us are lies concerning ourselves and the hope of purpose and calling.

Helmet of Salvation: The helmet protects our heads. This is where our brain is and where thought process operates. Salvation is the key to protecting those thoughts. It is the knowledge that our salvation has already been secured through the death and resurrection of Jesus that gives us the freedom to think lofty thoughts of Life Calling. When we don't keep that helmet on, we fall into the despair of seeing our failing and weakness, and we give up trying to accomplish anything of value.

Sword of the Word: The sword is the only offensive weapon mentioned in the armor. In our fight against evil forces that would have us believe we have no Life Calling, we can attack these forces with God's Word. The promises we find in the Bible completely defeat such lies. That is why these scriptural insights in each chapter are just as important as the Concepts section which outlines the theory of Life Calling.

Prayer in the Spirit: At the end of the list of armor, an activity is given. It is not a piece of armor; it is something we should do once the armor is on. Pray. And it is not just prayer on our own. It is prayer in concert with the Spirit of God. Romans 8:27 helps us understand the importance of this Spirit-enhanced prayer in relationship to our Life Calling. "And he [God] who searches our hearts knows the mind of the Spirit, because the Spirit intercedes for the saints in accordance with God's will." This kind of prayer keeps us on the right path of Life Calling.

One of the biggest mistakes we can make while trying to discover, discern, and then pursue our Life Calling it is to discount or underestimate the role of supernatural forces in this process. Those forces of evil want to keep us from our purpose. But those forces of good are greater and will help us prevail—if we make use of them.

> **PERSONAL REFLECTION** Are you trying to fight your battles in life on your own, or are you taking advantage of the full armor of God? How can you make sure that your are putting on this armor on a daily basis?

SCRIPTURAL INSIGHT 5 *Ultimately the Battle Belongs to the Lord*

"Don't be afraid," the prophet answered. "Those who are with us are more than those who are with them." And Elisha prayed, "Open his eyes, Lord, so that he may see." Then the Lord opened the servant's eyes, and he looked and saw the hills full of horses and chariots of fire all around Elisha. 2 KINGS 6:16 & 17

It is important to look at this passage of scripture after we have looked at Ephesians 6. Sometimes people look at Ephesians 6 and conclude that there can be no hope if such a supernatural force of evil is working against us. That was the conclusion of Elisha's servant. Let's back up and set the scene for these verses.

The nation of Aram was at war with the nation of Israel. Every time the king of Aram led his army to attack, the army of Israel knew they were coming and would escape. The reason for this was that the prophet Elisha was informed of their plans by God and would tell the king of Israel before it happened. When the king of Aram found out about this, he was furious and sent a force of horses and chariots to surround the city where Elisha was in hopes of capturing him and doing away with this advantage Israel had. When Elisha's servant saw this, he was greatly afraid and cried out to Elisha in despair. And that's where our verses for today begin. Elisha tells him not to worry because their side had more horses and chariots than Aram had. Now you have to realize that Israel didn't have any horses and chariots, so the servant was likely wondering what in the world Elisha was talking about. Then Elisha prayed that his servant would be given spiritual vision. When he was, he saw the hills full of horses and chariots of fire driven by spiritual forces from God—quite likely, angels. In the end Israel won a victory and Aram quit attacking Israel.

There is a remarkably organized force of evil identified in Ephesians 6 that is dedicated to keeping you from discovering your Life Calling. If you had to face this force on your own, you would have every reason to be afraid. But here is the good news. Those who are with us are more than those who are with them. The key to spiritual victory in your pursuit of your Life Calling is not to increase your ability to fight the forces of evil. It is, rather, your ability to stay close to the forces of heaven that will surround you if you let them. Your ability to do this will greatly increase your spiritual strengths.

PERSONAL REFLECTION Do you fear the forces of evil more than you trust the forces of heaven in your life? How can you increase your spiritual strength by developing your ability to see with spiritual eyes?

INSIGHT

 **Discovery**

How can the Discovery Guides help you identify and understand your *spiritual strengths*?

T **THEORY**	Religion and Philosophy classes and programs are a good place to study about spiritual strengths. You can also explore this domain in churches around your college. There are a vast number of books and authors who write on this subject. Explore sources that write in an area of spirituality of interest to you.
E **EXAMPLES**	Find people who live strong spiritual lives. Observe them and find time to talk to them. Ask them to share with you how they discovered and developed these spiritual strengths. Often these people will live outside the limelight, so you will need to seek them out.
A **ASSESSMENT**	The domain of spiritual strengths has a wide variety of assessments associated with it. These explore a variety of elements in the realm of spirituality. One that has shown a great deal of usefulness for college students is the Hope Scale developed by C. R. Snyder. A very effective spiritual assessment correlated directly to Life Calling as it is carried out in service is the *Intrinsic Motivation Assessment Guide & Evaluation (IMAGE)*. This assessment has been correlated to motivational potential in career and service. Similar to other assessments, *IMAGE* is much better understood when administered and debriefed by someone trained in how to use it.
C **COUNSEL**	Professional counselors and life coaches are trained to help you explore spiritual strengths. Your college and university may also have spiritual centers and chaplains that can help. Most churches in your area should have pastoral counselors willing to talk with you. Additionally, family members, teachers, and friends know you well and can give you valuable insights about your spirituality.
H **HISTORY**	The development of spiritual concepts and life is as well documented throughout history as any domain of the Strengths Matrix. Take time to read the many rich works written in the field of spirituality. Also search for historical biographies of notable people who have lived strong spiritual lives. Select some of these and learn from their experiences.
E **EXPERIENCE**	Engage in a variety of spiritual experiences. These experiences will help you cope with the pressures of college, and they will help you understand yourself better as a spiritual being.
R **REFLECTION**	Take time to reflect about your spiritual life. Reflect on what brings both spiritual energy and spiritual rest to you. Reflect on your disposition or attitude about spirituality and spiritual strengths in general and yours in particular.

▶ Story

The sun was moving toward the west as the six remained sitting beside Walden Pond, and longer shadows fell across the grass and the water. The peacefulness of the setting made it hard to leave. The talk moved from decision making to Thoreau's writing and philosophy. This led to questions about Ralph Waldo Emerson, whose name they had seen often in the area. This led to discussion about transcendentalism, which led to the exploration of the whole concept of spirituality. The pond and the woods were definitely having their effect on the six.

"So where does spirituality fit into strengths, Adam?" Diana asked.

"Actually, I think it is what rounds out our strengths," Adam replied.

"Explain what that means," Justin inquired.

"I guess it starts with what we mean by spiritual or spirit," Adam continued. "To me it is some aspect of us that's really not a part of our physical nature. It enables us to get direction on a supernatural level and then respond, I think, in a manner of service."

"You mean like Joan of Arc?" Lorena asked.

Adam hesitated. "I'm not sure that's what I had in mind. I suppose she represents one level of this. Joan of Arc reportedly experienced miraculous events with no rational explanation. I don't think

many of us are going to have that happen in our lives. I think with us it's more a case of experiencing thoughts and impressions that clearly do not come from our own minds, but provide us with crucial information that guides us."

"Is that like our conscience?" Abriella asked.

"I think so, but I'm not really sure," Adam replied. "But somehow it all seems to come together and motivate us to act … like something inside us pushing us forward. I think it also influences how we go about serving others."

"What kind of motivations?" Lorena asked.

"Ever read Paul's letter to the Romans?" Adam asked.

"Yes." Lorena answered as if she had been insulted.

"Paul listed seven," Adam explained. "I think I remember them all."

"Let's test you out!" Ryan urged him with a smirk.

"The first motivation he listed was *prophesying*," Adam began.

"Okay, that sounds more like we're back to Joan of Arc," Lorena interrupted.

"I know what you mean," Adam replied. "But I don't think that's what Paul had in mind. I think that's more our modern interpretation of what it means to prophesy. I think when Paul was writing, he was thinking more about your capacity to perceive right and wrong and then respond by publicly speaking out about your convictions."

"That's Lorena," Ryan broke in. "She's always telling us what to do."

Lorena turned, spreading her hands with the palm turned upward accompanied by a look on her face that begged the unspoken question, "Me?"

"But you know what?" Ryan continued. "I don't really mind. Most of the time I need someone telling me what to do, and Lorena usually has good judgment and makes good sense."

The others all looked at each other with confused looks on their faces. The relationship between Lorena and Ryan had become nearly impossible to figure out.

Adam continued, "The second motivation Paul called *mercy*."

"That's easier to understand, and it is definitely Diana," Justin responded. "She's always trying to keep peace with all of us. That's no easy job, especially between Ryan and Lorena." Everyone laughed.

"The third motivation was *exhorting*," Adam said.

"I think I know what that means," Abriella said, "but I've never been quite sure."

"I think it is the idea of encouraging people to take action in their lives," Adam replied, "and start bringing some practical solutions to the problems in life they are facing. You know, give them some steps of action they should take to overcome problems."

"That's you, Ryan," Abriella spoke first. "You always are trying to keep us upbeat, and you always have practical advice."

"I don't know how practical it is," Lorena said sarcastically. Ryan gave her a soft punch on the shoulder.

"The fourth motivation was *teaching*," Adam moved on. "This is discovering truth through careful research and then clearly presenting this to others in such a way that makes it easy to learn."

"Adam," the others all said in unison, looking first at each other and then at Adam.

"I guess I must be guilty, then," Adam laughed. "So let's continue on discovering truth. The fifth motivation was *governing* or *managing*. That's pretty obvious—organizing and coordinating other people's activities and setting goals for them."

"That's got to be Justin," Diana said. "He's always trying to keep us organized."

"And hardly ever able to succeed," Justin said, laughing, and the others joined in.

"The sixth motivation was *serving*," Adam continued. "I think this means helping others fulfill needs and complete tasks."

"That has to be Diana," Lorena said. "I don't know how any of us would survive if Diana wasn't there to help us do it." Diana's face turned a little red accompanied by a shy smile. Justin gave her a quick hug.

"I know I've messed up Paul's order. But the last motivation I haven't mentioned yet is *giving*," Adam said. "I think this is investing money and support in people and projects that are worthy of that support."

There was an awkward pause for several seconds after Adam spoke. Finally Lorena broke the silence. "I'm not sure that any of us qualify for this one." The others nodded their heads in agreement.

"Whoa!" Ryan exclaimed. "We forgot Captain Nemo and Mrs. Nemo. They seem pretty generous with the funding."

"You know, I think you're right about my dad," Diana said. "He's always looking for ways to help people accomplish their dreams. The funny thing is that the more he gives away, the more he keeps getting so he can give that away too. I've never been able to quite figure it out."

"You're dad's the greatest," Adam observed. "And so is your mom. You're lucky to have them." The others agreed. It was late in the afternoon, and their time at Walden Pond had come to an end. The explorers stood and began to walk back up the path to the parking lot and the motorhome. A long road trip lay ahead for the next day.

 **Exercises**

Understanding Your Intrinsic Spiritual Motivations Through *IMAGE*

One of the best assessments related to the *Spiritual Strengths* related to intrinsic motivation to serve was developed by Bill Millard and is administered by Life Discovery. This assessment is called the *Intrinsic Motivation Assessment Guide & Evaluation (IMAGE)*.

In most schools or institutions offering a course that uses this textbook, IMAGE is included as part of that course. If not, we highly recommend that you take the *IMAGE* from Life Discovery Interactive. If you are able to complete this online assessment, you will receive a comprehensive Evaluation Report. This report will provide you with:

- Your results including: Your Pilot Motivation and a delineation of your Proactive and Reactive Motivations.
- An in-depth discussion of your Pilot Motivation and your Proactive Motivations.
- A general discussion of all seven intrinsic motivations.

Work with your class instructor, or someone else in your institution who is qualified to interpret *IMAGE* results, and this person will facilitate you in your understanding of the results and how to use them in your life.

What Motivates You to Serve?

If you are unable to complete Exercise 1, complete this exercise as an alternative introduction to understanding your intrinsic motivations and how these can be used as you develop spiritual strengths in serving others.

One area of your spiritual strengths can be found in what spiritually motivates you to serve other people. When individuals respond to other people, situations and needs around them, they are motivated to work, think and react differently based on the varying strengths of seven built-in service motivations that you learned about in the Concepts section of this chapter.

The short *IMAGE QuickLook* assessment that follows can give you an introductory look at the intrinsic motivations working within you. However, it is important to note that this is not meant to produce the statistically analyzed and validated results obtained by the *Intrinsic Motivation Assessment Guide & Evaluation (IMAGE)* tool from Life Discovery Interactive. You will need to complete that validated assessment to obtain validated results. *QuickLook* rather gives you an introduction to the IMAGE discovery process and stimulates your thinking about spiritual intrinsic motivation.

The fourteen questions in *IMAGE QuickLook* relate to motivations that may or may not apply to you. Understanding these can determine what motivates you to serve others and how well you fit into a life design. Not all of the motivations will apply to you. This in no way reflects on you as a person. It just means that **you are unique**.

▶ IMAGE *QuickLook*

Answer each question as you **believe it applies** to you. Do **not** answer as you think it **should** apply to you or as you **wish** it applied to you. Don't be afraid to use "Almost Always", "Almost Never", or any of the other possible answers if appropriate.

If you have difficulty in deciding which answer best applies to you, the following is a good guideline in determining how often a situation fits your motivational makeup:

Over 90% = **Almost Always**
71%–90% = **Usually**
30%–70% = **Sometimes**
10%–29% = **Rarely**
Less than 10% = **Almost Never**

Once you have made your self-evaluation, place the number corresponding to the answer you selected in the box to the right of the answers.

1. How often do you respond to a situation with other people by organizing and coordinating the activities and efforts of others?

   Almost Always = 9   **Usually = 7**   **Sometimes = 5**   **Rarely = 3**   **Almost Never = 1**   ☐

2. How often do you attempt to solve a problem by trying to find out what is right and wrong in people, ideas, and/or situations

   Almost Always = 9   **Usually = 7**   **Sometimes = 5**   **Rarely = 3**   **Almost Never = 1**   ☐

3. How often do you support other worthwhile projects with your own money?

Almost Always = 9   **Usually = 7**   **Sometimes = 5**   **Rarely = 3**   **Almost Never = 1**   ☐

4. How often do you identify with the hurts and/or emotions of others?

Almost Always = 9   **Usually = 7**   **Sometimes = 5**   **Rarely = 3**   **Almost Never = 1**   ☐

5. How often do you engage in careful research to discover the truth about something?

Almost Always = 9   **Usually = 7**   **Sometimes = 5**   **Rarely = 3**   **Almost Never = 1**   ☐

6. How often do you solve problems for others by outlining practical steps of actions they should take to overcome these problems?

Almost Always = 9   **Usually = 7**   **Sometimes = 5**   **Rarely = 3**   **Almost Never = 1**   ☐

7. How often do you clearly present information to others in such a way that it will be easy to learn?

Almost Always = 9   **Usually = 7**   **Sometimes = 5**   **Rarely = 3**   **Almost Never = 1**   ☐

8. How often do you find practical ways to help others meet their physical needs?

Almost Always = 9   **Usually = 7**   **Sometimes = 5**   **Rarely = 3**   **Almost Never = 1**   ☐

9. How often do you publicly speak out about your inward convictions about issues of right and wrong?

Almost Always = 9   **Usually = 7**   **Sometimes = 5**   **Rarely = 3**   **Almost Never = 1**   ☐

10. How often do you help others solve problems by setting goals for them to meet in their activities and efforts?

Almost Always = 9   **Usually = 7**   **Sometimes = 5**   **Rarely = 3**   **Almost Never = 1**   ☐

11. How often do you wisely use and invest your money to provide support for worthwhile projects?

Almost Always = 9   **Usually = 7**   **Sometimes = 5**   **Rarely = 3**   **Almost Never = 1**   ☐

12. How often do you look for legitimate physical needs others have?

Almost Always = 9   **Usually = 7**   **Sometimes = 5**   **Rarely = 3**   **Almost Never = 1**   ☐

13. How often do you find yourself providing comfort to those who are in emotional distress?

Almost Always = 9   **Usually = 7**   **Sometimes = 5**   **Rarely = 3**   **Almost Never = 1**   ☐

EXERCISES

14. How often do you try to encourage others through counsel and advice?

Almost Always = 9   **Usually = 7**   **Sometimes = 5**   **Rarely = 3**   **Almost Never = 1**   ☐

a. Place the score from the question in the box beside its corresponding number in the following chart. Add the two scores on each line to the right of the letters in the left-hand column. Place the sum in the boxes in the column on the far right.

P	#2		+	#9		=	
C	#4		+	#13		=	
E	#6		+	#14		=	
T	#5		+	#7		=	
M	#1		+	#10		=	
H	#8		+	#12		=	
G	#3		+	#11		=	

b. Based on the scores you have obtained, rank the results from most frequent (1st) to least frequent (7th). Place the number in the small circle beside each letter in the wheel below. *Use a different ranking number for each description; no two descriptions should be rated the same.* If you have two scores that are equal, use the chart after the wheel and make a choice as to which one takes precedent over the other.

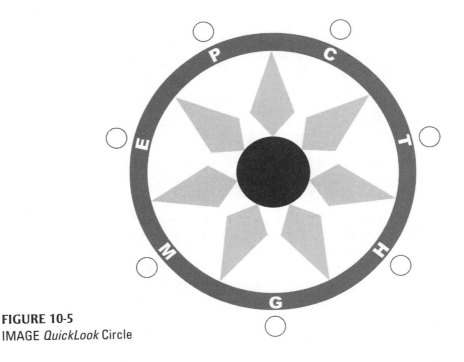

FIGURE 10-5
IMAGE *QuickLook* Circle

P	You tend to first determine what is right and/or wrong in the situation and then speak out about your convictions (*Proclaiming*)
C	You tend to first identify the hurts and/or emotions of individuals in the situation and then provide comfort for those emotional needs (*Comforting*)
E	You tend to first look for practical steps of action appropriate for the situation and then advise those involved on how to take these steps of action (*Exhorting*)
T	You tend to first carefully study to understand the situation and then present this information to those involved in a way that is clear to learn (*Teaching*)
M	You tend to first organize the situation by setting goals for those involved to meet and then coordinate their activities and efforts (*Managing*)
H	You tend to first look for practical needs or tasks others in the situation have and then physically assist them to meet these needs and tasks (*Helping*)
G	You tend to first use your own financial or material resources to solve a problem or support the efforts of others trying to work with the situation (*Giving*)

c. Observe the responses you ranked as the top three (1–3). In the space below, describe how you think these responses can reveal what motivates you in the way you serve other people.

   (1) _____

   _____

   _____

   (2) _____

   _____

   _____

   (3) _____

   _____

   _____

d. Refer back to the Classroom section discussing intrinsic motivation and correlate this to your answers in "c." What spiritual strengths do these motivations reveal in your life?

   _____

   _____

   _____

   _____

   _____

EXERCISES

e. How can these spiritual strengths help you discover your Life Calling?

_____

_____

_____

_____

_____

f. What courses or majors could help you cultivate these spiritual strengths?

_____

_____

_____

_____

_____

EXERCISES

EXERCISE 3

Expanding Your Understanding of Your Intrinsic Motivations by Using the *IMAGE 360*

1. Identify four different people who know you and who love and care for you. Choose the four so that they represent each of the following categories:
   - Parent _____
   - Teacher (present or former) _____
   - Friend _____
   - Younger sibling or relative _____

2. Provide all of the people you have identified with a copy of the *IMAGE 360* (not the Mirror) chart below and ask them to rank the seven intrinsic motivations based on what they've seen in your life. Let them know that the top three are the most important, so if they are unsure once they get beyond the top three, it is okay to leave them blank. Encourage

IMAGE 360	Description	Use numbers from 1 to 7 to rank how strong you've seen the intrinsic motivations in the columns to the left operating in me.	Can you give me an example of when you have seen me serving others in this way?
Proclaiming	You tend to first determine what is right and/or wrong in the situation and then speak out about your convictions.		
Helping	You tend to first look for practical needs or tasks others in the situation have and then physically assist them to meet these needs and tasks.		
Teaching	You tend to first carefully study to understand the situation and then present this information to those involved in a way that is clear to learn.		
Exhorting	You tend to first look for practical steps of action appropriate for the situation and then advise those involved on how to take these steps of action.		
Supporting	You tend to first use your own financial or material resources to solve a problem or support the efforts of others trying to work with the situation.		

(Continued)

EXERCISES

IMAGE 360	Description	Use numbers from 1 to 7 to rank how strong you've seen the intrinsic motivations in the columns to the left operating in me.	Can you give me an example of when you have seen me serving others in this way?
Governing	You tend to first organize the situation by setting goals for those involved to meet and then coordinate their activities and efforts.		
Comforting	You tend to first identify the hurts and/or emotions of individuals in the situation and then provide comfort for those emotional needs.		

them to give an example for the top three. If they have examples for others beyond the top three, let them know you would value those as well.

3. Now record the rankings you have personally determined in Exercise 1 or 2. Share an example of where you have seen the intrinsic motivations operating in your life.

IMAGE Mirror	My ranking of the seven intrinsic motivations	What has been my most fulfilling experience serving others based on this intrinsic motivation?
Proclaiming		
Helping		
Teaching		
Exhorting		
Supporting		
Governing		
Comforting		

1. Compare the top three intrinsic motivations you identified for yourself to the top three identified by others in the IMAGE 360. What do others see in you that you may not see in yourself? What can you learn about your perception of yourself?

2. Reflect on what you learned in Exercise 1 or 2 and Exercise 3 and summarize below what they have revealed to you about yourself.

Millard, B. (1992–2008). *Intrinsic Motivation Assessment Guide & Evaluation*. Marion, Indiana: Life Discovery Publications.

Millard, B. (1992–2008). *IMAGE QuickLook*. Marion, Indiana: Life Discovery Publications.

The following resources may be useful to you in your continuing exploration of Life Calling as you look at your Unique Design and your *spiritual strengths*.

Kise, J.A.G., Stark, D., and Hirsh, S.K. (2005). Lifekeys: Discover Who You Are. Bloomington, Minnesota: Bethany House Publishers.

Geen, R.G. (1995). *Human Motivation: A Social Psychological Approach*. Pacific Grove, CA: Brooks/Kole Publishing Company.

Oglilvie, L.J. (1984). *Freedom in the Spirit*. Eugene, OR: Harvest House Publishers.

Schwen, M.R., and Bass, D.C., Eds. (2006). *Leading Lives That Matter: What We Should Do and Who We Should Be*. Grand Rapids, Michigan: Erdmans Publishing Co.

Smith, C.S., and Denton, M.L. (2005). *Soul Searching: The Religious and Spiritual Lives of American Teenagers*. New York: Oxford University Press.

Smith, C.S., and Snell, P. (2009). *Soul in Transition: The Religious and Spiritual Lives of Emerging Adults*. New York: Oxford University Press.

Smith, G.T. (2011). *Courage and Calling: Embracing Your God-given Potential*. Downers Grove, Illinois: Intervarsity Press.

Wagner, C.P. (2005). *Discover Your Spiritual Gifts: The Easy-to-use, Self-guided Questionnaire That Helps You Identify and Understand Your Various God-given Spiritual Gifts*. Ventura, CA: Regal Books.

Yancey, P., and Brand, P.W. (2004). *In the Likeness of God*. Grand Rapids, Michigan: Zondervan.

Yohn, R. (1987). *Discover Your Spiritual Gift and Use It*. Wheaton, IL: Tyndale House Publishers.

REFERENCES

Driven by Passions

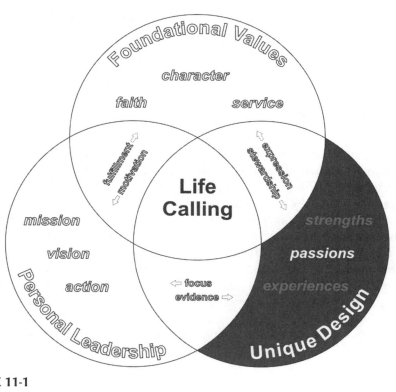

11

FIGURE 11-1
Life Calling Model Focusing on Passions

The second main component of the Life Calling Model is *Unique Design*. The second element of this design is formed from ***passions***.

CHAPTER OBJECTIVES

1. Articulate a working definition for passions related to Life Calling
2. Understand the nature of passions
3. Explain the difference and developmental relationship between interests, desires, and passions
4. Begin identifying passions in your life

If you have men who will only come if they know there is a good road, I don't want them. I want men who will come if there is no road at all.

DAVID LIVINGSTON

CONCEPTS

KEY TERMS

Compel = steer you toward a course of action
Desire = wish, crave, or long for as for something that brings satisfaction or enjoyment
Force = energy or power to influence, affect, or control
Impel = cause you to actually start moving in the right direction
Interest = attraction to or curiosity about something; fascination with something captivating
Propel = keep you moving forward or onward in the right direction
Sacrifice = to surrender or give up, or permit injury or disadvantage to, for the sake of something else

▶ Concepts

A sad thing happens to people on the road from childhood into their teen and college years and then life beyond. Somewhere along that road, they lose their ability to dream. When they were young, they would imagine all sorts of things and pretend they were great people. Then somewhere or sometime they were told that such dreams were foolish and that they could never achieve anything like that. But that's not the saddest part to this story. The saddest part is that they began to believe what they were told and gave up dreaming and turned their backs on the passions they once had. They started following paths somebody else outlined for them and entered careers somebody else recommended. In those careers they performed tasks somebody else gave them and were evaluated by somebody else's opinion. And at the end of their lives, they look back with some level of remorse because they realize they gave up on their dreams and abandoned their passion and instead lived somebody else's life. In other words they ended up only impersonating themselves rather than living out their own true lives.

Such a life has no passion because passion begins with dreams. Do you still have any dreams as you start your college experience? What do you care about more than anything else in life? Do you have any idea what that is? What do you care about more than anything else in your college experience? The clearer you are about the answer to that question, the more likely you are to have the potential for passion in your life. You also bring greater focus to your time in college. One of the real challenges we face in our search for a Life Calling relates to whether or not we have passions in our lives that can help guide us to that purpose.

I am a cyclist. I have what others might consider a pretty advanced Trek bicycle that I can easily carry around with one hand. I can ride it at pretty high speeds. Yet I am not now, nor have I ever been, a threat to the riders in the Tour de France or any other professional bike race. What makes the difference between a professional athlete and an avid enthusiast like me? One of the most critical factors is passion. There is a certain drive that leads accomplished athletes, musicians, artists, and others to set everything else aside and endure the grueling schedule of practice and workouts needed to reach that high level of performance in their area. And to be honest, I don't have that level of drive as a cyclist, so I have to be satisfied with my average level of performance.

Passions Defined

In this section of the book, we are looking at the second major component of the Life Calling model, *Unique Design*. We saw that it has three main elements—*strengths*, *passions*, and *experiences*. The second of these elements is made up of our *passions*, exactly what we have been talking about in the previous paragraphs. We define *passions* as deep forces in our lives that burn within our hearts and often drive the actions or paths we take. Passions that lead athletes, musicians, or artists to succeed are more than just interests. Passions that can lead to our discovery of a Life Calling are more than just interests as well. Passions are deep forces that compel, impel, and propel. To be a passion that leads to a Life Calling, the deep force must be *compelling*, which means it needs to produce an overwhelming pressure that stirs us to take action. To be a passion that leads to a Life Calling, the deep force must be *impelling*, which means it needs to exert a moral pressure that leads us to act because it is the right thing to do. Finally, to be a passion that leads to a Life Calling, the deep force must be *propelling*, which means it causes action that moves us forward or onward.

Passions Developed

How does such a deep force form in our lives? Figure 11-2 illustrates three tiers or levels that build to create passion at the Life Calling intensity.

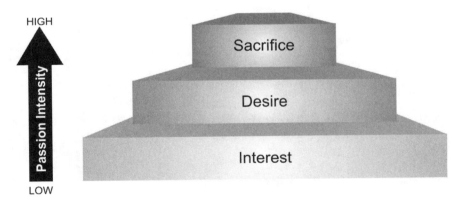

FIGURE 11-2
Three Levels of Passion

Level 1—Interest. The initial stage of passion development starts with our interests. These are options in life that attract our curiosity. The key word is *curiosity*, a condition in which the novelty of something makes you want to learn more about it. Although we may find our fascination aroused at this level, we certainly do not know enough about it to make major moves in our lives. Ironically, many career counselors rely heavily on assessments of interests as a source to guide clients in selecting career paths. It is not surprising that such advice has limited success in helping people find an overriding purpose for their lives.

CONCEPTS

Level 2—Desire. The second stage of passion development occurs as we identify interests we would definitely pursue if we had no limitations. At the level of desire, there is more than just curiosity involved. Now wishes and longings enter the picture. We find that certain interests bring us pleasure and enjoyment, and we find ourselves pursuing them with greater intensity. Still, we have not yet achieved true passion. There is a big difference between wanting and enjoying something and being convinced that we need to pursue it no matter the cost. That requires the next level.

Level 3—Sacrifice. The final stage of passion development comes when our desires reach an intensity where we care enough about them that we would be willing to set aside other interests or desires and dedicate (in some cases even risk) our life for these passions. That qualifier truly sets this level apart from the other two. To reach this intensity, the desire must bring a deep satisfaction to our lives, something that gives us a sense of meaning, significance, and hope, as discussed on a spiritual level in Chapter 10. Something this intense is rare. It is easy to be interested or curious about a lot of things. We can also find that our list of desires can be quite long. But when we ask ourselves what it is that we would be willing to dedicate our lives to—or even risk our lives for—then we will find that the list shortens dramatically. If we were to graph an inventory of the numbers we have in these categories during our lifetime, it would probably look like the graph in Figure 11-3. The dramatic impression left by that illustration clearly helps us to see why sacrificial passions are the ones that can truly help us discover our Life Calling. These are the ones that really matter in our lives.

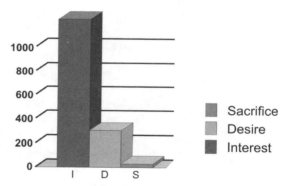

FIGURE 11-3
Comparison of Interest, Desire and Sacrifice in Your Life

Problems with Identifying Passions

One of the real problems with discovering our passions starts at the interest level. In our society today it is often hard to distinguish what are really our own interests and what are the interests of others that have been thrust upon us. This can come from peer pressure or the aspirations of parents hoping to bring success into our lives. It can also come from media and advertising seeking to move us in a direction favorable to their financial or social interests. So it is important for us to take time to think carefully about our interests, desires, and passions to know that they are really ours.

On the other hand, peers, parents, and other mentors do play a role in the exploration of interests that may become passions. They introduce us to areas we might not otherwise explore. They also model to us their own excitement about areas of interest, and we become intrigued to explore them.

Concepts Summary

When looking at the various strengths, we consistently emphasized that one of the most effective ways to discover them was to listen to what others who know us well say about us. This is not the case with passions. Although others might help us explore interests, it is almost impossible for another person, even those very close to us, to know what passions reside in our hearts at the sacrificial level. So how can we determine if something is our passion? A combination of contemplation and reflection provides the best source of information. When we take time to quietly do this and ask ourselves those deep questions related to meaning, significance, and hope, we will begin to distinguish the true passions from those that are nothing more than interests or desires.

CONCEPTS

Insight

In Proverbs 4:23 this good advice can be found: "Above all else, guard your heart, for it is the wellspring of life." The Concepts section of this chapter helped us see that the passions of our heart form an important component that can be a "wellspring" calling us to our Life Calling. Other scriptures provide additional insight concerning our passions.

SCRIPTURAL INSIGHT 1 *The Highest Level of Passion Comes from an Undivided Heart*

Teach me your way, Lord, that I may rely on your faithfulness; give me an undivided heart, that I may fear your name. PSALM 86:11

What are you fervent about? What would you really like to do in life? We have defined *passion* as a deep force that burns within our hearts that compels, impels and propels the actions or paths we take in life. This occurs when these driving forces are singular. Psalm 86:11 describes an "undivided heart." This is the kind of passion that leads to a Life Calling.

The word passion is used in a rather widespread context of meanings. On the shallow end, it is used to describe sexual feelings. On the deepest end, it is used to describe the sufferings of Jesus during the period following the Last Supper through his crucifixion. In the Life Calling Model, we have chosen to define passion at the deeper level, which is not achieved until we are ready to sacrifice our lives for our passion. Sacrifice does not mean we have to die for our passion, but it does mean we are ready to dedicate our lives for our passion.

When passions rise to this level of sacrifice in our lives, they compel us by steering us toward right courses of action. They are like that voice described in Isaiah 30:21, "Whether you turn to the right or to the left, your ears will hear a voice behind you, saying, 'This is the way; walk in it.'"

Secondly, when passions rise to a level of sacrifice in our lives, they will also impel us by causing us to actually start moving in the right direction. This is the kind of drawing force described in Isaiah 2:3. "Many peoples will come and say, 'Come, let us go up to the mountain of the Lord, to the house of the God of Jacob. He will teach us his ways, so that we may walk in his paths.'"

When passions rise to a level of sacrifice in our lives, they will also propel us to keep moving forward or onward in the right direction. Again we can turn to Isaiah (Isaiah 40:29-31) for a description of this.

He [the Lord] gives strength to the weary and increases the power of the weak. Even youths grow tired and weary, and young men stumble and fall; but those who hope in the Lord will renew their strength. They will soar on wings like eagles; they will run and not grow weary, they will walk and not be faint

If you are struggling with focus in your search for a Life Calling, you might want to ask yourself if you have a confused or divided heart. If that is the case, you may need to return to the prayer of Psalm 86:11 and ask the Lord to give you an undivided heart that can become the compelling, impelling, and propelling passion leading to a Life Calling.

> **PERSONAL REFLECTION** Do you hear a lot of voices in your heart or do you feel that it is undivided? Why not ask God to give you an undivided heart that can produce true passion in your life?

SCRIPTURAL INSIGHT 2 *Develop Interests That Are Based on Values*

Each of you should look not only to your own interests, but also to the interests of others. PHILIPPIANS 2:4

At one time or another as I grew up, I had interests in being a trash collector, pilot, baseball player, astronaut, military officer, lawyer, journalist, world explorer, park ranger, actor, billionaire, ship captain, spy, even the President of the United States. I ended up in careers where I have worked as a teacher, geologist, business owner, pastor, life coach, and leader—none of which were on my original list. So what happened? The answer is found in the relationship of interests to passions.

As we ascend toward passions at a Life Calling level of sacrifice, *interests* are at the first and lowest level. Interests form a fascinating window into who we are. They say a lot about our makeup and wiring. But they are not the foundation on which a Life Calling will be discovered because they are usually caught up in an attitude of self-centeredness and self-interest.

This is what led the Apostle Paul to advise us in Philippians 2:3&4, "Do nothing out of selfish ambition or vain conceit, but in humility consider others better than yourselves. Each of you should look not only to your own interests, but also to the interests of others." Paul goes on in verses 5-11 to tell us that our attitude should be the same as the attitude that Jesus had which led him to sacrifice his life on the cross. This remarkable passage in scripture certainly lets us know that our passions must go far beyond just self-interests if they are to guide our search for a Life Calling. Unfortunately, the interest surveys used so often in career exploration rarely go beyond the self-interest level and end up causing confusion in our search for a Life Calling.

Later in Philippians 2:20&21 Paul commends Timothy to the people of Philippi. "I have no one else like him, who takes a genuine interest in your welfare. For everyone looks out for their own interests, not those of Jesus Christ."

There is nothing wrong with us having interests. Curiosity is a good thing. It helps us consider many options in life, just like all those interests I had growing up. However, the problem with a life guided only by our interests is that it may not look out for the interest of Jesus. It rather tends to focus on our own interests, and a self-centered life will never lead to discovery of a true Life Calling. It is when we move into the two higher levels of passion—which we will look at in the next two devotions—that we begin to move more in a direction of looking outside our own self-centered concerns and into the realm of purpose.

> **PERSONAL REFLECTION** What are your interests in life right now? Are they guided by self-interests, or by higher values?

SCRIPTURAL INSIGHT 3 > *Shape the Desires of Your Heart*

Trust in the Lord and do good; dwell in the land and enjoy safe pasture. Take delight in the Lord and he will give you the desires of your heart. Commit your way to the Lord; trust in him and he will do this: He will make your righteous reward shine like the dawn, your vindication like the noonday sun. PSALM 37:3-6

The second level on our climb toward Life Calling passions is our *desires*. Psalm 37:4 speaks of our getting the desires of our heart and is often misinterpreted to mean that whatever we want we will get if we trust enough in the Lord to give it to us. Let's look at this passage in its fuller context of verses 3 through 6:

Three important conditions set up qualifications for receiving the desires of our heart—trusting in the Lord, taking delight in the Lord, and committing our ways to the Lord.

First, when we trust in the Lord's ways as being good, our desires will be for those good ways. David put it this way in Psalm 20:7&8—"Some trust in chariots and some in horses, but we trust in the name of the Lord our God. They are brought to their knees and fall, but we rise up and stand firm."

Second, when we delight in the Lord, our desires will be for that in which we delight—the Lord and his ways. In Paul's thorough discussion of love in 1 Corinthians 13, he makes this observation in verse 6, "Love does not delight in evil but rejoices with the truth." When this happens, our desires will be consistent with what God wants.

Third, when we commit our ways to the Lord, we will restrict our desires to only those ways that are of the Lord. Paul discusses this in Romans 8:5 by describing two different types of people. "Those who live according to the sinful nature have their minds set on what that nature desires; but those who live in accordance with the Spirit have their minds set on what the Spirit desires."

The passage in Psalm 37 ends by giving us an accountability assessment to make sure our desires are in this context. The desires must lead to righteousness and justice. When we experience desires of our heart at a level that matches this context, then we have reached a level of passion that is part of our Life Calling. When this happens we can experience another promise found in the Psalms: "May he give you the desire of your heart and make all your plans succeed" (Psalm 20:4).

> **PERSONAL REFLECTION** > Are the desires of your life based on trust and delight in the Lord and a commitment to his ways? Do your desires lead to righteousness and justice? How can you increase this in your life?

SCRIPTURAL INSIGHT 4 > *Save Your Life by Losing It*

Then he [Jesus] called the crowd to him along with his disciples and said: "Whoever wants to be my disciple must deny themselves and take up their cross and follow me. For whoever wants to save their life will lose it, but whoever loses their life for me and for the gospel will save it. What good is it for you to gain the whole world, yet forfeit your soul?" MARK 8:34-36

Finally, we reach the Life Calling level of passions when we arrive at a sacrificial attitude. Jesus made this clear in his challenge to those wanting to be his disciples. One of the greatest causes of confusion in searching for a Life Calling is the concentration on our own self-centered interests, desires and passions. We have consistently seen in our study so far that Life Calling is primarily found in an attitude of service to God and to others. This is what Jesus meant when he said that if we want to save our life, we must be willing to lose it.

The apostle Paul was a leader among the Jews when a new passion was put in his heart during an encounter with Jesus on the road to Damascus. He sacrificed everything else in his life to follow this passion. An amazing list in 2 Corinthians 11:24-28 describes how hard this was.

> Five times I received from the Jews the forty lashes minus one. Three times I was beaten with rods, once I was pelted with stones, three times I was shipwrecked, I spent a night and a day in the open sea, I have been constantly on the move. I have been in danger from rivers, in danger from bandits, in danger from my own people, in danger from Gentiles; in danger in the city, in danger in the country, in danger at sea; and in danger from false believers. I have labored and toiled and have often gone without sleep; I have known hunger and thirst and have often gone without food; I have been cold and naked. Besides everything else, I face daily the pressure of my concern for all the churches.

But in all of this, Paul did not try to take glory for himself. These were instead his words: "May I never boast except in the cross of our Lord Jesus Christ, through which the world has been crucified to me, and I to the world" (Galatians 6:14).

In Romans 12:1 Paul put this same challenge to us as he did for himself: "Therefore, I urge you, brothers and sisters, in view of God's mercy, to offer your bodies as a living sacrifice, holy and pleasing to God—this is true worship."

When we are willing to do this, we have risen to the sacrificial level of passions that truly means we have found a significant factor making up our Life Calling.

PERSONAL REFLECTION ⟩ What do you care about enough in your life that you are willing to put everything else aside to pursue it? What keeps you from offering your life as a living sacrifice to God?

SCRIPTURAL INSIGHT 5 ⟩ *The Chosen Are Few*

For many are invited, but few are chosen. MATTHEW 22:14

Those words from Matthew 22 come at the end of a parable Jesus told about people being invited by a king to a wedding banquet for his son. The point Jesus was making was that though God has called many to follow his way of sacrifice, few actually respond.

Jesus expressed the same thought using a different metaphor in Matthew 7:13&14. "Enter through the narrow gate. For wide is the gate and broad is the road that leads to destruction, and many enter through it. But small is the gate and narrow the road that leads to life, and only a few find it."

INSIGHT

Figure 11-3 in the Concept sections showed the frequency distribution of interests, desires, and sacrifice as they relate to passions. We have lots of interest. Our interests that grow into desires are fewer. At the core of our lives, however, the number of things for which we are willing to sacrifice our other interests and desires is very small.

When self-interests or other distractions take precedence in our lives, they confuse this pattern. They can lead us to believe that our interests are the same thing as our desires and that there is no need to sacrifice in order to achieve those things that mean the most to us. This is what happened in the life of the rich young ruler we looked at in chapter 9. Jesus called on him to sacrifice his wealth and follow Jesus. But his self-interests kept him from reaching that sacrificial level of passion.

This is illustrated in the story found in Judges 7 of Gideon forming an army to defend Israel against the Midianites. He started out with a force of 32,000 warriors. But when he gave those who had fear in their hearts a chance to leave, 22,000 left and only 10,000 remained. He then took them to a spring, and those that lapped up water quickly (they could quickly be ready to fight) were the ones that would form the fight force. Those who took too much time to kneel down and drink were dismissed. The final count? 300 warriors. That's a little less than one percent of his original force. There's where the real passion of sacrifice existed. In the end, as you may know from the story, these 300 achieved a very intriguing victory. We need to look in our hearts and find what it is that will lead us to take the sacrificing actions of those 300. These are the true passions that can lead to a Life Calling.

> **PERSONAL REFLECTION** ⟩ Do you have passions in your life that will lead you to sacrifice? Or have your self-interests kept you, like the rich young ruler, from being willing to sacrifice?

▶ Discovery

How can the Discovery Guides be most useful to help you understand and use your *passions*?

T THEORY	Study of social and behavioral sciences can help you explore your passions. Although this study is often pursued in formal classes, you can also pursue it in your own personal reading as well. Start creating a list of books that will aid your exploration. Ask others for recommendations.
E EXAMPLES	Observing people who have deep passions and who live these passions out in their lives is a very valuable source for learning about passions. Keep a constant search for such people. Many times you will find them in positions you may not have thought of, such as food servers, groundskeepers, janitors, secretaries, and others that may not be in the limelight of your institution. Seek out a mentor relationship with one of these types of person.
A ASSESSMENT	Many assessments measure interests. The Strong Interest Inventory is one of the most widely used. It is based on the Holland Occupational Themes. You might want to use some of these to help you get started in exploring passions. Keep in mind, however, that these tools do not measure passions at the sacrificial level defined in this chapter.
C COUNSEL	Professional counselors and life coaches are trained to help you explore interests and passions in your life. Your college and university will likely have a counseling center with trained personnel to help you. Additionally, family members, teachers, student life personnel, pastors, and friends know you well and can give you valuable insights about yourself.
H HISTORY	The classics and historical biographies are full of stories dealing with notable people who have lived out lives of passion. Select some of these and learn from their experiences.
E EXPERIENCE	Pursue areas of interest as you are going through college. You can find these in your residence life, in your classes, in your student clubs and governments, in work, and in community service. You will discover which of these interests grow into strong desires and the few that will inspire you to sacrifice other interests to pursue them.
R REFLECTION	Take time to reflect on your entire life to explore what really is a passion in your life. Take time to also reflect on your current experiences as well.

DISCOVERY

▶ Story

The *Nautilus* had traveled west on Interstate 90 through Massachusetts into New York. After passing through Albany, the route turned west for the most part. The travelers found the concept of a toll road interesting, if not necessarily desirable.

"At least highways are free in California," Justin remarked.

"Well, not really," Ken replied from the cockpit. "Gas tax is very high in California. The tax probably more than makes up the price of tolls back in these eastern states."

The journey continued on to Buffalo, where they headed north to Niagara Falls. Ken maneuvered the *Nautilus* into the Niagara Falls KOA Kampground. It was late in the day by the time they were settled, so the explorers decided to delay their visit to the falls until the next morning.

The day dawned clear and warm—perfect weather for viewing Niagara Falls.

"We're less than a mile west of the falls. I say we walk and save Captain Nemo the frustration of trying to navigate the *Nautilus*." Ryan had become good friends with Diana's father during the trip and was always looking out for him. Ken saw a lot of his younger self in Ryan and enjoyed talking with him. Sometimes they got carried away to the point of embarrassing Diana, but Ryan loved it.

The others quickly agreed with Ryan—all, that is, but Lorena.

"A mile's a long walk. Are we sure we don't want to ride?" she asked.

"If anybody needs the walk, it's you, Lor," Ryan responded. "You're too soft and out of shape. We've got to toughen you up." Lorena rolled her eyes.

"Fine, I guess," she sighed. "If I have to." With that the explorers started their walk.

It took about 25 minutes to reach the lookout point at Niagara Falls. Ryan had pointed out that it would have only been 15 minutes if Lorena had put her heart into the trek. Lorena had observed that Ryan should put a cork in his mouth. The others had encouraged them to focus on the beauty of nature, even though they all knew this was a futile request.

The spectacular Horseshoe Falls that most people picture when they think of Niagara Falls is in Canada. The American Falls, although impressive, is not nearly so breathtaking, so the explorers were actually in Ontario, Canada, standing along the railing of the observation point as they looked down at Horseshoe Falls.

"That's a lot of water going over the edge!" Abriella exclaimed.

"It's the third largest in volume in the world," Lorena replied.

"Really? How much is it?" Abriella asked.

"Over 600,000 gallons per second," Lorena said matter-of-factly.

"Where do you find all that junk?" Ryan asked, half intrigued and half in scorn.

"I read," Lorena stated tersely.

"So do I," Ryan countered.

"I read books," Lorena replied with an arrogant tone in her voice. Everybody else but Ryan laughed.

"It seems like there would be a lot of energy in that much water," Adam commented. "Do they harness the energy in any way?"

"On the American side of the border, downriver, there's a power plant that generates more than 2.4 million kilowatts of electricity," Lorena informed them. "And on the Canadian side, there's another facility that's the largest in Ontario."

"Lor, you're better than having an encyclopedia along with us," Adam laughed.

"Yeah, except there aren't any pretty pictures," Ryan added.

Lorena hit him. "I wish I had that kind of energy or power inside of me driving my life right now," Abriella said, half to herself and half to the others.

"You do," Justin replied. "You've got your passions about life. They drive you with the same force that Niagara Falls has."

"Is that like you and your carpentry, Justin?" Diana asked. "You seem to find it so fascinating."

"I'm not sure," Justin replied. "I know I love to build things, but I'm not sure that love really drives me. There's a difference between interests and passions. I'm not sure which carpentry is with me."

"How do you know when something is a passion in your life and not just an interest?" Abriella asked.

"Take a look at the falls there," Justin said, pointing at the water. "You might wonder what it would be like to go over them in a barrel."

"Whoa! That would be one fabulous ride!" Ryan exclaimed.

"Wondering about the ride would be like an interest. It's something you're curious about," Justin explained.

"I don't think I have that kind of interest," Abriella said, biting her lip fearfully as she looked at the powerful falls.

"That's all right. Let's use Ryan as the example. He has that interest," Justin continued.

"Right on!" Ryan agreed. "I'm ready."

"Now if we took the railing away here and set a barrel down at the edge of cement there, would any of us go up to the edge? Probably none of us except Ryan," Justin explained. "His interest would be growing. It would become a desire—something that he would definitely like to do."

"Let's just go ahead and push him over now and get it over with," Lorena suggested.

Ryan grabbed her as if he was going to push her over the edge, and she screamed.

"So where does the passion come in?" Abriella asked Justin.

"Okay, here is the real key to recognizing passion in your life. If Ryan was willing to get in the barrel and float out into the river, then that would indicate passion," Justin explained. "Ryan would be willing to put his life on the line at that point. That is life-energizing passion in my mind."

"Great explanation, Justin," Adam observed. "I've never thought of it quite like that."

"Wow! I'd have to think carefully to figure out what in my life drives me at that level," Abriella added.

"I don't think there are that many things driving any of us at such a level," Justin replied. "I think a lot of people say they have passion about something, but really it's no more than an interest or maybe a desire. My guess is that most of us have fewer than ten real passions. Maybe even fewer than five."

"That's how I feel about being a doctor," Lorena said confidently. "I know it will take a lot of work and that I'll have to sacrifice other things to succeed at it. But I'm willing to make that sacrifice."

"You're probably right, Lor," Justin said. "And that's probably why the rest of us are having a harder time figuring out what we want to be in life. We haven't discovered that level of passion yet in our lives."

"I've got a passion. Well, maybe it's just a desire," Diana laughed. "I'd like to ride on the boat that goes up to the Falls."

"That sounds fun," Adam replied. "I'm in." The others all agreed as well, and the group of explorers headed off to board the *Maid of the Mist*.

STORY

▶ Exercises

Name: _____ Date: _____ Class: _____ Section: _____

Life Dreaming

Remember what you read at the beginning of this chapter? How a sad thing happens to people on the road from childhood into their teen and college years and life beyond when they lose their ability to dream? How because of this they end up only impersonating themselves rather than living out their own true lives?

How can you keep that from happening in your life? How can you instill passion back into your life? It starts by exploring your dreams about your life. One of the best places to explore your dreams focuses on the areas most important to you. These likely include where to live, what kind of positions you would have in your career, what kind of family life you would like, recreational activities you would be able to pursue, what kind of service you would like to be able to give to others, what you would do for relaxation, what kind of spiritual life you would maintain, what your financial situation would be like, etc.

A. Describe your life dreams in the eight areas listed below.

B. Revisit these dreams and rate them using the following scale:

> *Interest*—option in life that attracts my curiosity
>
> *Desire*—interest I would definitely pursue if I had no limitations
>
> *Passion*—desire I would be willing to dedicate or give my life for

Area	DREAM
Location	
Rating	❑ Interest ❑ Desire ❑ Passion
Career	
Rating	❑ Interest ❑ Desire ❑ Passion
Family	
Rating	❑ Interest ❑ Desire ❑ Passion
Recreation	
Rating	❑ Interest ❑ Desire ❑ Passion

(Continued)

EXERCISES

Area	DREAM
Service	
Rating	❑ Interest ❑ Desire ❑ Passion
Relaxation	
Rating	❑ Interest ❑ Desire ❑ Passion
Spiritual life	
Rating	❑ Interest ❑ Desire ❑ Passion
Finances	
Rating	❑ Interest ❑ Desire ❑ Passion

Adapted from *LifeQuest: Planning Your Life Strategically in the Will of God.* Copyright © 1992–1996 A.W. Millard, Jr. Used by permission.

C. Which of the dreams did you rate as passions?

_____

_____

_____

_____

_____

D. What do you need to do to allow these dreams to *compel* you (drive you toward a course of action in your life)?

_____

_____

_____

_____

_____

EXERCISES

E. What do you need to do to allow these dreams to *impel* you (cause you to actually start to move in the right direction in your life)?

_____

_____

_____

_____

_____

F. What do you need to do to allow these dreams to *propel* you (keep you moving toward your goal in life)?

_____

_____

_____

_____

_____

EXERCISES

Starting to Look at Majors with Interest

Exercise 2 adapted from *The Essential Handbook for Academic Success* by The California University Regents. © 1998 by Kendall/Hunt Publishing Company. Used with permission.

Assessment questions adapted by UCLA Career Planning Center from *Coming Alive From Nine to Five* by B. N. Michelozzi, Mayfield Publishing Company. Used with permission.

So far we have concentrated on helping you think of passion at the level of sacrifice. It is useful, however, to also explore at the interest level because this is often where passions start to develop.

▶ Directions:

Circle the numbers of statements that clearly feel like something you might say or do or think—something that feels like you.

1. It's important for me to have a strong, agile body.
2. I need to understand things thoroughly.
3. Music, color, or beauty of any kind can really affect my moods.
4. People enrich my life and give it meaning.
5. I have confidence in myself that I can make things happen.
6. I appreciate clear directions so I know exactly what to do.
7. I can usually carry/build/fix things myself.
8. I can get absorbed for hours in thinking something out.
9. I appreciate beautiful surroundings; color and design mean a lot to me.
10. I love company.
11. I enjoy competing.
12. I need to get my surroundings in order before I start a project.
13. I enjoy making things with my hands.
14. It's satisfying to explore new ideas.
15. I always seem to be looking for new ways to express my creativity.
16. I value being able to share personal concerns with people.
17. Being a key person in a group is very satisfying to me.
18. I take pride in being very careful about all the details of my work.
19. I don't mind getting my hands dirty.
20. I see education as a lifelong process of developing and sharpening my mind.
21. I love to dress in unusual ways, to try new colors and styles.
22. I can often sense when a person needs to talk to someone.
23. I enjoy getting people organized and on the move.
24. A good routine helps me get the job done.
25. I like to buy sensible things I can make or work on myself.
26. Sometimes I can sit for long periods of time and work on puzzles or read or just think about life.
27. I have a great imagination.
28. It makes me feel good to take care of people.
29. I like to have people rely on me to get the job done.

30. I'm satisfied knowing that I've done an assignment carefully and completely.
31. I'd rather be on my own doing practical, hands-on activities.
32. I'm eager to read about any subject that arouses my curiosity.
33. I love to try creative new ideas.
34. If I have a problem with someone, I prefer to talk it out and resolve it.
35. To be successful, it's important to aim high.
36. I prefer being in a position where I don't have to take responsibility for decisions.
37. I don't enjoy spending a lot of time discussing things. What's right is right.
38. I need to analyze a problem pretty thoroughly before I act on it.
39. I like to rearrange my surroundings to make them unique and different.
40. When I feel down, I find a friend to talk to.
41. After I suggest a plan, I prefer to let others take care of the details.
42. I'm usually content where I am.
43. It's invigorating to do things outdoors.
44. I keep asking why.
45. I like my work to be an expression of my moods and feelings.
46. I like to find ways to help people care more for each other.
47. It's exciting to take part in important decisions.
48. I'm always glad to have someone else take charge.
49. I like my surroundings to be plain and practical.
50. I need to stay with a problem until I figure out an answer.
51. The beauty of nature touches something deep inside me.
52. Close relationships are important to me.
53. Promotion and advancement are important to me.
54. Efficiency, for me, means doing a set amount carefully each day.
55. A strong system of law and order is important to prevent chaos.
56. Thought-provoking books always broaden my perspective.
57. I look forward to seeing art shows, plays, and good films.
58. I haven't seen you for so long; I'd love to know how you're doing.
59. It's exciting to influence people.
60. When I say I'll do it, I follow through on every detail.
61. Good, hard physical work never hurt anyone.
62. I'd like to learn all there is to know about subjects that interest me.
63. I don't want to be like everyone else; I like to do things differently.
64. Tell me how I can help you.
65. I'm willing to take some risks to get ahead.
66. I like exact directions and clear rules when I start something new.
67. The first thing I look for in a car is a well-built engine.
68. Those people are intellectually stimulating.
69. When I'm creating, I tend to let everything else go.
70. I feel concerned that so many people in our society need help.
71. It's fun to get ideas across to people.
72. I hate it when they keep changing the system just when I get it down.
73. I usually know how to take care of things in an emergency.
74. Just reading about those new discoveries is exciting.
75. I like to create happenings.
76. I often go out of my way to pay attention to people who seem lonely and friendless.

77. I love to bargain.
78. I don't like to do things unless I'm sure they're approved.
79. Sports are important in building strong bodies.
80. I've always been curious about the way nature works.
81. It's fun to be in a mood to try or do something unusual.
82. I believe that people are basically good.
83. If I don't make it the first time, I usually bounce back with energy and enthusiasm.
84. I appreciate knowing exactly what people expect of me.
85. I like to take things apart to see if I can fix them.
86. Don't get excited. We can think it out and plan the right move logically.
87. It would be hard to imagine my life without beauty around me.
88. People often seem to tell me their problems.
89. I can usually connect with people who get me in touch with a network of resources.
90. I don't need much to be happy.

▶ Scoring Your Answers

To score, circle the same numbers below that you circled on the exercise:

R	I	A	S	E	C
1	2	3	4	5	6
7	8	9	10	11	12
13	14	15	16	17	18
19	20	21	22	23	24
25	26	27	28	29	30
31	32	33	34	35	36
37	38	39	40	41	42
43	44	45	46	47	48
49	50	51	52	53	54
55	56	57	58	59	60
61	62	63	64	65	66
67	68	69	70	71	72
73	74	75	76	77	78
79	80	81	82	83	84
85	86	87	88	89	90

EXERCISES

Now add up the number of circles in each column:

R __10__ I __14__ A __5__ S __6__ E __7__ C __3__ **TOTALS**

What are your three highest scores?

1st _____ I _____

2nd _____ R _____

3rd _____ S _____

▶ **Dimensional Analysis**

Holland's Group	Characteristic Interests	Characteristic Personal Traits	Characteristic Occupations
Realistic (R)	Activities that involve the precise, ordered use of objects, tools, machines and animals and include agricultural, electrical, manual, physical and mechanical things and activities. Example: Working on cars.	Present-Oriented Thing-Oriented (rather than people or data) Conforming Practical Shy	Engineering Skilled Trades Agricultural and Technical Occupations
Investigative (I)	Activities that involve the exploration and examination of physical, biological and cultural things to understand and control them: sometimes includes scientific and mathematical activities. Example: Reading fiction.	Analytical and Abstract Rational Curious Intellectual Introverted	Scientific, Analytical and some Technical Occupations
Artistic (A)	Activities that involve the use of physical, verbal or human materials to create art forms or products; includes activities and things related to language, art, music, drama and writing. Example: Listening to music.	Creative Expressive Rely on Feelings Imaginative Non-Conforming Idealistic	Musical Artistic Literary and Dramatic Occupations
Social (S)	Activities that involve interaction with other people for enjoyment or to inform, train, develop, cure and educate. Example: Entertaining guests.	Sensitive to needs of others Friendly Outgoing Persuasive Tactful	Teaching Ministry Social Welfare and other "Helping People" Occupations
Enterprising (E)	Activities that involve interaction with other people to reach organizational goals or economic gain; leadership, interpersonal and persuasive activities included. Example: Working for a community action or political organization.	Aggressive/ Assertive Self-Confident Ambitious Sociable Persuasive	Sales Supervisory and Leadership Occupati...
Conventional (C)	Activities that involve the precise, ordered use of data, e.g., keeping records, filing materials, organizing numerical and written data, clerical, computational and business. Example: Working as a treasurer for a political campaign.	Practical Conforming Efficient Accurate Orderly Set in Ways	Accounting Computational Secretarial and Clerical Occupations

If you are in the process of selecting a college major, how can this evaluation help you in your selection? If you have already selected a major, how does this evaluation confirm or call into question your selection?

Use the Dimensional Analysis chart to correlate your three highest scores with possible occupational areas.

Use these occupations to fill in the evaluation chart below:

Then evaluate each as to its appropriate level of attraction to you:

- Interest = something that attracts your curiosity
- Desire = something you would definitely pursue if you had no limitations
- Passion = something you would be willing to sacrifice most other pursuits for in order to pursue this

Occupation	Interests	Desires	Passions
Ministry			X
Social welfare			X
"Helping people"			X
Scientific		X	

▶ References

The following resources have been used in this chapter.

Millard, B. (1996). *LifeQuest: Planning Your Life Strategically*. Ventura, CA: Life Discovery Publications.

The California University Regents. (1998). *The Essential Handbook for Academic Success*. Dubuque, IA: Kendall/Hunt Publishing Company.

Michelozzi, B.N. (1999). *Coming Alive from Nine to Five*. Mountain View, CA: Mayfield Publishing Company.

The following resources may be useful to you in your continuing exploration of Life Calling as you look at your Unique Design and your *passions*.

Holland, J.L., and Gottfredson, G.D. (1996). *Dictionary of Holland Occupational Codes*, 3rd ed. Odessa, Florida: Psychological Assessment Resources Inc.

Schwen, M.R., and Bass, D.C., Eds. (2006). *Leading Lives That Matter: What We Should Do and Who We Should Be*. Grand Rapids, Michigan: Erdmans Publishing Co.

Smith, G.T. (2011). *Courage and Calling: Embracing Your God-given Potential*. Downers Grove, Illinois: Intervarsity Press.

Shaped by Experiences

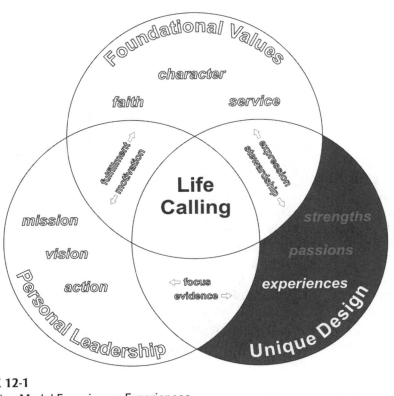

12

FIGURE 12-1
Life Calling Model Focusing on Experiences

Two roads diverged in a wood and I—I took the one less traveled by, and that has made all the difference.

ROBERT FROST

The second main component of the Life Calling Model is *Unique Design*. The third element of this design is comprised of our ***experiences***.

CHAPTER OBJECTIVES

1. Understand the effect of life experiences on your own design as a person
2. Identify the critical factors that impact a life experience
3. Identify and articulate experiences that have shaped your life

CONCEPTS

▶ Concepts

When you finally leave high school and arrive at college, you don't get there with a blank slate. You carry along with you a great deal of personal history. You may have been the valedictorian of your high school graduating class and have a great deal of optimism about how you will do in college. On the other hand, you might be coming into college on academic probation because of your struggles in high school and are worried whether or not you are up to the challenge ahead. You may be the only child in a happy family where your parents paid a great deal of attention to you and made you feel special. Or you may be one of four kids in a family where your parents divorced when you were very young, and you have had to fight to get any attention. You may have lost a good friend to a car accident. You may have struggled with physical or mental illness. And the list could go on. Whether your history was good or bad, it has had a definite impact on who you are today.

Recently I led a group of students enrolled in a leadership class on an expedition to a series of indigenous villages deep in the jungles of Costa Rica. The hike to one of the villages required us to make several river crossings through deep, rapid-flowing water. I was swept away in one crossing, pulled down by the current under the water, and nearly drowned. An overwhelming feeling of terror gripped me as I fought to get back to the surface so I could breathe. But just when I thought there was no hope and that I would die, spiritual strength from God and a strong emotional commitment to my family gave me energy I did not think I had, and I was able to finally find a rock underwater that I used as a platform to push myself up to the surface, where I was able to breathe again. Others from the team came and helped me get from the rock out of the river and back onto dry land. As you read this, you no doubt could even begin to feel a little of the terror just by hearing the story. You can imagine the impact it has had on my life. In fact, I had to get help dealing with the posttraumatic stress on my return home because I would relive the event every night in my dreams.

It is amazing, however, to begin uncovering lessons that this experience has taught me about my life. For instance, I learned that when you are down to your last breath, it is relationships that matter, not money, jobs, positions, titles, or accomplishments. I also learned that the relationships that matter most are those to whom you are the closest. There are enough of these lessons that I am collecting them into a short inspirational book entitled *Lessons from the Bottom of the River*.

Life experience has a great impact on shaping us into the persons we are. Each of us has dramatic experiences that have changed our lives. Reflecting on these is important to the process of discovering our Life Calling.

Strengths, *passions*, and *experiences* comprise the three main elements of our *Unique Design*, the second major component of the Life Calling model. Defining the third of these elements, *experiences*, is rather simple. Our *strengths* and *passions* are developed and shaped in a distinct pattern based on the unique situations, influences, and occurrences we encounter throughout our lives. These can be endowed with blessings, triumphs, and achievements, or they can be burdened by misfortunes, ordeals, and trials. Either way, these experiences will shape us and will help determine the Unique Design we take into our Life Calling.

Why is this important when considering our Unique Design? Two individuals could have similar strengths. It is also possible, though less likely, that these two individuals could have the same passions. But even if this was the case, their experiences in life would be different, and this would result in the two individuals ending up quite different from each other, even though they shared so many similarities.

Critical Forces

How do we begin to understand these life-changing experiences? An effective way to evaluate our life experiences is to analyze the three critical forces that influence them (Figure 12-2).

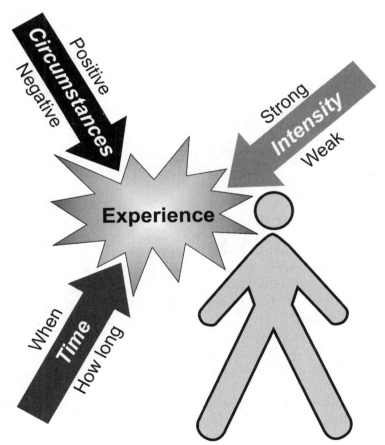

FIGURE 12-2
Critical Forces Impacting a Life Experience

CONCEPTS

Circumstances: The quality of the elements that affect an experience in our life. Positive experiences tend to shape us in a reinforcing manner. Negative experiences tend to shape in a reactionary manner. If you grew up in a family where you and your siblings did a lot of things together and got along well, you will likely be a person who expects to have good relationships and who enjoys social interaction. If, on the other hand, you grew up in a family where you felt your siblings always picked on you, you might have become the kind of person who is always approaching relationships in a combative manner, and you might find that close relationships are difficult for you to establish or maintain.

Intensity: The level of influence this experience has on our life. Obviously, experiences of high intensity tend to have more of an impact on our lives than those of low intensity. For example, breaking up with someone you were seriously dating for several years will affect you more than having a casual friend move to another town.

Time: The point of time in our life in which this experience occurred, and the length of time it lasted. Although things that have happened recently in our lives will be more present in our memories, that does not mean they will have the greatest shaping influence on our lives. Developmental psychologists have found that in certain periods in our lives we are more vulnerable to certain types of shaping events. Phobias, for instance, have a greater tendency to develop in childhood. It is not just when some experience occurred, but also how long it lasted. It is easy to understand that if you were a child who was permanently placed in a foster home by a single parent who no longer was able to take care of you, it will have a much greater impact on you than having to live for one year with a grandparent while your parents regained some financial stability.

Example from the Physical Earth

A good example of how these three shaping forces work can be found in the realm of geology. Carbon is a very important element on this earth. It is the basis for all plant and animal life. Elemental carbon compounds are those compounds on earth formed of nothing else but carbon. When this elemental carbon undergoes varying experiences, it forms different minerals. The experiences vary by the heat and pressure involved. This is similar to the life experiences we encounter. Coal is formed from carbon that has gone through minimal heat and pressure. When carbon experiences a greater amount of heat and pressure, it may well form graphite. When tremendous amounts of heat and pressure are put to bear on carbon, diamonds may be formed.

An important thing to notice in this illustration is that based on the experience, different forms of carbon occurred. Each of these forms has different valuable uses. Coal is the best source of fuel among the three. Graphite is the best lubricant, and when it is placed in a pencil, it also serves as the best writing material. Diamonds, on the other hand, have great value in the industrial world because of their hardness. Because of their beauty, they also form the best candidate of the three to be incorporated into jewelry. Can you imagine the reaction of a woman who would be offered an engagement ring containing a one-carat piece of coal or graphite?

Learning from the Experiences of Others

So far we have been looking primarily at our own personal experiences, and these have the greatest impact in shaping who we are. However, we also have been affected by the experiences of others. This can be as close as parents or other family members to classic history of others who lived thousands of years ago. One of the reasons most colleges and universities require students to study some history and social science is because of the value that understanding these experiences of others can have in helping us understand ourselves.

Concepts Summary

The lesson we can learn from this is that our experiences shape us into different people who will find that our compatibility with various callings in life correlates to the persons we have become. How can we recognize this in our lives? One of the best ways is through what we will call "autobiologs." These are historical journals we create by reflecting back on our lives and chronicling the experiences that may have had an impact on making us who we are. We can create these from our own memories, but it is also very valuable to interview others who have been close to our lives. We will look at this more in the Exercises section of this chapter.

 Insight

The words of David in the twenty-third Psalm provide a picture of what our life experiences can be like.

> The Lord is my shepherd, I lack nothing. He makes me lie down in green pastures, he leads me beside quiet waters, he refreshes my soul. He guides me along the right paths for his name's sake.
>
> Even though I walk through the darkest valley, I will fear no evil, for you are with me; your rod and your staff, they comfort me.
>
> You prepare a table before me in the presence of my enemies. You anoint my head with oil; my cup overflows.
>
> Surely your goodness and love will follow me all the days of my life, and I will dwell in the house of the LORD forever.

A common theme throughout the Bible is that the events of our lives will shape who we are and who we become.

SCRIPTURAL INSIGHT 1 ▶ *All Things Can Work Together for Good*

And we know that all things work together for good to them that love God, to them who are the called according to his purpose. ROMANS 8:28 (KJV)

Without a doubt, this is the most important scripture that applies to experiences we face in life. We first quote it here from the classic King James Version. *Experiences* are the third element in our Unique Design. We define *experiences* as the unique situations, influences and occurrences we encounter throughout our life. These can be blessings, triumphs or achievements, or they can be misfortunes, ordeals or trials. No matter what quality they have, these experiences shape us and definitely impact our Life Calling.

At the end of my junior year in high school, my dad decided to move from California to Massachusetts. I had gone through elementary, middle school, and nearly all of high school with my friends. I was really upset with my father for making this move. Six months later I found out that I was very sick and that if I had not been taken to a world-renowned health center in Massachusetts that specialized with my problem, I would have died. God used what seemed to me like a terrible life experience to accomplish something remarkably good in my life.

When we love God and respond to his call to follow him, all of our experiences will work together in a good way to develop our Life Calling. Now let's look at the passage as quoted with a slight difference in Today's New International Version, the version we have been using consistently in this book. "And we know that in all things God works for the good of those who love him, who have been called according to his purpose."

The thought that is added from this interpretation is that when we are in relationship with him, God actively works through our experiences to bring about good in our lives that will guide our Life Calling.

What we can learn from Romans 8:28 is that our life experiences form one of the best places to explore when searching for our Life Calling. The passage also encourages us to start moving forward in life as part of our search. As we experience life, whatever takes place will be woven into our Life Calling—in other words, it will continue to evolve as we encounter these events. In the next four devotions we will look at four remarkable stories from the Bible that illustrate this.

> **PERSONAL REFLECTION** > Are you harboring bitterness for things that have happened in your life that you really feel should not have been? How can you learn to entrust these to God to work with and accomplish good in your life?

SCRIPTURAL INSIGHT 2 > *What Others Intended for Evil God Can Redirect for Good*

Then Joseph said to his brothers, "Come close to me." When they had done so, he said, "I am your brother Joseph, the one you sold into Egypt! And now, do not be distressed and do not be angry with yourselves for selling me here, because it was to save lives that God sent me ahead of you. Genesis 45:4&5

The first example we will look at from the Bible comes from the story of Joseph. Joseph's brothers sold him into slavery. He was purchased by Potifar. Potifar recognized Joseph's trustworthiness and put him in charge of Potifar's household. Joseph developed good management skills. Some time later Potifar's wife falsely accused Joseph of adultery. He was put in prison.

Joseph's management skills learned in Potifar's home were recognized by the warden, and Joseph was put in charge of all the other prisoners. He worked in this position for several years. In that position, Joseph came in contact with the Pharaoh's cupbearer and baker who had been thrown into prison. Joseph interpreted their dreams. The butler was restored to service and promised to put in a good word for Joseph.

The butler forgot until two years later when Pharaoh needed a dream interpreted. The butler mentioned Joseph. Joseph interpreted the dream. Pharaoh elevated him to second in command over all of Egypt. In that position, Joseph was able to take care of Jacob, his father, and all his family during a terrible famine, no doubt sparing them from extinction were they to face the famine on their own.

From the time Joseph was sold into slavery until the time he became second in command over Egypt, twenty years had passed. For a good share of those years, things seemed to be going against Joseph. If anyone had a right to be bitter about life experiences, he certainly did. But he did not harbor such bitterness. When he talked to his brothers, he told them that the plans they had for evil were used by God to accomplish great good.

During all those years that seemed to be problematic, God continued to work for Joseph's good, weaving together a Life Calling that would accomplish great service to God's plan.

> **PERSONAL REFLECTION** > Have you learned to trust God with your life experiences? How can you start to view the things you see as hardships in your life as building blocks God can use to accomplish great things through you?

INSIGHT

> **SCRIPTURAL INSIGHT 3** *Choose the Hardships of God Over the Pleasure of Sin*

Since then, no prophet has risen in Israel like Moses, whom the LORD knew face to face, who did all those miraculous signs and wonders the Lord sent him to do in Egypt—to Pharaoh and to all his officials and to his whole land. For no one has ever shown the mighty power or performed the awesome deeds that Moses did in the sight of all Israel. DEUTERONOMY 34:10-12

The next example we will look at from the Bible comes from the story of Moses. Several hundred years after Joseph, new leaders had taken over Egypt and had enslaved the Israelites. Moses was born during this time when the Pharaoh of that era had ordered all baby Israelite boys to be drowned in the Nile River. Moses' mother put him in a basket and floated him on the river. Pharoah's daughter took a bath in the river and found Moses in the basket and decided to keep him as her own child. She hired a Hebrew woman to nurse him while he was a baby (the woman happened to be Moses' real mother).

When he was weaned, Moses went to live with his adopted mother in Pharoah's palace. Moses was highly educated as a member of Pharoah's family. He was also trained in military command. At age forty, he quite likely was in line to become the next Pharaoh. However, at that time he intervened in a situation between an Egyptian and an Israelite, killing the Egyptian. Pharaoh got mad and decided to kill Moses.

Moses fled to Midian and herded sheep for forty years. It was at that point that God decided to deliver the Israelites from their slavery in Egypt. And he had a perfectly qualified person to lead this deliverance—Moses. Moses was highly educated in Egyptian thinking, so he would know how to deal with the new Pharaoh; highly trained in military organization, so he would be able to organize large numbers of people; and highly developed in patience from leading sheep for forty years, so he would be able to deal with the ignorant, complaining Israelites. A perfect Life Calling!

Hebrews 11:24-26 sums it up with these words:

By faith Moses, when he had grown up, refused to be known as the son of Pharaoh's daughter. He chose to be mistreated along with the people of God rather than to enjoy the fleeting pleasures of sin. He regarded disgrace for the sake of Christ as of greater value than the treasures of Egypt, because he was looking ahead to his reward.

> **PERSONAL REFLECTION** Do you have a hard time figuring out how all of the things you have done in life can be brought together for anything valuable in your life? Are you looking just for pleasure and good times, or are you willing to suffer disgrace for the sake of Christ?

> **SCRIPTURAL INSIGHT 4** *Humble Yourself Before God*

A hand touched me and set me trembling on my hands and knees. He said, "Daniel, you who are highly esteemed, consider carefully the words I am about to speak to you, and stand up, for I have now been sent to you." And when he said this to me, I stood up trembling. Then he continued, "Do not be afraid, Daniel. Since the first day that you set your mind to gain understanding and to humble yourself before your God, your words were heard, and I have come in response to them. DANIEL 10:10-12

The next example we will look at from the Bible comes from the story of Daniel. A millennium after the Exodus led by Moses, the Israelites have been conquered by the Babylonians who decided to take the cream of the crop into captivity. One of these captives, Daniel, was a member of the Jewish royal family. He was a young, good-looking man with no physical defect. He was well educated and a quick study. Daniel was highly talented and well qualified, so Nebuchadnezzar, the king, had him taken into his palace rather than having him killed or imprisoned.

Once in the palace, Daniel learned the language and the literature of the Babylonians. He and his three Hebrew colleagues surpassed the wisdom of all the Babylonians by ten times over! He then interpreted Nebuchadnezzar's dream and spared the lives of all of the wise men. He helped Nebuchadnezzar run Babylon and became one of the king's closest confidants. God used this relationship to guide Nebuchadnezzar and ultimately bring him into a spiritual relationship with God.

When Belshazzar became king, Daniel dropped back from the forefront, but when writing showed up on the wall at Belshazzar's feast, he called on Daniel who read the message (which wasn't very good news for Belshazzar). Belshazzar and the Babylonians were conquered that night by the Persians.

Darius, the Persian king, appointed Daniel to be one of the three highest rulers in the nation. Others were jealous and tried to trap him for his habit of prayer. He ended up in the lions' den, but Daniel was joined by angels who shut the lions' mouths. Daniel was then made the highest ruler next to the king. He continued to be a leader under King Cyrus, and he was influential in helping Cyrus decide to allow the Jews to return to their homeland.

It is quite likely that Daniel neither planned on nor wanted any of the events that beset him, but God worked good in all of them and accomplished a great Life Calling through Daniel.

> **PERSONAL REFLECTION** ⟩ Have you humbled yourself before God in considering your life experiences? Are you spending your time resenting your life experiences or trying to understand them?

SCRIPTURAL INSIGHT 5 ⟩ *By the Grace of God I Am What I Am*

For I am the least of the apostles and do not even deserve to be called an apostle, because I persecuted the church of God. But by the grace of God I am what I am, and His grace to me was not without effect. 1 CORINTHIANS 15:9&10

The last example we will look at is the Apostle Paul in the New Testament. He was a highly respected Jew of the tribe of Benjamin. He was considered a Hebrew of Hebrews—the top of the line. He was a highly educated Pharisee who knew every aspect of the law. He had been trained by Gamaliel, a leading authority in the Jewish Sanhedrin and celebrated scholar of the Mosaic Law. Paul had no tolerance for people who did not fully support the Jewish religion. He was faultless when it came to legalistic righteousness. On top of all of this, he was a Roman citizen—no small fete for a Jew in those days. Paul was on the fast track to Jewish leadership.

INSIGHT

Paul thought his purpose in life included getting rid of the followers of Jesus. He collaborated in the stoning of the Christian martyr Stephen. He then obtained documents authorizing him to go to Damascus and take prisoner anyone who was a follower of Jesus. He was determined to wipe out this hated sect.

What a terrible life! Most of us would have no use for such a person. But God saw all of this as useful material for taking a man and using him to shape the Christian religion rather than wiping it out. All Paul lacked was a willingness to be this man, so God took care of that with a bright light on the road to Damascus.

After Paul's conversion to Christianity, everything did not suddenly turn into a bed of roses. As we saw in Chapter 11, his life was marked by one hardship after another. But look at Paul's words from the passage at the beginning of this devotion: "By the grace of God, I am what I am." God used Paul's life experiences—good and bad alike—to develop a person who had more impact on the development of Christianity than any other person except Jesus himself. What a Life Calling!

As we look back at the four examples in the devotions of this chapter, at face value, almost everything that happened to Joseph, Moses, Daniel and Paul seemed to be leading them away from what we might have chosen in outlining their Life Callings. Yet God used every event in their lives to craft the calling he wanted for them. God will do the same for us if we allow him to do so.

INSIGHT

> **PERSONAL REFLECTION** Are you letting your life move forward with events that you turn over to God? Are you allowing God to work them together for good in your life and in his plan for using you in service? How can you learn to let your experiences become the God-mastered building blocks of your Life Calling?

◗ Discovery

How can the Discovery Guides help you understand how your life *experiences* have shaped you and how can you benefit from this?

T **THEORY**	Study of social and behavioral sciences can help you explore the role of life experiences in shaping your Life Calling. This study can be pursued in both formal classes and in your own personal reading as well. Start creating a list of books that will aid your exploration. Ask others for recommendations.
E **EXAMPLES**	Talk with people who have lived full lives. Learn from them how their experiences have shaped them. Keep a constant search for such people. As has been pointed out several times before, many times you will find these kinds of people in positions you may not have thought of, such as food service, groundskeepers, janitors, secretaries, and other places that may not be in the limelight of your institution. Seek out a mentor relationship with a person who has lived a rich life full of life-shaping experiences.
A **ASSESSMENT**	Assessment of personal experiences takes on a different nature from other assessments. It is more of a process that involves life mapping and writing of autobiographies and personal history in narrative writing. Construction and study of anthropological charts can provide valuable information as well.
C **COUNSEL**	Professional counselors and life coaches are trained to help you in evaluating the experiences of your life. Your college and university will likely have a counseling center with trained personnel to help you. Additionally, family members, teachers, student life personnel, pastors, and friends know you well and can help you identify important experiences in your life.
H **HISTORY**	The classics and historical biographies are full of stories dealing with notable people who have lived lives full of rich experiences. Select some of these and learn from their experiences.
E **EXPERIENCE**	This whole area of observation involves life experiences.
R **REFLECTION**	Take time to reflect on your entire life to explore what impact the experiences you have encountered have had on who you are. Take time to also reflect on your current experiences as well and how all of these are shaping your Life Calling.

DISCOVERY

▶ Story

The boat ride on the *Maid of the Mist* had been an exciting and very wet adventure. The explorers had also returned to Niagara Falls that night to see the monstrous cascade lit by colored lights. The next day they boarded the *Nautilus* to continue their journey. They traveled back to Buffalo, where they rejoined Interstate 90 and headed west. They traveled through Cleveland, which, for some odd reason that they never could figure out, hosted the Rock 'n' Roll Hall of Fame. They passed through South Bend, Indiana, where Lorena pointed out Notre Dame as part of her ongoing—if unsolicited—list of outstanding schools. The trip had been marked by several severe thunderstorms that accompanied a cold front moving through the area. Fortunately, there was no hail, and the winds had not been bad enough to stop traffic. Still, the crew of the *Nautilus* was glad when this leg of their journey came to an end.

They had decided to camp at Indiana Dunes State Park for the evening and take the train into Chicago the next day. This way they could avoid traffic and the challenge of maneuvering the *Nautilus* in a big city. As the day waned, the six decided to walk along the beach that bordered Lake Michigan. The sun would not set until well after 9 pm, so there was plenty of light left in the day.

Silence marked the first part of the walk. A slight breath of wind passed through the leaves of the trees that lined the beach, and the small waves gently slapped against the sand. The explorers found these waves intriguing and different compared to those of the Pacific back home in Seahaven.

Lorena finally broke the conversational lull. "Why are you so stable, Adam?" The attention of everyone else was instantly captured.

"What do you mean, Lor?" Adam asked.

"Well look at all the rest of us," Lorena continued. "Ryan and I are always at each other's throats. Abriella seems almost ashamed that she hasn't figured out her life. Justin's not sure what's going on. Diana is … well, you know … Diana is Diana."

"What's that supposed to mean?" Diana asked.

Lorena ignored her. "But you always seem to have it all together. It's been that way ever since I can remember."

"First of all, I don't have it all together," Adam answered. "I have questions and uncertainty about my life just like you."

"So how can you stay so calm when you have that uncertainty inside you?" Lorena probed further.

"When I was ten years old, my uncle, my dad's brother, was promoted to vice-president of a pretty big company in LA. He was in his early forties," Adam replied. "He'd focused his life on getting that job. He neglected my aunt and my cousins to work for the promotion. He had worked in that VP job for only two weeks when he had a massive heart attack and died. At his funeral I told myself that when I grew up, I would never let the same thing happen to me. Even though I was young, I promised myself that I would live a balanced life."

"How does that keep you calm with us?" Abriella wondered.

"I try to evaluate everything by looking at the bigger picture," Adam explained. "That way I don't overreact to situations."

"What if that experience hadn't happened in your life, though? Do you think you'd be the same?" Abriella asked.

"I doubt it," Adam answered. "I think to a great extent we're all the product of our life experiences."

The discussion wandered on for several minutes, but as the daylight was fading, the six decided it was time to return to the motorhome. The next day they would visit Chicago.

The crew of the *Nautilus* woke early the next day and headed for the South Shore Line station near the park. They boarded the train and rode it into the city. After a couple of transfers, they got off the train and walked one block west to the Willis Tower. They purchased tickets to the Skydeck on the 103rd floor of the Tower. This would place them 1,353 feet above the ground. The cold front that had gone through the area on the previous day had left the air unusually clear and crisp in Chicago. The view from the Skydeck was spectacular. They were able to see four different states—Illinois, Indiana, Michigan, and Wisconsin.

"I wonder where the lady lived who had the cow that kicked over the lantern that started the fire that burned down Chicago?" Ryan asked. The others laughed because his question sounded a lot like the song "The House that Jack Built."

"Let's go around to the south side of the Skydeck," Lorena suggested. When they got there, she directed their attention about a mile south and a little west. "Do you see the university campus across the river?"

"Yeah," Ryan answered.

"Well the O'Leary house was just a couple of blocks east of that." Lorena put her arm over Ryan's shoulder and pointed. "Just on the other side of the freeway you can see there beside the university."

"Do you know everything? How do you know where this house was?" Diana asked in a somewhat frustrated tone.

"I read it in the tour guide book last night in the park," Lorena responded as she continued to point.

"Okay, I think I see it," Ryan replied.

The others all looked intently as did quite a few other tourists visiting the Skydeck, even though they did not know what it was they were looking at.

"You talk about experiences changing your life," Justin said, "there's an experience that sure changed people's lives. I bet Mrs. O'Leary was a different person after that."

"The cow too," Ryan agreed, and the others laughed.

"It's funny how some experiences are such life changers, while others have hardly any impact at all," Abriella reflected.

"I think the circumstances play a big part in that," Adam suggested. "What is the nature of the events that make up this experience in our life?"

"Probably so," Abriella said. "A fire like that was pretty intense. It can't help but have a strong influence. Adam's uncle dying obviously was an intense event in his life, so that's why it had such a strong impact on him."

"Don't you think when it happened makes a difference?" Lorena asked. "Adam was vulnerable at that young age."

"And not just the point of time, but how long it lasts as well," Justin added.

"Good point," Lorena said, nodding.

"Please excuse." A foreign tourist speaking with a strong accent interrupted them. "Do all American young people talk like this? I not realize you so mature."

The explorers were startled when they realized that others outside their own circle had been listening to their discussion.

"Believe me," Adam replied with a sheepish grin, "we aren't always like this. You caught us on a good day." The explorers and the tourists all laughed.

STORY

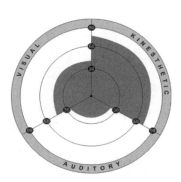

FIGURE 8-4
Learning Styles Grid Example

B. Use the TOTALS you have calculated to fill in the diagram below. The labels correspond to the initials used in the inventory above: V=Visual, A=Auditory, K=Kinesthetic. Use a pencil or pen to shade in the wedge for each of the categories out to the corresponding score you calculated for that category. Figure 8-4 gives an example of what this will look like.

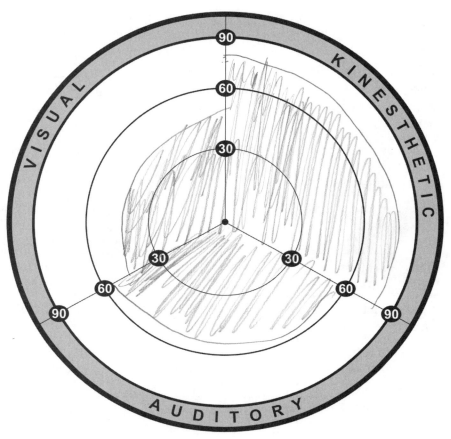

FIGURE 8-5
Learning Styles Grid

C. Look at the diagram you have produced and answer the following questions:

1. How would you classify the appearance of your diagram?
   - One wedge dominates the other two
   - Two wedges are near equal with the third quite a bit weaker
   - All wedges are nearly equal

I like Kinesthetic + auditory and should learn how to apply this

2. What does this indicate to you about the way you prefer learning? How can you maximize this in your learning strategies?

3. Most teachers in college tend to rely on *auditory* learning for their classes. How does this match with your preferred learning style? What strategy can you use to match or compensate for this?

I can use that

17. When I think back on a party I have gone to the, I find it easiest to remember	2	the faces of the people there, but not the names	1	the names but not the faces	3	the things I did and said while I was there
18. If I see the word "d-o-g", I immediately	2	think of a picture of a particular dog	1	say the word "dog" to myself silently	3	think about the feeling of being with a dog (petting it, running with it, etc.)
19. When I am trying to concentrate, I am distracted most by	2	things I see	3	noises I hear	1	feelings or sensations that are uncomfortable
20. When I am not sure how to spell a word, I usually	1	look it up online	2	sound it out	3	don't worry about it
21. When I am standing in a long line at the grocery store, I usually	2	look at the tabloids and other magazines	1	talk to the person next to me	3	fidget and shift my weight from one foot to the other
22. When I talk with others, I like to	1	use illustrations to explain my points	2	use a variety of words to make our conversation richer	3	use my hands to communicate my points
23. When I am alone, I often	1	daydream about places I'd like to be	2	talk to myself	3	try to stay physically active
24. At my school I am best at	1	visual arts	3	musical arts	2	sports or dance
25. In order to learn how to do something, I need to	1	see a diagram or illustration of how it should be done	2	listen to someone explain how to do it	3	actively participate in an activity related it to it
26. I am most skilled at	2	designing graphs, charts, and other visual displays for a class	3	making a speech to a class about a project I have completed	1	leading others in a group physical activity related to a class
27. The classes I get the most out of usually have	1	video clips and other pictures that illustrate points	2	an interesting teacher who gives good lectures	3	lots of hands-on activities
28. If I am lost, I prefer to	2	look at a map	1	call someone for directions	3	drive around until I figure where I am
29. My friends would say that I primarily	2	Show how things should be done	1	Tell how things should be done	3	Just do the things that should be done
30. My favorite activity in first grade was	1	show-and-tell	2	listening to stories read by my teacher	3	recess
TOTALS	49	V	56	A	75	K

EXERCISES

15
56
49
180

	V		A		K	
6. When I sit in a class, I	*2*	jot down notes with diagrams or pictures reflecting what I am learning	*3*	enjoy discussing issues and hearing other points of view	*1*	would rather be somewhere else and so spend my time doodling
7. In my spare time I would rather	*1*	watch television, go to a movie, or read	*2*	listen to my iPod (or other MP3 player), a CD or play a musical instrument	*3*	engage in a physical activity of some kind
8. When I get a new piece of electronic equipment, I prefer to	*1*	read the manual, follow instructions and then get it to work.	*2*	listen to an experienced person explain how to get it to operate	*3*	just figure out how to do it myself by trying it
9. When I read a book, I	*3*	sometimes stop and stare into space, imagining the scene I just read about.	*2*	frequently move my lips and speak under my breath.	*1*	fidget a lot, because I really do not like to read.
10. When I study for a test, I prefer to	*1*	read notes, read headings in a book, and look at diagrams and illustrations	*3*	have someone ask me questions, or repeat facts silently to myself	*2*	write things out on index cards and make models or diagrams.
11. When I listen to music, I often *19*	*1*	daydream about things that go with the music	*2*	hum along with the music	*3*	move my body with the music, such as tapping my foot or fingers
12. When I am working at solving a problem, I usually	*2*	make a list, organize the steps, and check them off as I do them	*1*	call my friends or someone who I think knows about the problem and talk to them about it	*3*	make a model of the problem or walk through what I think is the solution in my mind
13. If I was reading a book just for fun and had to choose among the following categories, I would prefer	*1*	a book with a lot of pictures in it	*2*	a book with a lot of conversation in it	*3*	a book where I answer questions and solve problems
14. If I go to a science museum, I will usually first	*2*	look around and find a map showing the locations of the various exhibits	*1*	talk to a museum guide and ask about the exhibits	*3*	go into the first exhibit that looks interesting, and play it by ear from there
15. I do not like going to a restaurant that has	*3*	lights that are too bright	*1*	music that is too loud	*2*	chairs that are too uncomfortable
16. I would prefer to take a(n)	*1*	art class	*3*	music class	*2*	physical education class

▶ Exercises

Caleb
Ostrander

Why does learning new skills and information seem to come so easily for some people, while others struggle? Is there one "right" way to learn something? Is there anything you can do to increase your personal learning power? The answers to these questions come from understanding how people learn, and especially how *you* learn.

But what happens if you figure out your preferred learning style and your teacher's instructional style and find they don't match? Should you drop the class in despair? No, you are going to need to develop strategies to match your learning style with a teacher's differing instructional style.

EXERCISE 1

Learning Style Inventory

A. Read the beginning statement in the column to the left in the table below, then read the choices for completing the statement given in the three columns to the right. Choose the statement that you believe most fits you and place the number "3" in the box immediately to the left of this statement. Then from the remaining two statements, choose the statement that you believe comes closer to fitting you and place a number "2" in the box immediately to the left of this statement. Then place a number "1" in the box immediately to the left of the remaining statement. When you have completed the inventory, use a calculator to total up the scores in each column and place the total in the appropriate box at the bottom of the inventory. As a check to verify that you added correctly, your three TOTALS scores should add up to "180."

	V		A		K	
1. My emotions can often be interpreted from my	1	facial expressions	2	voice quality	3	general body language
2. I keep up with current events by	1	reading the paper thoroughly when I have time	3	listening to the radio or watching TV news	2	quickly reading the paper or spending a few minutes watching TV
3. If I have work with others in a group project, I prefer communicating with them	3	in face-to-face meetings	1	by talking to them on the phone	2	text messaging
4. When I'm angry, I usually	3	clam up and give others the "silent" treatment	1	am quick to let others know why I'm angry	2	clench my fists, grasp something tightly, or storm off
5. When studying to remember something, I do best by:	2	reading it several times and keeping it in a visible place	1	saying it to myself over and over	3	writing it down

EXERCISES

(Continued)

Dealing with Stress

Caleb Ostrander

Our level of emotional strength has a direct impact on our level of stress. Learning how to manage our emotions is one of the four emotional abilities identified in emotional intelligence theory.

The transition from high school to college is almost always a time of stress. Consider just a few of the differences listed below:

HIGH SCHOOL	COLLEGE
Theme papers	Research papers
Some reading	Lots of reading
Processing facts	Processing ideas
Imposed discipline	Self-discipline
Minimal amount of homework	Significant amount of homework
Moderate pace	Twice-as-fast pace
Living at home	Living with roommates (who you may not know)

1. There may be additional sources of stress in your life. The list below has been created by combining elements from a number of studies related to the cause of stress. Look down through it and check off items that you are experiencing or have experienced in the last year. The items with shading represent more serious causes of stress.

☐	Death of parent or sibling
☐	Divorce of parents
☐	Martial separation of parents
☐	Jail term
☐	Death of close family member
☐	Personal injury or illness
☐	Loss of job for any reason
☐	Change in your personal health
☐	Change in health of a family member
☐	Gain of new family member
☐	Change in financial state (either you or your family)
☐	Death of close friend
☐	Change in jobs
☐	Breaking off a relationship with a girlfriend/boyfriend
☒	Conflict with parents

EXERCISES

☒	Conflict with close friend
☐	Change in responsibilities at work
☒	Outstanding personal achievement
☒	Leaving home for school for the first time
☒	Begin or end school
☐	Change in living conditions
☐	Revision in personal habits
☐	Trouble with boss or coworkers
☐	Conflict with roommate(s)
☐	Change in work hours or conditions
☒	Change in residence
☐	Change in schools
☐	Change in college major
☐	Change in recreation
☐	Change in church activities
☐	Change in social activities
☐	Financial concerns
☒	Change in sleeping habits
☐	Change in number of family get-togethers
☒	Change in eating habits
☒	Vacation
☐	Christmas alone
☐	Minor violations of the law
☐	Violations of rules at your school

EXERCISES

2. Record your findings:

   Number of boxes checked with darkest shading ___ *0* ___

   Number of boxes checked with medium shading ___ *5* ___

   Number of boxes checked with no shading ___ *4* ___

3. Understand your findings:

   What can you learn from this? It is probably easy for you to figure out that the greater the number of boxes you checked, the higher your level of stress will be. If more of the boxes you checked have shading, then the level of stress will be even higher.

Learning Atmosphere

Write in the "My Preference" column what you believe to be your preferred learning atmosphere after reading the element and the prompts given.

Stimuli	Elements	Prompts	My Preference
Environmental	Sound	Do you prefer it quiet?	No
		Do you prefer to study with sound?	Slight Sound
	Light	Do you prefer bright light?	No
		Do you prefer dim light?	Yes
	Temperature	Do you prefer a warm environment?	No
		Do you prefer a cool environment?	Yes
	Design	Do you prefer to sit at a desk?	No
		Do you prefer softer more informal seating?	Yes
Emotional	Motivation	Do you learn by self-motivation?	Yes
		Do you need to be motivated by others to learn?	No
	Persistence	Do you generally finish what you start by staying focused?	No
		Do you get bored or distracted easily and need breaks or small goals?	Yes
	Responsibility	Do you always try to meet the expectations given by your instructor?	Yes
		Do you prefer to complete assignments meaningful to you?	No (well yes, but not like the other one)
	Structure	Do you prefer clear directions before completing assignments?	No
		Do you prefer assignments that allow you to choose how you complete them?	Yes
Sociological	Self vs. Pair	Do you prefer to work alone?	Yes
		Do you prefer to work with another person?	No
	Solo vs. Teams	Do you prefer assignments in which you are totally responsible?	Yes
		Do you prefer assignments where responsibility is shared by a group?	NO!!!

	Feedback from Authority	Do you prefer a lot of feedback from your instructor?	No
		Do you prefer to have more autonomy and work independently of your instructor?	Yes
	Variety vs. Routine	Do you prefer one way of learning rather than a variety of ways?	No
		Do you prefer a variety ways of learning rather than one way?	Yes
Physical	Perceptual	Do you prefer to learn information in patterns and broad concepts?	Yes
		Do you prefer to learn information in detailed, smaller pieces?	No
	Intake	Do you prefer to be eating and drinking while you learn?	No
		Do you find eating and drinking distracting while you are learning?	Yes
	Time	Do you prefer to learn earlier in the day?	Yes
		Do you prefer learn later in the day?	No
	Mobility	Do you find it difficult to sit still for a long time while you learn?	Yes
		Do you find it easy to sit still for a long time and learn?	No
Psychological	Global/Analytic	Do you prefer an open and free environment for working?	Yes
		Do you prefer a more traditional environment for working?	No
	Right/Left Hemisphere	Do you prefer to learn in a logical and compartmentalize manner?	Yes
		Do you prefer to learn in a holistic and creative manner?	No (sometimes)
	Impulsive/Reflective	Do you often approach your learning with a "leap before your think" philosophy?	No
		Do you often approach your learning by "scrutinize before moving" philosophy?	Yes

What did you learn about yourself from doing this exercise?

I learned ways that I can improve my studying and learning environment by forming it to my strengths and preferences.

▶ Exercises

Caleb
Ostrander

Exploring Your Own Emotional Intelligence

EXERCISE 1

Questions in four brief surveys can lead you in further self discovery to understand your emotional intelligence. It is important to note, however, that this is a self-assessment dependent on your self-awareness to determine its accuracy. In the area of emotional intelligence, this is usually not the case. Thus, these questions do not measure actual skills, knowledge or abilities. You will need to complete the validated assessment *MSCEIT* to accomplish this.

Adapted from *Teaching Emotional Intelligence Skills* by David Caruso and Susan Kornacki. Copyright 2006, EI Skills Group. Used by permission.

Take a few minutes to answer and then score the questions in each section to determine your ability in that area.

Identifying Emotions Quiz: Select the response that best describes you.

I am aware of my feelings		
a	☐	Always aware of how I feel
b	☒	At times am aware of my feelings
c	☐	Don't pay much attention to my feelings
Express my emotions		
a	☐	My emotional expressions allow others to understand how I feel
b	☐	Can show some of my emotions
c	☒	Not good at expressing my emotions
Read other people's emotions		
a	☒	Always know other's emotions
b	☐	Usually pick up on other's emotions
c	☐	Mis-read people's emotions at times
Read subtle, non-verbal emotional cues		
a	☐	Almost always read between the lines and pick up on how the person feels
b	☒	At times, I can read non-verbal cues such as body language
c	☐	Don't pay much attention to this
Monitor my emotions		
a	☐	Almost always aware of my emotions
b	☒	Usually
c	☐	At times

(Continued)

EXERCISES

Aware of how the surroundings influence people's moods		
a	☐	Almost always
b	☒	Usually
c	☐	At times

Accurately identify the emotions artists express in their work		
a	☐	Almost always
b	☒	Usually
c	☐	At times

Aware of manipulative emotions		
a	☒	Almost always
b	☐	Usually
c	☐	At times

Accurately identify how others feel based on their body language		
a	☒	Almost always know when a person is trying to manipulate me
b	☐	Usually
c	☐	At times

Able to detect 'phony' people		
a	☒	Almost always
b	☐	Usually
c	☐	At times

▶ **Scoring**

There are two ways to score this brief self-quiz. Give yourself 0 points for each "c" response, 1 point for each "b" response and 2 points for every "a" response. Another way to view these results is to reflect on how many "a" responses you gave yourself. The "a" level responses indicate that a person displays a high level of expertise in that area.

"a" responses score __4__

"b" responses score __5__

"c" responses score __1__

Once again, note that this is not a validated EI test! The purpose is to stimulate your thinking about these EI abilities.

▶ What Do Higher and Lower Scores Mean?

People who score higher on this survey might be seen as possessing the qualities, and engaging in the behaviors, in the left-hand column.

Skilled	Unskilled
Knows what people feel	Misreads people's feelings
Will talk about feelings	Doesn't talk about feelings
Comfortable showing feelings	Never shows feelings
Expresses both positive and negative feelings	Does not know how to express feelings
Reads people accurately	Fails to identify how others feel
Good at recognizing own feelings	Misunderstands own feelings

Using Emotions Quiz: Select the response that best describes you.

Can generate an emotion		
a	☐	Yes, for all basic emotions
b	☒	For many emotions
c	☐	Rarely, or with difficulty
Before an important meeting requiring me to be in a high-energy mood		
a	☐	I always get into a positive, energetic mood
b	☒	I sometimes 'psych' myself up for it
c	☐	I keep my mood just the same
Influence of emotions on my thinking		
a	☐	Emotions focus me on what's important
b	☒	Emotions have little impact on me
c	☐	Emotions may distract me
I feel what others feel		
a	☒	Almost always
b	☐	Usually
c	☐	Rarely
When someone describes a powerful emotional event		
a	☒	I feel what they feel for all basic emotions
b	☐	My feelings change a bit
c	☐	My feelings stay the same

EXERCISES

(Continued)

My emotional imagination is…		
a	☐	Very strong
b	☐	Somewhat powerful
c	☒	Not well developed
Can feel all basic emotions on demand		
a	☐	Almost always
b	☐	Usually
c	☒	Rarely
I have a lot of shared feeling for other people – I feel what they feel		
a	☐	Almost always for almost all people
b	☒	Frequently for most people
c	☐	At times, or for a few people or feelings
Emotions focus me on what is important or what is going on around me		
a	☐	Almost always
b	☐	Usually
c	☒	Rarely
I match my mood to the demands of the task at hand		
a	☐	Almost always
b	☒	Usually do this
c	☐	Rarely

▶ Scoring

There are two ways to score this brief self-quiz. Give yourself 0 points for each "c" response, 1 point for each "b" response and 2 points for every "a" response. Another way to view these results is to reflect on how many "a" responses you gave yourself. The "a" level responses indicate that a person displays a high level of expertise in that area.

"a" responses score ___1___

"b" responses score ___5___

"c" responses score ___3___

Once again, note that this is not a validated EI test! The purpose is to stimulate your thinking about these EI abilities.

▶ What Do Higher and Lower Scores Mean?

People who score higher on this survey might be seen as possessing the qualities, and engaging in the behaviors, in the left-hand column.

Skilled	Unskilled
Uses emotions to be creative	Purely practical, logical, and concrete
Inspires people	Doesn't motivate others
Focuses on what's important when emotions are strong	Forgets what's important when upset
Emotions improve their thinking	Feelings are flat or distracting
Can feel what others are feeling (empathy)	Emotions are self-absorbed and not influenced by others' feelings
Feelings help to inform and change beliefs	Doesn't know how feelings influence thinking

Understanding Emotions Quiz: Select the response that best describes you.

My emotional vocabulary is		
a	❏	Highly complex and rich
b	☒	About average
c	❏	Not very large
My understanding of why people feel the way do usually yields		
a	❏	Excellent insights
b	☒	Some good insight
c	❏	Not a lot of valuable information
My emotional what-if thinking		
a	❏	Yields accurate predictions of people's reactions
b	☒	Results at times an ability to predict feeling
c	❏	Tends to not project how people *will* feel
When I try to determine what causes emotions, I		
a	❏	Am able to understand the causes of all basic emotions
b	❏	Often link the emotion to a cause
c	☒	Believe that emotions don't always have a cause
My knowledge of how emotions change and develop is		
a	❏	Highly differentiated for all emotions
b	☒	Reasonably developed
c	❏	Limited

(Continued)

EXERCISES

I understand how contradictory emotions (such as love and hate) can be felt at the same time		
a	☐	For all emotion combinations
b	☐	For many emotion combinations
c	☒	For a few emotion combinations
I am able to discover the causes of people's emotions		
a	☐	Almost always
b	☒	Often
c	☐	At times
I can predict how people's feelings will change		
a	☐	For almost all people and all basic emotions
b	☐	For many people and many basic emotions
c	☒	For some people and some emotions
I can come up with the exact word to describe my feelings		
a	☐	Almost always
b	☒	Usually
c	☐	At times
I can predict how someone *will* feel if something happens to them		
a	☐	Almost all the time
b	☒	Usually
c	☐	On occasion

▶ Scoring

There are two ways to score this brief self-quiz. Give yourself 0 points for each "c" response, 1 point for each "b" response and 2 points for every "a" response. Another way to view these results is to reflect on how many "a" responses you gave yourself. The "a" level responses indicate that a person displays a high level of expertise in that area.

"a" responses score ___0___

"b" responses score ___7___

"c" responses score ___3___

Once again, note that this is not a validated EI test! The purpose is to stimulate your thinking about these EI abilities.

EXERCISES

▶ What Do Higher and Lower Scores Mean?

People who score higher on this survey might be seen as possessing the qualities, and engaging in the behaviors, in the left-hand column.

Skilled	Unskilled
Makes correct assumptions about people	Misunderstands people
Knows the right thing to say	Says things to upset people
Makes good predictions about what people may feel	Is surprised by how people feel and behave
Has a sophisticated emotional vocabulary	Finds it hard to explain feelings
Understands that one can experience mixed conflicted feelings	Experiences on-or-off emotions, with few shades of gray
Has vast emotional knowledge	Has only a basic understanding of emotions

Managing Emotions Quiz: Select the response that best describes you.

My feelings are clear		
a	☐	Almost always
b	☒	Usually
c	☐	At times

I process strong emotions		
a	☒	In order not to exaggerate or minimize them at all times
b	☐	Much of the time
c	☐	So as to minimize them and control them

I can change a bad mood or emotion when the situation requires it		
a	☒	Almost always
b	☐	Often
c	☐	Usually

I can maintain a good mood or emotion when the situation requires it		
a	☒	Almost always
b	☐	Often
c	☐	Usually

I use imagery, breathing, or relaxation to manage my emotions		
a	☒	Almost always when needed
b	☐	Usually when necessary
c	☐	At times

(Continued)

EXERCISES

I can keep a good mood going		
a	☒	Almost always
b	❑	Usually
c	❑	At times

I can influence others to maintain or change their mood or emotion when this is necessary in order to focus their thinking in a more productive way		
a	❑	Almost always
b	☑	Usually
c	❑	At times

I am able to change a bad mood		
a	☒	Almost always
b	❑	Usually
c	❑	Rarely

When I experience an unpleasant event or mood, I		
a	❑	Almost always stay open to it
b	☒	Sometimes try to ignore it
c	❑	Tend to suppress the feeling

My decisions blend logic with a gut feel for the right thing		
a	☒	Almost always
b	❑	Usually
c	❑	At times

▶ Scoring

There are two ways to score this brief self-quiz. Give yourself 0 points for each "c" response, 1 point for each "b" response and 2 points for every "a" response. Another way to view these results is to reflect on how many "a" responses you gave yourself. The "a" level responses indicate that a person displays a high level of expertise in that area.

"a" responses score ____7____

"b" responses score ____3____

"c" responses score ____0____

Once again, note that this is not a validated EI test! The purpose is to stimulate your thinking about these EI abilities.

▶ What Do Higher and Lower Scores Mean?

People who score higher on this survey might be seen as possessing the qualities, and engaging in the behaviors, in the left-hand column.

Skilled	Unskilled
Emotions focus attention, inform decision making, and energize adaptive behavior	Emotions are distracting and derail adaptive behavior
Can "psych up," calm down, or maintain a mood as desirable	Is a slave to passions and acts impulsively
Can cheer others up, calm them down, or manage others' feelings appropriately	Has no intentional impact on others' feelings, has unintentional impact on others' feelings
Is open to one's feelings and the feelings of others	Shuts off feelings and represses them
Leads a rich emotional life	Leads and emotionally impoverished life

Read through the results and then complete the follow reflection exercise:

A. We identified four emotional strengths in the Concepts Section. What did the quiz reveal about your strength in each area?

1. *IDENTIFYING EMOTIONS: fundamental ability to recognize feelings and emotions.*
   - ❑ Strong
   - ☑ Moderate
   - ❑ Weak

2. *USING EMOTIONS: ability to know which emotions or moods are best for different situations.*
   - ❑ Strong
   - ☑ Moderate
   - ❑ Weak

3. *UNDERSTANDING EMOTIONS: ability to recognize and grasp emotional information.*
   - ❑ Strong
   - ☑ Moderate
   - ❑ Weak

4. *MANAGING EMOTIONS: ability to regulate emotions in yourself and in other people.*
   - ☑ Strong
   - ❑ Moderate
   - ❑ Weak

B. What did you learn about your emotional strength from this exercise?

I am very good at managing emotions, but struggle or am mediocre in other aspects of emotions. I especially need to work on understanding emotions.

EXERCISES

C. Were you surprised?

This did not really surprise me although I did
expect to have a little better understanding of
emotions. I definitely knew managing emotions
would be a strength

D. How can this knowledge help you in dealing with the pressures of schoolwork and relationships?

I would definitely say this could help me by encouraging
me to reach out to others who can understand my
emotions for clarity on why I am feeling the pressures
that I am.

EXERCISES

 Exercises

A life map is a way of looking at your past experiences as a collective influence on your life. This influence has had a great impact on shaping who you are and what Life Calling you have to fulfill. The following exercises will help you create a life map.

Creating Your Life Map

EXERCISE 1

▶ Identifying Life Experiences

The following are some questions to ask yourself in helping to identify these experiences:

1. Where were you born?
2. What places have been significant to you? Why?
3. What places have been significant to your family? Your neighborhood?
4. What moves have you made—from one house to another or one school district to another?
5. What friends have you made?
6. Any grandparents or other relatives who have died?
7. Any pets?
8. What about births of brothers/sisters?
9. Any time you got hurt?
10. When have you won something?
11. Do you remember a special birthday?
12. Has there been a divorce in the family?
13. Do you remember doing something embarrassing?
14. Has there been an unexpected death in family, friends, or neighborhood?
15. Do you remember the day you fell in love with someone?
16. Do you remember the day you fell out of love with someone?
17. Has there been a memorable event that happened to you during a sport or game?
18. Did you have a regular chore to do when you were young? What was it?
19. Where did you go to school?
20. Brainstorm with "I remember…" Give 3 minutes to write as many as possible… then pick the top 10

▶ Organizing Life Experiences

1. Chose 10 of the most important memories listed in Exercise 1
2. On a blank paper number from 1 – 10 (One is worst, 10 is best) and place the events accordingly
3. Make sure to label each event with the appropriate date (i.e. 1995)
4. On a separate sheet record each memory as a graphic image or "icon" (you can use computers for help with graphics) (It can be as detailed as you want it to be)—write a brief description next to each icon or image to explain what it means
5. Final draft timeline:
   a. Create a graph on a sheet of paper with the following:
      • A timeline that runs across the bottom of the graph.
      • A best-to-worst scale that runs down the left-hand column of the graph, with the score of "10" (best) at the top of page and the score of "1" (worst) at the bottom of page
   b. Using a dot, position the ten events on the graph based on when the event happened and how it rates on the best-to-worst scale
   c. Connect dots with lines
   d. Insert images or "icons" next to the dots of each event

EXERCISES

▶ **Reflecting on Life Experiences**

1. Use the Life Map you created in Exercise 1 to reflect on your life as a whole and also to identify high times and low times in your life:

_____

_____

_____

_____

_____

2. How have these experiences helped to shape you into the person you are today?

_____

_____

_____

_____

_____

3. How can you use these experiences to help other people? Is this part of your Life Calling?

_____

_____

_____

_____

_____

EXERCISES

Writing Your Autobiography

1. Use the material you have created in Exercise 1 to start writing an autobiography of yourself.

2. Focus on three major things:
   - Who you are in life
   - What life means to you
   - What your outlook on the future is

3. Interview your parents and other family members to help you create a genealogical history.

4. Gather information about your ethnic and cultural history.

5. Concentrate on writing one event or experience at a time. This is like planting a tree in the forest. Eventually, after you have planted many trees, you will have an entire forest—the story of your life!

6. Try to use narrative writing as you work on this assignment. This will make it more interesting for you to revisit from time to time as you continue to explore your Life Calling.

▶ References

The following resources have been used in this chapter.

Trent, J.T. (1998). *Life Mapping*. Colorado Springs, CO: Waterbook Press.

The following resources may be useful to you in your continuing exploration of Life Calling as you look at your Unique Design and your *experiences*.

Bennet, W.J., ed. (2008). *The Moral Compass: Stories for a Life's Journey*. New York: Touchstone.

Palmer, P.J. (2000). *Let Your Life Speak*. San Francisco: Jossey-Bass.

Schwen, M.R., and Bass, D.C., Eds. (2006). *Leading Lives That Matter: What We Should Do and Who We Should Be*. Grand Rapids, Michigan: Erdmans Publishing Co.

Smith, G.T. (2011). *Courage and Calling: Embracing Your God-given Potential*. Downers Grove, Illinois: Intervarsity Press.

Section II Conclusion

Unique Design

In Section II we discovered that though there may be a universal similarity to the foundational values we hold about reality, ourselves, and others, we will express these in a different manner based on our unique design as individuals. Like the proverbial snowflake, every person who has ever lived possessed a unique design.

Each person has a unique set of strengths that is the key to success in life. This unique set of strengths is made even more distinct as it interacts with our unique passion. Finally, our strengths and passion undergo intense molding and shaping as we encounter a variety of good and bad experiences in life. The experiences we encounter will be different than anyone else's. And it is this difference that gives rise to a unique Life Calling for each of us.

As we search to discover our Life Calling, the deeper we explore and further analyze all of the elements that make up our unique design, the greater will be our insight into our Life Calling. This really is where the search for a Life Calling begins to separate one person from another. Our unique design also provides the "focus" for concentrating our search. What we will find will give us the significance to our lives that is part of the universal need experienced by all humans.

Personal Leadership

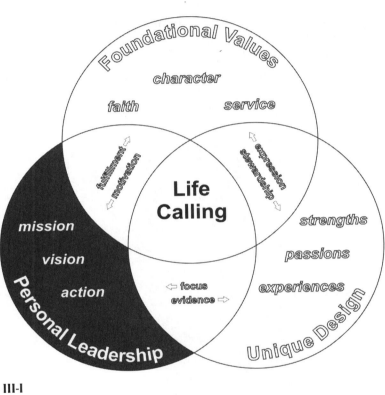

FIGURE III-I
Life Calling Model Focusing on Personal Leadership

Section III deals with the third main component of the Life Calling Model—
Personal Leadership.

Our foundational values and unique design set the stage that enables us to discover how to implement our Life Calling through personal leadership. If we do not go beyond reflecting on our values or becoming engrossed with our design, we will end up being little more than a statue on a pedestal. Somewhere in our search for a Life Calling we have to begin taking action. That is where personal leadership comes into play.

Let's look at what we mean by the concept of personal leadership. For the purpose of this study, we will define it as *taking action to bring about change in your everyday situation by mobilizing resources around you to accomplish a desired vision.*

In Section I, we concluded that there is an intentional place for each one of us in the universe. In Section II we discovered that not only is our place in the universe intentional, but it is also unique and each of us is designed specifically to fill our place. In other words, we were both meant to be and designed to be! Now the question arises, what do we do about this? The answer to this question will emerge as a personal leadership strategy. If we go back to our defintion, we discover three important stages we must travel through on the way to bringing about the change we desire. The first stage is to develop a sense of mission. In the second stage, this becomes clearer as we begin to visualize how things could be better if the mission is accomplished. Finally, in the third stage we outline and put into action a strategy to bring about positive change in the world.

In this section we will examine the definition of personal leadership a little more deeply and then explore the three major factors that determine our personal leadership—mission, vision, and action—and the strategy they provide for achieving our Life Calling.

Pursuing Your Life Calling through Personal Leadership

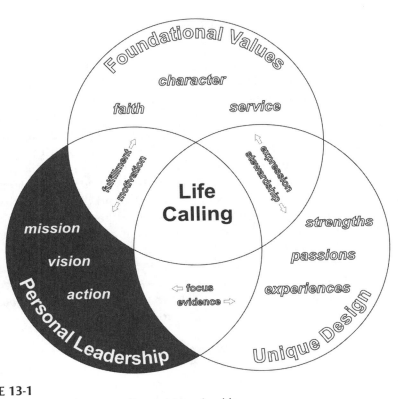

13

FIGURE 13-1
Life Calling Model Focusing on Personal Leadership

"Every day the opportunity for leadership stands before you...each day brings you opportunities to raise important questions, to speak to higher values, and surface unresolved conflicts. Every day you have the chance to make a difference in the lives of people around you."

RONALD HEIFETZ AND
MARTY LINSKY

The third main component of the Life Calling Model is *Personal Leadership*. We need to use this chapter to expand the Section III introduction and explain what we mean by the concept of personal leadership before we focus in on the three major factors that will determine our success in exercising personal leadership.

CHAPTER OBJECTIVES

1. Understand a general concept of leadership
2. Contrast and appreciate the difference between personal and positional leadership
3. Explain how personal leadership can form the framework for carrying out our Life Calling

KEY TERMS

Ambition = a compelling desire for some type of achievement or distinction

◗ Concepts

(This chapter has been adapted by permission from *Three Levels of Leadership* (Millard, 2012).)

A number of years ago, my colleague Jim Laub and I were asked to provide our university with a broad definition of "leadership." We both are Professors of Leadership and have studied the subject for quite some time. Yet we found ourselves working on this assignment for quite a while before we were satisfied. We finally arrived at this definition: "Taking action to effect change by mobilizing others to accomplish a shared vision." You probably already detected that we were attempting to craft a definition that did not immediately restrict the definition's application to established positions of formal leadership. We both believe that leadership occurs at many levels and can be effective on all of these levels if it is properly understood. I have slightly revised our original definition: "taking action to bring about change in your area of influence by mobilizing others to accomplish a shared vision." You will also notice that the definition has been personalized with the word "you" so that you can start imagining yourself in that role. Let's look at how this plays out on three broad levels that contain most, if not all, categories of leadership: *formal positional leadership, informal positional leadership*, and *personal leadership*.

Formal positional leadership. This level of leadership is recognized in established positions of leadership, so it is both formal and positional leadership. This includes the President of the United States, a general, the CEO of a corporation, a church pastor, or the president of the college or university you are thinking about attending. We would adapt our definition for this level of leadership to be "taking action in a formal position to bring about change among those under your authority by mobilizing them to accomplish a shared vision." Unfortunately, those are the kinds of people that often come to mind when you think about leadership, and so you often don't think of yourselves as leaders.

Informal positional leadership. Life Calling culminates when you make a difference in the world, and this begins with a decision to act in the true meaning of the word *leadership*. In order to make a better world, the world needs more of these kinds of leaders. Citizenship requires leadership. So does professional success. If you can lead no one, your education is incomplete. True, the majority of you probably won't be high-level formal leaders. But think about this: sometime in your life you will likely be some form of a director, a teacher, or an entrepreneur. And you will almost certainly at some point chair a committee, head a project, propose an idea to neighbors or colleagues, or parent a child. Each and every one of these roles or activities requires you to exercise a position of leadership.

This is what we could consider as *informal positional leadership*. This level of leadership truly fits the basic definition "taking action to bring about change in your area of influence by mobilizing others to accomplish a shared vision." In other words, leadership doesn't have to be a formal, exalted position or a permanent status. It is rather as the definition states: taking actions that bring about change in one's area of influence (that could be any setting) by mobilizing others (they don't have to be a formal group) to accomplish a shared vision that leads to a better future. And this is many times most effectively done from an informal position of leadership.

Personal leadership.   But what about those cases where a person is making a difference in a manner that does not involve any type of role? We need a definition of leadership in the Life Calling Model that allows us to consider this as well and does not depend on any kind of position related to others. So let's adapt the basic leadership definition to form a version that will allow for personal leadership: "taking action to bring about change in your everyday situation by mobilizing resources around you to accomplish a desired vision."

A study of hundreds of leaders at all three levels has led to the conclusion that when leadership is effective in more formal positions, it has been preceded by those same leaders being effective first in less formal positions. This leads to the proposal that leadership should first emerge on the personal leadership level, then further be developed on the informal positional leadership level, and only after that should sometimes be called for on the formal positional level. Figure 13-2 illustrates how one level should lead to another. It also shows how each level of leadership maintains dynamics of the previous levels. In other words, informal positional leadership maintains the dynamics of personal leadership, and formal positional maintains the dynamics of both personal leadership and informal positional leadership.

In order to better understand Personal Leadership, it will help to examine more extensively all three levels of leadership and the qualities within each that become the catalysts for developing that corresponding level of leadership. It is important to understand that these qualities can be developed.

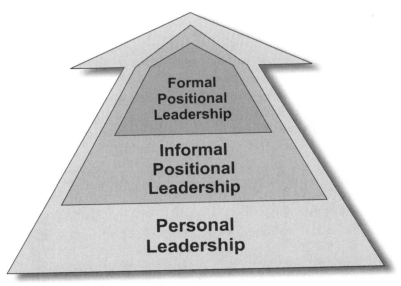

FIGURE 13-2
Three Levels of Leadership

The mistaken belief is that some people are born with them and some are not, and this is what determines leadership potential. While some might be born with gifts and aptitudes that make it easier for them to develop the qualities, they will still need to go through the rigor of developing them. And while others might be born with less of these gifts and aptitudes and find the qualities harder to develop, they still can discover ways to develop them and begin to practice some level of leadership.

Personal leadership: Taking action to bring about change in your everyday situation by mobilizing resources around you to accomplish a desired vision. The five qualities listed below are important catalysts that help produce personal leadership.

1. *Principles*

   People who take action to bring about change that leads to a better future do so because they have an inner compass guided by strong moral and ethical principles. They are determined to do the right thing. They are the kind of people who are honest and whose words are dependable. They are open and do not hide the true reality of a situation from those they associate with or lead. They are genuine—what you see is what you get at all times. This produces personal leadership that leads by principles instead of popularity or manipulation.

2. *Conviction*

   Next, people who decide to make a difference in the world around them become convinced this is the right thing to do based on the principles they hold. Conviction in many ways is similar to the *passions* at a sacrificial level that were examined in Chapter 11. Conviction *compels* people in a way that stirs them to want to take action. Conviction *impels* people in a way that transforms moral principles into moral actions. Finally, conviction *propels* people forward into the actual process of taking action. People with these kinds of convictions do not rationalize the convictions away by telling themselves that it is none of their business or that others should suffer the consequences of bad decisions. People of conviction believe that if good can be done, it should be done.

3. *Initiative*

   Next, people who are convinced that they should make a difference in the world around them respond to an inner willingness to take initial steps toward making that difference, and then follow through. This attitude arises primarily from an *internal sense of responsibility*. The following contrast is one of the greatest predictors of leadership—whether it is formal, informal, or personal.

Internal Sense of Responsibility	External Sense of Victimization
Individuals believe that under the guidance of God and the strength he gives them, their life and behavior is for the most part governed by their own personal decisions and actions.	Individuals believe that their life and behavior is for the most part ruled by the decisions and actions of other people or other external circumstances.

An *internal sense of responsibility* is sometimes referred to as an *internal locus of control*. Whether or not they are in formal positions, people who end up making a difference in the world around them *believe they can make a difference* and take action.

4. *Insight*

People who make a difference in the world also have a capacity to discern the hidden nature of things and generate solutions to perplexing challenges. So the next catalytic component leading to personal leadership is to develop good ideas. The minds of people with good personal leadership are incubators constantly giving birth to new possibilities and concepts. These are where visions begin. Often these insights begin out of what could be called "inspired annoyances." Something comes into a person's life that disturbs the person or bothers the person in such a way that it displeases, troubles, or irritates the person. Many people just get mad when this happens. But the person exercising personal leadership moves beyond displeasure or anger and begins to look for solutions to the underlying problem causing the annoyance. Most of the great inventions of the world came about through this process. The bottom line related to personal leadership is this: it is hard to change circumstances around you if you have nothing to offer. Your attempts to convince others will appear hollow and will raise suspicion that you are making claims that you cannot fulfill.

5. *Trailblazing*

The final component to be considered in people who decide to make a difference in the world is *trailblazing*. People who exhibit this quality are not afraid to chart a course that identifies a better place to be. They are also willing to then guide others on their journey to that better place. These leaders are not afraid to take risks if it is necessary to reach the better place. They are willing to take the path not taken. They are not like super cautious people who will not move ahead unless they are convinced that they know exactly what will happen, that no danger exists, or that the desired outcome will definitely be reached. I joke with these types of people that they are like the lady who would never go see a movie unless she had seen it one time before. If you think about that for a minute, you will realize she will never see a movie with that rule. Trailblazers are able to (1) recognize the path before others do, (2) travel the path themselves, and (3) reveal the path to others.

Informal positional leadership: Taking action to bring about change in your area of influence by mobilizing others to accomplish a shared vision. This second level of leadership moves to the level of mobilizing other people. It is more than just changing your own personal situation. It now involves changing other people's situations as well. We still are not talking about recognized formal positions of leadership, but we are talking about people of **influence**. Kubicek (2011) believes that influence is the engine of true leadership. He suggests that it might be the most potent and underutilized professional resource on earth. As personal leadership moves from an individualistic focus to a focus of influencing others, all the qualities of personal leadership will still be needed to be effective on this level. But we need to bring into play additional qualities that will help produce influence that can mobilize others. The five qualities listed below become catalysts that help produce informal positional leadership.

1. *Credibility*

   If a person is going to be a leader who can influence others, it starts with other people believing that the leader is a credible person who is worthy of their confidence and trust. In many ways, credibility is to *informal positional leadership* what initiative is to *personal leadership*. Initiative is your belief you can make a difference, and so you take action. Credibility is the belief of others that you can make a difference, so they take action to follow you. This is why others are willing to listen to you to begin with. This credibility is built to a large extent on the principles, convictions and insights that were developed in personal leadership. It is important to note, however, that when a leader loses credibility with those led, it is nearly impossible for the leader to ever regain it, and the leader's influence will disappear.

2. *Inspiration*

   One of the primary reasons people emerge into informal leadership is their ability to inspire others. The insights they developed in personal leadership intrigue others to eagerly follow these ideas. This starts, however, by a person moving beyond personal leadership into the realm of influential interaction with others. In other words, inspirational leaders begin to share the insights they developed in personal leadership. In the Sermon on the Mount, Jesus proposed that people who light a lamp do not put it under a bowl where it will be blocked from shining. He said, "Instead they put it on its stand, and it gives light to everyone in the house. In the same way, let your light shine before others, that they may see your good deeds and glorify your Father in heaven." (Matthew 5:15-16). These words of Jesus reveal two important aspects of sharing insights that inspire. First, communicating good ideas to others in a way that they can understand is important. Second, and just as important, the example that these emerging leaders demonstrate in their own lives reinforces their credibility and evokes others to aspire to follow them as a leader.

3. *Persuasion*

   If emerging leaders are going to be able to mobilize others, they will have to be able to persuade people to take action. This starts with the *insights* identified as a quality of personal leadership and builds on the *inspiration* discussed in the previous paragraph. Leaders of other people need to be able to effectively communicate these inspirational insights in a manner that clearly explains the concept, benefits, and value of the idea. If this level of communication is truly influential, it will compel others to want to change and take action because the ideas make sense, are appealing, and are worth adopting.

4. *Empathy*

   Influential people who others look to for leadership are empathetic. They are able to understand and imaginatively enter into the experience and feelings of another person. They instinctively ask themselves "what if" questions whenever they consider courses of action that they will ask those led to pursue, always trying to see things from the viewpoint of those led, rather than just the viewpoint of the leader. A mistaken belief is that empathy is something a person is born with or without. In reality, empathy grows out of emotional strengths and can be developed and enhanced if a person seeks it and begins to practice it.

5. *Partnership*

People who emerge from personal leadership into informal positions of influence join with others to move toward a vision through partnerships. They are not "lone rangers" who have to be in control and always be the winner who gains all the glory. Instead, they work collaboratively alongside others to develop and accomplish shared goals. This kind of partnership between the leader and the follower is more like a flat circular relationship than a vertical ladder. The circle is characterized by equality and mutual respect and a commitment to learn from each other, whereas the ladder is characterized by dominance and subordination.

Formal positional leadership: Taking action in a formal position to bring about change among those under your authority by mobilizing them to accomplish a shared vision. The third, and final, level of leadership is found where a person is in a recognized, formal position of authority over other people. Command and control now come into play. But here is a key concept: all the qualities of personal and informal positional leadership must be developed in a person before entering this level of leadership if the person is going to be effective. However, there are additional qualities that will be necessary if this formal position of authority is to be exercised effectively. The five qualities listed below become catalysts that will help make formal positional leadership successful.

1. *Serving*

Servanthood is a mindset in a leader that places the needs of those led before your own self-interests. This is what Jesus advocated for leadership when he instructed his disciples:

> "You know that the rulers of the Gentiles lord it over them, and their high officials exercise authority over them. Not so with you. Instead, whoever wants to become great among you must be your servant, and whoever wants to be first must be your slave—just as the Son of Man did not come to be served, but to serve, and to give his life as a ransom for many." (Matthew 20:25-28).

The 6th century B.C. Chinese philosopher Laozi suggested that "Enlightened leadership is service, not selfishness. The leader grows more and lasts longer by placing the well-being of all above the well-being of self alone."

Placing the needs of those led before your own self-interests, however, does not mean you are always giving as if you were an endless fountain. Go back to the quality of partnership developed at the level of *informal positional leadership.* The interaction between the leader and the follower is more like a circle of relationship characterized by mutual respect. Hence, there is a commitment by both the leader and the follower to not exploit each other.

CONCEPTS

With this mindset as a leader, authority and responsibility are shared rather than hoarded by the leader. Why is this attitude so important? Servanthood guarantees that leadership is only engaged in when the good of those led is truly the focus. Those led can trust that they are not being exploited or manipulated. Entering leadership with any other mindset leads to suspicion and mistrust.

2. *Modeling*

When looking at the level of *informal positional leadership*, we discovered that *credibility* and *inspiration* were two important qualities. Credibility was the quality that made the emerging leader someone you could believe in and want to follow. Inspiration took that even further by calling for leaders to demonstrate in their own lives the ideas they were proposing to others. In other words, they were modeling the way. As a person moves into a formal position of leadership, modeling the way needs to become an intentional and regular practice. When Jesus entered into a leadership relationship with the disciples, he did not start off by giving them a list of tasks to complete. Instead, he said "Follow me." Leaders in formal positions need to be role models for all that they ask followers to do, as well as for the values they promote. Leaders will seldom be successful at asking others to do something if they are unwilling to do it themselves.

3. *Positioning*

An important understanding of leadership can be discovered in the formal structure adopted by leaders in relationship to those they lead. Let's look at three different ways this can be structured.

a. **Above**: When leaders see their position primarily one of power, privilege, or possession, they tend to behave as if they are vertically superior to those they lead and are above demanding action or behind driving the led. There is no question that some decisions made by leaders in formal positions will require a top down approach and many key decisions require a clear supervising process of responsibility and accountability. We can't get away from the fact that positional leaders have authority and are expected to use it. This is especially true when quick decisions have to be made, when ultimate accountability is needed, when personnel matters have to be addressed, or when a final decision cannot be made by consensus. But it is important to realize that when this style of authority is exercised, it is based primarily on fear as a motivator, it produces mostly compliance rather than growth, it creates resentment more than understanding, and it results in resistance more than synergy. This is not a recipe for dynamic growth. Accordingly, if an organization is to flourish in a healthy manner, the above aspect of formal positional leadership will be required less than 5 percent of time.

b. **Ahead**: When leaders see their position primarily as a responsibility to be out in front modeling the way, they tend to enter into relationships with those they lead that promotes individual development, increases appreciation of diversity, demonstrates an internal locus of control for those led, and results in a sense of self-worth. And the reason for all of this is that when this style of authority is exercised, it is based primarily on trust as a motivator. Leading from ahead has some limitations. It still is focused to a great extent on the formal position, lacks sufficient fluidity for maximizing team dynamics, and can lull the follower into an unhealthy dependence on a benevolent leader. Because of this, if an organization is to flourish in a healthy manner, the <u>ahead</u> aspect of formal positional leadership should be exercised less than 45 percent of time.

   c. <u>**Alongside**</u>: When leaders see their position primarily as an opportunity to collaborate with their fellow workers, they tend to develop relationships, better described as peer relationships than vertical relationships. When this happens, the formal position of leadership is not the focus. In fact, the interactions among leadership, managers, and followers could better be described as a circle of relational action. Needs are addressed by the person with the best strengths set to deal with them. Functions are not bound in rigid systems correlated to a single leader. Ability to adapt quickly to varying situations is increased. Everyone is encouraged to strive for the highest level of collaborative synergy. When this style of authority is exercised, it is based primarily on respect and value as a motivator. Leading from <u>alongside</u> also has some limitations. Lines of responsibility and authority could be confusing, a pay structure might be hard to determine, and it might be unclear about who is responsible for supporting the worker if such support is needed. As the saying goes, "If everyone rules, no one rules." Hence, the <u>alongside</u> aspect of formal positional leadership will likely be appropriately exercised less than 50 percent of time

4. *Envisioning*
   Leadership researchers Kouzes and Posner (2010) put forward the premise that "the capacity to imagine and articulate exciting future possibilities is a defining competence of leaders." But for leaders in formal positions to be effective in the vision process, they must go beyond just imagining the future. They have to help bring that future into reality. This can best be seen in three roles they must exercise in the Dream Cycle of leadership. The first role is that of <u>dreamer</u>. In this role the leader imagines a better future or way of doing things. At this stage, boundaries are avoided and creativity is allowed to run free. The second role is <u>dream-caster</u>. In this role the leader helps those led to catch the same vision. If we go back to our definition of leadership, we find that change will be brought about by "mobilizing others to accomplish a shared vision for a better future." The sooner a leader can transform a vision from being "my vision" into becoming "our vision," the better the likelihood that the vision will be achieved. And more than just catching and endorsing the vision, the hope should be that those led will expand and enhance the vision. The third role is that of <u>dream-maker</u>. In this role the leader provides the resources for empowering those led to accomplish the shared vision. One definite capability of most persons in formal positions of leadership is that they have the greatest access to resources. Good leaders find ways to open up these resources to those they lead so that visions can be pursued.

5. *Investing*
   The most effective leaders at any level are those who truly care about the people they lead and invest in them. This can clearly be seen with those in formal positions of leadership in how much they make those

they lead a priority. This priority can be discerned in four key areas. First of all, it is impossible for leaders to inspire and empower those they lead if they are not willing to make them the top priority and spend <u>time</u> with them. The most effective leaders are more concerned about being available to those they lead than those who are over the leader. Second of all, effective leaders make it a priority to provide adequate resources to those they lead. This includes staffing, budget, facilities, equipment, and supplies necessary to be successful in carrying out the responsibilities that have been given to them. Third of all, effective leaders do not buy into the "need-to-know" myth that leads many organizations to stifle the flow of information. Instead, effective leaders believe that the more information that can be provided to those led in their efforts, the better off they will be in carrying out those efforts. Last of all, in most cases successful leaders have a great deal of life experience, including work and leadership experience, that can provide valuable insights to people whom they lead. Effective leaders find opportunities to share this appropriately with the people they lead.

Bringing It All Together

In order to better understand *personal leadership*, we have looked at it in contrast to *informal positional leadership* and *formal positional leadership*. We considered fifteen catalytic qualities that enhance leadership development, and we divided these into groups of five and correlated them to the three levels of leadership. It is important to realize, however, that this categorization is somewhat arbitrary. In other words, all fifteen of the qualities will be valuable at any of the levels. For example, *serving* is a quality that was identified as producing a better leader in a formal position. But it is also a quality that will also make a person a better personal leader as well.

Let's return to our basic working definition of leadership. Four key elements stand out: *vision, action, mobilization*, and *change*. A vision for a better future leads to a decision to act. Early on, this action involves sharing the vision with others. As they buy into the vision and share it, they mobilize around the vision. Ultimately, this mobilization brings about the change originally envisioned and desired. Interestingly enough, this change will probably produce new visions, so this becomes a cycle. A vibrant continuing leadership cycle is the kind of leadership that can truly make the world around you a better place.

This leadership cycle can happen on all three of the levels of leadership that we have considered. So let's take the leadership cycle with its four elements and place the three levels of leadership inside of it as the engine by which the cycle can be implemented. This provides us with a good leadership model (Figure 13-3).

Each of the four key elements in the leadership cycle will have a different manifestation within the three levels of leadership. For example, *vision* many times remains more of an individual dream at the *personal leadership* level. But when *vision* moves into the *informal positional leadership* level, it becomes a shared vision held jointly by the leader and the led in a spirit of collaborative development. *Vision* has the greatest capacity to be realized, however, when a

FIGURE 13-3
Leadership Model

person is in *formal positional leadership* helping to open up the resources that can make accomplishing the *vision* a possibility.

Back to the Beginning

We started this chapter by saying we needed to explain what we mean by the concept of *personal leadership* before we focus in on the three major factors of *mission, vision, and action* that will determine our success in exercising personal leadership. We provided that explanation in a general concept of leadership that contrasted *personal leadership* with two levels of *positional leadership*. But now let's finish the concepts section of this chapter by returning our focus to *personal leadership* and how *personal leadership* can form the framework for carrying out our Life Calling. At the beginning of Section III, we proposed three important stages we must travel through on the way to bringing about the change we desire in our Life Calling. The first stage is to develop a sense of a mission. In the second stage, this becomes clearer as we begin to visualize how things could be better if the mission is accomplished. Finally, in the third stage we outline and put into action a strategy to bring about positive change in the world. So if we take the five catalytic qualities that help build *personal leadership* and combine them with these three stages, we can produce a personal leadership model for implementing our Life Calling (Figure 13-4).

FIGURE 13-4
Personal Leadership Model

High impact *personal leadership* occurs when all five components are in place and are leading the person to develop a mission directed toward a desired vision for a better future. This vision-directed mission then stirs the person into action, moving the person toward that vision. This is the concept of implementing one's Life Calling. In the next three chapters we will look at the role of mission, vision, and action in helping us achieve our Life Calling.

► Insight

One of the great themes running throughout the Bible is that of personal leadership. Countless stories can be found of individuals who make a decision to change the circumstances in which they find themselves. There are also plenty of stories of people who could have made a difference for good and chose not to.

SCRIPTURAL INSIGHT 1 ► *Personal Leadership Starts with Strong Principles*

So Potiphar left everything he had in Joseph's care; with Joseph in charge, he did not concern himself with anything except the food he ate. Now Joseph was well-built and handsome, and after a while his master's wife took notice of Joseph and said, "Come to bed with me!"

But he refused. "With me in charge," he told her, "my master does not concern himself with anything in the house; everything he owns he has entrusted to my care. No one is greater in this house than I am. My master has withheld nothing from me except you, because you are his wife. How then could I do such a wicked thing and sin against God?" And though she spoke to Joseph day after day, he refused to go to bed with her or even be with her. GENESIS 39:6-10

Joseph demonstrates a very important quality of personal leadership. He does not wait until a situation is upon him to determine his course of action. Long before Potiphar's wife tried to seduce him, Joseph developed strong moral principles in his life that he relied on as an inner moral compass to guide his actions. He didn't have to ask himself *I wonder if this would be okay?* He knew and wasn't afraid to say "no" or to suffer the consequences of staying true to his principles.

This takes us back to Chapter 3 where we examined *character* and discussed the problem of *moral silos*. When we don't build a strong faith and then live that faith out consistently in our lives, we end up with no moral compass, and the enticements of the world can easily overpower us. When that happens, any hope of understanding and living out a Life Calling begins to fade.

So how can we take action to make sure this does not happen in our lives? First, put effort into building a strong faith that embodies moral virtues and principles. Second, determine in your heart to live out those principles. Third, make those principles the basis for your decisions in any situation that arises in your life. If you do this, you will not be caught off guard, unsure of what you should do. Instead, you will be taking the right actions to bring about beneficial change in your life.

> **PERSONAL REFLECTION** ⟩ What are the moral principles you have determined for your life that you can turn to when someone tries to convince you to do something you know you shouldn't? What can you do to continue building these principles in your life?

SCRIPTURAL INSIGHT 2 ► *Personal Leadership Happens When You Are Convinced This Is the Time*

When Esther's words were reported to Mordecai, he sent back this answer: "Do not think that because you are in the king's house you alone of all the Jews will escape. For if you remain silent at this time, relief and deliverance for the Jews will arise from another place, but you and your father's family will perish. And who knows but that you have come to royal position for such a time as this?" ESTHER 4:12-14

We looked at Esther's story earlier in this book. Let's take another look, but this time let's focus on Mordecai. Mordecai was a trusted servant in the palace of the king. As a Hebrew captive in a foreign land, he had a good thing going compared to others. When Haman turned against the Jews and plotted a scheme to exterminate them, Mordecai could have remained in the background hoping that someone else would come up with a solution. But he didn't. Instead, he was convinced that he needed to do something. He suggested to Esther that maybe she had been placed her position for such a time as this. But that suggestion came from the conviction in Mordecai's heart that he too was in the place that he was for such a time as this.

Just think what would have happened if Mordecai had not acted on his conviction. History is filled with stories of ruthless rulers who have carried out ethnic cleansing, and King Xerxes would no doubt have done the same. But Mordecai's actions turned the course of events. No wonder the Jewish people still celebrate this story to this day in the Purim holiday.

> **PERSONAL REFLECTION** ⟩ Think about a problem you are dealing with right now. Is there something you should be doing to make the situation better? What is keeping you from taking action based on your convictions?

SCRIPTURAL INSIGHT 3 ▶ *Personal Leadership Requires an Inner Belief That You Can Do It*

I know what it is to be in need, and I know what it is to have plenty. I have learned the secret of being content in any and every situation, whether well fed or hungry, whether living in plenty or in want. I can do all this through him who gives me strength. PHILIPPIANS 4:12-13

If anyone had reason to take on the attitude of a victim, it would have been the Apostle Paul. Look at this list found in 2 Corinthians 11 of the things that had happened to him:

- had to work harder than most
- been in prison
- been flogged severely
- exposed to death many times
- received 39 lashes five different times
- beaten with rods three times
- pelted with stones
- shipwrecked three times
- 24 hours adrift in the open sea
- gone without sleep
- known hunger and thirst
- often gone without food

- been in danger from:
  ✓ rivers
  ✓ bandits
  ✓ his own people
  ✓ Gentiles
  ✓ those in the city
  ✓ those in the in the country
  ✓ those trying to capture him
  ✓ perils of the sea
  ✓ false believers
  ✓ cold
  ✓ nakedness

If you were to experience that kind of life, wouldn't you be tempted to say "my life and behavior is ruled by the decisions and actions of other people or other external circumstances?" Yet what does Paul say in Philippians 4:13? "I can do all this through Him who gives me strength." In spite of everything that had happened to him, Paul maintained a strong *internal sense of responsibility*.

> **PERSONAL REFLECTION** Are you making up a long list of the bad things that are happening to you and using it as an excuse for not taking action in your own situation? Or are you saying that in spite of all that is happening to you, you still believe that you can make a difference and can do whatever it takes through the strength Jesus gives you? How can you develop a stronger internal sense of responsibility based on the strength Jesus gives you?

SCRIPTURAL INSIGHT 4 *Personal Leadership Is Fueled by Good Ideas*

The next day Moses took his seat to serve as judge for the people, and they stood around him from morning till evening. When his father-in-law saw all that Moses was doing for the people, he said, "What is this you are doing for the people? Why do you alone sit as judge, while all these people stand around you from morning till evening?"

Moses answered him, "Because the people come to me to seek God's will. Whenever they have a dispute, it is brought to me, and I decide between the parties and inform them of God's decrees and instructions."

Moses' father-in-law replied, "What you are doing is not good. You and these people who come to you will only wear yourselves out. The work is too heavy for you; you cannot handle it alone. Listen now to me and I will give you some advice, and may God be with you. You must be the people's representative before God and bring their disputes to him. Teach them his decrees and instructions, and show them the way they are to live and how they are to behave. But select capable men from all the people—men who fear God, trustworthy men who hate dishonest gain—and appoint them as officials over thousands, hundreds, fifties and tens. Have them serve as judges for the people at all times, but have them bring every difficult case to you; the simple cases they can decide themselves. That will make your load lighter, because they will share it with you. If you do this and God so commands, you will be able to stand the strain, and all these people will go home satisfied." EXODUS 18:13-23

Jethro was Moses' father-in-law. He had no official position of leadership in the emerging nation of Israel. Yet he was willing to exercise personal leadership in his relationship with Moses. He could see that Moses was wearing himself out in leading the Israelites. Jethro thought about it and came up with a good idea, and he shared it with Moses. Moses followed his advice, and he found his burden of leadership easier to bear.

Jethro could have stayed out of the situation. He wasn't the leader, so why not just let Moses work this out? He also could have gone to Moses and said, "You need to do something. You're going to kill yourself!" Or he could have left Moses on his own to figure out what to do. Instead, Jethro had an *insight* on how to make things better, and he offered it to Moses.

Good leadership at any level is enhanced by valuable insights. But if these insights are going to have a positive impact, they need to be shared. They don't have to be pushed, but they at least need to be shared. Where there are no insights, there probably isn't any real leadership taking place.

> **PERSONAL REFLECTION** When you have a good idea, do you share it with others, or do you keep it to yourself out of fear that it might be ridiculed or ignored? What good idea do you have for your life right now that you are not acting on? What do you need to do to change this?

SCRIPTURAL INSIGHT 5 *Personal Leadership Will Ultimately Require You to Take Risks*

The LORD had said to Abram, "Go from your country, your people and your father's household to the land I will show you. I will make you into a great nation, and I will bless you; I will make your name great, and you will be a blessing. I will bless those who bless you, and whoever curses you I will curse; and all peoples on earth will be blessed through you."

So Abram went, as the LORD had told him; and Lot went with him. Abram was seventy-five years old when he set out from Harran. GENESIS 12:1-4

Most of us find security in familiar circumstances. We feel comfortable in our homes. We feel like we better understand our own demographic groups than we understand others, and that our own demographic groups better understand us. We feel safest and most protected when we are in our own country. So imagine God coming to you and telling you to leave your home, your people, and your country and head off to some place you have never been nor even heard of. Wouldn't you be tempted to say to God, "I'm going to need to think about that" before you took any action?

Abram, in contrast, said "Okay," and he packed his things and took off for who-knows-where. Incidentally, if you are wondering, *is Abram the same person who later was named Abraham*, the answer is "yes," so that gives you a hint to the rest of the story. He did end up receiving all those blessings God promised. But he didn't have any of that when he set off from Harran.

He definitely exhibited the quality of *trailblazing*. He charted a course that identified a better place to be and then guided others on their journey to that better place. He took risks that were necessary to reach that better place. He was willing to take a path he had not taken before. In doing all of this, he demonstrated personal leadership that resulted in him becoming the physical father to the Jews and to many others in the Arab world. He also became the spiritual father to all Jews, Christians and Muslims. These religions make up over 60 percent of the world's population.

> **PERSONAL REFLECTION** Are you willing to step out and try something new in your life that might even seem a little risky? Or do you always "play it safe?" How can "playing it safe" actually hinder your relationship with God? What could you do that would help you start to become more of a *trailblazer* in your life?

INSIGHT

 Discovery

How can the Discovery Guides help you understand and develop *personal leadership* in your life?

T **THEORY**	Find courses in leadership offered at your school and enroll is some of them. There are many books written about leaders. Start developing a bibliography on leadership and then start reading these books. Talk to people who you see as good leaders and ask them to recommend books for you to read.
E **EXAMPLES**	Start observing people in your institution who are making a real impact. Many times you will find they are not necessarily in formal positions of leadership. They may be in positions you wouldn't normally think of, such as food servers, groundskeepers, janitors, secretaries, and other positions that may not be in the limelight of your institution. Start asking these people to meet with you for lunch or coffee and talk to them about what has led them to become the type of personal leaders they are.
A **ASSESSMENT**	There are quite a few assessments that measure leadership aptitude, skills, and mindsets. You might want to use some of these to help you develop leadership in your own life.
C **COUNSEL**	Finding a person in leadership who can serve as a mentor to you during your college years. You can learn a lot about leadership from a good mentor. Also seek out others in various levels of leadership for their advice.
H **HISTORY**	The classics and historical biographies are full of stories dealing with leaders. Select some of these and learn from their experiences.
E **EXPERIENCE**	Get involved with activities going on in your college or university and start trying to make a difference yourself. You can find these in your residence life, in your classes, and in your student clubs and governments. You will discover that this is a great way to start developing leadership traits in your own life.
R **REFLECTION**	Take time to reflect on what you have learned about your *personal leadership* in the other six activities of discovery. Consider how you can implement what you are learning in your life.

DISCOVERY

▶ Story

It had been a full couple of days in Chicago. The explorers were glad to be camped by Lake Michigan, where a stroll along the beach could calm the stress of a busy day filled with sightseeing. Early on the third morning, however, the visit had come to an end. The crew loaded everything into the *Nautilus* and headed out.

They followed Interstate 80 south of Chicago and traveled to the intersection of Interstate 55. There they turned south, heading for Springfield, capitol of Illinois and home to Abraham Lincoln for twenty-four years, though he was actually born in Kentucky. The explorers decided to stop and visit Lincoln Home National Historic Site. The house had been restored to appear as it had in the 1860s.

The six stood looking at a display highlighting Lincoln's quotes about slavery.

"What do you think caused Lincoln to take up this struggle?" Adam wondered. "Other presidents had been faced with the issue of slavery. What made Lincoln the one to act?"

"For Lincoln it just came to a point where something had to be done. I'm not so sure that it was the slaves themselves or their need to be free that made him act," Abriella observed. "I think it was more the tearing apart of the nation that demanded attention. He was convinced that it was a matter of principle that the nation be held together a unified nation."

"And it appears that he believed that it was his responsibility to do something about it," Adam added.

"So what do you think, Captain Nemo?" Ryan turned toward Ken Neimon. "You're the head of your company. What makes a person a leader like Lincoln?"

Diana's father looked back at Ryan. "I think both Abriella and Adam have identified important qualities. I've rarely found anyone to be a good leader who does not have strong principles and a conviction that these principles should guide action. But I think the greatest quality is the belief that it is their responsibility to take action and the accompanying belief that they have the ability to do so."

"Is that the kind of leader Mr. Neimon is?" Abriella asked Kim Neimon, his wife and Diana's mother.

"Well he certainly has strong convictions," Kim replied. "And he definitely has a strong internal belief that he can make a difference. I remember when he started the company, others said it wouldn't work. But Ken said, 'Kim, I know that I can make this work.' And he did."

"He sure did," Diana added.

"I'd say the Captain has done pretty good for himself," Ryan said. "I hope your success rubs off on me," Ryan slapped Ken Neimon on the back.

"Well it might not hurt to study how to do it as well," Lorena said with disdain in her voice. "Successful leadership doesn't infect you like a disease. You have to work hard at it. But then I guess you wouldn't know about that, Ryan."

Ryan ignored Lorena and turned back to Ken Neimon. "So what's your advice to a budding innovative leader like myself?"

Lorena rolled her eyes.

"Here's my advice," Ken Neimon replied. "When you hear everybody else complaining in despair that there is no hope in a situation, take a good hard look. There is probably something they are missing, and that is your opportunity to do something significant. I tell the workers in my company that what others see as threats, we should look at as opportunities."

"I'm not sure most of us think like that," Adam replied.

"You're right," Ken Neimon replied. "That's probably why there aren't very many good leaders."

"I don't think I'll ever be that kind of leader," Diana said to her dad and the others.

"Why do you say that?" Adam asked.

"People like you are always in positions of leadership where they can offer those ideas and make a difference," Diana answered. "But people like me are not in those kinds of positions. I guess we were just destined to be followers."

"Maybe you have too narrow of a concept of leadership, honey," Ken Neimon said to his daughter. "Not all leadership comes from official positions. In fact, some of the best leadership I see in my company comes from workers who are not in a formal position, but still believe they can make a difference."

"I've seen that quality in you, Di," Adam said to Diana.

"Thanks, Adam," Diana replied. "But I'd still love to be a leader like you."

"Don't be so sure," Adam responded.

They completed their tour of the Lincoln Home and then reboarded the *Nautilus*. Their journey continued on south and then west to St. Louis, Missouri, where they drove right by the Gateway Arch.

Ken was glad that he had a GPS navigation system in the motorhome. It guided him to an RV park less than two miles west of the Gateway Arch. It was late in the day, and everyone was ready to crash, leaving the sightseeing until the following day.

The next morning the explorers ate a quick breakfast in the *Nautilus* and then boarded a bus into the Convention Center. From there it was a short walk to the Gateway Arch.

"Tell us again what this Arch represents," Justin asked Lorena.

"It's intended to reflect the spirit of the early pioneers and their effort to open up the American West," Lorena replied. "It's also a tribute to Thomas Jefferson, whose dream inspired the spread of our nation to the west."

"How high is it?" Diana asked with a somewhat concerned voice.

"630 feet," Lorena answered.

"And we're going up there?" Diana nervously asked.

"Yes, Diana. It isn't that bad." Lorena was somewhat exasperated.

The trams that travel up the Arch on the inside could only hold five people, so they divided themselves into two groups of four. Lorena, Abriella, Ryan, and Justin went in one tram, while Adam, Diana, and her parents boarded the next one.

The air was quite clear, as it had been in Chicago, so there was good visibility from the top of the Arch. The travelers could see nearly thirty miles.

"Remember how we were talking about leadership yesterday at the Lincoln Home?" Abriella asked. The others nodded their heads. "I wonder what led people to risk everything and head out west." She pointed through the window toward the West.

"My guess is that it was predominantly a combination of circumstances," Adam replied. "Things weren't great back in the east where they lived, and they saw the West as a chance to start new lives for themselves, probably with greater opportunities."

"It's like Captain Nemo," Ryan added. "He said what others see as threats, he looks at as opportunities. He doesn't wait for someone else to show the way. He takes off and blazes the trail himself, and he has reaped the rewards."

"Hey you guys, do you think we can continue this discussion back down on the ground?" Diana obviously did not feel comfortable with the height of the tower, and she certainly did not like the view out the windows because they were on the lower angle of the Arch's triangular shape, and you could see straight down to the ground.

"A little squeamish, are we?" Ryan teased.

"Yes!" Diana answered emphatically with no sense of shame or apology.

"I think I've seen enough," Adam said. "I'm ready to go down with you." Adam always seemed to look out for Diana.

They all loaded back into the trams and headed down. They then went to the nearby Mississippi River for a paddleboat tour, which Ryan had wanted to do from the time they had first begun planning the trip. The explorers situated themselves on the top

STORY

deck of the boat where they could enjoy the sun and the view.

"Okay, Adam. Up in the Arch you said that the pioneers saw moving to the West as an opportunity." Lorena was ready to resume the discussion they were having at the top of the Arch. "Do you think this happens in everyone?"

"I don't know," Adam replied. "It seems like a piece is missing. What do you think, Mr. Neimon?"

Before Ken Neimon could answer, his wife Kim responded. "I think you will find that missing piece in Ken. The successful moves he has made with our company have always been preceded by innovative ideas and insight he has in the financial world. It's crazy. Others say there is no hope in a situation, and at the same time Ken sees it as a great opportunity and suggests an intriguing solution to the problem."

"Initiative really needs to go hand-in-hand with insight," Ken added.

"Yesterday we were talking about Lincoln. How do you think what you just said applied to him?" Adam asked.

"I think when the Confederate States seceded, most people saw that as the end of the United States," Ken Neimon answered. "But Lincoln saw it as an opportunity not only to maintain the Union, but also to eliminate the dark stain of slavery once and for all. That's the insight it takes to be a good leader."

"Give us an example, Captain," Ryan said.

"Well, a few years ago we were in a really tight spot financially as a company, and the board of directors made a decision to cut some of our employees." The six gathered around Ken Neimon while Kim, his wife, stood a little bit apart from the group. "We really didn't want to make cuts because these were all really good employees. When

the word got out about the decision, two of the workers asked if they could have two weeks to come up with another plan, and I agreed. At the end of the two weeks, they came back to me and said that all the workers had agreed to take a pay cut to save the jobs. I was amazed and proud of them. I agreed that all of us in executive roles would take cuts as well. I also promised that when we rebounded as a company, we would pay them bonuses for taking such an action. Nobody lost their job and the bonus they received after the rebound more than made up for the pay cut. The personal leadership of the two, even though they weren't in any recognized position, made a big difference in our company. I truly considered them important leaders."

"Is a person like you born with your trailblazing spirit, Captain Nemo, or can it be developed?" Ryan asked.

"To be honest with you, Ryan, I think it is a little bit of both," Ken Neimon answered. "There is no doubt that some people are born with a more daring spirit than others. But I also believe that willingness to take reasonable risks and step out ahead of others can be developed in anybody. What about you? Do you see it in your life, Ryan?"

"I don't know if I see it on land in my life," Ryan replied. "But I do think I see it on the waves. Sometimes you just get a feeling that this is the right wave, and you start paddling on your board to catch it. A lot of times the others out there don't even see it and dive under the wave. But you catch it and end up with a fabulous ride."

"So it's too bad that such insight and leadership never make it onto land beyond the breaking waves," Lorena said in a sarcastic voice.

The others all decided maybe it was best just enjoy the scenery.

 Exercises

Assessing Principles of Integrity

Personal Leadership begins with principles that provide integrity to your personal leadership. There are many different elements of integrity you could look at in your life, but a good place to start is with common practices that you are experiencing right now.

Use the following assessment to evaluate practices in your life related to honesty, openness, and genuine principles associated with integrity. The statements in the left-hand column ask how often you would do certain things. Read these and then place a check in the appropriate box to the right under the response that corresponds to your own history. Remember, you will learn more about yourself with an honest appraisal than you will with self-flattery. Total the number of entries in each column. Higher scores in the two right-hand columns indicate a higher history of integrity in these areas of practice. Higher scores in the left-hand columns indicate a contrary history.

How often would you...	Often	Sometimes	Rarely	Never
Fake or exaggerate an illness in order to gain an excused absence from a class for which you were not prepared?				
Turn in work as yours that is really someone else's or that you have copied from the Internet?				
Flatter a person even when you know you really do not mean it?				
Claim to have done something in your past that in reality you did not do?				
Hide troubling information from another person because you are afraid of the consequences of telling them?				
Set up barriers to keep people from finding out what you are really like?				
Try to be like someone else who you think is more successful or popular instead of being who you really are?				
Discard your values and principles when it hurts your popularity?				
Avoid people who you know are being unfairly attacked if you think it will bring you criticism or rejection?				
TOTALS				

1. What do these results indicate to you about the principles you hold in your life and the integrity you exercise in living out these principles?

2. What could you do to strengthen this area in your life?

EXERCISES

EXERCISE 2

Assessing Initiative

We discovered earlier that an *internal locus of control* (initiative) is one of the greatest predictors of leadership.

Use the following assessment to evaluate your attitude concerning why things happen in your life. The statements in the left-hand column present a situation. Read these and then select one of the two choices given to the right. Place a check in the appropriate box that corresponds to the choice that is the stronger attitude of yours. Remember, you will learn more about yourself with an honest appraisal than you will with self-flattery. Total the number of entries in each column. A higher score in the column under "Choice 1" indicates you have a stronger belief in an *internal locus of control*. A higher score in the column under "Choice 2" indicates a stronger belief in an *external locus of control*.

Situation		Choice 1		Choice 2
When I succeed…		it is largely a matter of my own effort		it is largely a matter of chance
My life is for the most part controlled…		by my own actions		by other people
Things happen in my life mainly…		as a result of my choices		as a series of random events
If I am not sure of the outcome of some action…		I take it on as a challenge		I avoid trying it
When I need others to do things my way…		I can convince them		I cannot convince them
My persistence and hard work		usually lead to success		usually don't matter
Like people in general, I am for the most part…		the master of my own fate		a victim of fate
I believe a lot of what happens to me…		depends on my use of my gifts and strengths		is a matter of luck or chance
Success in my relationships with other people is for the most part…		dependent on my own efforts and actions		largely a gamble
When it comes to student life in my college, I believe my involvement…		can make a significant difference		cannot make a significant difference
TOTAL		**Internal Locus of Control**		**External Locus of Control**

EXERCISES

1. What do these results indicate to you about where you believe the locus of control is in your life?

2. What could you do to strengthen an internal locus of control in your life?

EXERCISES

Assessing Servanthood

Earlier in this chapter, we identified servanthood as catalytic quality necessary for effective leadership in formal positions. However, servanthood is a quality necessary for all levels. It needs to be a fundamental principle in personal leadership, and it needs to be a key quality in leaders in informal positions if they are to establish credibility that will give them influence with their associates.

Use the following assessment to evaluate your mindset when you are in a role of leadership with your friends or are asked to lead out on a project or are in a formal position. Read the situation in the left-hand column, and then place a check in the appropriate box to the right next to the response that corresponds to your attitude or actions most of the time. Remember, you will learn more about yourself with an honest appraisal than you will with self-flattery. Total the number of entries in each column. A higher score in the left-hand column indicates you have a stronger servant-minded attitude concerning leadership. A higher score in the middle column indicates you have a stronger position-focused attitude concerning leadership that can result in a patronizing approach. A higher score in the right-hand column indicates a stronger self-centered attitude concerning leadership that often results in an autocratic approach that disregards the attitudes of those led.

	Mindset centered on others		Mindset centered on position		Mindset centered on self
I view myself as:	Serving those I lead		Superior to those I lead		The most important
I view those I lead as:	Counterparts of our leadership equation		Dependent on my direction as leader		Primarily to help me as the leader
My actions are characterized by	Mutual respect		Condescending attitudes		Dictatorial acts
I consider my position as a	Trust to faithfully carry out		Podium for imparting my ideas		Throne for imposing my wishes
My relationship with those led is:	Interconnected with those I lead		Vertically elevated above those I lead		Upwardly isolated from those I lead
The flow of power is:	Directed from me to those I lead		Diverted to me from those I lead		Demanded by me from those I lead
Responsibility is:	Shared by me with those I lead		Bestowed by me upon those I lead		Hoarded by me from those I lead
Knowledge is:	Disbursed among those I lead and me		Imparted by me to those I lead		Restricted to me
Communication is:	Open		Monitored		Quarantined
Emotional energy is mostly:	Emerging synergy		Resignation and compliance		Fear and resentment
TOTAL	**Servant-minded**		**Position-focused**		**Self-centered**

1. What do these results indicate to you about your approach to leadership?

2. What could you do to strengthen servanthood in your life and leadership?

Strengthening Your Personal Leadership

Compare your results from Exercised 1-3 with the descriptions of these three qualities given earlier in concepts section of this chapter. As you consider the results of your self-assessment, you may want to take actions that will help you build stronger qualities within that can make you a more effective leader. The next two sections can help you accomplish this.

A. Learn about leadership.

Did you know that many people who hold official positions of leadership, even in your own institution, have had more formal education in how to drive their cars than they have in how to lead other people? One of the greatest misconceptions about leadership is that, rather than being something you can learn, it is something that you are born with or that somehow falls upon you. Over the last five decades, leadership researchers have shown this to be a myth. While people may be born with certain traits that can help them with leadership, the far greater portion of what it takes to be an effective leader is something that needs to be learned. You can pursue that learning process while you are in college. Here are some places you can look to for leadership education:

Classes .... A rapidly increasing number of colleges and universities are offering formal academic training in leadership studies. Many of these programs lead to a minor in Leadership, and the number of schools offering majors in Leadership is increasing as well. Enroll in a foundational Leadership course offered by your institution. Consider going even further and adding a Leadership minor to whatever program you are considering. Almost every major offered in college is enhanced by a leadership minor when you enter the job-seeking world after college.

Experiential learning .... Many colleges and universities have adventure leadership learning centers associated with their campuses. The initiatives used in these centers can greatly help you develop some of the internal qualities that can produce credibility as a leader. If your campus has such a center, get involved with it. If not, ask where the nearest adventure leadership program is and see if you can participate in it.

Workshops .... Leadership training is likely an important part of Student Development on your campus. Seek out programs offered, such as leadership work-shops. These are great ways to learn about leadership without the pressure of a formal academic course.

Seminars .... Your college or university may have periodic seminars related to leader-ship. Often these may include nationally renowned speakers who are authorities on leadership development. Ask your advisor or Resident Director if such seminars are offered at your school.

Conferences .... Regional and national conferences are an excellent source of leadership education. Consider attending one of these conferences during your col-lege experience. The *International Leadership Association* is rapidly becoming the premiere professional association in the area of leadership studies. You might want to check it out first.

Books .... Finally, a vast number of books are published every year on the subject of leadership. You can learn a lot just by reading. Talk to some leaders who you respect at your college or university and ask them for recommendations concerning books you might read to start your leadership education.

B. Start to take on leadership roles.

As you begin to learn about leadership, one of the best ways to continue learning is to actually get involved in leadership activities. You can start in the areas right around you. Here are a couple of suggestions:

Classes: Instead of assuming a passive role in the classes you are taking, like most students do, take on a more active leadership role.

1. Ask questions
   - Critical thinking is an important part of leadership.
   - If necessary, think through your questions ahead of time.
2. Suggest alternate learning activities to your professor
   - Learn what kind of personality your professor has so you can be more effective in your suggestions.
   - Good leadership starts with being a good learner about people.
3. Challenge ideas with which you disagree
   - Learn to think through the reasons why you disagree before you voice them.
   - Learn to present your challenges in a way that is the least threatening.

Study groups: Many classes you take will include projects in which you will work with several other students in the class. Be willing to take on leadership roles in these groups.

1. Volunteer to coordinate your group
   - Organizing people and getting them to work together is an important skill often required in formal positions of leadership.
2. Volunteer to give reports to the class for the group
   - Leaders who know how to speak are more effective. Seek out roles to learn and practice this skill.
3. Volunteer to run a committee meeting
   - Set the agenda for the meeting and then stick to it.
   - If you can learn how to run a committee in a way that is efficient and engaging, you will greatly increase your effectiveness as a leader. Committees are a common reality in most formal leadership roles.

Consider taking more formal leadership roles in your areas of involvement. Here are some possible areas to consider:

Clubs

- Take leadership roles in clubs on your campus.
- If you are part of a fraternity or sorority, take on leadership roles.

Sports

- Take a leading role in encouraging your team toward excellence.
- Consider a captain's role on a sports team.

Drama

- Try out for a leading role in a play.

Music

- If you are in a music group and there is a place for student leadership, consider taking one of those roles.

EXERCISES

Service organization

- Become involved with leadership in a service organization on your campus or in the surrounding community.

As you develop more confidence in leadership, you want to take on a higher level of involvement. The following are two good areas to consider:

Student Government

- Run for office.
- Run a campaign.
- Serve on an advisory committee.
- Lead out in a movement addressing an issue.

Public Politics

- Voting is a form of leadership because it makes you an agent of change, so vote!
- Take time to learn about the candidates and issues so that you can vote intelligently.
- Get involved with local, state, regional, and national campaigns.

While the suggestion has been made to get involved with more formal roles of leadership, don't confuse leadership with formal positions. Go back to the definition given at the beginning of this exercise. Leadership is "taking action to bring about change by mobilizing others to accomplish a shared vision." You can do that in any relationship. You don't need a formal title of recognition. You can start where you are at right now by taking leadership with your roommates or your group of friends. The ancient Chinese philosopher Confucius taught that "a journey begins with a single step."

▶ References

The following resources have been cited in this chapter.

Heifitz, R.A., and Linsky, M. (2002). *Leadership on the Line: Staying Alive Through the Dangers of Leading*. Boston, Massachusetts: Harvard Business School Publishing.

Millard, B. (2008). "A New Look at Leadership" in *Life Purpose Explorations*. Winter.

The following resources may be useful as you explore the concept of *Personal Leadership*.

Bass, M.B., and Riggio, R.E. (2006). *Transformational Leadership*. Mahwah, NJ: Lawrence Erlbaum Assoicates.

Blanchard, K., Hybels, B., and Hodges, P. (1999). *Leadership by the Book*. New York, NY: William Morrow and Company.

DePree, M. (1989). *Leading Without Is an Art*. New York, NY: Dell Publishing.

DePree, M. (2003). *Leading Without Power*. San Francisco: Jossey-Bass Publishers.

DePree, M. (2008). *Leadership Jazz*. New York, NY: The Doubleday Publishing Group.

Gladwell, M. (2002). *The Tipping Point: How Little Things Can Make a Big Difference*. Boston: Back Bay/Little, Brown & Company.

Goffee, R. & and G. Jones (2006). *Why Should Anyone Be Led by You?: What It Takes To Be an Authentic Leader*. Boston, MA: Harvard Business School Press.

Greenleaf, R.K. (2008). The Servant as Leader. Westfield, IN: The Greenleaf Center for Servant Leadership.

Heifitz, R.A. (1994). *Leadership without Easy Answers*. Boston, Massachusetts: Harvard Business School Publishing.

Hunter, J.C. (1998). *The Servant: A Simple Story about the True Essence of Leadership*. Rocklin, CA: Prima Publishing.

Jensen, R. (2001). *Achieving Authentic Success: 10 Timeless Life Principles That Will Maximize Your Real Potential*. San Diego, CA: Future Achievement International.

Kellerman, B. (Ed.). (2010). *Leadership: Essential Selections on Power, Authority, and Influence*. New York, NY: McGraw Hill.

Kotter, J. (1996). *Leading Change*. Boston: Harvard Business School Press.

Kotter, J., and Cohen, D. (2002). *The Heart of Change: Real Life Stories of How People Change Their Organizations*. Boston: Harvard Business School Press.

Kottter, J., and Rathergeber, H. (2006). *Our Iceberg Is Melting*. New York: St. Martin's Press.

Kouzes, J.M. and Posner, B.Z. (2007) *The Leadership Challenge. 4th Edition*. San Francisco: Jossey-Bass Publishers.

Kouzes, J.M. and Posner, B.Z. (2010) *The Truth about Leadership*. San Francisco: Jossey-Bass Publishers.

Kouzes, J.M. and Posner, B.Z., (1993). *Credibility: How Leaders Gain and Lose It, Why People Demand It*. San Francisco, CA: Josey-Bass Publishers.

Kouzes, J.M. and Posner, B.Z., (2006). *A Leader's Legacy*. San Francisco, CA: Josey-Bass Publishers.

Kubicek, J. (2011). *Leadership Is Dead: How Influence Is Reviving It*. New York, NY: Howard Books.

Lencioni, P. (2002). *The Five Dysfunctions of a Team*. San Francisco: Jossey-Bass.

Malphurs, A. (2003). *Being Leaders: The Nature of Authentic Christian Leadership*. Grand Rapids, MI: Baker Books.

Manz, C.C., and Neck, C.P. (1999). *Master Self-leadership: Empowering Yourself for Personal Excellence*. Upper Saddle River, NJ: Prentice Hall.

Maxwell, J.C. (1998). *The 21 Irrefutable Laws of Leadership*. Nashville, TN: Thomas Nelson.

Millard, B. (2002). *Servanthood—A Right Attitude Necessary for Effective Leadership*. Marion, Indiana: Life Discovery Publications.

Millard, B. (2008). "A New Look at Leadership." *Life Purpose Explorations*. Winter.

Millard, B. (2009). "Circle of Relationship vs. Chain of Command." *Life Purpose Explorations*. Winter.

Millard, B. (2006). "Servant-Leadership—a Needed Z-axis for two-dimensional leadership thinking" in G.P. Barnes (Ed.), *Servant First* (Chapter 12). Indianapolis: Precedent Press.

Millard, B. (2003). *ChangeQuest: A Process for Modifying Your Organization*. Ventura, California: Life Discovery Publications.

Millard, B. (2002). *Servant-Leadership: Not Just a Pious Pursuit—It Works!* Marion, Indiana: Life Discovery Publications.

Northouse, P.G. (2007). *Introduction to Leadership: Concepts and Practice*. Thousand Oaks, CA: Sage.

Northouse, P.G. (2010). *Leadership: Theory and Practice. (5ᵗʰ Ed.)* Thousand Oaks, CA: Sage.

Rima, S.D. (2000). *Leading from the Inside Out*. Grand Rapids, MI: Baker Books.

Schwen, M.R., and Bass, D.C., Eds. (2006). *Leading Lives That Matter: What We Should Do and Who We Should Be*. Grand Rapids, Michigan: Erdmans Publishing Co.

Wilkes, C. Gene. (1998). *Jesus on Leadership: Discovering the Secrets of Servant Leadership from the Life of Christ*. Wheaton, IL: Tyndale House Publishers.

Wren, J.T. (1995). *The Leader's Companion: Insights on Leadership through the Ages*. New York, NY: The Free Press.

Wren, T.J., Riggio, R.E., and Genovese, M.A. (Eds.). (2009). *Leadership and the Liberal Arts*. New York, NY: Palgrave MacMillan.

REFERENCES

Leading from a Sense of Mission

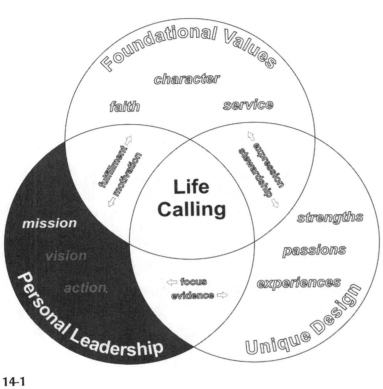

14

FIGURE 14-1
Life Calling Model Focusing on Mission

> *The kind of work God usually calls you to is the kind of work that you need most to do and that the world most needs to have done...The place God calls you to is the place where your deep gladness and the world's deep hunger meet.*
>
> FREDERICK BUECHNER

The third main component of the Life Calling Model is *Personal Leadership*. There are three important stages that must be addressed if we hope to be successful in carrying out effective Personal Leadership in our lives: *mission*, *vision*, and *action*. Let's stop for a moment and explain what we mean by these three terms.

Mission defines the fundamental purpose of your existence, succinctly describing why you exist and what you are meant to do with your life.
Vision depicts a long-term view of the way your world will look in the future if you are successful in carrying out your mission.
Action describes the strategy that culminates in you actually fulfilling your mission.

In this chapter we will explore **mission**, the first stage of developing Personal Leadership.

CHAPTER OBJECTIVES

1. Understand how a sense of mission emerges from encountering and responding to different circumstances in the world

2. Explain how people are drawn in unique ways to different types of people, locations, opportunities, and problems within the world

3. Encounter and respond to different types of people, locations, opportunities, and problems

4. Begin identifying what types of people, locations, opportunities, and problems have a draw on your life

KEY TERMS

Ambition = a compelling desire for some type of achievement or distinction

Articulate = to make distinct and clear

Circumstances = existing conditions or surroundings

Draw = cause to move in a particular direction by or as if by a pulling force

Location = place of settlement, activity, or residence

Opportunity = situation or condition in a good position, or with a good chance or prospect for advancement or success

Philosophy = a system of principles used for guidance in practical affairs

Problem = any question or matter involving danger, doubt, uncertainty, or difficulty

Values = the things one believes have relative worth, merit, or importance

Virtue = moral excellence

◢ Concepts

According to our definition of Personal Leadership, the primary focus is *taking action to bring about change through a mission directed toward a desired vision*. Where does that strong sense of mission in our lives come from? A sense of mission emerges from an inwardly-developed conviction that there is some good that needs to be brought to the world in which we live. This conviction in part grows out of the passions we studied in Chapter 11. As this passion-born conviction evolves, it begins to define the reason for our existence and embody our philosophies, ambitions, virtues and values. As our conviction becomes more clearly articulated, it provides us a sense of direction and guides the decisions we make and the actions we take. At that point it becomes our *mission* in life—a key component of our Life Calling, and this starts us on our way to exercising personal leadership.

How does all of this happen in our lives? Let's look at where you are right now. As you think about starting college, have you asked yourself where in the world you want to go when you graduate and who you want to be working with when you get there? Many times if you can start with the end in mind, you can have a better idea of how to start. Think about your family vacations as an example. Would you start planning what to take on a vacation or which car to drive before you knew where you were going? That wouldn't make any sense. Instead, you start by talking about where you would like to go. Then you plan the vacation around that destination. That's what we mean by having the end in mind.

One of the greatest mistakes you can make in trying to discover your Life Calling is failing to narrow your focus when trying to identify your mission in life. You cannot be everything to everybody in every situation. How can you avoid this dilemma? A good place to start is asking the question "To what types of needs in the world do you feel drawn?" That drawing force you sense is an intricate part of who you are and is one of the most important factors you should analyze as you try to figure out your mission and ultimately, your Life Calling.

In Buechner's quote at the beginning of this chapter, he proposed that our calling in life will best be found where the *"work that you need most to do and that the world most needs to have done"* come together. When this convergence takes place in our lives, we find the greatest conviction that leads us to a sense of mission, and we exercise the highest level of stewardship of those strengths, passions, and experiences that have been entrusted to us in our lives.

What, then, are those needs in the world that draw us? A rather long list could likely be created. In order to keep a manageable focus, we will look at four major categories of needs for the purpose of our study: people, location, problems and opportunities. Each of these categories draws us in its own unique way, independent of the other three. Looking at the categories from a different perspective, however, reveals that they have an interacting relationship as well.

People and locations form a northern and southern hemisphere in Figure 14-2. Individuals who are in the northern hemisphere find that they are drawn more to the needs of specific people groups than they are by the needs

FIGURE 14-2
World Draw Hemispheres

of a location. Individuals who are in the southern hemisphere are drawn more by needs related to locations than they are to the needs related to specific people groups.

Opportunities and problems form an eastern and western hemisphere in Figure 14-2. Individuals who are in the eastern hemisphere find they are drawn more by situations and conditions related to difficulty, struggles and peril in the world. Individuals who are in the western hemisphere find that they are drawn more to situations and conditions favorable for innovation, progressive accomplishment and personal development.

Drawn to People

We should have a love for all people and serve them with compassion and respect. That should be part of our Foundational Values, as we discovered in Chapter 4. However, for some the strongest draw in the world is to work with specific groups of people. This attraction may form around age groups. Some might discover that they find greater enjoyment working with small children, while others may enjoy working with the elderly. Still others might prefer working with teenagers, or others might be drawn toward college students or young adults. Gender creates another drawing force. Some may feel more comfortable working with men, whereas others may be drawn to work with women. Ethnicity can be a drawing force for some people—a strong draw to work with certain groups of people who have a common racial, national, linguistic, or cultural heritage. Language may be a drawing factor with certain people. For instance, a person might be fluent in Spanish and feel drawn to work with people who speak Spanish only or primarily.

We need to realize that although all of these groups are worthy, there is nothing wrong with the fact that we are drawn to certain ones and not to others. If this is a dynamic working within us, the affinity to work with certain people groups clearly should be considered in narrowing the focus of our Life Calling. This affinity should be considered as a part of who we are.

Drawn to Locations

The second draw to consider is *locations*. Some people find that they are drawn to specific locations in the world. When we hear the term *location*, we usually think of countries or regions, or more specifically cities or villages in the world. But the draw of a location might also be an issue of vicinity such as being close to extended family, or we might feel drawn to live and work in the area in which we grew up. Location might also have to do with climate. Some people feel most comfortable in warmer climates, whereas others prefer cool climates. Some prefer arid climates, whereas others would rather be in a tropical climate. Some really like four seasons. There might be a temptation at first to think that the draw of a location is not as worthy as other factors considered in discovering our Life Calling. Yet with some people, this is a major issue in the way they are wired, and we need to recognize that there is nothing wrong with the fact that some are drawn to certain locations and not to others. Again, if this is a dynamic working within us, the affinity to certain locations clearly should be considered in narrowing the focus of our mission. This affinity should be considered as a part of who we are.

Responding to Problems

The third draw we will consider is *problems*. Some people find themselves drawn to challenge specific difficulties, struggles and perils in the world. For example, a person might feel drawn to work with the challenges of single-parent families or children with no parents. Another good example of this would be a person who responds to working with people in poverty. Issues related to national conflicts would be another good example of problems that might draw people in this third hemisphere. Spiritual confusion, disease, lack of education, and environmental pollution are other good examples. The list is very long. Not one of us has the inclination or skill set to address every one of those areas of problems. Instead, we should accept that it is okay to be drawn to specific problems versus all problems. And we should accept that it is okay that some are drawn more to solve problems than others are.

Drawn to Opportunities

The final draw we will consider (and there are likely others) is *opportunities*. For some people opportunities might be more important than the locale. For instance, the drawing force might be working with family situations or working with people who have made certain lifestyle choices related to social, spiritual, or other issues. Some people find their greatest draw in life is related to political situations or causes. Others find themselves drawn to working with people who face certain legal challenges. Another example would be the draw to work with people who are struggling with economic issues in their lives. Once again, we need to realize there is nothing wrong with the fact that we are drawn or respond to certain opportunities and not to others. This can help us narrow the focus of our mission. Our preference for certain contexts and situations is a part of who we are.

What Are You Encountering Right Now?

If you are not sure about which needs in the world are drawing you, then examine what types of people, locations, opportunities, and problems within the world you find yourself most often encountering. Often the reason you have such encounters is because you are internally drawn there even though you may not be aware of the drawing force. The exploration of these drawing forces in the world forms a critical stage in our Life Calling discovery because what we find out will begin to point us in certain directions. As we enter this exploration, however, we will find that an interesting dynamic emerges, as illustrated in Figure 14-3.

For some, the draw of circumstances comes from just one of the components; for example, someone who is primarily attracted to working with kids. For others it may involve two of the components. Still others might have three components drawing them. The majority of people, however, have some

CONCEPTS

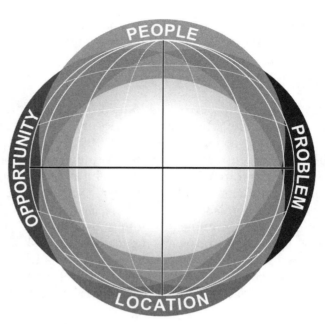

FIGURE 14-3
Interaction of Drawing Forces

level of draw from all four of the components, as illustrated in Figure 14-3 by the larger light section in the middle. Exploring the four components is an important step in defining our Life Calling.

Further Questions about Mission

There are four key questions to ask about a person's mission. 1) Who is the target of your mission? 2) What is it that you are doing? 3) What makes your mission distinct? 4) Why are you doing it? We have discovered how to find the answer to the first question. How do we find answers for the other three? As we continue to explore and understand all nine elements in the three components of the Life Calling Model, answers to the second and third questions will become clearer. Right now you might be tempted to think *I wouldn't be taking this course or reading this book if I had those answers*, and you would probably be right! But be encouraged to persist in your exploration, and answers will come. As for the fourth question, we will see in the next chapter on *vision* how we can begin to understand why we will do what we will do.

Concepts Summary

It is easy to see that when all four components are drawing us, there may be a complex set of choices we will have to sort through in assessing this area of our Life Calling. We might be tempted at this point to complain that this is making life more complicated rather than helping us simplify the Life Calling discovery process. That is a valid observation. The problem many of us encounter, however, is that we do not have the patience to explore the complexity of what draws us into service in the world, and we end up making choices derived from pressure and guilt. When we do this, we rarely find satisfaction or fulfillment in what we do and often end up full of resentment and bitterness. Life Calling is complex, but learning where to look for answers and being willing to continue this search throughout our life makes the discovery a lot more successful.

▶ Insight

Stewardship and service form the very core of a Life Calling. But these need to be guided and informed by our response to the needs of the world. The Bible has important insights that can direct us as we explore these circumstances.

SCRIPTURAL INSIGHT 1 ▶ *Our Call to Serve the World Is Not Optional*

Then Jesus came to them and said, "All authority in heaven and on earth has been given to me. Therefore go and make disciples of all nations, baptizing them in the name of the Father and of the Son and of the Holy Spirit, and teaching them to obey everything I have commanded you. And surely I am with you always, to the very end of the age." MATTHEW 28:18-20

As we develop a *Personal Mission* in our Life Calling, the first step is to examine what types of circumstances in the world attract us. These can be focused on people, locations, opportunities, or problems within the world. It is important to realize that we cannot be everything to everybody in every situation.

We start today with a scripture that contains the most universally accepted mandate for world service—what is often referred to as the Great Commission.

There are six important concepts in this passage that can guide the development of our personal mission and set the context for our overall Life Calling.

1. *Go*: Our personal mission and our Life Calling are implemented by moving outside of ourselves toward others. It is impossible to discover our Life Calling when we are unwilling to enter into service. Service is where Life Calling is carried out; it is also where we find out a lot about our Unique Design.

2. *Make disciples*: At the beginning of this book we stated that Life Calling is something more than a college major, job, position, title, profession or life's work. In this scripture we find out what that "more" is. No matter what shape our Life Calling takes or in what venue it takes place, it should be carried out with a prevailing intent to bring other people into a correct relationship with Jesus.

3. *Baptize*: Two actions help us "make disciples." The first action is restoration. Our Life Calling should always keep us aware of how we can help others discover how they can be reinstated into a relationship with Jesus no matter what path they have followed in becoming separated from him.

4. *Teach*: The second action is reformation. As we interact with others in our Life Calling, we need to find ways to instruct each other on how to redirect our lives so that they become more consistent with God's design for the universe and for our specific place in the universe.

5. *All authority*: Two remarkable statements are made at the beginning of the passage and at the end of the passage that should give us tremendous hope and confidence in our Life Calling. At the beginning Jesus says the basis for the effectiveness of the Great Commission is the fact that all authority in heaven and earth has been given to him. When we bring our Life Calling into connection with Jesus' power, with that kind of backing, we will not fail.

INSIGHT

6. *I am with you*: At the close of the statement Jesus reassures us that he will be right there with us through it all. We can pursue our Life Calling knowing that we are never alone.

> **PERSONAL REFLECTION** ⟩ How have you responded to the Great Commission? Do you see the Great Commission as part of your Life Calling?

SCRIPTURAL INSIGHT 2 ⟩ *Do What You Are*

The body is not made up of one part but of many. Now if the foot should say, "Because I am not a hand, I do not belong to the body," it would not for that reason cease to be part of the body. And if the ear should say, "Because I am not an eye, I do not belong to the body," it would not for that reason cease to be part of the body. If the whole body were an eye, where would the sense of hearing be? If the whole body were an ear, where would the sense of smell be? But in fact God has placed the parts in the body, every one of them, just as he wanted them to be. If they were all one part, where would the body be? As it is, there are many parts, but one body. 1 Corinthians 12:14-20

The next passage of scripture we look at balances the concept that Life Calling includes a universal commission with the concept that Life Calling needs an individual focus. The Apostle Paul examines the dynamics of Christians working together and uses the analogy of a human body.

Eyes cannot be everything for the body, nor can ears. They each have their own areas of responsibility in the body. That is what Paul recommends for each of us as we work together. We need to find our individual focus and be diligent in carrying out our Life Calling within that focus.

There's a temptation to say this relates to our unique design, not our personal mission. While 1 Corinthians 12:14-20 certainly does apply to our unique design—specifically our strengths—it also applies to our personal mission. As we saw in Matthew 28, we are called to take our Life Calling into the world. But we cannot be everywhere. One of the greatest failings with conscientious people involved in service is to say "yes" to everything. The problem is they usually burn out quickly. If we really examine ourselves closely, we will find that we are not drawn to all areas. We usually find ourselves drawn to specific circumstances in the world. When starting to look at these circumstances, we will find that there are different components that draw us. Some of us are drawn to work with certain groups of people. Others of us are drawn more to specific locations. Still others are drawn by opportunities we see. Some of us may be drawn to work with specific problems. And there probably are others as well.

The important point in all of this is that it is okay to be drawn to some areas and not to others. That's part of how God communicates to us concerning our Life Calling.

> **PERSONAL REFLECTION** ⟩ What circumstances in the world are drawing you? How is God speaking to you through these drawing forces?

SCRIPTURAL INSIGHT 3 ⟩ *Recognize the People Who Need Your Response*

On the contrary, they saw that I had been entrusted with the task of preaching the gospel to the Gentiles, just as Peter had been to the Jews. Galatians 2:7

What did Buechn mean when he said we are called to the place where our deep gladness meets the world's deep hunger? There are deep emotions in our hearts that respond positively to certain circumstances in the world more than others. Sometime these circumstances relate to certain groups of people. We may find ourselves most attracted to or most effective with certain groups of people. This does not mean that we don't care about other groups of people. In Matthew 22:37-40 Jesus responded to a question about what the greatest commandment is. "Love the Lord your God with all your heart and with all your soul and with all your mind. This is the first and greatest commandment. And the second is like it: Love your neighbor as yourself. All the Law and the Prophets hang on these two commandments." So we are expected to love everyone.

But that doesn't mean we will be equally drawn to or effective with all groups of people. Paul found he was more effective preaching to the Gentiles, while Peter was more effective preaching to the Jews. Certainly personal circumstances played a role in this. Because of his history, Paul was not very popular with Jews, especially Jews who were in any type of leadership. Part of this was because Paul's message was very radical. Many Jews felt that his disregard for circumcision and other Jewish laws was an affront to their religion. Peter seemed to weave his delivery of the gospel into a more subdued approach that, while not compromising the gospel, made it easier for Jews to listen to him.

God used these differences in approaches to spread the gospel in a remarkable way. Without the inclusion of the Gentiles, Christianity would have remained a small sect within Judaism. God can similarly use your affinity to certain people groups to accomplish his plans. Examining your draw to certain people groups is one good area to explore in searching for your Life Calling.

> **PERSONAL REFLECTION** > What people groups in the world are drawing you? What do you think God is saying to you through these drawing forces?

SCRIPTURAL INSIGHT 4 > *Recognize the Locations That Need Your Response*

But you will receive power when the Holy Spirit comes on you; and you will be my witnesses in Jerusalem, and in all Judea and Samaria, and to the ends of the earth. ACTS 1:8

It would be easy to misinterpret the Great Commission in Matthew 28 as a call for each one of us to go into all the world. However, that is not practically possible today, and it certainly was not possible in the time Jesus gave this commission. The only way we can interpret this commission is to see it as a call for each of us to go to different areas. In the end, the sum of our travels will cover the entire world.

Just like we discovered with people groups, we will find that we will be drawn to specific locations in the world. The drawing forces may come from a variety of circumstances. That doesn't matter. God can use any of those circumstances to get the people he wants to the places he wants. After the crucifixion of Jesus, several of his disciples headed back to the Sea of Galilee. Why? Because it was where their families and friends lived and they felt comfortable there. That is often the draw of a location. On the other hand, Paul had a dream where a man from Macedonia was begging Paul to come and help him.

Even though Paul was originally drawn to a different location, he changed his plan and went to Macedonia because he felt there was a real need.

The passage in Acts 1 proposes an orderly approach to locations for the preaching of the gospel. That could be the drawing force that directs our steps. The point is that different elements can be used to draw us to certain locations, and that is okay. There is one other key point, however, to be found in Acts 1. The receiving of power from the Holy Spirit was the indication of readiness to move toward the specific locations. An affinity to people groups or locations alone is not the complete indication of readiness or Life Calling. Spiritual power is much more important.

James gives a good perspective concerning how to consider our draw to different locations or circumstances. In James 4:13-15 he says,

> Now listen, you who say, "Today or tomorrow we will go to this or that city, spend a year there, carry on business and make money." Why, you do not even know what will happen tomorrow. What is your life? You are a mist that appears for a little while and then vanishes. Instead, you ought to say, "If it is the Lord's will, we will live and do this or that."

As we consider the different factors in the world that draw us to them, we always need to evaluate them in the larger context of the Lord's will. When we place that as the highest priority, we will be more effective in finding our Life Calling.

PERSONAL REFLECTION ⟩ What locations in the world are drawing you? What do you think God is saying to you through these drawing forces?

SCRIPTURAL INSIGHT 5 ⟩ *Recognize the Opportunities and Problems That Need Your Response*

Then Philip ran up to the chariot and heard the man reading Isaiah the prophet. "Do you understand what you are reading?" Philip asked.

"How can I," he said, "unless someone explains it to me?" So he invited Philip to come up and sit with him. ACTS 8:30-31

Philip had been sent south on the road from Jerusalem to Gaza by an angel. It was along this road that he came into contact with a top treasury official working for the queen of Ethiopia. The Spirit had told Philip to stay near the chariot in which this Ethiopian official was riding. When Philip came close to the chariot, he heard the man reading from the book of Isaiah. And that's where the passage from Acts begins.

What we can see from Philip's actions is that he was responding to both an opportunity and a problem. The opportunity was made known to him by an angel and the Spirit. I am sure all of us would like that to happen in our lives as well. However, opportunities are more often discovered by relationships we have with others. Once Philip responded to the opportunity and came in contact with the chariot, he discovered a problem. The man did not understand what he was reading in the book of Isaiah. Philip responded to this and helped explain the passage. Once he had shown the man how this scripture was talking about Jesus, the Ethiopian official believed and wanted to be baptized, and Philip baptized him.

This was a singular event, and Philip went on to other opportunities and problems. The lesson we can learn from this, however, is to be ready to respond when the drawing forces of opportunities and/or problems present themselves to us.

Look at this list of well-known characters from Hebrews 11: Noah, Abraham, Isaac, Jacob, Joseph, Moses, Rahab, Gideon, Barak, Samson, Jephthah, David, and Samuel. According to Hebrews 11 these characters all shared the common trait of strong faith. If you look at their stories, however, they also shared another common factor. They all faced problems—in some cases opportunities—and responded strongly when the drawing forces presented themselves.

Opportunities and problems will likely change throughout our lives, but each time they change they will help us discover our Life Calling.

PERSONAL REFLECTION > What opportunities or problems in the world are you encountering right now? What do you think God is saying to you through these?

INSIGHT

▶ Discovery

How can the Discovery Guides help you understand the *needs of the world* that are drawing you right now and help you identify a mission for your life that can respond to these needs?

T THEORY	Studying circumstances in the world covers a broad area of subjects from geography to intercultural studies to social problems to human behavior to language and many more areas. Much of what forms a good liberal arts education will provide you with opportunities to study circumstances in the world. If you approach classes in the core curriculum that make up your liberal arts or general education as opportunities to expand your understanding of the world and its needs, you will find the classes more meaningful.
E EXAMPLES	The experiences of others are a very good place to learn about circumstances in the world and their drawing forces. Seek out people with a rich variety of experiences and find time to talk to them. As you start to feel certain drawing forces in your own life, find someone with a lot of life experience who has been drawn in a similar direction and ask them to mentor you in this area.
A ASSESSMENT	Formal assessments do not really play a major role in helping you determine what needs in the world are drawing you.
C COUNSEL	People speaking into your life can be powerful sources of guidance and strength in relationship to circumstances in the world. Additionally, family members, teachers, pastors, student development and residence life personnel, and friends know you well and can give you valuable insights about what they see in your life drawing you.
H HISTORY	The classics and historical biographies are full of stories dealing with people who have felt drawn in specific ways to serve others. Select some of these and learn from their experience. Also, learning about the history of cultures, situations, problems and other circumstances can help you understand them better.
E EXPERIENCE	Get involved with activities going on in your college or university that can introduce you to a wide variety of circumstances in the world discussed in this chapter. You can find these in your residence life, in your classes, and in your student clubs and governments. There will also be opportunities in the community that surrounds your college or university. In addition, give strong consideration to studying abroad for a semester. This will be a rich experience in helping you determine your Life Calling.
R REFLECTION	Take time to reflect on what you have learned in the other six activities of discovery about what circumstances in the world are drawing you. Consider if any of these needs is becoming stronger than the others and if it might be a call on your life.

DISCOVERY

▶ Story

Even in the comfort of the *Nautilus*, the 850 mile trip from St. Louis to Colorado seemed like a long ride. The travelers joked that long stretches of wheat fields across Kansas were only broken up by an occasional cornfield.

"I don't know how you stay awake, Captain Nemo," Ryan said. "Kansas is pretty much one big field."

Ken Neimon laughed. "Yeah, but I bet you don't have any trouble getting a loaf of bread."

"Good point, Captain," Ryan responded.

The motorhome continued its monotonous trek across Interstate 70. Adam finally broke the hypnotic hum of the motorhome. "Hey, Abi, yesterday you said you weren't sure that it was the issue of slavery that drew Lincoln into this struggle of the Civil War. Do you think it didn't matter?"

"Are you saying he didn't care about the slaves?" Lorena asked disdainfully.

"No, of course not," Abriella answered. "I just think that his concern about the slaves was not the drawing factor. I think it was the problem situation with the nation. I face that all the time. As an African American, I realize the struggle that's always there for equality and civil rights, but I don't find that to be the drawing cause in my life."

"That's an interesting observation, Abi," Adam said. "It probably *is* easy for people to stereotype you into what you ought to care about."

"That's a hard thing for me," Abriella replied. "Sometimes I have a hard time figuring out what it is in the world that's drawing me."

"I know what you mean," Justin agreed. "Sometimes I feel like there isn't anything drawing me, and then at other times I feel like I am being drawn by everything. In either case, I don't feel any direction in life."

"Exactly," Abriella replied. "My life experiences have not led me down a path that causes me to be drawn to that struggle as much as some others are. You guys are part of the blame." She had a grin on her face.

"How so?" Adam asked.

"Well, we've all been together as friends for over twelve years," Abriella responded. "It has never mattered that I'm African American or that Justin's family originally came from Korea or that Lorena was born in Mexico. We're just all friends. We've always been that way."

"That's so true," Adam said. "It's probably what's kept us all so close over these years. We've never focused on our differences."

"Except Lorena," Ryan broke in. "She's against people not going to college."

"I'm not against people who don't go to college. I'm just against lazy, dumb loafers like you," Lorena said, laughing.

"Adam, up in the Arch yesterday you said that the pioneers were drawn to the West by circumstances." Diana was ready to resume the discussion rather than allow Ryan and Lorena to fight. "Do you think all of us are drawn in that way?"

"In a way, yes," Adam replied. "We're drawn to different things, and I think it's important for us to realize that. I think this unique draw helps to shape our purpose in life."

"So give us an example," Justin pressed Adam. "What's drawing you?"

"I'm still trying to figure that out," Adam replied. "I find myself drawn to the public arena. I'd like to help make our government a more respected part of our lives."

"Right on, man," Ryan said. "Those guys need all the help they can get."

"What about the rest of you?" Adam asked. "What kind of draw do you feel?"

"You already know the answer for me," Lorena quickly answered. "I'm drawn to the medical needs people have."

"I'm drawn to kids," Diana said. "Whatever I end up doing in life, I want it to be involved with kids."

"I'm drawn to the sea," Ryan half-jokingly said. "Whatever it takes to keep those waves coming."

Lorena rolled her eyes in disgust.

"I've always had a desire to work with families," Abriella said. "I feel like they need all the help they can get. But I also love anything that has to do with the arts."

"What about you, Justin?" Adam asked, turning toward him.

"I'm not sure. Maybe it would be to make school more interesting," Justin said in a reflective voice. "They should make school interesting and meaningful enough so guys like Ryan would see its value."

"Fabulous," Ryan replied sarcastically. "I would hate to see the other poor kiddies coming after me have to suffer like I did."

"Oh, brother," Lorena said, sounding disgusted.

"So what am I suppose to do now?" Diana asked. "I may know who I feel drawn to, but I'm not sure what that means."

"I'm not sure," Adam answered.

"I bet the Captain does," Ryan injected. "Captain Nemo, you need to help you poor, struggling daughter."

Ken Neimon laughed. "Okay, I'll see what I can do for her. I read once that the place God wants you to be is where your passions and the world's needs meet. So I think that's where you begin. You know what you are passionate about, so start looking for people who are associated with this passion and what their needs are. You might want to explore developing skills related to those needs."

"Are you saying that if I feel passionate about working with kids, I should start thinking about what their greatest needs are?" Diana asked her father.

"Sure seems like that would be a good place to start," he answered.

"Good advice, Captain," Ryan joined in. "I need to start looking at how I can help my people develop better surfboards." A big grin spread across Ryan's face.

"I think I'm feeling carsick," Lorena said with disgust. "What you need to do is install screens to read iBooks on surfboards so all of your people, as you call them, could develop some intelligence."

"Did you know that Einstein liked to surf?" Ryan asked with a straight face.

"No he didn't!" Lorena emphatically responded.

"Check it out. I'm afraid your almanac brain might have found its limits," Ryan pushed back.

The others laughed. They were pretty sure that Ryan was making this up. But then again…

"Hey look!" Justin exclaimed. "A sign welcoming us to Colorado."

A look of relief appeared on most faces: relief from the long trip…and relief from the Lorena-Ryan fight-club.

Exercises

Magnets of the World

A sense of mission emerges from your encounter with and response to different types of people, locations, opportunities and problems in the world. As these encounters or responses take place, you will begin to experience a drawing towards these people, locations, problems and opportunities.

Examples of "people" factors that might be drawing you:
- Age groups
- Specific races or ethnic groups
- Gender

Examples of "location" factors that might be drawing you:
- Specific country
- Certain type of climate
- Living close to extended family
- Scenic surroundings
- Specific regions of a country or the world
- Preference for either an urban or rural setting

Examples of "problem" factors that might be drawing you:
- Poverty
- Famine and malnutrition
- Life-threatening diseases
- Poor health practices
- Lack of education
- Abnormal psychological and emotional conditions
- Dysfunctional marriages and families
- Threats to the Earth's environment
- Spiritual ignorance or dysfunction
- Legal

Examples of "opportunity" factors that might be drawing you:
- Spiritual leadership
- Creative expression in writing or the visual and musical arts
- Desire to have a family
- Scientific exploration and innovation
- Financial investment and growth
- Sales and marketing
- Radio, television, movie, and theater performance or production
- Political leadership
- Professional sports
- Outdoor recreation programs
- International travel
- Intellectual study, advancement and teaching

It is impossible for any one person to respond to every type of person, location, problem, or opportunity in the world. Most people, if they reflect deeply enough, will discover that they are drawn to specific people, locations, problems, or opportunities.

▶ Responses to the Circumstances

In the charts that follow, reflect and discuss what types of people, locations, problems, or opportunities in the world you feel drawn to.

Types of People	Describe
	Explain

Types of Locations	Describe
	Explain

	Describe	
Types of Problems		
	Explain	

	Describe	
Types of Opportunities		
	Explain	

▶ Encounters with Circumstances

Sometimes people have a hard time identifying the drawing forces in their lives. If this is the case, then a good place to start looking to see what draws you in your life regarding this is to examine what types of people, locations, opportunities and problems in the world you most often encounter. Go back through the previous charts and reflect and discuss what types of people, locations, problems and opportunities within the world you find yourself most often encountering. Give examples of these.

▶ Reflection

As you look through your responses to the Magnets of the World, what do you think is beginning to be revealed to you about your mission in life?

Starting to Develop a Personal Mission Statement

In the Concepts section we discovered that there are four key questions to ask about a person's mission. In this exercise you will begin to answer those questions.

1. Who is the target of your mission?

   Use what you wrote in Exercise 1 to answer this question. Which do you think you find yourself drawn to more:

   ☐ Specific groups or types of people
   - If so, what are they? _____
   ☐ Specific location
   - If so, where is it, and who are the people associated with this location? _____
   ☐ Specific problem
   - If so, what is it, and who are the people associated with this problem? _____
   ☐ Specific opportunity
   - If so, what is it, and who are the people associated with this opportunity? _____

2. What is it that you are doing?
   a. What is it that the people you identified in #1 need most to have done for them?
   b. Based on the strengths and passions you identified in previous chapters, what would you like most to do for these people?
   c. Do your strengths and passions match the needs of the people you identified?

3. What makes your mission distinct?
   a. What could you do for these people that not only matches your strengths and passions, but also would be somewhat different than what everyone else is doing?
   b. What would you need to do in order to better develop what you want to do and give it more uniqueness?

4. Why are you doing it?
   a. How does what you want to do match the Foundational Values we studied in Section I?
   b. How does what you want to do match your own personal values?

   Use the answers you gave to the previous four questions and try writing them into a single personal mission statement for you life.

▶ References

The following resources have been used in this chapter.

Buechner, F. (1993). *Wishful thinking: A Seeker's ABC*. San Francisco: HarperSanFrancisco.

The following resources may be useful as you explore the role of *mission* in continuing your exploration of Personal Leadership and Life Calling.

Millard, B. (2012). *LifeQuest: Planning Your Life Strategically, 2nd ed*. Marion, IN: Life Discovery ePubs.

Schwen, M.R., and Bass, D.C., Eds. (2006). *Leading Lives That Matter: What We Should Do and Who We Should Be*. Grand Rapids, Michigan: Erdmans Publishing Co.

Inspired by a Vision

15

FIGURE 15-1
Life Calling Model Focusing On Vision

The third main component of the Life Calling Model is *Personal Leadership*. We identified three important stages that must be addressed if we hope to be successful in carrying out effective Personal Leadership in our lives: *mission, vision*, and *action*. In this chapter we will explore **vision**, the second stage of developing Personal Leadership.

CHAPTER OBJECTIVES

1. Understand the role of vision in forming a personal mission to carry out one's Life Calling
2. Explain what a vision is
3. Identify the important components that create a good vision
4. Begin developing your own life

CONCEPTS

KEY TERMS

Dream = see in one's mind something of beauty, charm, value, or desirability

Imagination = ability to see in one's mind something that is not real in the immediate setting

Inspiration = ability to arouse an animating, quickening, or exalting influence

Picture = mental image representing something in a graphic sense

Task = job, assignment, chore, or act of work to be carried out

▶ Concepts

As you concentrate on starting your college journey, graduation from college is probably not at the forefront of your thoughts. But have you at least once allowed the picture to pass though your imagination of marching across the stage and receiving your diploma? Imaginary pictures and dreams play an important role in our lives because they give us the inspiration to start or continue journeys. Have you ever wondered what it is that drives mountain climbers to risk their lives scaling dangerous peaks such as Mount Everest, K2, the Matterhorn, or the most deadly of mountains—Annapurna in Nepal? In talking with mountain climbers, I have discovered a common theme emerging. They all had a dream about being at the top of the mountain and seeing the view before they ever started the climb. This dream was great enough to motivate them to overcome the fears they had about the many perils they would face on the journey up the mountain.

We can take this concept and apply it to all areas of our lives. The dream must be greater than the challenge! This is an especially important place to start as you look ahead toward your college *experience*. There will certainly be challenges ahead. Some of these will seem so formidable that they will strike a great deal of apprehension and fear in you. Without a strong inspiring dream, those fears can easily overcome you, even to the point of stopping your journey. So it is very appropriate, indeed critical, to take time at the beginning of your college experience to paint a picture—a vision—that you can continually return to for encouragement during your journey.

That takes us to the second factor in the last of the major components that form the Life Calling Model—*vision*. In Chapter 13 we defined *vision* as a picture depicting a long-term view of the way your world will look in the future if you are successful in carrying out your mission. This picture is produced in our mind by our imagination. As simple as that may sound, it turns out to be one of the most difficult things for people to accomplish in our society. When people are asked to describe a vision they have, almost all of them respond by describing plans of action or tasks they will accomplish. But if we return to our definition, we will clearly discover that *vision is a picture, not a task*.

VISION = PICTURE
VISION ≠ TASK

In the previous chapter we examined the concept of world needs as drawing forces that focus our efforts and attention. These provide the fertile soil for our vision. We now need to ask ourselves, "When I think about the needs within the world I identified, what kind of picture of a better place do I envision in my mind that includes me playing some part in bringing this vision to fruition?"

This requires us to put our creative imagination to work. Anyone can do this. Dewitt Jones (2006), a well-known photographer for the National Geographic, stated, "We all have great creative potential within us. To begin to connect with it, we first have to define it. Let me offer a definition: *creativity is the ability to see the ordinary as extraordinary.*" That's what we need to do to set before us a vision in our lives—*see the ordinary as extraordinary*. Jones also believes creativity is "*just falling in love with the world.*" He goes on to say,

> Think about it. First, when we're in love with something, it really is extraordinary. We see its uniqueness, feel its potential, celebrate its excellence, are open to its growth. Second, when we're in love with something we take care of it; we treat it with respect and compassion. Finally, when we're in love with something we find ourselves in touch with a source of incredible energy…we call it passion.

One of the best examples of this kind of passionate vision can be found in the "I Have a Dream" speech of Dr. Martin Luther King, Jr. Standing on the steps of the Lincoln Memorial in Washington, D.C., on August 28, 1963, Dr. King delivered one of the most memorable speeches in U.S. history. In the preceding chapter where we looked at needs of the world and the forces within these needs that draw us, we identified four—people, location, context, and problems. Dr. King was responding to all of these, including African Americans (people force), the United States and specifically the South (location), racial bigotry (contextual force), and equal rights (problem force). As his speech neared its end on that day in 1963, Dr. King wanted to paint a picture of his vision for responding to this world-drawing force. He painted that picture with words rather than outlining a plan or listing the tasks.

In one word picture Dr. King depicted descendants of former slaves and slave owners sitting at the same table. In another picture he dreamed of his own children living without being judged by their color. In still another picture, there were black children joining hands with white children and walking together. His last picture exploded with the vision of being free at last.

> You can find the full text, video and audio of this inspiring vision by logging onto the Web site: http://www.americanrhetoric.com/speeches/mlkihaveadream.htm

Dr. King went on to literally give his life to bring about this vision. It is important to note, however, he started with a vision. A Personal Mission that is not fueled by a vision will lack power and endurance.

How do visions such as this come about? A variety of approaches provide an answer to that question, but whatever the approach, these three ingredients will help them be true life-changing visions:

1. *Imagination*. When you think of the forces in the world that are drawing you, allow a process to take place in your mind of forming a conscious

idea or mental image of something you have never before wholly thought of in reality. Then try to place yourself in that future.

2. *Inspiration.* As the imagination process takes place, let the voices of your spirit, soul, and heart speak as loud as your mind and body. In other words, don't be too quick to rush toward plans and tasks. First, let the dream paint itself fully and completely.

3. *Independence.* As these inspiring dreams begin to emerge in your imagination, guide them toward your own images rather than those of others. Don't be bound by the past or the limits others have tried to place on you.

As we continue to paint life-changing visions into our Life Calling, we need to use three important brushstrokes. First, we need to paint with a senses-related brushstroke—what will the future we envision look like? Second, we need to paint with an emotions-related brushstroke—how will others and I feel in this future world? Finally, we need to paint with a relationships-related brushstroke—how will people relate to each other differently in this envisioned future?

Concepts Summary

When we begin to dream visions about the future, we will find that they emerge from the question, "What will I be like if the future I envision comes about?" But our dreams will also address the larger question, "What will the world be like if the future I envision comes about?" Some are daring enough to even ask what the universe will be like if the future they envision comes about. Few people are willing to dream at this level, but the ones who do are the people who bring about truly great changes. They are also the ones who steadfastly discover and pursue their Life Calling—no matter the cost.

Why is it so important to have a clear vision in our Life Calling? Every Life Calling takes a person along a path that will sooner or later encounter challenges. If we are to continue beyond the challenges, our vision must be greater than the challenges. If it is, we will conquer the challenges and move on. If it is not, we will turn back and follow a path that has no real purpose or calling.

◗ Insight

When you hear the word "vision", especially when it is associated with the Bible, you probably think of some phenomenon that foretells the future. When the Bible speaks of visions, however, more times than not these were pictures of how a life well-lived should look. In fact, prophets throughout the Bible story spent far more time proclaiming messages of reform and issuing calls to holy living than they did predicting the future. So it is within this context of vision that we can look to the scriptures for insight about the role of vision in our own lives.

SCRIPTURAL INSIGHT 1 ◗ *Your Life Calling Will Perish Without a Vision*

Where there is no vision, the people perish: but he that keepeth the law, happy is he. PROVERBS 29:18 KJV

In the last chapter we observed that the people, locations, opportunities and problems within the world to which we are drawn provide fertile soil for developing a picture of our Life Calling. When we respond to these circumstances, we need to picture a better place for these circumstances—a picture that includes us playing some part in creating this better place.

The adage found in Proverbs 29:18 readily points out the critical necessity for vision in our Life Calling. Once again, we first quoted it here from the classic King James Version. Let's take a look at the instant replay of this proverb, only this time let's read it from *The Message* paraphrase: "If people can't see what God is doing, they stumble all over themselves; but when they attend to what he reveals, they are most blessed."

This is precisely what happens in pursuing a Life Calling. If there is no vision that helps us imagine what God is doing in those circumstance to which we are drawn, we will end up stumbling all over ourselves, trying anything and everything, struggling in multiple careers, and finding little or no satisfaction or success.

We return once again to Hebrews 11:13-16 which we have visited several times in this book. Vision is really what was fueling their faith.

> All these people were still living by faith when they died. They did not receive the things promised; they only saw them and welcomed them from a distance, admitting that they were foreigners and strangers on earth. People who say such things show that they are looking for a country of their own. If they had been thinking of the country they had left, they would have had opportunity to return. Instead, they were longing for a better country—a heavenly one. Therefore God is not ashamed to be called their God, for he has prepared a city for them.

Here are the key words when it comes to vision: "They did not receive the things promised; they only *saw* them and welcomed them from a distance" (emphasis added). Throughout the Bible, visions were sent by God to prophets so that they might inspire people into righteous action: images, beasts, flying wheels with eyes, unclean animals in a sheet, four horsemen, plagues, and scarlet prostitutes on scarlet beasts. There is no shortage of imagery. The key to remember is that visions were always employed as a bridge from an undesired condition to hoped-for action. We may have an initial sympathetic response to people, locations, opportunities, or people in the world, but without a vision, it will likely go no further than feelings of sympathy.

> **PERSONAL REFLECTION** ⟩ What picture is God giving you right now as you look at your place in the world? What can help you learn better how to see pictures in your life that can lead to purpose?

SCRIPTURAL INSIGHT 2 ⟩ *Open Your Eyes*

And Elisha prayed, "O Lord, open his eyes so he may see. Then the Lord opened the servant's eyes, and he looked and saw the hills full of horses and chariots of fire all around Elisha. 2 KINGS 6:17

We have returned to a story told in 2 Kings 6 that we visited in Chapter 10, where the capital city of Israel had been surrounded by the invading armies of Syria. The servant of Elisha is terribly afraid and cries out to Elisha (verse 15): "Oh, my lord, what shall we do?"

Elisha gave a remarkable answer (verse 16): "Don't be afraid. Those who are with us are more than those who are with them." At this point, Elisha's servant must have figured that Elisha was either insane or really poor with numbers. But Elisha lifted up the request to God in our verse for today.

Don't you think the servant's hopes greatly increased at that point? I think so! The vision now inspired him to see victory where without it he had only seen defeat. That is the key role of visions in our Life Calling. They help us to see possibilities where we formerly saw only challenges. They help us see victory where without them we only see defeat.

Let's go back to the story in 2 Kings 6. The victory was spectacular as well, with the enemy smitten with blindness; Elisha then led them into a trap; the king of Israel wanted to kill the enemy; Elisha instead gave them a feast and sent them home! Crazy? But the raids against Israel ended. Why could Elisha do this? He saw a vision. There is a song that asks God to open our eyes because we want to see Jesus, even to reach out and touch him.

The song points out a problem in the Christian walk. We have never seen Jesus or God. The entire relationship exists outside of the reach of our physical senses. That's where vision can come into play. Visions take place in our thoughts and spirits rather than the retinas at the back of our eyeballs. In *Explorer's Guide* we learned that in our lives the dream must be greater than the challenges we face. Our Life Calling will be filled with many challenges, and in many cases what we want to accomplish will be something we have never seen in our lives. Our only hope at such times will be that same prayer Elisha offered: "*O Lord, open my eyes so I may see.*"

> **PERSONAL REFLECTION** ⟩ What is keeping your eyes closed right now and preventing you from seeing a vision for your life? What can help you open your spiritual eyes and see God's vision for you?

INSIGHT

SCRIPTURAL INSIGHT 3 ▶ *Be Sure to Look at Everything*

"Don't you have a saying, 'It's still four months until harvest'? I tell you, open your eyes and look at the fields! They are ripe for harvest." JOHN 4:35

Not all visions were science fiction thrillers! John 4:1-42 recounts the familiar story of Jesus and his disciples stopping in Sychar, a town in the middle of Samaria, a region Jews avoided. Jesus and his disciples had not eaten for quite some time on the journey, so the disciples went on into town to get some food. Jesus did not go with them; instead he sat down beside what was known as Jacob's Well. While he sat there, a Samaritan woman came to draw water from the well and entered into the well-known discourse that ultimately led her to believe that Jesus was the Messiah. Jesus was energized by this spiritual dialogue, but when the disciples returned, they were far more concerned about basic needs. Listen to the interchange between Jesus and the disciples in verses 31-34:

> Meanwhile his disciples urged him, "Rabbi, eat something."
> But he said to them, "I have food to eat that you know nothing about."
> Then his disciples said to each other, "Could someone have brought him food?"
> "My food," said Jesus, "is to do the will of him who sent me and to finish his work."

Jesus was trying to paint a picture for his disciples that would inspire them to see something greater than just meeting their own physical needs. He is setting a vision for them. He continues on with this in verses 35 through 38:

> "Don't you have a saying, 'It's still four months until harvest'? I tell you, open your eyes and look at the fields! They are ripe for harvest. Even now those who reap draw their wages, even now they harvest the crop for eternal life, so that the sower and the reaper may be glad together. Thus the saying 'One sows and another reaps' is true. I sent you to reap what you have not worked for. Others have done the hard work, and you have reaped the benefits of their labor."

The problem that the disciples had was they were bound by what they saw with their ordinary eyes. When Jesus called on them to open their eyes and look at the fields, he was challenging them to look with a different type of vision—spiritual vision. If we are going to find our Life Calling, we will need to open our spiritual eyes and see the vision of God at work.

> **PERSONAL REFLECTION** ▶ Do your physical eyes keep you from seeing what is visible only with your spiritual eyes? How can you change this?

SCRIPTURAL INSIGHT 4 ▶ *Look Forward to a New Heaven and a New Earth*

But in keeping with his promise we are looking forward to a new heaven and a new earth, where righteousness dwells. 2 PETER 3:13

INSIGHT

Peter, one of Jesus' disciples, would use a similar approach to help inspire people to be ready for Jesus' second coming (2 Peter 3:10-14):

> But the day of the Lord will come like a thief. The heavens will disappear with a roar; the elements will be destroyed by fire, and the earth and everything done in it will be laid bare.
>
> Since everything will be destroyed in this way, what kind of people ought you to be? You ought to live holy and godly lives as you look forward to the day of God and speed its coming. That day will bring about the destruction of the heavens by fire, and the elements will melt in the heat. But in keeping with his promise we are looking forward to a new heaven and a new earth, where righteousness dwells.
>
> So then, dear friends, since you are looking forward to this, make every effort to be found spotless, blameless and at peace with him.

The vision is quite vivid—thief in the night; heavens disappearing with a roar; elements destroyed by fire; earth laid bare. Not too appealing, but wait! There is an alternative—a new heaven and a new earth! But there is one little catch. This is the home of righteousness. The solution? Make every effort to be found spotless, blameless and at peace with Jesus!

Peter was drawn to help people turn from failure to victorious living, and to help do this, he very effectively utilized a vision to inspire people to take action to live holy lives. Without the vision, they would have had a harder time deciding to take the action. This same concept holds true for us as we discover our Life Calling. If we don't have a vision, we will have a hard time making a decision to take action that can lead us to carry out our Life Calling. The more vivid the visions we paint as we begin to uncover our Life Calling, the more powerful will be the inspiration to compel us toward our calling.

PERSONAL REFLECTION > What kind of vision of a new heaven and a new earth do you see that can help you attain your Life Calling? Is your vision inspiring you to live a life that is spotless, blameless and at peace with God?

SCRIPTURAL INSIGHT 5 > *Lift Up Your Eyes*

Lift up your eyes and look about you: All assemble and come to you; your sons come from afar, and your daughters are carried on the hip. ISAIAH 60:4

Isaiah served as a prophet to the Jews as their nation declined. In fact Israel had split into two nations—Israel and Judah. The nation of Israel went downhill quickly and was conquered by its enemies. Judah had a little more spiritual strength, but it too was headed downward morally and physically toward captivity. It was during this period that Isaiah prophesied. Many of his messages warned of the dire results that would befall the people of Judah if they did not change their ways. In chapter 60, however, God realized that the people needed a vision of what the future held for them when they finally returned to him. He gave Isaiah a vision of hope to share with the people of Judah. It was in this spirit that Isaiah said in verse 4, "Lift up your eyes and look about you." Listen to his words shared in the three verses that preceded verse 4:

> Arise, shine, for your light has come, and the glory of the Lord rises upon you. See, darkness covers the earth and thick darkness is over the peoples, but the LORD rises upon you and his glory appears over you. Nations will come to your light, and kings to the brightness of your dawn.

What elements of this vision make it a source of hope and encouragement—even in a time of despair and discouragement? First, it calls for action. "Arise, shine, for your light has come." A good question we should ask ourselves as we consider our Life Calling is whether or not the light of God has come to our lives. Second, the vision gives the promise of something better ahead. "Nations will come to your light, and kings to the brightness of your dawn." We need to have a promise in our lives of something better coming ahead.

Just making up our own vision and giving ourselves false hope will do us no good. The hope of something better coming in the future needs to rest on God's promises. Once again, we are taken back to the Foundational Values we discussed at the beginning of our look at the Life Calling Model. Our faith is built around our assumptions about God and belief in his promises. These can become the fertile soil from which the seeds of vision can sprout and give us hope. These can become the dreams that will be greater than the challenges that we will face as we pursue our Life Calling. The first verse we looked at in this chapter said that without a vision, the people perish. At the end of this chapter, we can look at the positive side of this concept—a vision will help us flourish in our pursuit of a Life Calling.

> **PERSONAL REFLECTION** ⟩ Do you have a vision in your life that can help you flourish in the pursuit of your Life Calling? What is keeping you from seeing a clear vision? What do you need to do to help you lift up your eyes rather than look downward?

INSIGHT

Discovery

How can the Discovery Guides help you see a *vision* for your life?

T THEORY	One of the criticisms of higher education is that formation of a personal vision is seldom a part of the formal curriculum of colleges and universities. Fortunately a number of books have been written on the subject, so you can pursue it in your own personal reading. Start creating a list of books that will aid your exploration. Ask others for recommendations.
E EXAMPLES	The example of other visionary people may be one of your best sources for learning how to see a vision in your own life. Find such people and make time to talk to them. Keep in mind, however, that these people may not be in the limelight of your institution.
A ASSESSMENT	Formal assessments do not really play a major role in helping you to form a vision for your life.
C COUNSEL	People speaking into your life can be powerful sources of guidance in the formation of vision. Finding someone who can serve as a mentor to you during your college years can make a great difference in your vision. Additionally, family members, teachers, pastors, student development and residence life personnel, and friends know you well and can give you valuable insights about what they see in your life.
H HISTORY	The classics and historical biographies are full of stories dealing with people who have great visions and who have followed these visions in their lives. Select some of these and learn from their experiences.
E EXPERIENCE	Start recording in some manner the pictures you are beginning to see when you start to consider the various needs of the world that have some draw on your life.
R REFLECTION	Take time to reflect on what you have learned in the other six activities of discovery about your vision. Is a vision starting to emerge that has the capacity to compel you forward in your life?

DISCOVERY

▶ Story

The *Nautilus* had crossed the Great Plains of America, and now the plains began to rise a little as they crossed into Colorado. When they reached the town of Limon, they turned onto US 24 and headed for Colorado Springs. The explorers were somewhat surprised as they pulled into the city. The name *Colorado* had evoked images of the Rocky Mountains, snowcapped peaks, and evergreen trees. What the explorers had not realized is that the eastern third of the state is a part of the American Prairie with plenty of grasslands, but few trees. Colorado Springs sits right at the border of this geographic change, and although it is adjacent to the Rockies, it is definitely a prairie town—unlike its ski resort cousins Aspen and Vail, which lay a little further to the west.

It was late in the evening as Ken finally reached the western side of Colorado Springs and settled the *Nautilus* into an RV site in the Garden of the Gods Campground. The travelers spent the next day exploring the Garden of the Gods, marveling at the strange and fascinating collection of colorful geologic forms and shapes. It was the following day, however, that everyone was looking forward to—they were planning on going to the top of Pikes Peak.

Pikes Peak dominates the scenery of Colorado Springs, looming over the High Plains of eastern Colorado. It is the most visited mountain in North America and the second most visited mountain in the world besides Mount Fuji in Japan. It is possible to drive to the top of this 14,110-foot mountain on a gravel road. In fact, this is the route that the race cars of the renowned Pikes Peak Auto Hill Climb follow. A 42-foot motorhome, on the other hand, is not designed for this curvy road, so the explorers decided on a different form of transportation to the top—the famed Pikes Peak Cog Railway.

The explorers boarded the train at the Manitou Spring Depot and began their journey upward. As the train traveled alongside a stream through the evergreen trees, Justin observed, "This is what I always thought Colorado would look like, not like the grassy hills to the east." The others agreed.

Further along the climb up the mountain began in earnest. After passing through bristlecone pine trees, some of the oldest living trees on earth, the train broke out above the timberline, where all trees stop growing. They finally reached the top.

"What an amazing view!" Abriella exclaimed. "You can see forever and ever."

"I know," Diana agreed. "Look at how tiny Colorado Springs looks down there, and look at how far those plains stretch out. I bet you can see clear into Kansas."

"Fabulous," Ryan added.

"Remember what I told you back in Seahaven?" Adam asked. "This is where the song 'America the

Beautiful' got its inspiration. I think there's a monument dedicated to it up here somewhere."

They searched for a few minutes and soon found a bronze plaque commemorating the 100th anniversary of the writing of the song's lyrics. They read together the first two verses that were engraved on the plaque:

> O beautiful for spacious skies,
> For amber waves of grain,
> For purple mountain majesties
> Above the fruited plain!
> America! America!
> God shed his grace on thee
> And crown thy good with brotherhood
> From sea to shining sea!
>
> O beautiful for pilgrim feet
> Whose stern impassioned stress.
> A thoroughfare of freedom beat
> Across the wilderness!
> America! America!
> God mend thine every flaw,
> Confirm thy soul in self-control,
> Thy liberty in law!

"Katherine Lee Bates painted a fabulous picture with these words," Adam said in awe. "It's like a vision of America. When you look out in all directions up here, it's easy to see how she was inspired to write this verse."

"You certainly can see the spacious skies." Justin pointed to the vast expanse above them.

"And those would be the amber waves of grain." Abriella pointed to the east. "The purple mountain majesties are all around us," Lorena announced as she pointed to the Sangre de Cristo Range, stretching across the southern vista and the Collegiate section of the Rockies on the western horizon.

"What about the fruited plain?" Diana asked. "I don't see much fruit down there."

"I guess that is where the vision kicks in," Adam replied, grinning at her. "You have to use your imagination."

"Wouldn't it be great if we had a mountain like this we could stand on and get a vision of what to do in our lives?" Abriella reflected.

"In a way, we do," Adam commented. "Remember back at Lincoln's Home and in St. Louis how we were talking about circumstances in the world that draw us, and we connect to?"

"Yes, I remember," Abriella answered.

"Well, what if we would just paint a picture in our minds of how it would be if things were better in all those circumstances?" Adam continued. "And if we want to be in this vision, we need to paint ourselves into the picture as playing some part in bringing this vision to reality."

"That's really cool, Adam!" Abriella exclaimed. "I've never thought about it that way. I need a picture like that in my mind to help me keep going when everything seems like it's too much for me."

"I heard it said once that the dream must be greater than the challenge," Adam replied.

"That makes sense," Abriella said.

"Hey, take a look out there to the north," Ryan said, breaking into their philosophical discussion. "Check out those skyscrapers in the distance. I'll bet that's Denver." The others all looked in the direction he was pointing and agreed.

"Oh no! Look at the time," Lorena said. "We'd better get back to the train. Remember, they said we were only allowed 40 minutes up here because most people begin to feel the effects of their quick change in altitude."

"To be honest, I actually have a slight headache," Diana said. "I guess I've been up here long enough. But then again, when I try to have a vision about my life, I get a headache too."

The others laughed. They headed back to the train to begin their descent down the mountain.

STORY

▶ Exercises

Creative Visions

An inspired vision is really a creative dream in response to drawing forces of the world. Earlier in the Classroom section we referred to the well-known photographer Dewitt Jones (2006). Here are four suggestions Jones gives from his experience with photography that he believes can help us create visions that can be applied to all challenges in life:

1. View the situation or the challenge from the right perspective.
2. Within that right perspective, identify the elements that are most critical.
3. Approach the situation or challenge with the understanding that there is more than one right answer.
4. Don't be afraid of making a mistake.

In Exercise 2, you will have the opportunity to engage in creative dreaming about some major aspects of your life. In Exercise 1, let's practice creative dreaming by looking at something smaller and closer to your present situation. Select a class you are currently taking or scheduled to take that could be described as one in which you really want to do well.

▶ Activity 1

1. Picture in your mind what you see as a successful outcome to this class.

2. Now to try to picture at least two other outcomes of this class that would also be acceptable to you. In other words, look at some different perspectives.

3. Which is the most desirable perspective? Which is the most realistic perspective? (They may be the same or different.)

▶ Activity 2

Based on the perspective you have chosen in picturing the successful outcome for this class, describe the following elements:

1. What would your grade be?

2. What would you feel like?

3. What would you know and understand?

4. What would your relationship be to the instructor and the other students?

5. Which of these elements do you believe are the most critical in this situation?

▶ Activity 3

It is important to approach the situation or challenge with the understanding that there is more than one right answer. In succeeding in this class, how can you apply this principle to the class you are assessing?

▶ Activity 4

Creative solutions to success in a class are often stifled by the fear of making a mistake.

1. What is your greatest fear about this class?

2. What other things could you do to in this class to succeed if the thing you feared actually did occur?

3. In the larger picture of your life, how important is success in this class?

4. What proactive actions could you take to keep the thing you fear from occurring in the first place?

Daydreaming

Paint a series of pictures in your life by answering the following question: if you could change any of the following for the better, even if it was just for this one day, what would it look like? What part would you play in bringing about the change? Use the lessons learned in Exercise 1 to help you envision these changes.

Your personal life

Your family life

Your church

Your school

Your community

Your nation

Your world

Your universe

How do these dreams relate to your Life Calling?

▶ References

The following resources have been used in this chapter.

Jones, D. (2006). "Seeing the ordinary as extraordinary: Techniques for unlocking your creative potential." Retrieved October 19, 2006, from http://www.dewittjones.com/html/seeing_the_ordinary.shtml

The following resources may be useful as you explore the role of *vision* in continuing your exploration of Personal Leadership and Life Calling.

Millard, B. (2012). *LifeQuest: Planning Your Life Strategically, 2nd ed.* Marion, IN: Life Discovery ePubs.

Schwen, M.R., and Bass, D.C., Eds. (2006). *Leading Lives That Matter: What We Should Do and Who We Should Be*. Grand Rapids, Michigan: Erdmans Publishing Co.

Putting It into Action

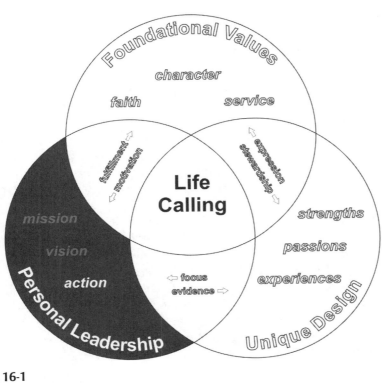

16

FIGURE 16-1
Life Calling Model Focusing on Action

The third main component of the Life Calling Model is *Personal Leadership*. We identified three important stages that must be addressed if we hope to be successful in carrying out effective Personal Leadership in our lives: *mission, vision*, and *action*. In this chapter we will explore ***action***, the third stage of developing Personal Leadership.

CHAPTER OBJECTIVES

1. Understand the role of action in forming a personal mission to carry out one's Life Calling
2. Explain how strategy leads to action
3. Identify the important components of a good strategy
4. Begin developing your own action plan

> ### KEY TERMS
>
> **Action** = something done or performed
> **Direction** = a line of thought or action or a tendency or inclination leading from one point of reference to another
> **Goal** = purpose toward which an endeavor is directed
> **Strategy** = a plan, method, or series of actions for obtaining a specific goal or result

▶ Concepts

As you think about the dream you have for the college experience ahead of you, what will keep you right now from achieving that dream? Or the dream for your life beyond college? The quote from Confucius at the beginning of this chapter exhorts us that any kind of long journey begins by taking a first step. But if we look at that concept in reverse, we will find another important concept. One of the most common barriers that keeps us from realizing our dreams is fear of taking the first step. How can you change that in your life?

As we bring our study of the Life Calling model to a close by looking at the final component of *Personal Mission*, we now consider the final factor that defines this mission—*action*. The reality is that we are little more than statues until we put our Life Calling into action. This really goes back to the concept of life congruence that we discussed in Chapter 3. When our Life Calling begins to unfold as we study all the other elements of the model, if we want congruence in our lives, we need to take actions consistent with what we have discovered. If we sense a drawing force to certain needs in the world yet do not respond to that draw, then no Personal Mission has taken place that follows a Life Calling. If we paint the most vivid picture in our minds of a noble future, yet we do not allow that vision to inspire our actions, then we had nothing more than a daydream and again no Personal Mission takes place that follows a Life Calling.

So how do we accomplish this? How do we take a vision and turn it into a reality in our lives? This is the point where many people fail to realize their Life Calling because they don't know how to put it into action. Four steps can help us cross the bridge from vision to action and avoid joining that group of people who never realize their Life Calling.

Step 1: Establish *directions* for your life based on your vision. These directions will be general at this point in the journey from vision to action. They are like the direction "East." Have you ever noticed that there is no "East Pole" on the earth? When you travel north, you finally arrive at the North Pole. The same is true when you travel south. But when you travel east, you never get to a precise spot that identifies "East." This is the kind of direction you will set at this time—you may not be able to define a spot that tells you if or when you got there, but you can certainly tell if you are headed in the right direction. Here is an example related to work: *I will work in the field of (and* *you could fill in this field based on your vision) even though I have not decided about a specific career or job in this field.* Setting that direction gets you pointed toward the right path in carrying out this aspect of your Life Calling.

Step 2: Set *goals* for your journey as you travel in the direction you have established in Step 1. Now you begin to apply more detail to your plan of action. If these goals are going to be effective, we need to make sure they have certain qualities—these qualities are often identified by the acronym SMART.

Specific. Your goals should set definite targets you wish to reach. They should be stated as simply, concisely, and explicitly as possible. Let's look at an example. When completing Step 1, let's say you had identified the educational field as a direction for your Life Calling. A specific goal could be to explore the career of teaching elementary school by working as a classroom assistant.

Measurable. Your goals should be put together in a manner that allows you to determine if and when you accomplish them. In the example we are following, the measurement would be whether or not we had actually worked as a classroom assistant.

Achievable. Your goals should identify an outcome that is realistic in relationship to who you are and the resources you have available. This is a critical point in which you need to integrate your Unique Design into your Personal Mission. In our example of working as a classroom assistant, you would want to ask the question of whether or not you have the time and skill set to do this. At the same time you need to make sure there is a certain level of challenge in the goal, otherwise it will not keep you moving forward in your Personal Mission.

Relevant. Your goals should relate to and support the vision you have painted in response to the world-drawing forces. In other words, your goals should help you turn your vision into a reality. In our example, the goal we set to serve as a classroom assistant is relevant to our desire to explore becoming an elementary teacher. To help clarify this, we should look at a goal that would not be relevant. For example, if we had set a goal for ourselves to work six months as a junior accountant, that would not be relevant to exploring the educational field.

Timed. Your goals need to be set within a realistic time frame. Deadlines need to be set to provide accountability. Failure to do this is the death knell for many a vision and Personal Mission. In our example we could state our goal to explore the career of teaching elementary school by working as a classroom assistant during the following month. This provides the urgency necessary to take action based on the goal and allows us the criteria for evaluating whether or not we took action.

Step 3: Develop a *strategy* that outlines specific steps you will need to take to accomplish your goals. Let's continue to follow the example of working as a classroom assistant. Your strategy could include the following steps: determining what hours you have available to do this work, identifying an elementary teacher you know who might be willing to allow you to work as an assistant, and finally, contacting the teacher. The important thing to remember about a strategy is that it is a plan of action intended to help you accomplish a specific goal. If this is to occur, the steps you identify in your action plan must be performance based. In other words, they need to be precise steps you will take.

Step 4:   Take the *actions* you outlined in your strategy. Remember what we said at the beginning of this chapter? We really are nothing more than statues until we put our Life Calling into action. Here is where that action starts. Up until now we have been learning, reflecting, analyzing, assessing, and planning. Now we begin to actually act on our plans. Using our example, we call the teacher we know and we let her know that we have a desire to work as a classroom assistant. This will help us explore elementary teaching as a career choice. We ask her if she would be willing to let us work with her next month. If she answers "yes," then we can begin expanding our strategy to outline how we will make this happen. If she says no, we can adjust our strategy to look for another teacher. At this point it is important to keep the process moving. We should not allow ourselves to become immobilized because we run into roadblocks. Our mind-set at this point should be to look for solutions, not excuses.

Concepts Summary

Why do we outline so much detail when looking at the *action* factor of our Personal Mission? If our Life Calling is ever going to materialize into Personal Mission, it will ultimately happen through action. As obvious as that seems, it is hard for many of us to implement this in our lives. In the middle of the last century, there was a popular song about the future based on the Spanish phrase "que será será." The English translation of these words is "whatever will be, will be."

Many of us operate our lives with that same attitude. The future is something we can't see, and so we just move ahead with a fatalistic mind-set that whatever will happen, will happen. This really takes us full circle back to Chapter 2, where we looked at our Foundational Values and, more specifically, at our faith. We defined this as the value we hold about reality. If we believe that the universe is a closed system with all aspects, including its history, predetermined before any event ever takes place, then we should join in singing "que será, será." On the other hand, if we believe that the universe is an open and dynamic system where history is made, not imposed, then we will want to create visions and take actions that can make our history a productive one.

Insight

In his letter to the early Christians, the Apostle James consistently exhorts that any life of faith needs to be accompanied by a life of action. If you have a purpose for your life and do nothing to accomplish it, then it is worthless. Our Life Calling will only experience fulfillment when we actually live it out. Scriptural insights can help us understand the need for this and the process that can make it possible.

SCRIPTURAL INSIGHT 1 ▶ *Move in the Right Direction*

So after they had fasted and prayed, they placed their hands on them and sent them off. ACTS 13:3

When our Life Calling begins to unfold as we study all the other elements of the model, we need to take actions consistent with what we have discovered. If we sense a draw to circumstances in the world yet do not respond to that draw, then no Personal Mission has taken place that follows a Life Calling. If we have a vision yet we do not allow that vision to inspire our actions, then again, no Personal Mission takes place that follows a Life Calling.

There are four steps that can help us cross the bridge from vision to action: directions, goals, strategy and action. Let's follow the life and ministry of the Apostle Paul as an example of how this occurs. In this Scriptural Insight, let's look at *directions*.

Acts 13:1-3 describes the start of Paul's first missionary journey on which Barnabas accompanied him.

> Now in the church at Antioch there were prophets and teachers: Barnabas, Simeon called Niger, Lucius of Cyrene, Manaen (who had been brought up with Herod the tetrarch) and Saul. While they were worshiping the Lord and fasting, the Holy Spirit said, "Set apart for me Barnabas and Saul for the work to which I have called them." So after they had fasted and prayed, they placed their hands on them and sent them off.

There was no route given and no timetable set. These were general *directions* at best. But they were enough to get the journey started. There is no doubt the other three steps were addressed by Paul and Barnabas. The story does not include that description. However, the story does let us know that the journey was a success.

Many times we don't move forward in pursuing our Life Calling until we think we know every step of the way and what the outcome of the journey will be. The problem is that many times we do not know these until we start the journey. There is an old saying that it is easier to steer a moving car. Like Paul and Barnabas who were commissioned and set off and then discovered their journey as they traveled, we need to commission our Life Calling, set off on the journey and discover where it takes us as we travel.

PERSONAL REFLECTION ▷ What are you waiting on that's keeping you from pursuing your Life Calling? What action could you take right now to start you on your journey?

INSIGHT

INSIGHT

Some time later Paul said to Barnabas, "Let us go back and visit the brothers in all the towns where we preached the word of the Lord and see how they are doing." ACTS 15:36

In this Scriptural Insight, we'll look at the second step that can help us cross the bridge from vision to action: *goals*. We move ahead in the story of Paul to the next chapter, Acts 15, and pick up the next part of his story. Our verse for this devotion shows that Paul wants to make plans.

Paul is proposing a second missionary journey. This time the description of the plan includes a little more detail. The goal is to visit all the towns where they had preached on the first missionary journey. In the end, Barnabas did not accompany Paul on the second journey. (Paul and Barnabas had a fight, but that is another story.) Barnabas was replaced by Silas.

We see the goal to visit all the previously visited towns played out in an interesting incident recorded in Acts 16. Paul had been to the province of Asia on the first journey and had a specific goal and timeline to revisit this area. This is where we pick up the story in verse 6 through 9:

> Paul and his companions traveled throughout the region of Phrygia and Galatia, having been kept by the Holy Spirit from preaching the word in the province of Asia. When they came to the border of Mysia, they tried to enter Bithynia, but the Spirit of Jesus would not allow them to. So they passed by Mysia and went down to Troas. During the night Paul had a vision of a man of Macedonia standing and begging him, "Come over to Macedonia and help us."

Sometimes our goals have to be changed and new ones established based on new information received. Paul quite clearly tried to achieve his original goal, but could not. So he set a new goal—go to Macedonia. This turned out to be a very valuable change of goals, because it was in the Macedonian region that Paul first visited Philippi where some of his greatest messages were given.

In James 4:15, counsel is given concerning goals: "You ought to say, "If it is the Lord's will, we will live and do this or that." This does not mean that goals, especially specific ones, are bad things. What James advises is that we keep our goals in the proper perspective of God's will, knowing that what we thought originally was God's will might change as it becomes clearer to us through our life journey.

> **PERSONAL REFLECTION** What would help you see the goals in your life that are part of God's will? Which of those goals do you see for your Life Calling during this next year?

For I resolved to know nothing while I was with you except Jesus Christ and him crucified.
1 CORINTHIANS 2:2

In this Scriptural Insight, we'll look at the third step that can help us cross the bridge from vision to action: *strategy*. During the second missionary journey, Paul visited Athens, a city wrapped up in its self-admiration and filled with people impressed by their own wisdom. Paul developed a strategy to get their attention. We see this played out in Acts 17:22&23.

Paul then stood up in the meeting of the Areopagus and said: "People of Athens! I see that in every way you are very religious. For as I walked around and looked carefully at your objects of worship, I even found an altar with this inscription: TO AN UNKNOWN GOD. So you are ignorant of the very thing you worship—and this is what I am going to proclaim to you.

Paul challenged the Athenians to consider the Christian God as that "Unknown God." The Athenians, who loved to conjecture, debate and speculate, wanted to hold more discussions on the matter. In the end, however, verse 34 indicates that only "a few people became followers of Paul and believed."

Paul went from Athens to the equally self-absorbed city of Corinth. When we read 1 Corinthians 2:1-5, however, we can see that he quite intentionally revised his strategy.

When I came to you, brothers, I did not come with eloquence or human wisdom as I proclaimed to you the testimony about God. For I resolved to know nothing while I was with you except Jesus Christ and him crucified. I came to you in weakness with great fear and trembling. My message and my preaching were not with wise and persuasive words, but with a demonstration of the Spirit's power, so that your faith might not rest on human wisdom, but on God's power.

Just because Paul saw the need to change his strategy does not mean that strategy is a bad thing. Jesus made that clear in Luke 14:28-32:

"Suppose one of you wants to build a tower. Won't you first sit down and estimate the cost to see if you have enough money to complete it? For if you lay the foundation and are not able to finish it, everyone who sees it will ridicule you, saying, 'This person began to build and was not able to finish.'"

"Or suppose a king is about to go to war against another king. Won't he first sit down and consider whether he is able with ten thousand men to oppose the one coming against him with twenty thousand? If he is not able, he will send a delegation while the other is still a long way off and will ask for terms of peace."

The lesson that we can learn from Paul's approach in Athens and then in Corinth is that strategy should never become a rigid track that holds us to a line even when it does not work. If we go back to the passage in 1 Corinthians, we will not see strategy discarded. Instead, we will clearly see a new strategy developed. This is quite typical of what will happen to each of us as we discover and pursue our Life Calling. It will evolve and plans will change as we learn new lessons.

> **PERSONAL REFLECTION** ⟩ What is your strategy for hearing from God concerning your Life Calling? How has that strategy changed throughout your life or as you have read this book?

SCRIPTURAL INSIGHT 4 ▶ *You Are Called to Action*

After Paul had seen the vision, we got ready at once to leave for Macedonia, concluding that God had called us to preach the gospel to them. ACTS 16:10

In this Scriptural Insight, we'll look at the third step that can help us cross the bridge from vision to action. That third, and last, step *is* action. Let's return to Acts 16 where Paul was forced to develop new goals and strategies based on the vision of that man in Macedonia begging him to "Come over to Macedonia and help us." The next verse in that story says, "After Paul had seen the vision, we got ready at once to leave for Macedonia, concluding that God had called us to preach the gospel to them." Once the goal was revised and the new strategy clear, action was taken.

We quoted James 2:17 at the beginning of this chapter where the Apostle James tells us, "Faith by itself, if it is not accompanied by action, is dead." We could return to Jesus' analogy of a wise man building his house on rock and the foolish man building his on sand. The rock scenario represented Jesus' words being put into action. The sand represented no action being taken. We could also return to the parable of the talents in Matthew 25:26&27. The master rebuked the servant who did not take action.

> His master replied, "You wicked, lazy servant! So you knew that I harvest where I have not sown and gather where I have not scattered seed? Well then, you should have put my money on deposit with the bankers, so that when I returned I would have received it back with interest.

The Bible is not a purely philosophical discourse, though there is plenty of good philosophy in the Bible. To the contrary, the Bible is a call to action! Our Life Calling will be tested by our action.

This call to action starts early. Proverbs 20:11 says, "Even small children are known by their actions, so is their conduct really pure and upright?" In a real sense, this takes us back to the Foundational Values at the beginning of the Life Calling Model and specifically to the element of "character." What we believe should be carried out in consistent actions that match our beliefs. Character is faith carried out in action.

If we are to discover our Life Calling, it will ultimately be found in action. We may have to redirect our actions or change courses as we learn more about our Life Calling, but eventually we need to get moving—to take action.

> **PERSONAL REFLECTION** > How are all other elements of the Life Calling Model being carried out in the actions of your life? What keeps you from moving forward in action?

SCRIPTURAL INSIGHT 5 > *Fight the Good Fight*

I have fought the good fight, I have finished the race, I have kept the faith. 2 TIMOTHY 4:7

Throughout our lives we will continue to explore our Life Calling and discover new aspects. When we do this, the more we will move forward in action, and the greater our discoveries will be about our Life Calling. This really is where Life Calling begins to become a reality and we sense fulfillment.

As Paul's life neared an end, he was able to look back at the same time he was looking forward, and his view in both directions was satisfying to him. He reflected on this in a letter to Timothy (2 Timothy 4:6-8).

> For I am already being poured out like a drink offering, and the time for my departure is near. I have fought the good fight, I have finished the race, I have kept the faith. Now there is in store for me the crown of righteousness, which the Lord, the righteous Judge, will award to me on that day— and not only to me, but also to all who have longed for his appearing.

Years of observing and conversing with thousands of people have revealed that there is a universal need experienced by all humans for a sense of meaning, significance and hope in their lives. Even in situations that seem like there could not be possibility for these, the desire still remains. In his classic book *Man's Search for Meaning*, Viktor Frankl shares his experiences as a prisoner in a Nazi concentration camp and what he did to find a reason to live. You might think that in such a situation, one would give up such a search. But that universal need still remained and was a driving force in Frankl's experience. The experience of Corrie ten Boom, another holocaust concentration camp survivor, reveals the same thing.

As an overriding purpose for our lives begins to develop, a sense of meaning develops from those Foundational Values we form. A sense of significance emerges out of the discovery of our unique design. But it is in this final component of the Life Calling Model where we begin to develop a personal mission and where a sense of hope arises. We see that there is something to do with our lives. We see, like Paul, that we can fight the good fight, we can run the right race, and we can keep the faith. Also, like Paul, we can look forward and see that our Life Calling does not end when this life ends. We see ahead the crown of righteousness that we will receive on the day of Jesus' appearing—the day on which we enter the next phase of our Life Calling and our Personal Mission!

> **PERSONAL REFLECTION** ⟩ Do you have a sense of meaning, significance and hope in your life? If not, what is keeping your from having that sense? Are you looking forward toward the day of Jesus' appearing when the next phase or your Life Calling begins?

INSIGHT

Discovery

How can the Discovery Guides help you start putting your Life Calling into *action*?

T **THEORY**	If you can find a class at your institution that studies the theory of strategic planning and action, enroll in it. This will help you no matter what field you pursue in your studies and in life. You will likely not be able to take such a class until your junior or senior year. Ask your advisor to help you find such a class. In the meantime, a number of books have been written on the subject, so you can pursue the study of strategic action in your own personal reading. Start creating a list of books that will aid your exploration. Ask others for recommendations.
E **EXAMPLES**	The examples of other people who have pursued their lives in a strategic manner can be one of your best sources for learning how to take action in your own life. Find such people and make time to talk to them.
A **ASSESSMENT**	Formal assessments do not really play a major role in helping you develop strategic action. However, well-developed processes can help lead you through such planning and take you to a point of action.
C **COUNSEL**	People speaking into your life can be powerful sources that can exhort you into action. Finding someone who can serve as mentor to you during your college years can make a great difference in developing a strategy and putting it into action. Additionally, family members, teachers, pastors, student development and residence life personnel, and friends know you well and can give you valuable insights about taking action in your life.
H **HISTORY**	The classics and historical biographies are full of stories dealing with people who have developed strategies for their lives and who have then taken action to live out these strategies. Select some of these and learn from their experience.
E **EXPERIENCE**	Start developing a plan for your next semester. This will help you learn how to strategize.
R **REFLECTION**	Take time to reflect on what you have learned in the other six activities of discovery about strategic action. Is a plan of action starting to emerge that has the capacity to guide you in the next few months of your life?

▶ Story

The *Nautilus* headed north out of Colorado Springs on Interstate 25 the next day. An hour later, the travelers passed right by the skyscrapers of Denver they had seen from the top of Pikes Peak the day before.

"The buildings of the capitol seem a lot bigger down here," Justin laughed. The others agreed.

The trip continued north along the eastern edge of the Rocky Mountains and on to Cheyenne, the capitol of Wyoming. From there they traveled to Casper and then headed in a more northwestern direction along the Wind River and on to Thermopolis.

"So what makes this such a hot town?" Ryan asked. The others all looked at him quizzically. "That's what the name of the town means," Ryan explained. "Hot city."

"I didn't know your vocabulary was that big," Lorena said in her usual sarcastic tone reserved for Ryan.

"Well, Ryan, there's your answer," Adam said, pointing to a sign up ahead.

"Home of the World's Largest Mineral Hot Springs," the sign revealed.

Leaving Thermopolis, they headed west for Yellowstone National Park. Entering the park through the East Gate, Ken Neimon headed for the Fishing Bridge RV Park … but at a crawl.

"Whoa!" Ryan exclaimed. "The traffic here is as bad as California! Right, Captain Nemo?" Ken Neimon agreed.

However, just when they thought the pace could not get worse, it stopped completely. Then they saw the reason—a large brown bear on the road. "What does that hump on its shoulders mean?" Diana asked.

"It means that we're dealing with a grizzly bear," Lorena answered. "Batten down the hatches and hope for the best." The explorers all watched intently out of the *Nautilus's* windows.

"Check out that crazy lady!" Justin pointed to a woman who had jumped from her car and was chasing after the bear with a camera, trying to get a close-up picture. "Let's watch and see if the bear eats her."

"Justin, that's terrible!" Diana scolded.

Any hopes for a bear-versus-woman conflict, though, were dashed as the bear ran off into the nearby woods. Justin's "crazy lady" stood by the side of the road with a disappointed look on her face. The traffic began moving again. It was not too long until the *Nautilus* was neatly berthed into a campsite in the RV park.

The next two days were filled with hot springs, geysers, moose, buffalo, trees, lakes, waterfalls, and wonder. It all culminated with the explorers standing in a circle along with hundreds of other people waiting for Old Faithful to erupt.

"It is not the largest or even the most regular geyser in the park," Lorena explained. "But it's the most popular."

They were not disappointed. In just another 3 minutes, the geyser spewed out steam and boiling water nearly 170 feet high, one of its better displays.

"Don't you wish life was this predictable?" Abriella asked. "I would give anything if I could just go and stand in a circle, wait for an hour and then have my life's direction erupt up out of the ground right before my eyes."

The others laughed with Abriella as they started to make their way back to the *Nautilus*.

"What do you think the key is, Adam?" Abriella asked. "Why is life so complicated?"

"I don't know," Adam replied. "Sometimes I think it's because we're unwilling to take action even when we do start to figure things out."

"Hmm." Abriella frowned. "I'll have to think about that."

They loaded into the *Nautilus* and headed south out of Yellowstone toward Grand Teton National Park, which lies adjacent to Yellowstone.

"Fab-u-lous!" Ryan stretched out his favorite word as they approached a vista where the full Teton Range came into view. "Now *those* are real mountains."

"As opposed to fake mountains?" Lorena asked mockingly.

"Oh, come on, Lor. Have you no appreciation for beauty and grandeur?" Ryan asked. "I suppose not. It takes somebody more cultured who has taste, like myself." The others burst out laughing while Lorena groaned.

The highlight of their visit to the Tetons had been anticipated from the earliest point in the trip's planning—a whitewater trip on the Snake River. The motorhome made its way to Jackson Hole. There they connected with Lewis & Clark River Expeditions in Jackson Hole (chosen primarily because they liked the name). The explorers had finally decided on joining a classic tour that used a larger standard raft custom-designed for the strength of the Snake River. Ryan and Justin had argued for the smaller 13-foot raft that would make it a significantly greater adventure. In the end, however, none of the girls felt comfortable holding their own in such a small raft that relied on their strength and follow-through to

keep them out of trouble. They were even more sure of this when the guide informed them that the river was running at about 20,000 cubic feet per second. This meant the famed "Lunch Counter" rapids would likely be at class IV with a 12-foot vertical height. The dramatic nearly-straight-down drop made the rapids look like a "lunch counter" at a diner. It also made for a scary ride.

"Fabulous!" Ryan was obviously excited about the size of the rapids. On the other hand, Diana's face paled with those words. She was not necessarily comforted when the guide went on to assure them that most of the other rapids would be class III.

The eight explorers plus the expert guide climbed into the raft and entered the river at West Table River Access in the deepest section of the Snake River Canyon.

"Can you *believe* the scenery in the canyon?" Adam asked, looking all around.

"How far are we going?" Diana asked nervously.

"About eight miles," the guide answered cheerfully.

"How far to the rapids?" Diana asked with even more anxiety and concern.

The guide laughed. "Just around a couple of bends in the river here. Just watch that other raft up ahead."

There had been significant screaming as the raft made its way through one series of rapids after another. Even with all that preparation, however, novices are not quite ready for the Lunch Counter Rapids when they see it.

"That other raft disappeared!" Diana screamed.

"Hold on tightly!" the guide commanded. "This is a big one."

The raft shot up and then plunged down into what the girls were convinced was the abyss.

"Whoa!" Ryan exclaimed, obviously having the time of his life.

The drenched expedition came back up in a few seconds, though it seemed a lot longer to Diana.

"That was some ride!" Justin shouted above the roar of the rapids.

They finally reached Sheep Gulch, where the trip ended, and they climbed into the vans that would take them back to Jackson Hole.

The explorers dried off and changed clothes in the *Nautilus*. Then they headed south toward Utah, where they planned to stay overnight at the Bear Lake KOA campground.

"Okay, Adam," Abriella slapped him on the back. "About that action business you were talking about at Old Faithful. Explain what you mean."

"Think about the whitewater trip," Adam said.

"I'm trying to forget it," Diana moaned.

"Don't be such a wimp," Ryan chided her.

Adam continued, "We started the adventure with a picture of it in our minds. It was like our vision. We knew what direction we were headed by the map the guide showed us. We had goals."

"To survive," Diana interrupted again.

"And we had a strategy," Adam went on. "The guide instructed us about how to paddle and how to secure ourselves in the raft. But all of that wasn't enough. We could be drawn to the adventure. We could have a vision of how exciting it would be.

We could have those directions, goals, and strategies. But when we were put into the river, if we hadn't started taking immediate action, then we would have been doomed for disaster. We could have easily gotten caught in that class V Three Oar Deal Rapid with the dangerous hydraulic."

"Do we have to bring that up again?" Diana asked unhappily.

"The point is that we didn't get caught because we were acting on our plan," Adam said emphatically. "I think that's how it is with our purpose in life as well. We have to think through all the stuff we've been talking about on this trip, but in the end we have to do more than think and talk. We have to act."

It was all finally starting to make sense to them.

STORY

Exercises

Taking Your Next Steps

You have made it to the last element of the Life Calling Model. Now it is time to start taking action. But you might be asking, "Where do I start?" Let's explore this by using mountain climbing as a pattern.

You study all the mountains and you decide you want to climb Mt. Everest. You look at pictures. Maybe you even visit Nepal and see Mt. Everest. In your mind you have a vision of the mountain with you on top.

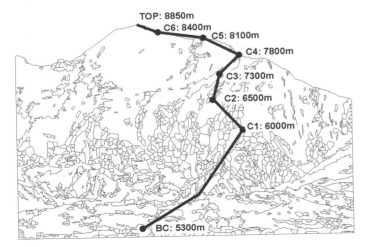

FIGURE 16-2
Vision of Mt. Everest

So far, however, it is still only a dream. There is no elevator to the top or any helicopters to take you there. You have to climb the mountain if you are going to turn your vision into a reality. So next you will need to determine a good route to the top. There are several choices, and each one will get you there. You decide on one that best fits your strengths and interests.

TOP: 8850m
C6: 8400m
C5: 8100m
C4: 7800m
C3: 7300m
C2: 6500m
C1: 6000m
BC: 5300m

FIGURE 16-3
Route to the top of Mt. Everest

You are one step closer to realizing your dream, but you are still not there. What you have is a map, so what are you going to do with that map? You begin to climb, but you don't try to go clear to the top in one climb. You would tire out and quit long before you made it. Your route has several camps identified, and you start by climbing from the base camp at 5300 meters, where you are at now, only to the first camp at 6000 meters. You succeed one step at a time.

▶ Activity 1

Let's use the mountain-climbing illustration as a guide to practice with an example that is right before you as you start college—the choice of a college major.

1. Let's suppose that as you completed your study of chapters seven and eight, you began to sense that an important part of your Life Calling is to help young children develop life skills that will lead them to successful lives.

2. In such a case, your choice of majors has been narrowed. Not all fields of study in college will lead you to this outcome. List three majors at your college or university that you think could lead you to the outcome of helping children, and list three that probably would not.

Probably Would	*Probably Wouldn't*
_____	_____
_____	_____
_____	_____

3. Let's suppose that you selected Elementary Education as the major most attractive to you in preparing you to help young children develop life skills. How can you know this is the right major for you?

   ✓ Identify four people you could talk to about Elementary Education—two professors and two persons teaching elementary school

Professors	*Teachers*
_____	_____
_____	_____

   ✓ Once you have identified these persons, if this was a real situation rather than an example, you would set up times to meet with these persons.

4. If after talking with people working in that field, you still felt that Elementary Education was a major you would like to check out, then the next step would be registering for the introduction class into that major in your next semester. This would be the equivalent of climbing to the C1 camp on your way up the mountain.

▶ Activity 2

Use the same pattern as we did in Activity 1 and actually apply it to your own situation.

1. Review all the elements of the Life Calling Model as they have applied to your life. Give special attention to areas you identified in chapters seven and eight related to world-drawing forces and vision. What have you begun to sense that could be an important part of your Life Calling?

_____

_____

EXERCISES

_____

_____

2. List three majors at your college or university that you think could lead you to the outcome of what you are sensing in your own life, and list three that probably would not.

Probably Would   *Probably Wouldn't*

_____   _____

_____   _____

_____   _____

3. Which of the majors listed as "Probably Would" is most attractive to you in preparing you to pursue your Life Calling?

_____

4. Identify four people you could talk to about this major—two professors and two persons working in this area.

Professors   *Practitioners*

_____   _____

_____   _____

5. Once you have identified these persons, contact them and set up times to meet with them to talk about this field of study and work.

Finding Points of Entry

In Exercise 1, we used the illustration of mountain climbing to help us explore how to start taking action in our Life Calling. In Figure 48, we identified a route to take us to the top of the mountain. Let's look at another version of that map of the mountain.

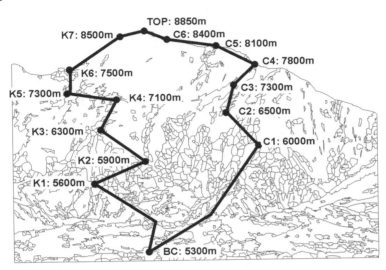

FIGURE 16-4
Two Routes to the top of Mt. Everest

Here we see on the map a second route to the top of Mt. Everest. It is easy to jump to the question "Which is the right route?" The answer, however, would be that both routes are "right." In other words, they both lead to the top. The challenges will vary depending on the route, but they both end up at the same place.

This will be the case many times as you move in the direction of taking action toward your Life Calling. One of the best ways to begin moving toward your vision is to identify likely scenarios (projected sequence of events—in other words, your route) that would lead you to this vision. Often it is easier to start with the vision and work back from this.

For example, Vision ⇦ Career to carry out vision ⇦ Major to prepare for career ⇦ GPA required to graduate with major ⇦ classes required for major ⇦ introductory class for the major

1. Describe the vision that you have begun to sense as an important outcome of your college experience.

_____

_____

_____

_____

2. Try to think of two or three most likely scenarios that would lead to your dream.

- Scenario 1

- Scenario 2

- Scenario 3

3. What would be the first step you would need to take to start down the paths of these scenarios?

- Scenario 1: Step 1

- Scenario 2: Step 1

- Scenario 3: Step 1

Chances are that if you are not taking any of these steps, you are probably not moving toward any of your dreams. Why not go ahead and take that first step right now?

4. What if you are on the wrong route? You might think it is safer to not take any route until you know for sure that it is the right route? But it is important to remember what we learned in the last chapter:

- Approach situations or challenges with the understanding that there is more than one right answer.
- Don't be afraid of making a mistake.

Here is an observation that is always true. If you take a route, there is always some chance that it may be a wrong one and you might not make it to the top of the mountain, but there is also just as good a chance that you will find a good route to the top. One thing is for sure: if you never start on a route, there is a 100 percent chance that you will not make it to the top of the mountain!

5. Look over the three scenarios (or however many you have developed). Select the one (or several) that is the most feasible and appealing to you.

6. Set *goals* for your journey as you travel the scenario you have chosen. Remember to make these goals SMART: specific, measurable, achievable, relevant, and timed.

> Here is one last observation from mountain climbing. When mountain climbers first put on their packs and begin the ascent, they often feel awkward and uneasy in those first few hundred meters of climbing. Their bodies are not used to the extra load and they begin question if they will make it or if they should have started in the first place. But as they continue hiking, they begin to adapt to the challenge and they develop a hiking pattern that will take them to the top.
>
> Don't be too quick to give up on adventures you choose as your explore your Life Calling!

◤ References

The following resources have been used in this chapter.

Millard, B. (2012). *LifeQuest: Planning Your Life Strategically, 2nd ed.* Marion, IN: Life Discovery ePubs.

The following resources may be useful as you explore the role of *action* in continuing your exploration of Personal Leadership and Life Calling.

Bolles, R.N. (2011). *What Color is Your Parachute? 2011: A Practical Manual for Job-Hunters & Career-Changers.* Berkley, CA: Ten Speed Press.

Hakim, C. (1994). *We are All Self-Employed.* San Francisco, CA: Berrett Koehler Publishers.

Schwen, M.R., and Bass, D.C., Eds. (2006). *Leading Lives That Matter: What We Should Do and Who We Should Be.* Grand Rapids, Michigan: Erdmans Publishing Co.

Millard, B. (2003). *ChangeQuest: A Process for Modifying Your Organization.* Marion, IN: Life Discovery Publications.

Section III Conclusion

Personal Leadership

In Section III we concluded that for our Life Calling to become a reality, we have to move beyond theory and self-assessment into action. Like the proverbial snowflake, every person who has ever lived possesses a unique design. If photographers go no further than "lights—camera," they produce nice still photographs. It is only when the director calls "lights—camera—action" that a movie is produced. The same is true with our lives.

Once we understand our Foundational Values and have discovered our Unique Design, we need to begin moving forward in Personal Leadership. To move in an effective direction, we need to determine a mission based on the types of people, situations, and needs toward which we are going to move. Once we have some idea of that direction, we need to begin painting a picture in our minds of what all this is going to look like in an ideal situation once it has been affected by us working through our Life Calling. Sure, it sounds audacious, but a good vision should be audacious if it is going to inspire us. Nobody is spurred into action by the lure of mediocrity. When the picture is clear enough that we can describe the images we see, then we need to outline and take the actual steps of action that move us toward the vision's reality and the fulfillment of our Life Calling.

The more we unwrap our Life Calling, the greater the clarity of our Life Calling will become. This really is where Life Calling begins to become a reality and where we sense fulfillment. Feelings of meaning, significance, and hope emerge, which is part of the universal need experienced by all humans, and an overriding purpose for our lives begins to develop.

The Rest of the Story

The six high school graduates and new national explorers slowly walked along the warm sand at McClellan State Beach. They had been back in Seahaven a little over a week.

"That's the best trip I have ever taken," Abriella said. "I learned so much about our country, but I also learned a great deal about my life and the rest of you. I feel a lot more prepared for college, even if I still plan to keep my options open for my major."

"I feel the same way," Justin added. "I wouldn't trade that experience for anything. You learn so much when you're willing to explore like we did. Sometimes I feel like society's trying to keep us from exploring like that when we go to college."

"Well, you guys, the way to keep that exploring spirit is to avoid college at all costs," Ryan announced.

"And end up poor and ignorant," Lorena chided him.

Ryan started after her to take a swing, but Lorena ran away. He kept up the chase.

The others began to separate a little as well. Diana found herself walking with Adam, and Justin and Abriella were more or less walking by themselves.

Ryan finally caught Lorena, but there was no hitting or joking. "Lorena." Ryan's tone was serious. "When you go to college, will you forget all about me?"

"No." Lorena's response had an uncharacteristic tenderness to it.

A little behind Lorena and Ryan, Diana turned to Adam. "I'm scared about what lies ahead."

"What do you mean?" Adam asked.

"I haven't had to face life without you being there for me or any of the rest us. You've been there for us since we were five." Diana's eyes began to mist and her voice cracked a little.

Adam grabbed her hand. "I'll still be there for you even when I'm away at school."

****

Abriella looked up at the banner welcoming the 25th Anniversary Class to the Seahaven High School alumni weekend. "I can't believe it's been this long," she said to her husband, who had dutifully accompanied her back to Seahaven for the celebration. Abriella was the owner of an art gallery in Malibu. She and her husband had driven up the coast to Seahaven that morning. They worked their way to the front of the auditorium, selecting seats in the third row. Traffic had been heavy and slow, but they had arrived in time for the Alumnus of the Year presentation. Abriella knew she would connect with her friends after the award ceremony.

The principal of Seahaven High School, Dr. Justin Park, came to the podium and welcomed the guests. This was followed by a musical selection played by the SHS Marching Band, although, of course, they did not march on this occasion. Finally it was time to announce the winner of the Alumnus of the Year award—the Golden Dolphin.

Dr. Park addressed the audience. "It gives me great pleasure to introduce to you our distinguished guest who will announce this year's recipient of the Golden Dolphin. He was the recipient of the award himself two years ago and is accompanied by his lovely wife, Diana Neimon Collins, another distinguished Seahaven alumnus."

Abriella leaned over toward her husband and whispered, "She's still as beautiful and in shape as ever."

"No better than you," he replied. She smiled appreciatively—even if she did not fully believe him.

Justin continued, "Ladies and gentlemen, the distinguished governor of California, the honorable Adam Collins." Justin reached out to shake Adam's hand as he came to the podium, but Adam gave him a hug instead. By this time the audience was standing with applause.

"Thank you, ladies and gentlemen," Adam said, motioning for the audience to sit down. "Nothing could give me greater pleasure than to make this award today. The recipient of this year's Golden Dolphin came to this award by a different route than most of his predecessors. There was probably a time when no one saw this coming. I know I was certainly once a doubter."

"Isn't that the truth," Abriella remarked to her husband. "So was I. I still can't believe it."

"This year's Alumnus of the Year has distinguished himself in many roles," Adam continued. "He is an entrepreneur who invented the AquaDyanmic Thruster. This propulsion device not only uses water as the medium for thrust, but also draws its energy from the hydrogen in the water. Of course his first application of the invention was to surfboards because he was tired of fighting the waves on the trip out to catch a wave. Now hardly any board does not have the small thrusters—a fact that has made a lot of money for our honoree." The audience laughed.

"But our honored guest has used that money for a good purpose." Adam resumed his introduction. "He created the Seahaven Oceanographic Institute, a world renowned research center to protect the oceans of the world. And of course, just last year he received the Nobel Prize for his research into the salinity of ocean currents that has revolutionized the way we look at our oceans and made it possible to predict ocean current temperatures and weather patterns with far greater accuracy. It has been estimated that this has saved billions of dollars for the nations of the world each year."

"I do not want to overlook one of the driving forces that helped our honored guest get to where he is today, and that is his lovely wife Lorena Rodriguez Williams, Chief of Pediatric Medicine at Seahaven Children's Hospital." Adam gestured toward Lorena, and she gave her husband a soft punch on the shoulder. The audience laughed and clapped.

"You don't know how true that is," Abriella whispered to her husband. "She is one tough lady."

Adam turned back to the microphone, "But most of all, this year's Alumnus of the Year is a very good friend. Ladies and gentlemen, I present to you this year's Alumnus of the Year and winner of the Golden Dolphin, Dr. Ryan Williams."

The audience stood with thunderous applause for its hometown hero. Ryan and Adam hugged each other, and then Adam presented Ryan with the Golden Dolphin.

Ryan stepped to the podium, raised the Golden Dolphin high over his head and then exclaimed the one word everybody in the audience was waiting to hear.

"Fabulous!"

The auditorium exploded into laughter, shouting, whistles, and even greater thunderous applause. Ryan motioned for his wife Lorena, Adam and his wife Diana, and Justin to join him. Then he looked down to the third row in the audience and beckoned Abriella to come up on stage as well. The friendship and history of the six was legendary in Seahaven. The trip was finally over.

Or was it? Ryan pulled a picture from his pocket and showed it to the other five. It was a beautiful ocean research vessel, and there across the bow was the name *Nautilus*. "Are you in?" he asked the others.

STORY

Epilogue

My parents were both successful professionals—my father was a psychologist and a college administrator, and my mother was a first-grade teacher. As a young child, I was taught to read and was enrolled in piano and trumpet lessons. I loved to dream up make-believe stories, but when I entered school, my teachers told me that daydreaming was a waste of time, and they structured my life around the acquisition of knowledge and the memorization of facts.

Problems began when my fifth-grade teacher told my class that the sun was the largest star in the universe. I loved astronomy and pointed out the teacher's error in front of the whole class. I was promptly sent to the principal's office. This became a pattern, and by the end of high school, I knew my principals better than my teachers. In the classroom, I excelled in creative projects, but did not study and, as a result, ended up with below-average grades. Teachers told my parents that I was a troublemaker with no future. My mother refused to believe them.

I compliantly went to college, though my less-than-stellar work in high school left no hope for any scholarships. I had no idea what I was doing and found my first semester boring. My work was mediocre in my English composition class, so I was not surprised when my teacher said that I did not belong in that section of the class—I was accustomed to being thrown out of classes. I was shocked when the teacher explained that I belonged in the honors section of the class. In the honors section, I was encouraged to write my creative dreams and earned the top grade in the class. With this experience as a catalyst, I began to excel in the rest of my college studies. By the time I graduated, I was at the top of my class. Despite the diploma in my hand, however, I still had no idea where I was going in life.

Although I was offered scholarships to pursue graduate studies in political science, history, and law, my search for life's meaning led me to seminary. That didn't work for me. Frustrated with my failure to discover my life's meaning in seminary, I dropped out and entered the Air Force's officer-pilot training program. The government put a freeze on pilot training soon after my entrance, and I was released. My career volatility became a family joke to everyone except my mother, who still expressed confidence in me.

I then decided to study public health, but after one semester switched to dentistry because I could make more money as a dentist than I could working in the public health sector. I was at the top of my dental school class when I realized that though I loved the science and health courses, I hated looking in people's mouths and drilling teeth. It seemed like that could be a problem in dentistry! Once more I dropped out and pursued graduate studies in secondary education. After completing my master's degree, I became a high school religion teacher. During my six years of teaching, I continued my pursuit of life's ultimate meaning. When a series of events eliminated that teaching position, I decided to pursue more graduate studies, this time in geology. After graduating at the top of my class, I went on to work for an oil exploration company. I stayed in this business for seven years and did reasonably well. However, in the office I was known more for helping the workers discover solutions to their life problems than I was for finding oil.

It then occurred to me that I had been helping people in this manner most of my life, and I began to see that this was the purpose for my life! I decided to leave the oil business and pursue helping others find purposes for their own lives. Suddenly, I was energized by my work, and my impact extended over the lives of many other people.

What compelled me to pursue so many different careers? Confusion coupled with a determined search for meaning, significance, and hope. At the heart of my actions and decisions, there was a driving need to find an overriding purpose for my life.

It was not until I made it a priority to not only seek that overriding purpose, but also to help those around me understand the same thing for their lives, that I discovered how to unleash the power of purpose. At that point, it became more than just a purpose. It became a Life Calling.

Everyone has a Life Calling. Discovering it and developing confidence in it is where problems arise. We often confuse Life Calling with our jobs, but Life Calling is larger than an occupation, more profound than a profession or life's work. These are worthy purposes in our lives, as are family relationships, community service, values, missions, and strengths. However, none of them by themselves constitutes our Life Calling. They are like individual rivers running into an ocean. The ocean is our Life Calling—where all the various purposes for our lives come together.

My pursuit of a Life Calling through relationships and circumstances was life changing for me, as well as for those around me. As this occurred, I concluded that for purpose to be unleashed at a level that propels us toward a Life Calling, it must overcome four major barriers.

First, for purpose to be unleashed at a level great enough to gain Life Calling status, it must become strong enough to overcome the selfishness of indifference. Most of us search for our life's purposes in the context of "it's all about me." But when we invest time and resources into helping others discover their Life Calling, our own Life Calling is better developed and discovered through examination of who we help and how. There is an inward and outward focus that must be pursued to discover our Life Calling.

Second, for purpose to be unleashed at a level great enough to gain Life Calling status, it must become strong enough to overcome the comfort of complacency. It always seems easier not to do anything, but doing nothing leads to nothing. When we take action, we plant the first seed of achievement. The discovery of our Life Calling requires us to be active explorers, not passive bystanders.

Third, for purpose to be unleashed at a level great enough to gain Life Calling status, it must become strong enough to overcome the fear of failure. Most of us fear failure. So we decide not to approach any significant challenges to avoid the opportunity for failure. The problem is that when we do this, we guarantee that we will never achieve anything significant. Most achievements occur as a result of many failures. Thomas Edison had far more failed inventions than he did successful ones, but he is remembered for his successful ones. If we hope to discover our Life Calling, we must be willing to take risks.

Fourth, for purpose to be unleashed at a level great enough to gain Life Calling status, it must become strong enough to overcome the avoidance of pain. Achievement always includes an element of change. Discomfort and pain are noticeable indicators of change and are nearly always encountered along the path to achievement. If pain is always avoided, then gain likely will be as well. In fact, it is when we face the painful circumstances of our lives that we often discover the clearest picture of our Life Calling. If we hope to discover our Life Calling, we must be willing to change.

When the various purposes in our lives combine into a Life Calling, an overriding and consistent context develops that motivates and guides a lifetime of endeavors and decisions. Until that happens, we will never overcome these four barriers.

As we have seen in this book, the discovery of our Life Calling emerges from exploration of three crucial life dimensions: foundational values, unique design, and personal leadership. These three crucial components of Life Calling are not isolated from each other. Instead, they are interactive and integrated. Our foundational values inspire the inward search for unique design with a sense of stewardship, whereas the inward search for unique design manifests expression to the values we hold. The foundational values we hold motivate our outward response through personal leadership, whereas the personal leadership fulfills the foundational values we hold. Finally, the unique design we possess gives focus to our personal leadership, whereas our personal leadership provides evidence of the unique design we possess as distinct individuals.

We encounter the dimensions of Life Calling in constantly reoccurring cycles. As each cycle takes place, we develop tools that help us explore more effectively each dimension. The value of this is best illustrated when painful circumstances occur. At that point, we are faced with a choice: we can choose to allow these circumstances to become baggage that weighs us down into hopelessness, or we can choose to use Life Calling discovery tools to incorporate these circumstances into strengths for the future. I had a hard time in elementary, middle, and high school. Some of the things I experienced still impact me today, but I have chosen to use those experiences to learn about the assets I possess and then incorporate them into my personal leadership.

The absence of any dimension greatly diminishes the potential power of our Life Calling. If there are no foundational values as an anchor, there will be no meaning to guide our search for a Life Calling, and we will find it hard to continue when life and circumstances get tough. If we ignore our unique design, there will be no clarity in our lives, our efforts will be misdirected, and we will fail to see the significance of our lives. If there is no outward response to the world through personal leadership then our Life Calling will remain unfulfilled, and we will fail to experience the hope that comes from service.

The good news is that all three of these dimensions can be discovered and developed. When we make this discovery and bring all the components together, we can unleash the power of purpose in our lives! We can follow it as an Explorer's Guide to Life Calling.

Appendix A

Solution to "Stranded in the Desert" Exercise

The Expert's Ranking

12 magnetic compass
10 book *Plants of the Desert*
1 rearview mirror
5 large knife
8 flashlight (4 batteries required)
9 .38-caliber pistol
4 one transparent plastic ground cloth (6 ft by 4 ft) per person
7 piece of heavy-duty, light blue canvas (20 ft by 20 ft)
2 one jacket per person
3 one 2-quart plastic canteen full of water per person
11 accurate map of the area
6 large box of kitchen matches

Rationale for the Expert's Ranking

The group has just been through a traumatic situation and most, if not all, of your group need to receive treatment for shock. Your group has five major problems to deal with: how to deal with dehydration, how to signal search parties, how to obtain as much drinkable water as possible, how to protect yourself from the cold at night, and how to gather food for the group if the group is not rescued within a few days.

If the group decided to walk out, traveling at night, all members will probably be dead by the second day. They will have walked less than 33 miles during the two nights. If group members decide to walk during the day, they will probably be dead by the next morning, after walking less than 12 miles. For the group to walk out, having just gone through a traumatic experience that has had considerable impact on the body, having few if any members who have walked 45 miles before, and having to carry the canvas and wear the jackets to prevent dehydration, would be disastrous. The group would also be harder to spot by search planes once they started to walk away from the site of the crash.

Appendix B

Increasing Your Effectiveness as a Writer

One of the biggest differences you will encounter as you move from high school into college is the amount of writing you will have to do. Almost every class you take will require one or more papers to be written. It is important that you develop good writing skills early in your college experience.

Power Writing

You can become an excellent writer by learning about the steps in POWER writing: Prepare, Organize, Write, Edit, and Revise.

Prepare

Plan your time. The first step in writing is to plan your time so that the project can be completed by the due date. Picture this scene: It is the day that the term paper is due. A few students proudly hand in their term papers and are ready to celebrate their accomplishments. Many of the students in the class are absent, and some will never return to the class. Some of the students look as though they haven't slept the night before. They look stressed and weary. At the front of the class there is a line of students wanting to talk with the instructor. The instructor has heard it all before:

- I had my paper all completed and my printer jammed.
- My hard drive crashed and I lost my paper.
- I was driving to school and my paper flew off my motorcycle.
- I had the flu.
- My children were sick.
- I had to take my dog to the vet.
- My dog ate my paper!
- My car broke down and I could not get to the library.
- My grandmother died and I had to go to the funeral.
- My roommate accidentally took my backpack to school.
- I spilled salad dressing on my paper, so I put it in the microwave to dry it out and the writing disappeared!

To avoid being in this uncomfortable and stressful situation, plan ahead. Plan to complete your project at least one week ahead of time so that you can deal with life's emergencies. Life does not always go as planned. You or your children may get sick, or your dog may do strange things to your homework. Your computer may malfunction, leading you to believe it senses stress and malfunctions just to frustrate you even more.

To avoid stress and to do your best work, start with the date that the project is due and then think about the steps needed to finish. Write these dates on your calendar or on your list of things to do. Consider all these components:

Project Due Date: _____

To Do	By When?
1. Brainstorm ideas	_____
2. Choose a topic	_____
3. Gather information	_____
4. Write a thesis statement	_____
5. Write an outline	_____
6. Write the introduction	_____
7. Write the first draft	_____
8. Include the bibliography or works cited	_____
9. Edit	_____
10. Revise	_____
11. Print and assemble	_____

Find a space and time. Find a space where you will work. Gather the materials that you will need to write. Generally writing is best done in longer blocks of time. Determine when you will work on your paper and write the time on your schedule. Start right away to avoid panic later.

Choose a general topic. This task will be easy if your topic is already clearly defined by your instructor or your boss at work. Make sure that you have a clear idea of what is required, such as length, format, purpose, and method of citing references and topic. Many times the choice of a topic is left to you. Begin by doing some brainstorming. Think about topics that interest you. Write them down. You may want to focus your attention on brainstorming ideas for 5 or 10 minutes, and then put the project aside and come back to it later. Once you have started the process of thinking about the ideas, your mind will continue to work, and you may have a creative inspiration. If the creative inspiration does not come, repeat the brainstorming process.

Gather information. Go to your college library and use the Internet to gather your information. As you begin to gather information on your topic, you can see what is available, what is interesting to you, and what the current thinking is on your topic. As you find information relevant to your topic, begin to write down information that you can use in your bibliography. The bibliography contains information about where you found your material. Write down the author, title of the publication, publisher, place of publication and date of publication. Note the major topics of interest in each publication that might be useful to you. Once you have found material that is interesting to you, you will probably feel motivated to continue your project.

Write the thesis statement.   The thesis statement is the key idea in your paper. It provides a direction for you to follow. It is the first step in organizing your work. To write a thesis statement, review the material you have gathered and then ask these questions:

- What is the most important idea?
- What question would I like to ask about it?
- What is my answer?

For example, if I decide to write a paper for my health class on the harmful effects of smoking, I would look at current references on the topic. I might become interested in some information about how the tobacco companies misled the public on the dangers of smoking. I would think about my thesis statement and answer the questions stated earlier.

- **What is the most important idea?** Smoking is harmful to your health.
- **What question would I like to ask about it?** Did the tobacco companies mislead the public about the health hazards of smoking?
- **What is my answer?** The tobacco companies misled the public about the hazards of smoking to protect their business interests.
- **My thesis statement:** Tobacco companies knew that smoking was hazardous to our health, but to protect their business interests, they deliberately misled the public.

The thesis statement helps me to narrow the topic and provide direction for the paper. I can now focus on reference material related to my topic: research on health effects of smoking, congressional testimony relating to regulation of the tobacco industry, and how advertising influences people to smoke.

Organize

At this point you have many ideas about what to include in your paper, and you have a central focus, your thesis statement. Start to organize your paper by listing the topics that are related to your thesis statement. Here is a list of topics related to my thesis statement about smoking.

- The tobacco companies knew that nicotine was addictive
- Tobacco companies minimized the health hazards in their advertisements
- How advertisements encourage people to smoke
- Money earned by the tobacco industry
- Health problems caused by smoking
- Statistics on numbers of people who have health problems and die from smoking
- Regulation of the tobacco industry
- How advertisements are aimed at children

Think about the topics and arrange them in a logical order that makes sense to you. Use an outline, a mind map, a flowchart, or a drawing to think about how you will organize the important topics. Keep in mind that you will need an introduction, a body, and a conclusion. Having an organizational structure will make it easier for you to write because you will not need to wonder what comes next.

Write

Get started. This might be the most difficult step. Many people are anxious about writing and are victims of "writer's block." You have writer's block if you find yourself staring at that blank piece of paper or blank computer screen, not knowing how to begin or what to write. Here are some tips for getting started and avoiding writer's block.

1. **Write freely.** Just write anything about your topic that comes to mind. Don't worry about organization or perfection at this point. Don't censure your ideas. You can always go back to organize and edit later. Free writing helps you to overcome one of the main causes of writer's block: you think it has to be perfect from the beginning. This expectation of perfection causes anxiety. You freeze up and become unable to write. Perhaps you have past memories of writing where the teacher made many corrections on your paper. Maybe you lack confidence in your writing skills. The only way you will become a better writer is to keep writing and perfecting your writing skills, so just write what comes to mind to start the writing process. Don't worry how great it is. You can fix it later. Just begin.

2. **Use brainstorming if you get stuck.** For five minutes, focus your attention on the topic and write whatever comes to mind. You don't even need to write full sentences; just jot down ideas. If you are really stuck, try working on a different topic, take a break, or come back to it later.

3. **Write the first sentence.** Begin with the main idea.

4. **Write the introduction.** It is the roadmap for the rest of the paper.

5. **Realize that it is only the first draft.** It is not the finished product, and it does not have to be perfect.

6. **Read through your reference materials.** These ideas can get your mind working. Reading can make you a better writer.

7. **Write a journal.** Writing a journal gives you practice at writing and makes it a habit.

8. **Break it up into small parts.** If you find writing difficult, write for five minutes at a time and put it away. Do this consistently, and you can get used to writing and can complete your paper.

9. **Find a good place for writing.** If you are an introvert, look for a quiet place for concentration. If you are an extrovert, go to a restaurant or coffee shop and start your writing.

10. **Beware of procrastination.** The more you put it off, the more anxious you will become and the more difficult the task will be. Make a time schedule and stick to it.

Save your work!   As soon as you have written the first paragraph, save it on your computer. Save your work in two places. Save it on your hard drive and save it on a disk. At the end of each page, save your work again to both of these places. When you are finished, print your work and save a paper copy. In this way, if your hard drive crashes, you will still have your work on a disk. If your disk becomes corrupted, you will still have the paper copy. Following these procedures can save you a lot of headaches. Any writer can tell you stories of lost work because of computer problems, lightning storms, power outages, and other unpredictable events.

Write the introduction.   The introduction includes your thesis statement and establishes the foundation for the paper. It introduces topics that will be discussed in the body of the paper. The introduction for the paper should include some interesting points that provide a "hook" or some motivation for the audience to read your paper. For example, for our paper on the hazards of smoking, begin with statistics on how many people suffer from smoking-related illnesses and premature death. Write about profits earned by the tobacco industry. Then introduce other topics: deception, advertisements, and regulation. The introduction provides a guide or outline of what will follow in the paper.

Write the body of the paper.   The body of the paper is divided into paragraphs discussing the topics that you have introduced. As you write each paragraph, include the main idea and then explain it and give examples. Here are some tips for good writing:

1. Good writing is clear thinking. Think about what you want to say and write it so the reader can understand your point of view.
2. Use plain and understandable language. Avoid using too many words and scholarly sounding words that get in the way of understanding.
3. Don't assume that the audience knows what you are writing about. Provide complete information.
4. Provide examples, stories, and quotes to support your topic sentence. Include your own ideas and experiences.
5. Beware of plagiarism. Plagiarism is copying the work of others without giving them credit for their work. It is illegal and can cause you to receive a failing grade on your project or even get you into legal trouble. You can avoid plagiarism by quoting the author's work and providing a reference indicating where you found the material. You can paraphrase the work of others by reading the ideas, looking away, and writing about the ideas in your own words.

Write the conclusion.   The conclusion summarizes the topics in the paper and presents your point of view. It makes reference to the introduction and answers the question posed in your thesis statement. It often makes the reader think about the significance of your point and the implications for the future. Make your conclusion interesting and powerful.

Include references.   No college paper is complete without citing references. References are cited as footnotes, endnotes, or works cited and the bibliography. You can use your computer to insert these references. There are various styles for citing references, depending on your subject area. There are computer programs that put your information into the correct style. Ask your instructor which style to use for your particular class or project. Frequently used styles for citing references include:

- The American Psychological Association (APA) style is used in psychology and other behavioral sciences. Consult the *Publication Manual of the American Psychological Association* (2001), 5th edition. Washington, DC: American Psychological Association. You can find this source online at: http://apastyle.apa.org/
- The Chicago style is used by many professional writers in a variety of fields. Consult *The Chicago Manual of Style* (2003) 15th edition. Chicago: The University of Chicago Press. You can find this source online at: http://www.chicagomanualofstyle.org/home.html
- The Modern Language Association (MLA) style is used in English, classical languages, and the humanities. Consult the *MLA Handbook for Writers of Research Papers* (2003), 6th edition. New York: Modern Language Association. This source is available online at: http://www.mla.org/

Each of these styles uses a different format to list the source of the information, but all include the following elements. Make sure that you write down this information as you collect your reference material. If you forget this step, it is very time consuming and difficult to find it later:

- The author
- The title of the book
- The publisher of the book
- The city where the book was published
- The title of magazine or newspaper article
- The publication date of the book or article
- The page number (and volume and number if available)

Here are some examples of citations in the APA style:

- Book (Include author, book title, city of publication, publisher, date of publication).
- Fralick, M. (2000). *College and career success.* Dubuque, IA: Kendall/ Hunt Publishing Company.
- Journal Article (Include author, title of article, name of journal, date, volume and number, pages).
- Fralick, M. (1993, Spring). College success: A study of positive and negative attrition. *Community College Review, 20* (5), 29–36.
- Web site (Include author's name, date listed or updated, title of Web site or article, the URL or address of the Web site, and the date you accessed

it. Some of these items may be missing on the Web site. Include as many of the above items as possible. Methods of citing information on the Internet are still evolving.)

Put it away for a while.   The last step in writing the first draft is easy. Put it away for a while and come back to it later. In this way, you can relax and gain some perspective on your work. You will be able to take a more objective look at your work to begin the process of editing and revising.

Edit and Revise

The process of writing involves writing quickly and then editing and revising leisurely. The editing and revising process allows you to take a critical look at your work and choose the best. It takes some courage to do this step. Once people see their ideas in writing, they become attached to them. With careful editing and revising, you can turn in your best work and be proud of your accomplishments. Here are some tips for editing and revising:

1. **Read your paper as if you were the audience.** Pretend that you are the instructor or person reading your paper. Does the paper make sense? Is it what you meant to say? I have read many papers and wondered what the sentences meant. Read what you write, and the result will be a more effective paper.

2. **Read paragraph by paragraph.** Does each paragraph have a main idea and supporting details? Do the paragraphs fit logically together? Use the cut-and-paste feature on your computer to move sentences and paragraphs around if needed. Check your grammar and spelling. Use spell-check and grammar check on your computer.

3. **These tools are helpful, but they are not thorough enough.** Spell-check will pick up only misspelled words. It will skip words that are spelled correctly but are not used correctly. To your spell checker the words *of* and *on* are spelled correctly, but they really change the meaning of your sentence. The spell-checker will not flag *their* or *there* because each is a correct spelling. To find such errors, you need to read your paper after the spell-check.

4. **Check for language that is biased in terms of gender, disability, or ethnic group.** Use words that are gender neutral. If a book or paper uses only the pronoun "he" or "she," half of the population is left out. You can avoid sexist language by making a few changes:

   Change this: The successful student knows his values and makes goals for the future.

   To this: Successful students know their values and make goals for the future.

   After all, we are trying to make the world a better place, with opportunity for all. Here are some examples of biased language and better alternatives.

Biased Language	Better Alternatives
policeman	police officer
chairman	chair
fireman	firefighter
draftsman	drafter
mankind	humanity
manmade	handcrafted
housewife	homemaker
lady	woman
crippled	disabled
American Indian	Native American
Negro	African American
Oriental	Asian American
Chicano	Mexican American, Hispanic

5. **Have someone else read your paper for clarity and meaning.** After you have read your paper many times, you do not really see it anymore. If you need assistance in writing, colleges offer tutoring or writing labs where you can get help with editing and revising.

6. **Look at your introduction and conclusion.** They should be clear, interesting, and concise. The introduction and conclusion are the most powerful parts of your paper.

7. **Prepare the final copy.** Check your instructor's instructions on the format required. If there are no instructions, use the following format:
   - Double space
   - Use a font of ten or twelve
   - Use one-inch margins on all sides
   - Use a three-inch top margin on the first page
   - Footnotes and endnotes are generally single spaced
   - Number your pages

8. **Prepare the title page.** Center the title of your paper and place it one third of the page from the top. On the bottom third of the page, center your name, professor's name, the class title, and the date.

Your Title

Your Name

The Professor's Name

The Name of the Class

The Date

---

9. **Follow instructions about using a folder or cover for your paper.** Generally professors dislike bulky folders or notebooks because they are difficult to carry. Imagine your professor trying to carry 50 notebooks to his or her office! Unless asked to do so, do not use plastic page protectors. Professors like to write comments on papers, and it is extremely difficult to write on papers with page protectors.

10. **Turn your paper in on time.** Some professors do not accept late papers. Others subtract points if your paper is late. Put your paper in the car or someplace where you will have to see it before you go to class.

11. **Reward yourself for a job well done!**

Appendix C

Being Successful in Oral Presentations

Studies by organizations such as the National Association of Colleges and Employers and the Association of American Colleges and Universities identify oral and written communication as one of the top characteristics employers look for in prospective employees coming out college. That is why both of these skills are encouraged and required in most of the classes you will take in college. In fact, nearly every college or university will require you to take a specific class that concentrates on developing writing skills and another class that concentrates on developing and delivering speeches.

I have had to make hundreds of speeches all over the world, yet I still get somewhat nervous when I am just about ready to give one of these speeches. I want to share with you several strategies I used to be successful.

The Knowing Strategy

1. Know your topic
   - Make sure you clearly understand the topic you have been assigned or have chosen.
   - Once you are clear on this, take time to read and study the topic—even if you think you already know everything there is to know about the topic (I have never met a person who really did know that much).
   - Gain some familiarity with all the topics, but concentrate on knowing the essential concepts.
   - Write out your explanation of the important concepts using your own words. Reread these explanations over and over until they are fixed in your mind.

2. Know your audience
   - Make sure you have a good idea of who you will be speaking to. Don't treat every audience as if it is the same as others.
   - Keep your words appropriate for your audience. This includes speaking at their level of comprehension (a speech to first graders should be different than a speech to a professional society), using words that do not violate their values, and keeping your explanations consistent with their understanding of your topic (if they have high understanding, don't insult them by speaking down to them; if they have low understanding, don't speak over their heads with concepts that presume they know the basics of your topic).

3. Know your parameters
   - When will you be speaking?
   - How long will you have to speak?
   - Who will be speaking before you?
   - How will you be introduced?
   - Is a question-and-answer time expected after your speech?

4. Know your setting
   Find out ahead of time as much as you can about the facilities, including:
   - Sound system
   - Type of podium
   - Stage arrangement
   - Seating arrangement of audience
   - Availability of media support (PowerPoint, video clips, music, etc.)
   - Computer setup (will you need to use your own laptop, or will there be a computer provided?)

The Script Strategy

In preparing your speech, think of it as a three-act play. Write your speech out ahead of time and practice it.

1. Act 1: Introduction
   - This part of your speech is your opportunity to let your audience know what it is that you will be speaking about. Here are a few good things to remember:
   - Keep it simple. Introduce the topic and three or four main points you will be addressing.
   - Catch their interest. The beginning of your speech will determine to a great extent whether or not your audience will continue listening to you or tune you out. Interesting quotes, personal experiences, current events, or humor can be an effective way to begin a talk. If you plan to use humor, make sure it is appropriate for that audience and that it will actually work.

2. Act 2: Main body
   - This part of your speech will be your chance to explain your topic and ideas.
   - Keep your main points at three to five in number.
   - Use illustrations to clarify your concepts.
   - If you are using PowerPoint or any other visual presentation support, use it to enhance what you are saying, not just to repeat what you are saying.

3. Act 3: Conclusion
   - This part of your speech will be your chance to leave your audience with a desire to do more concerning your topic: further study, change of personal practice, rally to your cause, or some other action.
   - Human interest and persuasion are good elements to use in a conclusion.
   - Keep your conclusion short and to the point. Don't keep repeating the phrase "in closing."

The Delivery Strategy

Here are some useful tips when you are actually giving the speech:

1. Dress appropriately for the occasion. It is better to dress slightly more formal than your audience than less formal unless your less formal dress is, in sense, part of your props.

2. Go to the restroom before you speak. You don't want that need to arise during your speech or while you are waiting to speak.

3. Make sure that there is water available in case you get an irritation in your throat while you are speaking.

4. Take some deep breaths or whatever else helps you to relax just before you speak.

5. A short time of prayer is always a good thing right before you speak.

6. Speak slowly and clearly. It is always good practice to speak more slowly in a presentation than you do in casual conversation.

7. Once you start talking, things usually start to get better.

8. Make eye contact with your audience. Look at a variety of people and avoid locking in on just one or two.

9. Your words will sound better if you are smiling.

10. If you make a mistake, just move on rather than making a big deal of it. Usually your audience has no idea that you made the mistake.

11. Keep an eye on the time, or have someone who will tip you off when your time is up.

The Personal Strategy

Most people are fearful of public speaking because they have convinced themselves of wrong ideas. Here are three of those wrong ideas:

1. My speech is a reflection of my self-worth.
   - Your success in a speech does not determine your worth as a person.
2. If I fail in my speech, I am a failure in life.
   - Your speech is only a small activity in your life. Don't let it loom larger than it really is.
3. The opinions of others are vital in determining who I am as a person.
   - You are the one who needs to decide who you are as a person. Whether people like your speech or not should not change this.

Appendix D

Getting Started with PowerPoint

In many of your class presentations, you will likely use PowerPoint as a visual aid. Knowing how to effectively use it will make PowerPoint that much more effective.

1. Start with the end in mind.

Answer the following key questions:
- ✓ What do you want to accomplish?
- ✓ Who is your audience?
- ✓ How much time do you have?
- ✓ Will there be more than one presenter involved?
- ✓ What is the size and configuration of the room in which you will be presenting?
- ✓ What kind of equipment will be available? (Computer, projector, remote control, software version, fonts, etc.)
- ✓ Will you need handouts?

2. Less is better than more.

3. Use images to liven things up.

Images can add life to your presentations. However, be careful not to overdo it. In fact, some of the most effective presentations use images and other special effects (music, video, and more) sparingly.

PowerPoint includes the **Microsoft Clip Organizer** (On the **Insert** menu, point to **Picture** and click **Clip Art**. On the **Insert Clip Art** task pane, click **Clip Organizer**) to help you find the art you want to use. Additionally, you can use your own images that you have stored on your computer.

To add an image to your presentation:

1. Display the slide in Slide view.
2. On the **Insert** menu point to **Picture** and click the type of picture you want to insert.
3. If you want to add clip art from the Clip Organizer, click **Clip Art**. The Insert Clip Art task pane appears so that you can tell PowerPoint what kind of art you're looking for.
4. If you have your own file you want to use, click **From File** and then find and click the image file.

5. Then Click **Open**. Present your data in a chart. If you have a lot of data to present, it is better to display this in a chart.
   - To find the commands you need for both charts and diagrams, on the **Insert** menu, click either **Diagram** or **Chart**.

Use **Rehearse Timings** to set the timing for your presentation. On the **Slide Show** menu, click **Rehearse Timings**.

- Practice. You'll feel better about what you're saying and when the slide transitions should occur.

Index